SYRIAC GRAMMAR,

WITH

A COURSE OF EXERCISES, A CHRESTOMATHY, AND A BRIEF LEXICON.

UHLEMANN'S

SYRIAC GRAMMAR,

TRANSLATED FROM THE GERMAN

BY ENOCH HUTCHINSON.

WITH A COURSE OF

EXERCISES IN SYRIAC GRAMMAR,

AND A

CHRESTOMATHY AND BRIEF LEXICON

PREPARED BY THE TRANSLATOR.

WIPF & STOCK · Eugene, Oregon

Wipf and Stock Publishers
199 W 8th Ave, Suite 3
Eugene, OR 97401

Uhlemann's Syriac Grammar
Translated from the German by Enoch Hutchinson, with a course of Exercises in Syriac Grammar and a Chrestomathy and Brief Lexicon Prepared by the Translator

By Uhlemann, Maxmillian and Hutchinson, Enoch
ISBN 13: 978-1-62564-031-4
Publication date 4/15/2013
Previously published by D. Appleton & Co, 1855

TRANSLATOR'S PREFACE.

The following translation was undertaken in accordance with the suggestion of several literary friends, and in view of an increasing desire among American students to become acquainted with a language in which the earliest and best version of the New Testament is generally admitted to have been made, and which is essentially the language spoken by our Saviour.

Uhlemann's Grammar is acknowledged by all to be a manual of rare excellence; and it is hoped that, in an English dress, it will be found to be well adapted to promote the progress of oriental philology in this country. Some of our helps of this kind, in the study of the Syriac, are too brief, and others are too voluminous. Uhlemann has aimed to present, within moderate limits, a work sufficiently extensive for ordinary purposes of instruction. The translator has endeavored to give as literal a translation as is compatible with perspicuity. He has added, where it seemed to be necessary, occasional explanatory notes. After having prepared an abridgment of the paradigms of verbs and nouns, following Winer's arrangement in his Chaldee Grammar, he, on the whole, concluded to insert the full paradigms as they stand in the original work, and not to make the attempt to improve a grammar so nearly faultless.

The translation is followed by a course of Exercises in Syriac grammar, which, if carefully studied, will, it is believed, materially facilitate the progress of the learner in an accurate knowledge of the elements of the language. After having read, with care, the introduction, and cursorily examined other parts of the grammar, the pupil may, at once, commence upon the Exercises, and merely consult the grammar (as directed in the introductory remarks to the Exercises) as a book of reference, in order to enable him to solve the difficulties with which he may meet in analyzing the first page of the Chrestomathy. The translator trusts that he shall not be considered as obtrusive in calling special attention to a method of analysis which he has found to be of great advantage in teaching classes in Hebrew. Some instructors have probably adopted a similar one, and others may have devised still better methods. This is submitted to the consideration of those teachers who have not already adopted a satisfactory one.

A brief Chrestomathy and Lexicon, prepared by the translator, follow the Exercises. The former is composed of selections from that beautiful edition of the Peshito Bible published by the British and Foreign Bible Society in London, in 1816, and reprinted in smaller type in 1826. It was executed for the use of the Syrian Christians in India. It was corrected for the press, as far as the Acts of the Apostles, by Dr. Buchanan, and completed by Rev. S. Lee, Professor of Arabic in the University of Cambridge. Several manuscripts were consulted, and the text is considered as very correct, though we have discovered in it some typographical errors.

In the Exercises, an extended analysis will be found of the first page of the Chrestomathy, and merely brief explanatory remarks on the remaining pages.

The basis of the Lexicon is that inserted by Uhlemann in his grammar, to which the translator has made many additions, having consulted the Syriac Lexicons of M. Trost, E. Castell, Ægidius Gutbier, and Æmilius Rödiger. The Lexicon is intended merely to include those words which occur in the Chrestomathy.

Some errors, in the author's numerous references to the Old and New Testaments, have been discovered and corrected. There are, probably, others which were not observed.

The translator trusts that this effort will be received with indulgence by the literary public. Errors will doubtless be found by teachers who may use the Manual, and he will be very thankful to receive suggestions from any quarter, by which a future edition, should it ever be called for, may be improved.

The publication of the work has been unexpectedly delayed, most of the stereotype plates, when nearly completed, having been destroyed by a disastrous fire.

The translator avails himself of this opportunity to express his obligations to Mr. W. W. Turner, late of the Union Thelogical Seminary of this city, T. J. Conant, D. D., of Rochester University, and J. G. Palfrey, D. D., formerly of the Theological School connected with Harvard University, for valuable suggestions; also to Mr. A. H. Guernsey, of this city, for important aid in the examination of the manuscript before going to press.

New York, Jan. 1855.

EXTRACTS FROM THE AUTHOR'S PREFACE.

The earlier sheets of this Text book, designed, principally, for academical instruction, had been printed, and that part of the Manuscript which contains the elementary principles and paradigms had been for a considerable time out of my hands, when the more comprehensive work of Professor Hoffmann made its appearance. In the preparation of this work my plan had especially led me to present, with as much brevity as was consistent with clearness, what is most essential for understanding the language in its grammatical forms. I was of the opinion that the more extended treatment of separate phenomena of the language might be dispensed with, since the greater portion of the Syriac forms may be explained from those of the Hebrew language; and in fact, a knowledge of the Hebrew implies an acquaintance with the principles of the Syriac. Upon a close examination of the above-mentioned work, I was convinced, that I had proceeded upon almost the same principles, had made a similar use of the older grammarians, such as Amira, Ludov. de Dieu, Buxtorf, Michaelis, and others, and had deviated only in the collocation of separate rules. Although I might have approximated more nearly to the work of Hoffmann, by isolated alterations, yet I deemed it advisable, where deviations existed, to follow my own views; as for example, in the tabular arrangement of derivative nouns. Following the older grammarians, I have introduced a separate paradigm of the nouns placed under Declension III.,* instead of classing them with the Segholate forms; this was done because the vowel entering into the inflection of these nouns is not an original one, as in the case of the Segholate forms, but is introduced on account of the difficulty of pronunciation. Real Segholate

* § 48, Decl. III.

forms, monosyllabic nouns, namely, those derived from verbs 3 rad. Olaph quiescent, belong rather, according to their principal inflection, to the substantive-stems of Declension V., and, in only a few instances, coincide with the Segholate forms. In preparing the Syntax, I have, like Professor Hoffmann, followed the *Lehrgebäude* of Gesenius; and like him, also, I have made use only of those passages of the Old Testament collected by Gesenius, in which the translator, unfettered by the Hebrew text, seems to have wrought more in accordance with the genius of his own language. In addition to this, I have frequently consulted the translation of the New Testament, as the oldest Syriac writing known to us;* Ephraemi Opera Syr., Romæ, 1743, tom. III., fol.; Barhebræi Chronicon Syr., ed. Kirsch. Lips. 1789; and Assemani Bibliotheca Orient. Clementino-Vaticana, Romæ, 1719, tom. III., fol.; so that a close and impartial examination will easily determine what has been added from my own not inconsiderable collections.† * * * * * *

BERLIN, *March*, 1829.

---

* In point of time the Peshito version of the Old Testament is the most ancient document extant in the Syriac language, though the New Testament was translated into Syriac from the original Greek about the same time. Michaelis supposes, that the Syriac version of both Testaments was made near the close of the first, or in the early part of the second century.—TR.

† The remainder of the Author's Preface relates mainly to his Reading Lessons, which we have not inserted, they being, in our opinion, too difficult for beginners —TR.

CONTENTS.

PART SECOND.

ETYMOLOGY, OR PARTS OF SPEECH.

CHAPTER I.

PRONOUNS.

CHAPTER II.

THE VERB.

PAGE

A. *Quiescent Verbs.*

B. *Defective Verbs.*

CHAPTER III.

THE NOUN.

CHAPTER IV.

PARTICLES.

PART THIRD.

SYNTAX.

CHAPTER I.

THE PRONOUN.

PAGE

CHAPTER II.

THE VERB.

CHAPTER III.

THE NOUN.

CHAPTER IV.

PARTICLES.

INTRODUCTION.

BRIEF HISTORICAL VIEW

OF THE

SYRIAC LANGUAGE AND LITERATURE.

1. The Syriac language (sometimes called the Western Aramæan, to distinguish it from the Chaldæan or Eastern Aramæan, with which it constitutes the Aramæan dialect of the Semitic family of languages), formerly extended over the whole northern part of Aram, from the borders of Palestine to Natolia, and from the Mediterranean to and beyond the Euphrates.* It degenerated at an early period, and, during the continual changes of government, particularly by the reception of Persian and Greek words, lost much of its original purity. Of its pure state, no written monuments have come down to our times. But at the beginning of the fourth century after Christ, the language enjoyed a flourishing period, and kept its place for a long time at Edessa as a written language. As from the earliest period the Palmyrene dialect was recognized as the principal one, so this period has been designated by the name of the Edessene Period. Moreover, at various times, mention is made of the Damascene, the Chalnic or Ctesiphontic, the Acharic or Nesibene, and the Maronite dialects. The essential difference between these consisted very likely in the pronunciation; this may be asserted with still more confidence in respect to the Nabatæan dialect. The ancient written language of Antioch or Commagene is still used by various Christian sects, in particular

* E. Rödiger says of the Aramæan language: "It was called Syriac in the form in which it appeared in the Christian Aramæan literature, and Chaldee when it appeared in the Jewish Aramæan writings." See Gesenius' Heb. Gramm., 15th edit. by Rödiger, Leipz. 1848; Einleitung, § 1. 2. b.—Tr.

by the Maronites, Nestorians, and Thomas-Christians of India, as their ecclesiastical language. So also the Zabians, or so-called St. John's Disciples, are said to make use of it, in their religious ceremonies. But as the language, as early as the eighth and ninth centuries, was greatly corrupted by the frequent use of the Arabic, and was driven by the Arabs from the cities in the tenth and eleventh, and from the villages in the twelfth and thirteenth centuries, it may be safely assumed that it is no longer in use as a vernacular language. Although several modern travelers of note, as Niebuhr and Brown, maintain that it is still spoken in some parts of Mesopotamia, about Raka, Edessa, and Damascus, as well as upon Lebanon, they are opposed by Ferrières Sauveboeuf and Volney, while Chateaubriand, Seetzen, Clarke, Joliffe, and Buckingham pass the matter over in silence; and Burckhardt only remarks, that the Maronites in the convent of Kashia use the Syriac, at the present day, as we do the Latin.*

Rem.—The LXX, even, use Syria, (Συρία, Σῦροι, Συριστί) in the wider sense, for the Old Testament אֲרָם (ܐܪܡ) comp. the Ἄριμοι in Hom. Il. ii. 783; Hesiod Theog. 304; Strabo Geog. i. 2. xi. 14; Stephanus Byzant. under Ἄριμα, and Bochart Geogr. S. ii. 5, 6); and the Greek and Roman Authors often confound Syria with Assyria (comp. Diod. Sic. ii. 13; Herodot. vii. 63; Strabo xvi. 2; Xenoph. Cyrop. vii. 5, 31; Lucian de Dea Syr. § 1; Oppian, Κυνηγ III. 402; Horat. Od. II. 11, 16; III. 4, 32. Justin. i. 2; Ammian Marcell. xxiii. 6. The Arabs call it الشام, as it lay at the left, when their faces were turned towards the east (comp. Abulfeda Tab. Syr. p. 5; Assemani Bibl. Orient. T. III. P. ii. p. 782.) In the earliest times this country was divided into several small nations, ruled by kings (comp. Jahn Bibl. Archäol. Thl. i. Bd. i. p. 51 seq.; Mannert Geogr. Bd. vi. p. 1 seq.; Vater Commentar über den Pentat. Bd. I. p. 152; Winer Bibl. Realwörterbuch, Bd. i. p. 51 seq.); of these, subsequently to the time of David, Zobah and Damascus are mentioned in the Scriptures, as the most powerful; David conquered them both (2 Sam. viii. 3 sq.; x. 6; 1 Chron. xix [xviii] 3, 4. sq), and Solomon kept possession of them

---

* Since Uhlemann prepared his grammar, it has been ascertained that the Nestorians use the Syriac language at the present day. Mr. Layard, in his admirable work on the ruins of Nineveh, says of the Nestorians (or Chaldæans as he incorrectly denominates them): "Most of their church books are written in Syriac, which, like the Latin in the West, became the sacred language in the greater part of the East." See Layard's Nineveh, chap. viii. Missionaries who are laboring among the Nestorians, bear testimony to the same fact.—Tr.

until Reson Ben-Eliada, who had been general of the king of Zoba (1 Kings xi. 23 sq.), re-established at Damascus a government independent of that of the Hebrews. Subsequently the Syrians were incorporated with the monarchies of the Assyrians (738 B. C.), the Persians (539 B. C.), and the Macedonians (331 B. C.). Though after the death of Alexander the Great, they arose again for a time under the Seleucidæ (301 B. C.), yet they again lost their independence by means of Pompey (64 B. C.), and their kings reigned only at Edessa, till the third century after Christ, when this kingdom came also under the Roman sway. At the division of the Empire, under Theodosius (395), Syria fell to the Byzantine Empire, after Jovianus had (A. D. 363) already surrendered Nesibis* to Sapores II, king of Persia. Afterwards it was taken possession of by the Arabs (636), and was subjected (660) to the Ommiades and several other Arabic royal families, whose dynasties were, in 1086, brought to a close by the Seljooks.† At the time of the Crusades, the Christians could maintain themselves there against the Seljooks but a short time (1097 and subsequently); and in 1171, Saladin wrested the country from them. In 1369, Syria became a prey to the marauding inroads of the Mongols under Timur; and it has now, for three centuries, sighed under the Turkish yoke (cf. Gatterer, Handbuch der Universalhist, Bd. I. p. 248 sq.; Beck, Weltgeschichte, Bd. I. p. 213 sq.; Heeren, Ideen über die Politik, u. s. w. Thl. I. p. 213 sq.; Rühs, Handbuch der Geschichte des Mittelalters, p. 152, sq.). The transition into broadness of pronunciation (πλατυστομον) seems not to have extended much beyond the time of the Babylonish captivity; and the Palmyrene Dialect, which is known to us by some inscriptions found among the ruins of Palmyra or Tadmor, and deciphered by Barthelemy and Swinton, may have grown up soon after Solomon, the founder of that city. In the Edessene Period, during which flourished Ephraem (died 378), Jacob Von Sarug, Isaac the Syrian, and Xenaias of Mabug, all of whom Jacob of Edessa, at the middle of the seventh century, recognizes as classical writers, theological learning was zealously cultivated (cf. Assem. T. III. P. II. p. 994). The Maronites on the Orontes and upon Lebanon, originally disciples and followers of St. Maro (cf. Assem. I. 496 sq.; Pfeiffer, in his Auszuge, p. 166 sq.; Gieseler, Lehrbuch der Kirchengeschichte, Bd. I. p. 675; Rühs, Handbuch der Geschichte des Mittelalters, p. 37) approximate to the ancient Syriac dialect; still more closely do the Nestorians (cf. Assem. T. III. P. II. p. 379), and the Thomas-Christians of India, who differ from the Nestorians only in name and place of residence (cf. Assem. a. a. O. pp. 413, 435. sq.; Pfeiffer, pp. 285, 484; Gieseler, Bd. I. pp. 417, 638), all of whom make use of it only as an ecclesiastical language; the two former speaking Arabic in common life, and the latter, the language

* A celebrated city and military post in Mesopotamia, generally written Nisibis.—Tr.
† Called, also, Seljuks, Seljouks, or Seljoukian Turks.—Tr.

of Malabar. Different from this is the dialect of the so-called Johannes-Christians, Mandæans, or Zabians (who are not to be confounded with a Mohammedan sect of the same name, in Maraccii Coran. Sur. II. p. 33 sq.; Assem. T. III. P. II. pp. 509-515; Pfeiffer, p. 510 sq.; cf. Gieseler, Bd. I. p. 66; Neander, Allgemeine Geschichte der christlichen. Religion und Kirche, Bd. I. Abth. II. p. 427), whose religious books are written in a corrupted Syriac, and which appears, from the numerous Ghebric expressions which occur in them, to have been drawn up in the Persian Irak. By the Nabatæan, according to Barhebræus (in Assem. T. I. p. 476) is to be understood the former language of the Syrian country-people. On the question, whether the Syrian is still a vernacular language, compare Niebuhr, Reisebeschr von Arabien, Bd. II. p. 352; Brown, Biblioth. der neuesten Reisebeschr. Thl. I. p. 489; Ferriéres Sauvebœuf, Mémoires historiques, etc., T. II. p. 169; Volney, Voyage en Syrie, etc., T. I. p. 331; and Burckhardt, Travels in Syria, etc., pp. 22, 186.

2. Syriac literature, which extends over almost all branches of knowledge, and in a special manner over the department of Theology, and possesses valuable works upon Oriental and Ecclesiastical History, flourished principally in the period between the fourth and tenth centuries of the Christian era. The language itself, which gave proof of its versatility of expression by the translations of Aristotle and other Greek authors, and by its accurate representation of mathematical subjects, had found, at an earlier period, in its own country, zealous cultivators in the departments of Grammar and Lexicography.

As the most ancient grammarians, whose works have been lost, history records the names of Achudemen (died 575), Joseph Huzita (died 580), Jacob of Edessa (died 698), who labored to restore the purity of the ancient language, Jesudenah (at the beginning of the eighth century), John Stylita (about 830), John, son of Chamis, Bishop of Themanum (850), and Honain, the physician (died 876). The first accurate grammar, however, was written by John Bar Zugbi, a Nestorian monk, at the beginning of the thirteenth century; about which time, also, Joseph Bar Malcon seems to have composed his *Rete Punctorum*, and Barhebræus (died 1286) to have made known his grammatical works. At the beginning of the sixteenth century, the study of the Syriac language was transplanted to Europe. Theseus Ambrosius learned the Syriac language from Syrians at Rome, in 1514, and became, in 1529, teacher to Albert Widmanstadt, who subsequently pursued the study under Simeon, Bishop of the Syrians upon Lebanon. Through the labors of these men, and of Moses von Merdin, whom

Ignatius, Patriarch of Antioch, had sent, in 1552, to Julius III. at Rome, and whose instructions were enjoyed by Andreas Dumas (Masius), the publication of the New Testament was effected in 1555. At the close of the sixteenth century, the grammatical study of the Syriac language was much promoted at Rome itself, by the Maronites Amira and Abraham Ecchellensis, whose copious grammatical works had already been preceded by the attempts of Theseus Ambrosius, Widmanstadt, Tremellius, Dumas, and Waser. They were followed, about the middle of the seventeenth century, by Isaac Sciadrensis and Joshua Accurensis. From this period onwards, the Syriac language has been grammatically pursued in Germany; partly independently of other languages, most copiously by the two Michaelises and Hoffmann; partly in connection with the Chaldee, as by Ludov. de Dieu and Jahn; or with the other Semitic languages, as by Buxtorf, Hottinger, Schaaf, Vater, and others.

The earliest attempts at Syriac lexicography were also made in the ninth and tenth centuries, in Syria, by Honain Isa or Joshua of Maruz, and Gabriel, the son of Bochtiesu. More important, however, are the contemporary works of Isa Bar-Ali (about 885), of Ananiesu Bar-Saru (about 900), and the most serviceable work of this kind by Abulhasan, Isa Bar-Bahlul (about 963,) which is still extant. The lexicons of Dumas, de la Boderie, Schindler, Crines, Buxtorf, Trost, Hottinger, Gutbier, Nicolai, Schaaf, and Zanolini, which have appeared since the sixteenth century, are confined to the New Testament, with which the Syriac literature in 1555 made its appearance in Europe. Ferrarius, and Edm. Castell, on the other hand, availed themselves of the above-mentioned Syriac works relating to the same subject, and John David Michaelis enriched the labors of the latter by valuable remarks and additions. The valuable work of Lorsbach, who compared all the Syriac works which had then been printed, besides a number of manuscripts, and collected the words and significations wanting in Syriac lexicons, still remains uncompleted. More recently, copious works have been promised by Bernstein and Quatremere, philologists of great merit in the department of Oriental literature. Glossaries are contained in the Chrestomathies of Michaelis, Kirsch, Tychsen, Grimm, Hahn, and Sieffert.

Rem.—Eusebius (Hist. Eccl. I. 13) cites the letter of Abgarus to Jesus, and the answer to it, as among the most ancient Syriac writings (cf. Assem. I. 554; III. P. II. p. 8; Gieseler, Bd. I. p. 74); and, in like manner, John is said to have written his Gospel in the Syriac language. But the most ancient Syriac work of undoubted authenticity, is perhaps the translation of the New Testament,* which must have existed as early as the second century (cf. Hug, Einleitung in die Schriften des N. T., Thl. I. p. 348 ; Gieseler, Bd. I. p. 123). That the Syrians considered their language to be richer than the Arabic is attested by Asseman (III. P. I. p. 326 sq.) ; and its capacity for rendering Greek authors may be judged from Barhebræus (Chron. p. 231. ed. Bruns), compared with Aristotle (Top. I. cap. 4). Abulpharagius, in his Historia Dynast., ed. Pocock, p. 147, mentions Theophilus of Edessa as the author of a successful translation of two books of the Iliad (cf. Assem. I. p. 521). In addition to the larger work of Asseman (Assemani Bibliotheca Orientalis Clementino-Vaticana, Romæ, 1729,) 3 vols. fol., and the abridgment of it by Pfeiffer, Erlangen, 1776, we possess a brief history of Syriac literature by Hoffmann, in Bertholdt's kritischem Journal der neuesten theologischen Literatur, Thl. XIV., pp. 225-291.

I. GRAMMARS.

Thesei Ambrosii, Introductio in Chald. linguam, Syriacam, etc., Papiæ, 1539.

Aug. Caninii, Institutiones linguæ Syriacæ, Parisiis, 1554.

Widmanstadii, Syriacæ linguæ prima elementa, Viennæ, 1555, 4to. ed. II. Antwerp, 1572.

Ioh. Merceri, Tabulæ in grammaticen linguæ Chald., quæ et Syriaca dicitur, Paris, 1560. 4to. Eiusd. grammatica Chald. et Syr. Vitebergæ, 1579, 8vo.

Imman. Tremellii, Grammatica Chald. et Syr. Genevæ, 1569, 4to. Appended also to his edition of the New Testament.

Andr. Masii, Grammatica linguæ Syriacæ (im Tom. VI. der Antwerp, Polygl.) 1573, fol.

Casp. Waseri, Institutio linguæ Syræ ex optimis quibusque apud Syros scriptoribus collecta. Lugd. Bat. 1594. 4to. Ed. II. Leidæ, 1619, 4to.

Georg. Amiræ, Grammatica Syr. sive Chald. etc. Romæ, 1596, 4to.

Christoph. Crinesii, Gymnasium Syr. h. e. linguæ Iesu Christo vernaculæ perfecta institutio, etc. Vitebergæ, 1611.

Io. Buxtorfii, Grammaticæ Chald. et Syr. libri III. Basil. 1615. Ed. II. 1650, 8vo.

* Hug, in his Introduction to the New Testament, says that the Translation of the New Testament was appended to that of the Old Testament, and that both were included under the same name, *Peshito*.—Tr.

Io. Casp. Myricæi, Grammatica Syro-Chaldæa. Genev. 1619, 4to.

Herm. Nicolai, Idea linguarr. Aramæarum per comparationem etc. Copenh. 1627, 8vo.

Abrah. Ecchellensis, Linguæ Syr. s. Chald. perbrevis institutio. Romæ, 1628, 16mo.

Ludov. de Dieu, Grammatica linguarr. orientt. Hebræorum, Chald. et Syr. inter se collaturum Lugd. Bat. 1628, ex recens. Clodii. Francof. ad M. 1683, 4to.

Isaac Sciadrensis, Grammatica linguæ Syr. Romæ, 1636, 8vo.

Ioh. Michael. Dilherri, Rudimenta grammaticæ Syr. Halis, 1637. Ed. II., 1646, 12mo.

Iosephi Acurensis, Grammatica linguæ Syr. Romæ, 1647, 8vo.

Io. Ernst. Gerhardi, Σκιαγραφία, linguæ Syro-Chald. Hal. Sax. 1649.

Andr. Sennerti, Ebraimus, Chaldaismus, Syriasmus, Arabismus nec non Rabbinismus, etc. Viteb. 1666, 4to. Eiusd. Chaldaismus et Syriasmus, etc., 1666.

Ioh. Henr. Hottingeri, Grammatica Chald. Syr. et Rabbinica Turic. 1652, 8vo. Eiusd. Grammatica quatuor linguarr. Hebr. Chald. Syr. et Arab. harmonica Turici, 1659, 4to (the Syriac also printed separately).

Briani Waltoni, Introductio ad lectionem linguarr. orientt. Hebr. Chald. Samarit. Syr. Arab. Pers. Armen. Copt. Lond. 1653, 12mo.

Io. Leusdeni, Scholæ Syriacæ lib. III. etc. Ultraiect. 1658, 8vo.

Guil. Beveridgii, Grammatica Syr. tribus libris tradita. Lond. 1658, 8vo.

Edm. Castelli, Brevis et harmonica quontum fieri potuit grammaticæ linguarr. Hebr. Chald. Syr. Æthiop. Arab. et Pers. delineatio. Lond. 1669 (preceding his Lex. Heptagl.)

Dav. Grafunderi, Grammatica Syriaca cum Syntaxi, etc. Viteb. 1665.

Io. Nicolai, Grammatica linguarr. Ebr. Chald. Syr. Arab. Æthiop. Pers.orientalium secundum prima præcepta delineata harmonica. Ienæ, 1670. 4to. Ed. II. Critica Sacra Francof. et Hamb. 1686.

Io. Altingi, Synopsis institutionum Chald. et Syr. Francof. ad M. 1676. Ed. VI. a Georg. Othone adornata, 1701, 8vo.

Christ. Cellarii, Porta Syriaca. Cizæ, 1677, 8vo. Eiusd. Porta Syriæ patentior, etc., 1682.

Henr. Opitii, Syriasmus facilitati et integritati suæ restitutus, etc. Lips. et Francof. 1678. 4to. in compendium redactus a *Christ. Ludovici* Viteb. 1669, 4to.

Car. Schafii, Opius Aramæum complectens grammaticam Chaldaico-Syriacam, Lugd. Bat. 1686, 8vo.

Io. Aug. Danzii, Aditus Syriæ reclusus, etc. Jenæ, 1689. Ed. III. 1715, 8vo.

Io. Ern. Gerhardi, Harmonia linguæ Chald. Syr. et Æthiop. Ienæ, 1693, 4to.

Herm. von der Hardt Syriacæ linguæ fundamenta. Helmst. 1694. 8vo. (Only Paradigms.)

Ge. Othonis Palæstra linguarr. orientt. Chald. Syr. Arab. Æth. Pers. etc. Francof. 1702. 4to.

Io. Phil. Hartmanni Hebraicæ, Chald. Syr. et Samarit. linguarum institutio harmonica. Francof. ad M. 1707. 4to.

Sam. Frid. Bucheri Thesaurus orientalis s. compendiosa et facilis methodus linguarr. orientt. etc. Francof. et Lips. 1725. 4to.

Christ. Bened. Michaelis Syriasmus i. e. grammatica linguæ Syr. Halis, 1741. 4to.

Io. David Michaelis Grammatica Syr. Halis, 1784. 4to.

I. G. Kals Grammatica Hebræo–harmonica cum Arab. et Aram. Amstelod. 1758. 8vo.

Iac. Ge. Christ. Adlerii Brevis linguæ Syr. institutio etc. Altonæ, 1784.

W. Hezel, Syrische Sprachlehre. Lemgo, 1788. 4to.

Ioh. Gottfr. Hasse Practisches Handbuch der Aramäischen oder Syrisch-Chaldäisch-Samaritanischen Sprache. Iena, 1794. 8vo.

Innoc. Fessleri Institutiones linguarr. orientt. Hebr. Chald. Syr. et Arab. Vratisl. Halis et Ienæ, 1787 et 1789.

Ol. Gerh. Tychseni Elementale Syr. Rostochi, 1793. 8vo. (Appended to his Chrestomathy.)

Io. Iahn. Aramäische oder Chaldäische und Syrische Sprachlehre für Anfänger. Wien 1793. 8vo. neu herausgegeben von *Oberleitner* Elementa Aramaicæ s. Chaldæo-Syriacæ linguæ etc. Viennæ, 1820. 8vo.

Ioh. Sev. Vater Handbuch der Hebr. Syr. Chald. und Arab. Grammatik. Leipzig, 1802 u. 1817. 8vo.

Thomas Yeates' Syriac Grammar, principally adapted to the New Testament in that Language. Lond. 1819. 8vo.

Hampus Tullberg Elementale Syr. P. I. et II. Lond. 1824. 8vo.

Paul Ewald Lehrbuch der syr. Sprache. Erlangen, 1826. 8vo.

Andr. Theoph. Hoffmanni Grammaticæ Syriacæ libri III. Halæ, 1827. 4to.

II. LEXICONS.

Andr. Masii Syrorum peculium. Antwerp, 1521. folio.

Fabr. Boderiani Dictionarium Syro-Chald. Antw. 1572. (Tom. VI. of the Antw. Polygl.)

Val. Schindleri Lexicon pentagl. Hanoviæ, 1612. 1649. Lond. 1635 Francof. 1653. 1695. fol.

Christoph. Crinesii Lexicon Syriacum. Viteb. 1612. 4to.

Ioh. Bapt. Ferrarii Nomenclator Syriacus. Romæ, 1622. 4to.

Ioh. Buxtorfii iun. Lexicon Chald. et Syr. Basil. 1622. 4to.

Martini Trostii Lexicon Syr. etc. Cothenis Anhalt. 1623. 4to.

Thomas a Novaria Nomenclator Syr. Romæ, 1636. 8vo.
Andr. Sennerti Lexici Chald. et Syr. compendium. Viteb. 1666. 4to.
Ioh. Henr. Hottingeri Etymologicum orientt. s. Lexicon harmonicum heptagl. etc. Francof. 1661. Turici, 1664. 4to.
Dav. Grafunderi Compendium Lexici, Syr. (Appended to his Syriac Grammar.)
Aegid. Gutbirii Lexicon Syr. Hamb. 1667. 8vo. (Appended to his New Testament.)
Edm. Castelli Lexicon heptagl. Lond. 1669. From this has been specially edited the Syriac, by J. G. Michaelis, under the title, Edmundi Castelli Lexicon Syr. Gotting. 1788. Tom. II. 4to.
Io. Fr. Nicolai Hodogeticum orientale harmonicum etc. Ienæ, 1670. 4to.
Christoph. Cellarii Glossarium Syro-Latinum. Cizæ, 1683. 4to.
Car. Schafii Lexicon Syr. concordantiale. Lugd. Bat. 1708. (Appended to the New Testament.)
Ant. Zanolini Lexicon Syriacum. Patav. 1742. 8vo. (Appended to the New Testament.)

III. CHRESTOMATHIES.

Ioh. Dav. Michaelis Syrische Chrestomathie Thl. 1. Göttingen, 1768. 8vo. Die II. Ausg. 1783. mit einem Glossar. u. Anm. vervollständigt unter dem Titel: *Ioh. Dav. Michaelis* Chrestomathia Syr. Ed. III. glossario adnotationibusque instructa a *I. Ch. Dœpke.* 1829.
I. C. G. Adleri Chrestomathia Syr. Hafn, 1784.
Ioh. Gottfr. Hasse Lectiones Syro-Arabico-Samaritano-Æthiopicæ Regiom. et Lipsiæ, 1788. 8vo.
Georg. Guil. Kirschii Chrestomathia Syr. Hofæ, 1789. 8vo. (Newly edited by Bernstein.)
Olai Gerh. Tychsen Elementale Syriacum etc. Rostochi, 1793. 8vo.
Henr. Ad. Grimm Neue Syrische Chrestomathie mit einem Glossarium u. s. w. Lemgo, 1795. 8vo.
Gust. Knoes Chrestomathia Syr. maximam partem e Codd. MSS. collecta. Gotting, 1807. 8vo.
Aug. Hahn et Sieffert Chrestomathia Syr. s. S. Ephraemi carmina selecta. Lips, 1825. 8vo. (With a Lex. Syr.)

SYRIAC GRAMMAR.

PART FIRST.

ELEMENTS OF THE LANGUAGE.

TABLE OF CONSONANTS.

Order.	NAME.		Initial.	Medial.	Final. Connected.	Final. Unconnected.	SOUND.	Numerical value.
1	Olaph	ܐܠܦ	ܐ	ܐ	ܐ	ܐ	*Spiritus lenis.*	1
2	Beth	ܒܝܬ	ܒ	ܒ	ܒ	ܒ	B, Bh, V.	2
3	Gomal	ܓܡܠ	ܓ	ܓ	ܓ	ܓ	G.	3
4	Dolath	ܕܠܬ	ܕ	ܕ	ܕ	ܕ	D, Dh (*th* in *this*).	4
5	He	ܗܐ	ܗ	ܗ	ܗ	ܗ	H.	5
6	Vau	ܘܘ	ܘ	ܘ	ܘ	ܘ	W or V.	6
7	Zain	ܙܝܢ	ܙ	ܙ	ܙ	ܙ	Z, ζ Gr., ç Fr.	7
8	Cheth	ܚܝܬ	ܚ	ܚ	ܚ	ܚ	Ch, or Hh.	8
9	Teth	ܛܝܬ	ܛ	ܛ	ܛ	ܛ	T.	9
10	Jud	ܝܘܕ	ܝ	ܝ	ܝ	ܝ	Y.	10
11	Coph	ܟܦ	ܟ	ܟ	ܟ	ܟ	K, Ch.	20
12	Lomad	ܠܡܕ	ܠ	ܠ	ܠ	ܠ	L.	30
13	Mim	ܡܝܡ	ܡ	ܡ	ܡ	ܡ	M.	40
14	Nun	ܢܘܢ	ܢ	ܢ	ܢ	ܢ	N.	50
15	Semcath	ܣܡܟܬ	ܣ	ܣ	ܣ	ܣ	S.	60
16	Ee	ܥܐ	ܥ	ܥ	ܥ	ܥ	ע Hebrew.	70
17	Phe	ܦܐ	ܦ	ܦ	ܦ	ܦ	P, Ph, F.	80
18	Tsode	ܨܕܐ	ܨ	ܨ	ܨ	ܨ	Ts.	90
19	Koph	ܩܘܦ	ܩ	ܩ	ܩ	ܩ	K guttural, Q.	100
20	Rish	ܪܝܫ	ܪ	ܪ	ܪ	ܪ	R.	200
21	Shin	ܫܝܢ	ܫ	ܫ	ܫ	ܫ	Sh.	300
22	Thau	ܬܘ	ܬ	ܬ	ܬ	ܬ	Th. T. Θ Greek.	400

CHAPTER I.

Written Characters and their Use.

§ 1. *Consonants.*

The Syriac, or West Aramæan Language, has an alphabet consisting, like that of the Hebrew and Chaldee, of twenty-two consonants. In common with the Arabic, it connects together the several letters of a word by horizontal lines at the bottom; from which arises a fourfold form, though essentially the same, according as a letter is initial, medial, or final, or is connected or unconnected with the preceding letter, as exhibited in the table on the preceding page.

Rem. 1.—The character exhibited in the preceding alphabet, is called *Peshito, i. e. the simple.* It is employed by the Maronites and Jacobites, and is said to have been invented by Jacob of Edessa in the seventh century. Besides this, Amira mentions the *Estrangelo*, not from στρογγυλος, *round*, (see Asseman Biblioth. Orient. T. III. P. II. p. 378.) which, according to Michaelis Gram. Syr., p. 15, means the *Gospel character* (scriptura evangelii). It was the basis of the Nestorian smaller character, to which the so-called *double* alphabet, used for inscriptions and titles of books, bears a strong resemblance. There is also the *Palmyrene* alphabet, found in inscriptions on the ruins of Palmyra or Tadmor, and the *Mandæan* or *Nabatæan* alphabet. The latter, in consequence of the amalgamation of the gutturals ܐ with ܥ, and ܗ with ܚ, consists of only twenty consonants. It is written in a continuous line, with four different forms of each letter, viz., the simple consonant, and the consonant with the vowels *a, i,* or *u.*

Rem. 2.—The letters ܐ, ܕ, ܗ, ܘ, ܙ, ܨ, ܪ, ܬ, connect only with the preceding letter. After one of these letters, therefore, ܕ, ܝ, ܙ, ܓ, stand unconnected; and also, with the exception of ܝ, always at the beginning of a word. The final letters are ܟ, ܠ, ܡ, ܢ, ܩ. ܐ before ܠ is written ܠܐ; and after it ܐ or ܠܐ. Double ܠ, at the end of a word takes the form of ܠܠ. The letter G, in words adopted from other languages, is written ܓ̰ . Several consonants, where they terminate a word, are slightly inflected upward; e.g. ܟ, ܒ, ܦ, etc.

Rem. 3.—The gutturals express the several gradations of guttural sounds from the weakest to the strongest. ܐ and ܗ may be compared with the *Spiritus lenis* and *Spiritus asper* of the Greek language (§ 12. 5. b). Deeper guttural sounds are ܚ (= the German ch) and ܥ which the Greeks express, sometimes by the *Spiritus asper*, and sometimes by γ. The sound of ܟ is formed in the fore-part of the mouth; that of ܩ farther back towards the throat. ܫ = שׁ sometimes stands for ς at the end of Greek words, and is pronounced, according to Amira, p. 9, *sc* before *e* and *i*. The aspirated consonants ܒܓܕܟܦܬ are, in some MSS., marked as such with a red point placed over them; the removal of the aspiration is indicated by the same sign beneath them (§ 5).

Rem. 4.—The division of consonants, with reference to the organs of speech, is the same as in Hebrew. But the gutturals ܐܗܚܥ occasion less difficulty than in Hebrew, as the *Sheva* and *Daghesh forte* are wanting in Syriac. Of the gutturals, in connection with ܝ and ܘ, it is to be remarked; *a*) that ܐ between two vowels has the sound of *y*; e.g. ܩܳܐܶܡ *ko-yem*; *b*) that ܘ quiesces in ܳ and ܽ (= *o* and *u*), and after ܰ and ܶ (= *a* and *e*), forms the dipthongs *au* and *eu*; *c*) that initial ܝ with ܺ = *i*, and even when ܐ is prefixed, it is pronounced *i*; e. g. ܐܝܗܽܘܕܳܐ *Ihudho*; *d*) that initial ܥ (§ 8. b) before ܗ is pronounced like ܐ; e. g. ܥܰܗܶܕ *ehadh*.

Rem. 5.—The letters of the Alphabet suffice for designating the numerals as far as 400 (Vid. Table of Consonants, Amira, p.12. sq). In compound numbers, the larger stand first; e. g. ܬܡܐ 441. From 500—900, the tens of 50—90 are denoted by a dot over the letter; e.g. ܣ̇ 600, ܦ̇ 800. Thousands are designated by ܼ placed under the units, ten thousand by ܼ, ten thousand thousand by ܼ. The numbers 20 and 50 are also expressed by double ܟܟ and ܢܢ, the final letters falling away where units are added. Fractional numbers are designated by a small line drawn obliquely downward, from left to right, over the letter which expresses the denominator of the fraction; e.g. ܒ̀ = ½, ܓ̀ = ⅓ &c.

§ 2. *Vowels in General* (*Vowel Letters and Vowel Signs*).

InSyriac, the vowel-letters ܐ, ܘ, and ܝ originally served to designate the vowels, and, at the time of Mohammed, the Syrians were acquainted with only three vowel-signs, which sufficed for their language, and which the Arabs appear to have borrowed from them. Afterwards the Monophysites sought to express the Greek vowels, and increased their number to seven (v. Asseman T. I. pp. 477, 478; Gesenius Lehrgeb. p. 34), and since the time of Theophilus of Edessa, in the eighth century, the Greek vowels appear to have been in common use. The Nestorians, on the other hand, make use of diacritical points (Asseman T. III. P. II. p. 378). The Monophysites or Maronites commonly use them only in doubtful cases.

Rem.—Even in the last century, the Maronite Gabriel Heva employed the vowel-letters to designate the vowels, making ܥ = *a*, ܐ = *o*, ܐ̇ = *e*, ܝ = *i*, and ܘ = *u* (v. Michaelis. p. 29).

---

§ 3. *Vowel Signs.*

The Syrians denote the vowels by diacritical points, or by characters formed from and in imitation of the Greek vowels, the latter mode being that now generally used. In ancient manuscripts both modes occur together.

FORM. Syriac.	FORM. Greek.	NAME.		SOUND.
—ܲ	—ܰ or —ܱ	Pethocho	(ܦܬܳܚܳܐ)	a.
—ܶ or —ܶ	—ܳ or —ܴ	Revotzo	(ܪܒܳܨܳܐ)	e.
—ܻ	—ܻ or —ܼ	Chevotzo	(ܚܒܳܨܳܐ)	i.
—ܿ or —ܵ	—ܳ	Zekofo	(ܙܩܳܦܳܐ)	o.
ܘ̣—, ܘ̇— ܘ̇—	ܘܼ—	Etzotzo	(ܥܨܳܨܳܐ)	u.

Rem. 1.—The names are derived from the form of the organ used in pronouncing the vowel. The Greek forms from which they are derived are easily recognized. ܽ— also occurs without ܘ = *u* in ܟܽܠ and ܡܟܽܠ. (For ܟܽܒܪܺܝܬܳܐ, Luke xvii. 29, stands more correctly ܟܶܒܪܺܝܬܳܐ Psalm xi 6). The first three vowel-signs may also be written beneath the consonants.

Rem. 2.—As to pronunciation, ܰ— seems to have denoted *a* and *ae*, though ܳ— was sometimes sounded by the Nestorians like *a* (V. Asseman T. III. P. II. p. 379). In foreign words it quiesces in ܘ. In ܽ— are contained both the German *ö* and *ü*.

Rem. 3.—As to quantity it may be assumed with some certainty that ܳ— is always long, and ܰ— always short; according to others, ܺ— with ܝ, ܳ— and ܽ— with ܘ are long; ܰ— is short, except in foreign words. Amira, on the other hand, maintains that ܰ— = *ă*, ܳ— = *ō*, and the others, even ܽ— with ܘ, are common. Some grammarians also denote the quantity of the vowels by different signs, thus;—

LONG.		SHORT.		
—	—	—	—	Revotzo.
	—		—	Chevotzo.
o—	·o—		o—	Etzotzo.

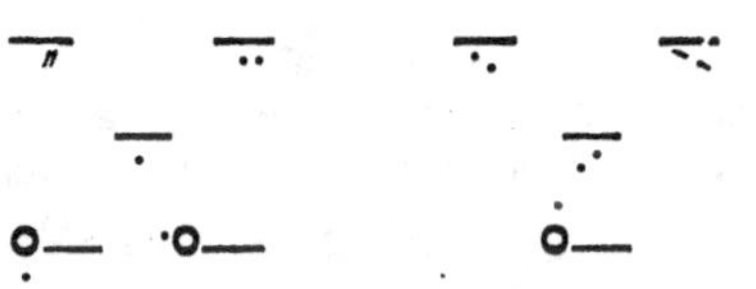

Rem. 4.—The dipthongs are formed with ܘ and ܝ. With Vau; *a*) with ܰ— preceding at the beginning or middle of a word, *au*; e. g. ܡܰܘܬܳܐ; *b*) with ܶܝ preceding, *oi* nearly (the German *eu*); e. g. ܐܦܠܝܘܗܝ; *c*) in the middle of a word, after ܺܝ, *iu*; e. g. ܢܦܫܝܘܗܝ; *d*) Vau doubled, the first with ܽ—, *ou* (according to Amira *u*). With Yud (besides the combinations *b* and *c* above); *a*) with a preceding ܰ—, *ai*; e. g. ܟܰܝܢܳܐ; *b*) with ܳ— in the middle and at the end of a word, *oi*; e. g. ܩܰܕܡܳܝܬܳܐ.

---

§ 4. *Diacritical Points which supply the place of Vowels.*

These were employed earlier than were the vowels, and

were used even after the invention of the vowels, by the Nestorians. The point which designates the suffix 3 sing. fem. ܗ̇ seems to have originated from that system.

REM.—According to Amira p. 51, ܗܘ=ܗ̇ܘ; while ܗ̇ܘ=ܗܘ̇; ܗܝ=ܗ̣ܝ; ܗܝ=ܗ̇ܝ. Ludov. de Dieu has treated this subject more definitely in his Grammar, p. 35 seq.; according to him the point when above the consonant denotes *a*, *o*, and *ŭ*, under it *e*, under ܝ and ܐ *i*, and under ܘ *ū*. The principal use of this point in the verb, is to denote the different persons and tenses (v. Amira, p. 51; Lud. de Dieu, p. 37). Throughout the preterite, with the exception of the 1 sing., it stands under the radicals. In the participle, it denotes, over the first radical, in Peal, ‗̊‗, in Aphel, ‗̊‗, or in Verbs med. Vau, ‗̂‗. In the imperative and infinitive it may be omitted or written underneath. The future takes it only under the radicals, not under the preformatives, with the exception of the 1 sing., where it stands above it (comp. Isenbiehl, Beobachtungen von dem Gebrauche des Syrischen Puncti diacritici bei den Verbis, Göttingen, 1773).

---

§ 5. *Kushoi and Rukok* (ܩܘܫܝ — ܪܘܟܟ).

1. According to Lud. de Dieu and Norberg, the Syrians have in fact the Sheva, and pronounce a vowelless consonant with a short half-sound of *ĕ*; e.g. ܢܩܘܡ pronounced *n^e kum*. Some Grammarians, as Amira, p.42, and the Zabians, use ‗̂‗. So too, according to Asseman, the doubling of consonants in pronunciation (Daghesh forte) occurs among the Oriental Syrians, and, according to the analogy of the Hebrew, in Pael and Ethpaal of Verbs ܥܡ̈ and ܟܠܠ̈.* But as the doubly written consonant falls away where analogy would require it to be retained (§ 8), this grammatical usage is still very doubtful. This duplication is retained only in foreign words.

2. Analogous with Daghesh lene is *Kushoi*, (i.e. *hardening*), a red point inserted over the aspirates, in manuscripts, which removes the aspiration. The retention of the aspiration is indicated by a point placed underneath, called *Rukok* (i. e. *softening*).

---

* It should be borne in mind that Sheva and Daghesh are not, in Syriac, denoted by any written characters, and appear only in pronunciation. —Tr.

Rem.—Some consider Kushoi to be Daghesh forte, which is denied by Amira and Gabriel Sionita. Lud. de Dieu, p. 25 sq., places it; *a*) at the beginning of words, except where ܡܘܕܠ precede, or where the preceding word ends in ܝ, ܘ, ܐ, in which case Rukok is retained; e. g. ܬܟܬܘܒܐ, ܠܟܬܒܐ; *b*) in the middle, after a quiescent letter; e. g. ܡܠܟܬܗ; *c*) after dipthongs; e. g. ܒܝܬ; ܡܘܬܐ, with the exception of ܐܝܟ *as*. Rukọk, on the contrary, occurs, besides the cases noted under *a* above; *a*) when one of the aspirates ends a syllable, but is in the same case hardened by a preceding vacant consonant; e. g. ܐܬܦܪܩ; *b*) when, according to Hebrew analogy, they follow a movable Sheva; e. g. ܦܘܪܩܢܐ; *c*) after an open syllable; e. g. ܐܒܐ. So too these consonants are not pronounced as aspirates in Pa. and Ethpa. of Verbs ܦܢ, when the ܢ preceding them has fallen away; e. g. ܐܬܟܠܝ from ܢܟܠ; and in verbs with the middle radical doubled, where, in Hebrew, Daghesh forte stands. Furthermore, here belong the letters in which one having fallen away before them, is to be compensated for, in the future and infinitive of verbs ܥܥ, or in general where Daghesh forte euphonic stands in Hebrew. These points do not occur in printed works.

---

§ 6. *Ribui* (ܪܒܘܝ).

1. To distinguish the plural of nouns and verbs from the singular written with the same consonants, the Syriac makes use of *Ribui*, *i. e.* two points placed horizontally over the word. This sign is still retained, like the vowels, in printed books. Thus, by means of these points ܡܠܟܐ is read ܡܠܟܐ̈ *the kings*, and distinguished from ܡܠܟܐ, *the king*. This sign is also used in the 3 plur. fem. pret. of Verbs 3 rad. Olaph in all the conjugations except Peal (§ 32), to distinguish it from 3 sing. masc.; e. g. ܐܬܩܠܣܝ̈ *they have praised themselves*, from ܐܬܩܠܣܝ *he has praised himself*. In like manner Ribui strengthens the distinction between the 3 plur. pret. masc. and fem., where the formatives ܘ and ܝ at the end sometimes fall away from the 3 sing. masc.; e. g. ܩܛܠ — ܩܛܠܘ, ܩܛܠܝ̈. The plurals, which are easily recognized, re-

main without this designation, though it is not omitted in plural forms with suffixes. In numerals the usage is arbitrary. *Some* mark with this sign only the feminines, and the forms with suffixes; e. g. ܬܪ̈ܬܝܢ, ܬܪ̈ܝܗܘܢ.

Rem.—Amira, p. 48, omits Ribui, when the plural form ܝܢ (§ 44) has the signification ܐܢܘܢ or ܐܝܬܝܗܘܢ, *i. e. they are*, but adopts the above-mentioned use in numerals, and uses it also with prepositions joined with plural suffixes (§ 16. c).

2. Ribui also serves to denote collectives; e. g. ܬܘܪܐ *a beeve*, ܬܘܪ̈ܐ *a herd of beeves.*

Rem.—When Ribui stands over ܪ (with the exception of the 1 sing. pret. and fut., and the participles Act. Pe., according to § 4. Rem.), or coincides with a diacritical point representing —, one of the points is omitted. When three points come together, one of them represents Kushoi.

---

§ 7. *Mehagyono and Marhetono.*

(ܡܪܗܛܢܐ — ܡܗܓܝܢܐ).

When an accumulation of consonants without vowels, occurs, and the Syrians wish to indicate that a monosyllabic word is to be pronounced as a dissyllable, or a dissyllabic word as a trisyllable, and so on, they place a line under the consonant to which a vowel (usually — more rarely —) is to be supplied; e. g. ܕܚܝܠܬܐ. This line is called *Mehagyono*, and denotes a removal of this accumulation in utterance (Diæresis). If, on the contrary, the voice is to hurry over these same consonants, a line is drawn above them, which is called *Marhetono*; e. g. ܕܡܬܐ.

Rem. 1.—Some Grammarians place Mehagyono only before ܠܡܐܡܪ and before ܫ in ܕܚܫܒܬܐ. Amira, p. 41. sq., compares the two with *Diæresis* and *Synæresis*, which may have been transferred from prosody into prose. (Vd. Chrestom. Syr. ed. Hahn et Sieffert, Lips. 1825. p. 11).

Rem. 2.—Sometimes a line is found over consonants; *a*) in numerals; e. g. ܝܒ 12; *b*) in abbreviations; e. g. ܡܫ for ܡܫܝܚܐ; *c*) over the particle of exclamation ܐܘ, to distinguish it from ܐܘ.

§ 8. *Linea Occultans.*

This line placed under consonants denotes; *a*) that the letter under which it stands is not pronounced; e. g. ܡܕ̱ܬܐ (§ 12. 1); *b*) that ܠ at the beginning of a word, followed by ܗ is to be pronounced weaker, and like ܐ; e.g. ܠ̱ܗܘܢ (vid. §1. Rem.4); *c*) that the letter quiesces, viz., in the imperf. of the pass. Ethpeel and Ethpaal; e. g. ܐܬ̱ܩܛܠ, pronounced *ethkatl*, and imp. from ܪܗܛ; which with the transposition of the first two radicals is ܗ̱ܪܛ (comp. § 12. 1).

Rem.—Some have extended this also to the imperatives Ethtaphal and Eshtaphal; but in the latter especially, it appears to be merely a diacritical designation of the imperat. As such it may in general be regarded as coming under *b* and *c* above.

§ 9. *Tone.*

1. The tone stands regularly upon the penultimate syllable; when the ultimate does not terminate in a movable consonant; e. g. ܡܠܟܐ, *Màlco.*

Rem.—In an accumulation of consonants, where by Mehagyono (§ 7) the penultimate syllable becomes the antepenultimate, the tone remains upon the stem-syllable.

It is more difficult to determine whether words, which, according to Amira, p. 462, have ܘ in the penultimate, follow the same rule; e. g. ܐܚܘܢܐ, and should be pronounced *áchuno* or *achúno.*

2. The tone is on the ultimate, when it ends in a movable consonant; e. g. ܢܠܒ; so too with ܘ and ܝ final, if they have arisen from ܘܬ and ܝܠ; e. g. ܡܠܟܘ from ܡܠܟܘܬ. vid. Amira, pp. 467—469.

§ 10. *Signs of Interpunction.*

The Syrians, who do not possess the Hebrew system of accents, divide their periods, according to Amira, p. 475, into protasis and apodosis, which again are subdivided into smaller parts, and include the more precise designation of subject and predicate. In this respect they designate; *a*) the separate members of the protasis with (:); *b*) the close of the protasis with (⁝), which is also the sign of interrogation; *c*) the separate members of the apodosis with (.·), which also marks longer interrogations; and *d*) the close of a period is marked by a point, which as it also occurs in the middle of a period, some consider to be the smallest mark of interpunction, and (❖) or (::) the largest point.

REM.—Amira, p. 479, mentions a point standing over a word which indicates a question, address, admiration, praise, command, and the like.

CHAPTER II.

PECULIARITIES AND CHANGES OF THE LETTERS.

---

§ 11. *General View.*

As the changes in the different parts of speech are effected partly by consonants and partly by vowels, this chapter is naturally divided into two parts. In the first place, those changes which take place uniformly, in accordance with fixed laws, in pronouns, verbs, and nouns, must be accurately distinguished from those which occur only in individual forms. Though the former class of changes will be here principally treated, yet in order to afford a proper connection between them, that which occurs universally will be first treated of, and that which takes place in special and individual cases will be appended, either independently or in remarks.

---

§ 12. *Changes of the Consonants.*

Of those changes in the radical consonants which Hebrew grammarians classify as Assimilation, Transposition, Falling away, Exchange, and Addition, the first only is wanting in Syriac. And this want is only in form, for in point of fact this feature exists in those cases where a letter is dropped in pronunciation by the occurrence of Linea occultans (§ 8. comp. Gesenius, Lehrgebaude, p. 132). Here should be noticed the following—

1. Consonants are dropped in pronunciation, by the occurrence of Linea occultans, as follows: A) *In General;* *a*) in nouns whose middle radical is doubled; e. g. ܡܐܢܐ *mano;* *b*) ܕ without a vowel before ܬ; e. g ܡܕܝܢܬܐ; *c*) ܗ in suffixes of the 3 masc. sing. ܝܗܝ, ܘܗܝ, ܢܝܗܝ, ܘܢܝܗܝ of the verb, and ܘܗܝ of the noun plural (v. Table to § 16); or when Linea occultans has arisen from theGreek *Spiritus asper*; e.g. ܪܗܘܡܝ ῾Ρωμη; *d*) ܘ in derivatives of verbs ܦܝ and ܦܐ, as ܦܘܩܕܢܐ from ܦܩܐ: B) *In particular* is this the case; *a*) with ܐ initial in ܐܢܫܝܢ, ܐܢܬܝܢ, ܐܢܫ, and in the pronoun ܐܢܐ in connection with the participle, ܩܐܡܐ ܐܢܐ; *b*) with ܗ, particularly in the following cases; *a*) in the pronouns ܗܘ and ܗܝ, with the throwing back of the vowel upon the preceding vacant consonant; e. g. ܟܠܗ ܗܘ; or with the falling away of the letter with the preceding vowel; e. g. ܩܫܐ ܗܘ pronounced *k*ᵉ *sheu;* in which case, however, before ܗܘ, — passes into — ; e. g. ܐܢܐ ܗܘ for ܐܢܐ; *β*) in ܗܘܐ (v. § 38) when it is an auxiliary verb; e. g. ܩܛܠ ܗܘܐ *he had killed*; *γ*) in ܢܗܒ for ܢܗܒ *to give*; *c*) with ܠ in ܐܙܠ *to go away,* when it should have a vowel which falls back upon the ܐ; e. g. ܐܙܠܬ for ܐܙܠܬ (v. § 28); *d*) with ܢ in the pronouns ܐܢܬ masc. and ܐܢܬܝ fem., and their plurals ܐܢܬܘܢ masc. ܐܢܬܝܢ fem., and in some other words; e.g. ܫܢܬܐ; and finally; *e*) with ܪ in ܒܪܬ *daughter;* (v. § 8).

Rem.—Linea occultans is retained under ܐ in nouns derived from those adduced under *a*; e.g. ܐܢܫܘܬܐ, ܐܢܬܬܐ, ܐܢܫܘܬܐ, and many others. It also occurs in ܐܢܐ, ܗܘ, and ܗܝ when they are used for the logical copula or substantive verb (comp. § 16. I., § 54. A. 3. *a* and *c*). In these pronouns, even when they stand pleonastically (§ 55. A), the logical copula is fundamentally involved, as is confirmed by the pleonastic use of ܗܘܐ (§ 68. A), which verb loses Linea occultans only when it is used absolutely in the sense of *to be, to become, to come to pass;* As to further inflection of ܢܗܘܐ compare § 29. 1. *Rem.*

2. *Transposed* is ܬ before sibilants in *Ethpe.*, *Ethpa.*, and *Eshta.*; e. g. ܐܣܬܠܟ from ܣܠܐ, ܐܣܬܘܕܝ from ܣܘܕܝ.

Rem.—ܬ is changed into ܛ after ܨ, into ܕ after ܙ; e. g. ܐܨܛܒܥ for ܐܬܨܒܥ, ܐܙܕܡܢ for ܐܬܙܡܢ. There is no transposition when ܬ is doubled in Ethpe. of Verbs ܥܥ and ܥܘ; e. g. ܐܬܬܣܝܡ (v. §31. 2). ܐ as middle radical is sometimes transposed; e. g. ܐܬܬܐܟܒ from ܟܐܒ. Also ܙ in the imperat. from ܙܗܛ (v. § 8).

3. *Dropped* are; *a*) ܐ with Linea occultans; e. g. ܡܪܢܐ for ܡܪܐܢܐ and as first radical in the 1 sing. fut. Pe. infin. and part. Pa. of Verbs ܦܐ (§ 28. 1); e. g. ܐܟܘܠ for ܐܐܟܘܠ; and in ܐܦܝ for ܐܦܐ; *b*) ܝ and ܢ as first radical, and ܘ as middle radical in Verbs ܦܝ (§ 29. 2), ܦܢ (§ 33. 1), and ܥܘ (§ 31. 1); e. g. ܡܦܩ from ܢܦܩ. Here belong such nouns as ܡܦܩܬܐ for ܡܢܦܩܬܐ The same is true also in respect to the middle radical of Verbs ܥܥ (§ 34. 1), and the nouns derived therefrom; *c*) one of two ܬ without a vowel standing between them; e. g. ܚܬܐ for ܚܬܬܐ. Also when three ܬ stand together in the fut. pass.; e. g. ܬܬܛܠܠ for ܬܬܬܛܠܠ. Finally ܬ falls away at the end of the fem. endings ܘܬ and ܝܬ; e. g. ܡܠܟܘ for ܡܠܟܘܬ.

4.—*Exchanged* are; *a*) the gutturals ܥ and ܐ before ܗ; e. g. ܐܗܝܡ for ܥܗܝܡ; *b*) in transferring Hebrew words into Syriac, ז passes into ܕ, צ into ܛ, ש into ܬ, sometimes ר into ܠ and ܢ; also ר of verbs ע״ו into ܗ; e. g

ܕܗܒܐ = זָהָב ; ܨܘܪܐ = צַוָּר ; ܬܘܪܐ = שׁוֹר ; ܬܪܝܢ = שְׁנַיִם ; ܒܪܘܬ = בְּרוֹשׁ ; *c*) ܬ, when transposed with sibilants, in the passive, goes over into ܕ and ܛ, according to Rem. 2. above; *d*) ܐ with ܬ in the construct state fem., and before suffixes (§§ 45, 46); and in the *Ethpe.* and *Ethpa.* of verbs ܦܐ (§ 28. 1 Rem. ; e. g. ܐܬܬܐܡܪ for ܐܬܐܡܪ.

Rem.—This last has been also applied to nouns derived from ܦܐ Verbs ; e.g. ܬܘܢܝܐ from ܐܢܫ. In many cases this usage is doubtful ; e. g. ܬܘܕܝܐ which may be derived from ܝܕܐ or ܐܘܕܝ. Hence the form ܬܘܕܝܬܐ is found. The derivatives from Aphel do not belong here ; e. g. ܬܘܪܒܝܬܐ from ܐܘܪܒܝ.

5.—*Added* are ; *a*) sometimes ܐ at the beginning, before a vacant consonant ; e. g. ܐܟܣܦܐ for ܟܣܦܐ ; ܐܫܟܚ for ܫܟܚ ; also in Greek words beginning with Σ ; e. g. ܐܣܛܕܝܘܢ = ϛαδιον ; *b*) ܗ to denote the *Spiritus asper* in Greek words ; e. g. ܗܪܘܡܝܐ Ῥωμαιος (§ 12. 1. A. c); even in compound words in the later Syriac ; e. g. ܣܘܢܗܘܕܘܣ συνοδος ; and in cases where ܗ does not represent *Spiritus asper ;* e. g. ܦܛܗܪܘܣ Πετρος ; *c*) ܢ is added where it supplies the place of Daghesh forte with Linea occultans ; e. g. ܢܓܢܒܪܐ = גִּבּוֹר ; ܐܢܬܬܐ = אִשָּׁה.

§ 13. *Quiescent Letters.*

The vowel-letters ܝ, ܘ, ܐ, and, according to some, ܗ also, quiesce in the preceding vowel.

Rem.—Here belongs only ܗ ; for ܗ̇ of the suf. 3 sing. fem. = הּ of the Hebrew.

The following letters quiesce :

1. ܐ final in ◌ܳ and ◌ܶ ; e. g. ܩܪܐ, ܩܪܶܐ ; ܐ medial in ◌ܳ and ◌ܶ ; e.g. ܡܳܐܢܐ, ܡܳܐܟܠ ; and if it have a vowel, this falls back upon the preceding vacant consonant ; e. g. ܢܶܐܢܐ for ܢܐܢܐ. And so in words transferred from the Hebrew ; e. g. ܟܐܒ = כְּאֵב.

Rem.— ܐ quiesces in ◌ܶ in ܟܶܐܦ݂ܳܐ, ܪܶܫܳܐ, ܐܶܐܕ and ܐܶܬܶܐܐ. In Greek words ι and αι are represented by ܐ◌ܺ, αι sometimes by ܐܝ◌ܺ; e.g. ܩܺܐܒܽܘܛܳܐ κιβωτος; ܩܺܐܪܳܘܣ καιρος. In the later Syriac ܐ stands for α and ε.

2. ܘ quiesces in ◌ܳ; e.g. ܩܳܘܡ, and sometimes ܘܘ; e.g. ܩܘܘܪܝܳܐ (§ 3. Rem. 4).

Rem. — In Greek words ܘ quiesces in ◌ܳ, in the termination ܘܣ = ος; e. g. ܦܺܝܠܺܝܦܳܘܣ = Φιλιππος. ܘܣ is also used for αις; e. g. ܐܶܪܟ݂ܳܘܣ = ἀρχαις. In the later language we find also ܐܶܬܺܝܢܰܘܣ = Ἀθηναις; ܐܶܪܟ݂ܰܘܣ = ἀρχας.

3. ܝ, medial and final, quiesces, in ◌ܰ and ◌ܺ; e. g. ܚܺܝܡ, ܐܶܬܺܝܟ݂ܺܝܠ. ܝ initial usually quiesces in ◌ܺ; e. g. ܝܺܕܰܥ, and ◌ܺ falls back upon the preceding vowelless prefix; e. g. ܘܺܝܕܥܶܗ for ܘܝܺܕܥܶܗ. Also between two consonants ܝ quiesces in ◌ܺ; e. g. ܐܺܢܬܬܳܐ for ܐܢܬܬܳܐ.

§ 14. *Vowel-Letters which are not sounded* (*Otiant*).

In the following cases ܝ, ܘ, ܐ, are not sounded;

1. ܐ in the pronouns 2 plur.masc. and fem. ܐܰܢ̱ܬܽܘܢ, ܐܰܢ̱ܬܶܝܢ conjoined with the participle to denote the present tense, e. g. ܩܳܛܠܺܝܢ ܐܢ̱ܬܽܘܢ pronounced *kotelitun*, in which case the ܢ of the participle is not sounded.

2. ܘ and ܝ at the end of words; *a*) in verbal endings without any vowel preceding (2 pret. sing. fem.; 3 plur. masc. and fem.; imperat. sing. fem. and plur. masc.; and 2 fut. sing. fem.); e. g. ܩܛܰܠܬܝ, ܩܛܰܠܘ; *b*) in the suffixes ܝ, ܟܝ, ܢܟܝ, ܘܗ̱ܝ, where ܝ is sounded only when followed by ܗܽܘ; e. g. ܒܰܟ݂ܝ ܗܽܘ pronounced *bekyu*; *c*) in ܐܶܬܡܳܠܝ *yesterday*, ܫܰܠܝ *rest*, and the like, which form ܝܳܐ in the emphatic state (§ 46. 1).

§ 15. *Changes in the Vowels.*

Although to a less extent than in Hebrew, the vowels in Syriac, undergo various changes and modifications in respect to formation and derivation, still they are *exchanged, transposed, dropped* or *added.*

1. They are *exchanged* partly in accordance with the genius of the language, and partly in transferring Hebrew and Chaldee words. The genius of the language requires the following exchanges of vowels; *a*) in the preformatives of the fut. and infin. Pe. in simple syllables, in Verbs ܦܳܐ, ܦܰܥ, (ܢܣܐ § 32), ܰ passes over into ܶ; e. g. ܢܶܩܛܽܘܠ, ܡܶܩܛܰܠ; but before gutturals and ܪ at the end of words, into ܰ; e.g. ܢܶܥܒܰܪ for ܢܶܥܒܽܘܪ; *b*) in the feminine with ܬܳܐ, ܬܳ, in the construct state, passes over into ܰ; e. g. ܡܰܠܟܬܳܐ construct state ܡܰܠܟܰܬ (§ 45. 2). In transferring words from the Hebrew and Chaldee, the following vowel changes may be noted; *a*) for ܳ the Syriac prefers ܳ; e. g. ܓܳܠܳܐ = גָּלָה; ܐܳܪܳܡ = אֲרָם; *b*) ֵ is exchanged in proper names mostly with ܺ; e. g. ܥܺܣܽܘ = עֵשָׂו; ܰ with ܶ; e. g. ܢܶܦܬܰܚ = יִפְתָּח; *c*) ֹ with ܽܘ; e. g. ܩܽܘܕܫܳܐ = קֹדֶשׁ; or with ܘ; e. g. ܝܰܘܡܳܐ = (Chald. יוֹמָא) יוֹם.

2. Vowels are *transposed*; A) *in general*; *α*) ܽ in the imperat. plur. masc. Pe. when a suffix is added; e. g. ܩܛܽܘܠܘ, with suffix ܩܽܛܠܽܘܗܝ; *b*) concerning the falling back of the vowel over ܐ, ܝ, or ܗܝ, upon prefixes, compare § 13. 1. 3; § 52. 1; § 53.1. Rem.; B) *in Particular*; *a*) in ܐܢܳܫ, whenever ܐ is vacant, the vowel of the ܢ falls back upon it; e.g. ܐܶܢܳܫ for ܐܢܳܫ (§12.1); *b*) in some nouns of the form ܩܽܘܕܫ, when a syllable is appended and in the emphatic state ܩܽܘܕܫܳܐ (§ 45. 3; § 48. A. Decl. IV); of the form ܩܦܰܣ, emphatic state ܩܽܦܣܳܐ; *c*) in ܩܽܘܒܠ and ܩܽܘܕܡ with ܠ prefixed, ܽ is placed before ܒ when ܒ and ܕ retain their ܳ; e. g. ܠܽܘܩܒܰܠ, ܠܽܘܩܕܰܡ. In ܟܽܠ when it enters into

composition, ܰ moves forward upon ܪ; e. g. ܒܪܢܫܐ, ܒܪܢܫܐ.

3. The vowel of a final mixed syllable is *dropped*, when an entire syllable is added at the end, especially when the last radical begins the new syllable; e. g. in the verb ܩܛܰܠ masc. ܩܶܛܠܰܬ fem.; in the nouns ܡܰܠܟ̣ܳܐ, ܡܰܠܟܳܐ.

Rem.—This vowel remains unchanged; *a*) when merely a formative letter, without a vowel, is added; e.g. ܩܛܰܠܗ from ܩܛܰܠ; *b*) when a syllable is added, if the stem-syllable remain a mixed one; e. g. ܩܛܰܠܬܽܘܢ from ܩܛܰܠ; and moreover; *c*) when the stem-syllable becomes a simple one, in the following cases; *a*) in the second form of the 3 fem.plur.pret.and 2 fem. plur. imperat.; *β*) where inHebrew Daghesh forte stands; e. g. ܥܰܡ emphatic state ܥܰܡܳܐ (עַם, עַמִּי); *γ*)in words ofDeclension I.masc. (comp. § 48.A). In ܥܶܒܶܪ emphatic state ܥܒܳܪܳܐ; ܩܽܘܕܫ emphatic state ܩܽܘܕܫܳܐ, the original vowel only reappears (comp. 48. A. Decl. IV).

4. Vowels are *added; a*) with ܐ, ܝ, and ܥ, at the beginning of words; ܐ and ܥ usually take ܰ and ܶ; e.g. ܐܶܩܛܽܘܠ (imp.), ܥܶܒܰܕ: but ܝ usually takes ܺ; e. g. ܝܺܠܶܕ; *b*) of two vacant consonants at the beginning of a word,the first takes ܰ; e. g. ܩܰܛܘܠܶܐ for ܩܛܘܠܶܐ; so also when two vacant consonants in the middle of a word follow ܳ; e. g. ܡܳܪܺܝܬܳܐ for ܡܳܪܝܬܳܐ; or when in Hebrew, the first has Daghesh forte; e. g. ܐܶܓܰܪܬܳܐ for ܐܶܓܪܬܳܐ from אִגֶּרֶת; or finally when three vacant consonants would come together in the middle of a word; e. g. ܐܶܬܩܰܛܠܰܬ for ܐܶܬܩܛܠܰܬ. This assumed vowel is sometimes ܶ; e.g. ܩܶܛܠܰܬ (pret. Pe.) from ܩܛܰܠ; or ܺ before ܝ, (v. § 13. 3), excepting in the emphatic state of the participle fem. pass. of Verbs ܠܝ in Pa., Aph., and Eshta., where ܰ is added to distinguish it from the active participle (comp. § 48. B. Decl.IV. Rem.). Finally ܘ is assumed in the emphatic state sing. of some words; e. g. ܡܰܠܟܽܘܬܳܐ from ܡܰܠܟܳܐ for ܡܰܠܟܬܳܐ; *c*) a vowel is assumed with ܘ between two vacant consonants: this vowel is ܰ when it stands at the beginning of a mixed syllable; e. g.

ܢܕܘܬܗܘܢ; but — when it stands in a simple syllable; e. g. ܢܕܘܬܐ. *d*) The assumption of a vowel is arbitrary, when there are two vacant consonants, of which the first can be attached to the preceding, and the second to the following syllable; e. g. ܡܕܒܚܐ and ܡܕܒܚܐ; if the second consonant be ܐ, —̂ must be assumed, for ܝ, ܘ and ܐ cannot stand without a vowel between two consonants.

PART SECOND.

ETYMOLOGY, OR, PARTS OF SPEECH.

CHAPTER I.

PRONOUNS.

§ 16. *Personal and Possessive Pronouns.*

The Personal Pronouns are divided into two classes: *Separate Pronouns*, which stand as separate words, and mark the nominative case; and *Suffixes*, consisting of syllables formed from the separate pronouns, which are appended to other parts of speech; appended to Verbs, they mark the accusative; appended to nouns, the possessive pronoun, or the relation of the genitive; and, with prepositions, they form the remaining cases.

TABLE OF PRONOUNS AND SUFFIXES.

	SEPARATE.	SUFFIXED TO VERBS.			SUFFIXED TO NOUNS.	
		a.	*b.*	*c.*	IN SING.	IN PLURAL.
Sing.		1. 2.				
1 c.	ܐܶܢܳܐ	ܢܝ، ܰܢܝ	ܢܝ	ܳܢܝ	ܝ	ܰܝ
2 m.	ܐܰܢ݇ܬ	ܳܟ	ܟ	*	ܳܟ	ܰܝܟ
2 f.	ܐܰܢ݇ܬܝ	ܶܟܝ	ܟܝ	ܽܟܝ·	ܶܟܝ	ܰܝܟܝ
3 m.	ܗܽܘ / ܗܰܘ	ܶܗ { ܰܘܗܝ / ܽܘܗܝ	ܗܝ / ܘܗܝ	ܳܘܗܝ	ܶܗ	ܰܘܗܝ
3 f.	ܗ̱ܝ / ܗܳܝ	ܳܗ̇ { ܳܝܗ̇ / ܶܝܗ̇	ܗ̇	*	ܳܗ̇	ܶܝܗ̇
Plur.						
1 c.	ܚܢܰܢ	ܢ ܰܢ	ܢ	ܳܢ	ܳܢ	ܰܝܢ
2 m.	ܐܰܢ݇ܬܽܘܢ	ܟܽܘܢ	*	ܳܟܽܘܢ	ܟܽܘܢ	ܰܝܟܽܘܢ
2 f.	ܐܰܢ݇ܬܶܝܢ	ܟܶܝܢ	*	ܳܟܶܝܢ	ܟܶܝܢ	ܰܝܟܶܝܢ
		SEPARATE FROM THE VERB.				
3 m.	ܗܶܢܽܘܢ / ܐܶܢܽܘܢ	ܐܶܢܽܘܢ			ܗܽܘܢ	ܰܝܗܽܘܢ
3 f.	ܗܶܢܶܝܢ / ܐܶܢܶܝܢ	ܐܶܢܶܝܢ			ܗܶܝܢ	ܰܝܗܶܝܢ

Remarks and Explanations concerning the Table.

I. *The Personal Pronoun.*

The second and third persons have two genders, while the first person is of the common gender. The fem. of the 2 sing., is denoted by ܝ appended to the masc. In the 3 sing. ܗܽܘ masc. and ܗܺܝ fem., are used rather in a demonstrative sense, while ܗܽܘ masc. and ܗܺܝ fem., are used in connectionwith adjectives and participles rather to designate the present tense. And so in the plur., the first forms given above are used rather substantively as nominatives, and the second as accusatives (comp. § 36). Concerning Linea occultans under ܐ and ܗ of the 1 and 3 sing., see § 12.1.

II. *Suffix Pronouns.*

A. Suffixes of the Verb.

In the suffixes, or abbreviated forms of the separate pronouns, an ancient obsolete form whose characteristic was not ܬ but ܟ, lies at the basis of the 2 sing. and plur. (comp. Gesen. Lehrgeb. 203).

Of the suffixes to verbs, given in the Table, those marked *a*, fall into two classes; the first of which are attached to consonants (with the exception of ܘ) in the forms of the regular verb; and the second mainly to the same forms of Verbs ܠܝ, and in part to the imperat. and fut. of the regular verb. The forms placed between 1 and 2, are common to both.

The suffixes marked *b* are appended to forms with ܘ and ܝ, which then quiesce in ـُ and ـِ. Where this form is wanting under *b* it is comprehended under *a*. Finally the suffixes under *c* are attached to the forms with ܘ, and also to the 2 sing. masc. and 3 plur. fem. pret. The forms wanting under *c* are comprised under *a*. On their mode of union, comp. §§ 36, and 37, and the accompanying Tables.

B. Suffixes of Nouns or Possessive Pronouns.

The suffixes of the noun (possessive pronouns) are attached, in nouns masc. sing., to the emphatic state (§ 45,) with the falling away, of ܐ ; e. g. ܡܰܠܟ, emphatic state ܡܰܠܟܳܐ, with suff. ܡܰܠܟܰܢ. In the plural they coalesce with the ending of the construct state ـܰܝ, so that they may be considered as attached to the final consonant of the noun; e.g. construct state ܡܰܠܟܰܝ, with suff. ܡܰܠܟܰܝܟ. Only in the 3 sing. masc. does ܝ pass into ܘ, and in the 3 sing. fem. ـܶ is the union vowel. In the noun fem. the suffix with a union vowel is attached to the emphatic state, with the falling away of ܐ, e. g. ܡܰܠܟܽܘܬܶܗ from emphatic state ܡܰܠܟܽܘܬܳܐ. In the remaining persons (1 sing. 2 and 3 plur.) suffixes sing. are attached to the construct state (v. § 46. 2); e. g. ܡܰܠܟܽܘܬܝ from the construct state ܡܰܠܟܽܘܬ, plur. ܡܰܠܟܽܘܬܰܢ from construct state ܡܰܠܟܽܘܬ.

Rem.—For the complete union of nouns and suffixes, compare §§ 46—48, and the accompanying Tables.

Besides, the possessive pronoun may be expressed in a separate form from the noun, by means of some form of ܕܺܝܠ (from ܕ = אֲשֶׁר chald. דִּי and ܠ) with a suffix, thus;

	Plural.			*Singular.*		
	FEM.	COMM.	MASC.	FEM.	COMM.	MASC.
1.		ܕܺܝܠܰܢ *our.*			ܕܺܝܠܝ *my.*	
2.	ܕܺܝܠܟܶܝܢ		ܕܺܝܠܟܽܘܢ *your.*	ܕܺܝܠܶܟܝ		ܕܺܝܠܳܟ *thy.*
3.	ܕܺܝܠܗܶܝܢ		ܕܺܝܠܗܽܘܢ *their.*	ܕܺܝܠܳܗ *her.*		ܕܺܝܠܶܗ *his.*

Rem.—This form, which corresponds with the German *der meinige* (mine)etc. occurring after a suffix to the noun, indicates an emphasis; e. g. ܘܬܰܠܡܺܝܕܰܝܟ ܕܺܝܠܳܟ, *but thy scholars.* Sometimes it signifies *relating to;* e. g. ܕܺܝܠܟܽܘܢ *to us.*

C. Suffixes to Particles.

The *Prepositions*, which were in part originally nouns, take suffixes sing. and plur. Singular suffixes are attached to ܒ *in*, ܠ the sign of the dative, ܠܘܳܬ *to*, ܡܶܢ *from*, ܒܳܬܰܪ and ܒܳܬܰܪ *after*, ܠܘܽܩܒܰܠ *towards*, *against*, comp. § 15. 2. Plural suffixes are attached to ܠܚܽܘܕ *aside*, *only*, ܒܠܥܳܕ *without*, ܚܕܳܪ or ܚܕܳܪܰܝ *about*, ܚܠܳܦ *for*, ܥܰܠ *over*, ܨܶܐܕ or ܨܶܝܕ *towards*, *after*, ܩܕܳܡ *before*, ܬܚܶܝܬ (ܬܚܶܝܬ before nouns) *under*. The suffix plural fem. occurs with ܡܶܛܽܠ *on account of*; e. g. ܡܶܛܽܠܳܬܗܶܝܢ; with both plural suffixes ܒܰܝܢܰܝܗܶܝܢ and ܒܰܝܢܳܬ *between*.

Rem.—For the complete union with suffixes, compare the Table belonging to § 52.

---

§ 17. *Other Pronouns.*

1. The *Demonstrative Pronoun* is declined as follows:

Plural. F.	C.	M.		*Singular.* F.		M.	
ܗܳܢܶܝܢ	ܗܳܠܶܝܢ (ܐܶܠܶܝܢ)	ܗܳܢܽܘܢ	*these.*	ܗܳܕܶܐ (ܗܳܕܳܐ)	*this.*	(ܗܳܢ) ܗܳܢܳܐ	*this.*

Rem.—Sometimes, in the sing., the fem. ܗܳܕܶܐ is united with the personal pronoun 3 sing. masc. ܗܽܘ and fem. ܗܝ, forming ܗܳܕܽܘ and ܗܳܕܶܐܗܝ. Sometimes ܗܽܘ and ܗܝ precede; e.g. ܗܽܘ ܗܳܢܳܐ *just this*, ܗܝ ܗܳܕܶܐ *just this*. The Chaldee ܐܶܠܶܝܢ is only used in comparisons; e. g. ܕܰܐܝܟ ܐܶܠܶܝܢ, or ܕܰܐܝܟ ܗܳܠܶܝܢ *such*.

2. The *Relative* for all numbers and genders is ܕ, *who*, *which*, *that*, and with the pronouns ܡܰܢ *c.* ܐܰܝܢܳܐ *m.* ܐܰܝܕܳܐ *f.* ܐܰܝܠܶܝܢ pl. *com.* preceding, it becomes interrogative.

Rem.— ܐܰܝܢܳܐ having a relative signification with ܕ following it, is an exception to the general rule.

3. The *Interrogative*; *a*) for persons of both genders and numbers is ܡܰܢ *who*. It unites with ܗܽܘ following, and

forms ܡܰܢܘ and ܐܰܝܢܳܐ masc. *who?* ܐܰܝܕܳܐ fem. *who?* *b*) ܡܳܢܳܐ and ܡܶܢ *what*, refer to things (ܡܳܢܳܐ, ܡܽܢܶܘ); *c*) ܐܰܝܠܶܝܢ refers to both persons and things.

4. The *Reciprocal* and *Reflexive Pronouns*. are formed partly by passives (§ 21. 2. § 22. 2. § 24. 2), or by the nouns ܢܰܦܫܳܐ *soul*, and ܩܢܽܘܡܳܐ *person*, with suffixes appended (comp. the Syntax).

CHAPTER II.

THE VERB.

§ 18. *General View.*

1. The Verb is, as in Hebrew, the most important of the parts of speech, since it lies at the basis of the formation of the others. Verbs may be divided into the three following classes, in so far as new verbal forms are derived from them in accordance with definite laws, or as a noun is to be considered as their stem: *a*) *Primitives*; e. g. ܟܬܰܒ *to write*, ܩܛܰܠ *to kill*; *b*) *Verbal Derivatives* (*Conjugations*); e. g. ܙܰܕܶܩ *to justify*, from ܙܕܶܩ; *c*) *Denominatives*, subsequent formations from nouns; e. g. ܥܰܣܰܪ *to tithe*, from ܥܣܰܪ *ten*; ܐܰܦܨܰܚ *to celebrate Easter*, from ܦܶܨܚܳܐ *Easter*.

2. The Stem-form in the 3 sing. masc. pret. consists usually of three radicals (verbum triliterum), and is pronounced as a monosyllable, by the help of ܰ placed over the middle radical in transitive, and ܶ in intransitive verbs.

3. From this are formed the Derivatives or Conjugations, which agree closely with the ground-form in the inflection of persons, and the principal characteristics of mood and tense. Modern grammarians have added a third conjugation, Shaphel, to the two originally derived from the ground-form. The passive is formed by prefixing ܐܶܬ, and has not only a passive but also a reciprocal and reflexive signification.

The Conjugations are as follows ;

	Active.			Passive.
1. Peal	ܩܛܰܠ	*to kill ;**	Ethpeel	ܐܶܬܩܛܶܠ
2. Pael	ܩܰܛܶܠ	*to murder ;*	Ethpaal	ܐܶܬܩܰܛܰܠ
3. Aphel	ܐܰܩܛܶܠ	*to cause to kill ;*	Ethtaphal	ܐܶܬܬܰܩܛܰܠ
4 Shaphel	ܫܰܩܛܶܠ	*to cause to kill* (*rare*)	Eshtaphal	ܐܶܫܬܰܩܛܰܠ

Rem.—All verbs do not have the whole of the conjugations; and where Pael and Aphel are found together, there is usually a difference in their signification; e. g. ܝܰܩܰܪ *to honor,* ܐܰܘܩܰܪ *to be burdensome.*

4. The Syriac, like the other Semitic dialects, has a Preterit and Future. It has, moreover, an Imperative in the passive, and two Participles, an active and a passive, in the active. The Hebrew Infinitive absolute and Infinitive construct are in Syriac united in one form (v. § 19.B.3).

Rem.—The other relations of time are supplied in the following manner; the Present is expressed by the participle with the personal pronoun following; the Imperfect and Pluperfect by ܗܘܳܐ (הָיָה), the former joined with the participle, the latter with the preterite. The Optative and Subjunctive, are contained in the future, to denote which more explicitly, ܗܘܳܐ is also frequently used (v. Syntax).

5. Verbs, finally, are divided into two principal classes, *Regular* and *Irregular*. In regular verbs the radical letters remain unchanged, while in irregular verbs, one of the radicals either falls away (*Defective Verbs*), or quiesces (*Quiescent Verbs*) v. § 27.

---

1. REGULAR VERBS.

§ 19. *The Inflection of Regular Verbs in General.*

The formation of Verbs, in respect to person, tense, and mood is effected, in general, by uniform laws. The irregular verbs are formed in a different manner, in particular

*Literally, *he killed*, etc. The infinitive being considered in English the ground-form of the verb, and for the sake of brevity, is uniformly used to represent the Syriac ground form 3 masc. sing.—Tr.

cases only, according to their special laws. It will therefore be most convenient to treat, under the regular verb, of whatever belongs to the universal analogy of the verb.

In the following Tables of the Inflection of Regular and Irregular Verbs, the following signs are used: The radical letters are denoted by *. The vowels which stand immediately over the *, belong to the inflection of transitive verbs; and those vowels which are separated from the * by .... belong to intransitive or guttural verbs, or denote other forms in equal use. Radical letters which have fallen away, are denoted in the Table of Irregular Verbs, § 27 by °. Those which take their place, stand over this sign.

1. TABLE OF PERSONAL INFLECTIONS.

	Singular.					Plural.				
	3 m.	3 f.	2 m.	2 f.	1 c.	3 m.	3 f.	2 m.	2 f.	1 c.
Preterit.	***	***ܬ	***ܬ	***ܬܝ	***ܬ	***ܘ	***ܝ ܝܢ	***ܬܘܢ	***ܬܝܢ	***ܢ ܢܢ
Future.	ܢ**ܘ*	ܬ**ܘ*ܝ	ܬ**ܘ*	ܬ***ܝܢ	ܐ**ܘ*	ܢ***ܘܢ	ܢ***ܢ	ܬ***ܘܢ	ܬ***ܢ	ܢ**ܘ*
Imperat.			**ܘ*	**ܘ*ܝ				**ܘ*ܘ	**ܘ*ܝ	

II. TABLE OF THE TEMPORAL INFLECTION OF REGULAR VERBS.

Eshtaph.	*Shaphel.*	*Ethtaphal.*	*Aphel.*	*Ethpaal.*	*Pael.*	*Ethpeel.*	*Peal.*	
ܐܫܬ***	ܫ***	ܐܬܬ***	ܐ***	ܐܬ***	***	ܐܬ***	***	*Preter.*
ܢܫܬ***	ܢܫ***	ܢܬܬ***	ܢ***	ܢܬ***	ܢ***	ܢܬ***	ܢ**ܘ*	*Future.*
The remaining	Imperative	like the	Preterit.	ܐܬ***	like Pret	ܐܬ***	*ܘ**	*Imperat*
ܡܫܬ***ܘ	ܡܫ***ܘ	ܡܬܬ***ܘ	ܡ***ܘ	ܡܬ***ܘ	ܡ***ܘ	ܡܬ***ܘ	ܡ***	*Infinit.*
	ܡܫ*** ....ܐ		ܡ*** ....ܐ		ܡ*** ....ܐ		*** } m. ...ܐ } f.	*Particip. Act.*
ܡܫܬ*** ....ܐ	ܡܫ*** ....ܐ	ܡܬܬ*** ....ܐ	ܡ*** ....ܐ	ܡܬ*** ....ܐ	ܡ*** ....ܐ	ܡܬ*** ....ܐ	*ܝ** } m. ܐ } f.	*Particip. Pass.*

A. *Personal Inflections* (comp. *Table* 1).

The inflection of persons is found in its most simple form in the preterit and imperative, where formative syllables are appended only to the stem (*Afformatives*). In the future the form is more complex, additions being received at the beginning (*Preformatives*), and at the end. The inflection is as follows;

In the 3 sing. pret. the simple verbal stem suffices for the masc.; but in the fem., ܬ, preceded by ܰ (= ָה), is appended and considered as a sign of that gender. The 3 plur., which has a two-fold gender, is distinguished in the masc. by the addition of the plural-sign ܘ, from which the fem. in its simple form is distinguished only by a silent ܝ instead of ܘ. In the same person of the fut. the inquiry into the origin of the preformative ܢ in the sing. masc. and the plur. masc. and fem., is a difficult one. The opinion that the ܢ had its origin in ܝ is opposed by the fact that among the Zabians this preformative exists, while there is no similarity between those two letters. More consideration is probably due to the derivation from ܗܘܐ and ܗܘܝܢ (comp. § 17). In the plur., the masc., in addition to the preformative ܢ, is distinguished as in the pret., by the plural-sign ܘ with ܢ paragogic, which causes the vowel of the last radical syllable to fall away. And thus the ܢ in the fem. reminds one of the paragogic final syllable נָה in Hebrew. The abbreviated form of the personal pronoun evidently appears in the 2 sing. and plur. Thus in the pret. sing., ܬ masc. and ܬܝ fem. are related to ܐܢܬ masc. and ܐܢܬܝ fem., as ܬܘܢ masc. and ܬܝܢ fem. are to ܐܢܬܘܢ masc. and ܐܢܬܝܢ fem. in the plur. The same is true of the preformative ܬ in the same person of the fut. sing. and plur. where the fem. sing., in order to designate the gender, takes ܝ final and ܢ paragogic, with a like influence upon the vowel of the preceding radical syllable. In the plur. the 2 pers. shares with the 3 pers., this same character at the end. In the 1 sing. pret. the original form of the ܬ with ܶ = תִי preceding, has not been shown. But in the plur. ܢ and ܢܝ, as well as ܐ before the

1 sing. and ܢ before the 1 plur. fut. refer us the more definitely back to ܐܢܐ and ܚܢܢ. Here too it should be noticed that the 1 plur. fut. is distinguished from the 3 sing. masc. which has the same form, by Ribui.

The preformatives of the fut. uniformly take ܶ except in Pael and Shaphel, where (with the exception of the 1. sing.) they are vacant, and in Aphel, where they take ܰ.

The imperative coincides with the future in respect to formatives at the end, except that the paragogic ܢ in the 2 sing. fem. and 2 plur. masc. falls away, the former person ending in the feminine sign ܝ, and the latter in the plural sign ܘ. In both cases in Peal, ܘ̇ is retained as the vowel of the radical syllable. Finally the fem. plur. ends with ܶܢ and the vowel of the final syllable is retained.

B. *Inflection of the Tenses and Moods* (*comp. Table* 11).

1. With the preterit (the characteristics of which are more specifically given in Table 11. and the section following), the imperative most nearly coincides. The imperat. Peal receives, in Verbs Med. A, between the second and third radicals, ܘ quiescing in ܳ; but in Verbs Med. E. and 3 Gutt. the middle radical takes ܰ. All the remaining imperatives are like preterits, except that in Ethpe. and Ethpa., Linea occultans stands under the middle radical with ܶ preceding.

Rem.—The same holds good in respect to the imperatives Ethta. and Eshta., if Linea occultans be admitted in them

2. The future is formed from the imperative by prefixing ܢ. In Aphel the characteristic falls away, and in passives ܐ of the formative syllable ܐܶܬ. In Ethpe. and Ethpa. after the rejection of Linea occultans, the vowels of the preterite re-appear.

3. The infinitives (of which the simple form denotes the gerund in *do* or the absolute state, but with ܠ prefixed denotes the construct state) are formed from the preterites by prefixing ܡ. They end (excepting in the Peal, where they coincide precisely with the preterit) in ܘ̇, and in the apoco-

pate feminine form, in ܬܵܐ, changing the vowel of the last syllable of the preterit into ـܘܿ.

4. The participles are formed from the preterit as follows ;—in peal, active form, the first radical takes ـܵ, and the second ـܸ ; in the passive form ـܝܼ is inserted between the last two radicals. In the other conjugations ܡ is prefixed, and ـܲ, in the second syllable of the active form, is changed, in passives, into ـܲ. But this distinction appears only in the absolute state of the masc., and even here is lost in verbs 3 Gutt., ܪ, and ܗ, the active form of which likewise takes ـܲ.

5. The preformatives of the fut., infin., and part., mostly take ـܸ; but in Aphel they take ـܲ, rejecting the ܐ according to No. 2; and in Pael and Shaphel they are without a vowel.

Rem.—For the reciprocal use of these twoTables, which suffice for the complete formation of the regular verb, it is to be remarked; that Table I. contains the personal inflection of Peal. The forms in Table II. in the inflection according to Table I., retain their characteristic vowels, and merely take from Table I. the afformatives with the vowels thereto belonging. Where, in pret. Peal, the vowel of the stem falls away, the remaining preterits also lose the vowel of the last radical syllable ; but Ethpe. takes ـܲ over the first radical, where this has ـܸ in Peal.* In the fut. the vowel of the last radical syllable is uniformly lost where ܘܿ falls away in Peal, except that in this case also in Ethpe. the first radical takes ـܲ. In imperatives the vowel of the last radical syllable is retained, as ܘܿ is retained in the imperat. Peal.

---

§ 20.

A. The ground form Peal — its Formation and Signification.

1. The usual form of Peal is ܩܛܲܠ (*transitive verb med. A*). Besides this the form with ـܸ (*med. E*) is always used

*The inflection of the different persons in the preterit should be noticed in order to perceive the verification of this remark. Tr.

for *intransitives;* e. g. ܝܬܸܒ *to sit,* ܩܪܸܒ *to be near.* To this class also belong *Verbs* ܥ̈ܐ, which throw back ܸ upon the first radical; e. g. ܟܐܸܒ *to feel pain,* or *derivatives* of Hebrew Verbs ע״ו; e. g. ܛܐܸܒ = טוֹב. The form Med. O. still appears in the Verb ܦܘܪ *to shudder.*

Rem.—With the inflection of Verbs Med.A. agree those with 3 rad. ܗ; e. g. ܫܡܗ *to name,* ܬܡܗ *to admire.* Verbs Med. E. retain ܸ, when in Verbs Med. A. ܲ stands in the radical syllable. In respect to the forms of the 3 plur. fem. pret. ܩܛܠܹܝܢ, ܩܛܠܹܝܢ and ܩܛܠܝ adduced by Buxtorf, the first is found only in Verbs ܠ̈ܐ and the second seems to have originated from crasis with the affix ܗܝܢ. There are instances to be found, though rare, in which ܲ is placed over the third radical in the 1 plur. ܩܛܠܢ. The apocopate form of the infinitive with ܘ is also sometimes found in Peal; e.g. Luke ix. 33. ܠܡܥܒܕܘ. In the imperat.plur.masc. with ܢ paragogic, ܘ final quiesces in ܘ; e.g. ܩܛܘܠܘܢ. Besides the 2 plur.fem.with ܝܢ Amira (p. 300) adduces another form,viz: ܩܛܘܠܹܝܢ. The imperat.ofVerbs Med. E.takes ܲ instead of ܘ; though the transitive form with ܘ is also found; e.g. ܩܪܘܒ from ܩܪܸܒ. Sometimes another form with ܸ occurs; e. g. Rom. xiii. 3. ܕܚܠ. More rarely the vowel of the imperat. differs from that of the fut. as in the Verb ܐܙܠ, fut. ܢܐܙܠ, imperat. ܙܠ. Not only the imperat. but the fut. of Verbs Med.E. and of those having the third rad. a guttural, take ܲ; e.g. ܢܚܣܪ. In the fut. 3 sing. fem. the form with ܝ attached is more frequent. Also a form of the fut. with ܸ; e. g. ܢܠܒܫ together with ܢܠܒܫ. Instead of the part. act. ܩܛܠ, the participial noun of the form ܩܛܘܠ, emphatic state ܩܛܠܐ, is often used. In the part. act. the emphatic state masc. and the absol. fem. are alike; e. g. ܩܛܠܐ. The active form ܫܚܝܢ (Mark xiv. 67), in immediate connection with ܫܚܢ (verse 54), is perhaps to be regarded as an error in transcribing. The passive form is always fully written; in intransitive verbs, the first radical sometimes takes ܲ. Passsive intransitives occasionally occur in an active sense, sometimes derived from transitives; e. g. ܛܥܝܢ *bearing*, ܐܚܝܕ *holding*.

To the inflection of the participle belongs also the idiom by which the present tense is expressed by abbreviated personal pronouns, appended, like afformatives, to the participle. But this formation occurs only in the 2 sing. and the 1 and 2. plur. masc. and fem., and is as follows:

Participle Passive. *Participle Active.*

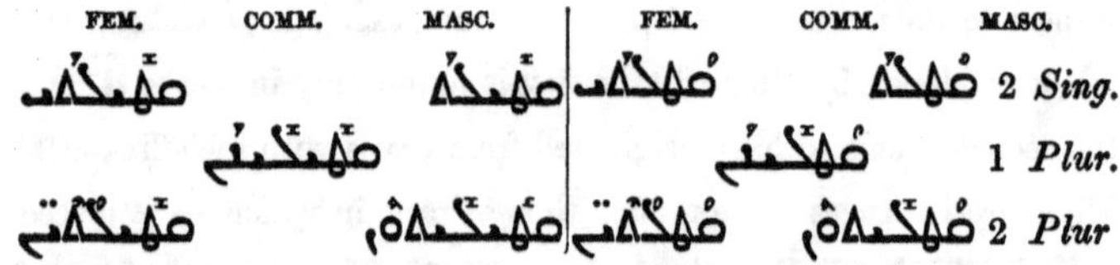

2. From the preceding remarks it appears that the signification of Peal may be transitive or intransitive. Sometimes we find both forms in the same verb. In some cases there is no difference of signification; e. g. ܠܥܣ and ܠܥܣ *to chew;* and in other cases there is a difference in signification; e.g. ܦܠܓ *to divide*, ܦܠܓ *to be divided.*

B. Derivative Conjugations.

§ 21. *Ethpeel.*

1. The characteristic of this conjugation, as in the other passives, is the formative syllable ܐܬ and the vowel ـَ or in Verbs 3 Rad. Gutt. ـَ, in the last syllable (vid. Amira, p. 278). The passive conjugations are distinguished from each other generally by the vowels over the radical letters, or by the addition of ܬ (*Ethta.*) or by the insertion of ܫ (*Eshta.*).

Rem.—Upon the transposition of the sibilants with ܬ see § 12. 2. The first radical takes ـَ in the 3 sing. fem. and 1 sing. pret., in all of the imperat., in the 2 sing. fem. and 2 and 3 plur. masc. and fem.

of the future, and finally in the part. excepting the absolute state masc. According to others ـܰ is used, but only in Verbs ܠܐ even when ܐ falls away; e. g. Acts. xx. 27. ܐܶܬܟܰܐܠܺܝܬ; ܐܶܬܟܰܠܺܝܬ. This usage however is confirmed neither by examples nor by Amira. The 3 sing. fem. and 1 sing. pret. the imperatives, 2 sing. fem. and 2 and 3 plur. masc. and fem. of the fut. and the part. excepting the absolute masc. cannot be distinguished, according to Lud. de Dieu p. 217, from the same persons of Ethpa. excepting when the first radical is an aspirate, which, in Ethpa. becomes hardened. The passive form ܐܶܬܩܛܶܠ is not mentioned by Amira. In the Verb ܫܡܥ, in Ethpe., ܺܝ is inserted between the two final radical letters. The infinitive however is excepted; e.g. pret. ܐܶܫܬܰܡܺܝܥ; infinit. ܡܶܫܬܡܳܥܽܘ.

2. The signification of *Ethpe.* is; *a*) *passive of Peal;* e.g. ܐܶܬܩܛܶܠ; *b*) *reflexive;* e. g. ܐܶܬܚܰܫܰܒ *to reflect by or upon ones self;* *c*) = *Peal* in intransitive verbs; e. g. ܗܦܰܟ and ܐܶܬܗܦܺܟ *to return;* *d*) sometimes *Ethpe.* is passive of *Aph.*; e.g. ܐܶܬܬܥܺܝܡ *to be embarrassed*, from ܐܰܬܥܶܡ.

---

§ 22. *Pael and Ethpaal.*

1. Both of these conjugations are characterized by ـܶ in the penultimate, and ـܰ, in Pa., in the ultimate syllable. The vowel is changed into ـܶ, in Verbs 3 Rad. Gutt. or ܪ, as it is in the passive. The preformative ܐ of the 1 sing.fut. Pa. alone takes ـܰ (comp. § 19. A. and B. 5). The imperat. Ethpa. with Linea. occultans and the part. fem. Ethpa. are like the same forms in Ethpe.

Rem.—The passive form ܐܶܬܩܰܛܶܠ does not occur in Amira. It is rejected also by *Buxtorf.* Amira remarks, p. 339, that in ܐܶܬܪܰܚܰܡ, the second radical takes ـܶ only in the imperat. (vid. Matt. ix. 27). Concerning the part. act. and pass. in Pa. vid. § 19. B.4. The form ܩܰܕܶܡܘ (Mark. x. 16) in pret. Pa. must be considered as an incorrect mode of writing, since ܩܰܕܶܡ (verse 32) is a participial noun.

2. The signification of Pa. is; *a*) *causative;* e. g. ܕܰܚܶܠ *to cause to be afraid*, from ܕܚܶܠ *to fear;* *b*) *intensive;* e.g. ܐܰܠܶܨ *to overwhelm* from ܐܠܰܨ *to press;* *c*) = Pe.; e.g. ܢܰܫܶܩ and ܢܫܰܩ *to kiss;* *d*) *to hold forth, to declare;* e. g. ܙܰܕܶܩ *to pronounce just.* The signification of Ethpa. is; *a*) *passive* of Pael; e. g. ܐܶܬܩܰܛܰܠ *to be murdered;* *b*) *reciprocal;* e. g. ܐܶܬܕܰܡܰܪ *to wonder within one's self;* *c*) = Peal; e. g. ܐܶܬܢܰܟܰܦ *to be made to blush*, i. e. *to blush* = ܢܟܶܦ.

---

§ 23. *Aphel and Ethtaphal.*

1. Aphel is characterized by ܐ placed before the stem, which quiesces in ◌ܰ. After the preformatives of the fut., infinit. and part., ܐ falls away, and its vowel falls back upon the preformative. ◌ܶ occurs in the second syllable, and, only in Verbs 3 Rad. Gutt. and ܪ, is ◌ܰ found in that syllable. In the passive, to compensate for the loss of the characteristic ܐ of Aph., ܬ mit ◌ܰ is inserted between the stem and the formative syllable of the passive ܐܶܬ. The final radical syllable takes ◌ܰ; e.g. ܐܶܬܬܰܩܛܰܠ.

Rem.—The characteristic ܐ of Aph. is retained after the preformative, in verbs, which lose a radical letter; e.g. ܡܰܐܚܶܐ from ܚܝܳܐ. Under the same rule should be placed Verbs ܥ̈ܥ; e. g. ܢܰܐܩܶܦ or ܢܰܩܐܶܦ. But the Verbs ܐܶܫܟܰܚ *to be able*, and ܐܶܫܬܺܝ *to drink*, do not belong here, since ◌ܶ already re-appears over ܐ. They are rather forms of Pe. with ܐ prosthetic, as is also shown by their further formation; e.g. fut. ܢܶܫܟܰܚ, infinit. ܡܶܫܟܳܚܽܘ (comp. § 20.Rem.), part. P. ܫܟܺܝܚ, and the passive ܐܶܫܬܰܟܰܚ. In respect to the participles of Aphel the same rule holds good as in § 22.1. Rem. compared with §19. B. 4. *Buxtorf* and others do not recognize the passive. Lud. de Dieu p. 238, approves of the abridged imperat. with Lin. occult.

ܐܬܬܩܛܠ. Later Grammarians however doubt the correctness of this form (Comp. § 8. Rem.).

2. The signification of Aphel is; *a*) *causative* as in Pael; e. g. ܐܩܪܒ *to bring forward;* and then it frequently takes two accusatives; e. g. ܐܠܒܫ *to cause to put on* (something upon some one); *b*) *imperative* or *permissive;* e. g. ܐܪܟܒ *to suffer to mount a horse;* *c*) *intransitive;* e. g. ܐܡܚܠ *to be weak;* *d*) = *Pael;* e. g. ܕܚܠ and ܐܕܚܠ *to frighten.* The passive has either the passive signification of Aphel or coincides with Pe.; e.g. ܥܡܪ *to dwell,* ܐܬܬܥܡܪ *to keep house.*

---

§ 24. *Shaphel and Eshtaphal.*

1. Shaphel is one of the conjugations, admitted into the paradigm at a later period (§ 18. 3). Its characteristic is ܫ with ◌ܰ prefixed to the stem, and ◌ܶ in the last syllable. In inflection it coincides with Aphel. In the passive (Eshtaphal) occurs the transposition of ܫ and ܬ and ◌ܰ appears in the last syllable. The preformative of Shaphel, like that of Pael, takes ◌ܶ only in the 1 sing. fut.

Rem.—In verbs which lose a radical letter, this conjugation sometimes furnishes a new stem; e. g. ܫܚܘܪ *to be black,* from ܫܚܘܪ, Shaph. of ܚܘܪܘܪ. The same is true in Eshtaphal. Thus ܐܫܬܘܚܪ furnishes the new quadriliteral ܐܫܬܚܪܪ.

2. The signification of these two conjugations is similar to that of Aph. and Ethtaphal. Shaphel is, in the examples still extant; *a*) *causative;* e. g. ܫܪܓܠ *to let fall;* *b*) *intensive;* e. g. ܫܚܠܦ *to exchange,* from ܚܠܦ *to change.* Eshtaphal has sometimes a passive and sometimes a reciprocal signification; or it forms intransitives; e.g. ܐܫܬܪܓܠ *to err, to sin.*

§ 25. *Conjugations occasionally used and Quadriliteral Verbs.*

The occasional conjugations (vid. Agrell in Otiolis Syr. p. 28 sq.) are similar to Pa. and Aph. and take, for the most part, their signification. They are also to be considered as quadriliterals. To verbs, which take the initial, prosthetic letters ܫ, ܣ, ܬ, and are,

A. similar to Aphel, belong; *a*) Maphel, ܡܰܣܟܶܢ *to make poor*, pass. ܐܶܬܡܰܣܟܰܢ *to become poor*; *b*) Saphel, ܣܰܪܗܶܒ *to permit to hasten* and *to hasten* = ܐܰܪܗܶܒ, pass. ܐܶܫܬܰܡܚܰܠ *to persecute*; *c*) Thaphel, ܬܰܠܡܶܕ *to teach.*

Rem.—For ܗܰܝܡܶܢ (ܐܰܡܶܢ vid. § 23. Rem.) no special form can be assumed, as similar examples do not occur.

B. Similar to Pael are those conjugations which insert ܝ, ܫ, ܪ, ܘ, after the first radical viz.; *a*) Pauel = Poel, usually transitive; e.g. ܓܘܰܙܶܙ *to chew the cud*, pass. ܐܶܬܦܘܰܪܰܙ *to become divided*; *b*) Paiel, transitive; e.g. ܣܰܝܒܰܪ *to suffer*; *c*) Pamel; e.g. ܫܰܡܥܶܠ *to remain*: *d*) Parel; ܟܰܪܓܶܠ *to dance*, pass. ܐܶܬܓܰܪܕܰܡ *to be cut off.*

C. Not very different from the last are also the quadriliteral verbs with prosthetic ܫ and final ܝ, viz.; *a*) Pali = Pael; e.g. ܫܰܡܠܝ *to domesticate*, pass. ܐܶܬܫܰܡܠܝ *to converse with one*; *b*). Palen, ܩܰܢܝܶܢ *to be master*, pass. ܐܶܬܩܰܢܝܰܢ *to make one a master.*

D. Here belong quadriliterals with a radical doubled = Pilel and Pilpel; *a*) Palel = Pael; e.g. ܫܰܥܒܶܕ *to reduce to slavery*; *b*) Pealel with its pass. ܐܶܬܚܠܰܡܠܰܡ *to dream*, and finally; *c*) Palpel (in Verbs ܥܥ); e.g. ܡܰܣܡܶܣ *to heal*, pass. ܐܶܬܦܰܪܦܰܥ *to be broken.*

Rem.—Those verbs, which are compounded of two ground forms, also belong here; e.g. ܐܶܣܬܰܡܩܰܪ *to blush*, from ܣܡܰܩ and ܣܰܪ. In quadriliterals formed from the Greek (e.g. ܦܰܣܩܶܦ *to elect a Bishop*).

a letter of the ground form frequently falls away; e. g. ܦܛܪܝܪܟ *to appoint as Patriarch.*

---

§ 26. *Verbs with Gutturals.*

Since the peculiarities of Guttural Verbs, are not marked in Syriac, as in Hebrew, either by Daghesh forte or Sheva, the irregularities in verbs of which the first and second radicals are gutturals are entirely wanting; and those only, of which the third radical is a guttural or ܪ, deviate, and those in but very few cases from the regular verb, in connection with which these deviations have already been cited. (Concerning Verbs ܦܐ, ܠܐ, and ܥܥ compare §§ 28, 30, 32). For more convenient reference, these cases of deviation are here brought together. These verbs take; 1) in the fut. and imperat. Peal, ܰ instead of ܘ; e. g., fut. ܢܥܡܪ; imperat. ܥܡܪ; 2) in like manner in the other conjugations, and in the part. act. Peal, they exchange the ܶ of the last syllable for ܰ; e. g. part. act. Peal, ܐܡܪ; pret. Ethpe. ܐܬܐܡܪ, fut. ܢܬܐܡܪ; Pa. pret. ܥܡܪ, fut. ܢܥܡܪ, imperat. ܥܡܪ, part. act. & pass. ܡܥܡܪ; Aph. Pret. ܐܘܕܥ, fut. ܢܘܕܥ, imperat. ܐܘܕܥ, part. act. and pass. ܡܘܕܥ.

Rem.—In the same manner in Pa. and Ethpa. are formed the following; ܒܝܐ *to console,* ܛܡܐ *to soil,* ܣܐܒ *to defile,* and ܐܬܦܐܝ *to be adorned* (comp. § 13. 1. Rem).

II. Irregular Verbs.

§ 27. *General View.*

1. Under *Irregular Verbs,* are to be comprehended, those in which there is a change in respect to one of the three letters of the ground form. Such letter either *quiesces* or *falls away* (*Quiescent and Defective Verbs*). A verb in which two let-

ters of the ground form are changed is said to be doubly anomalous (*Verbum dupliciter imperfectum*).

2. The *Quiescent Verbs* are the following; verbs with 1. rad. Olaph (ܦܐ), ܐܟܠ; 1. rad. Jud (ܦܝ), ܝܠܕ; med. rad. Olaph (ܥܐ), ܫܐܠ; med. rad. Vau and Jud (ܥܘ، ܥܝ) ܩܘܡ (ܩܘܡ), ܣܝܡ; and 3 rad. Olaph (ܠܐ) ܓܠܐ.

To defective verbs belong those with 1. rad. Nun (ܦܢ); e.g. ܢܦܩ, and med. rad. doubled (ܥܥ); e.g. ܒܙܙ.

Rem.—Here, and frequently in subsequent sections, the designations of classes of verbs are taken from the position of the radicals, of the Verb ܦܥܠ (= פעל), by which the variations affecting the radical letters of irregular verbs are kept in view.

VERBS ܐܢ ; ܐܢ. § 32.

Part. Pe.	Imperat. Pa.	Fut. Pe.	Pret. Pe.	
***	***	ܢ***	***	ܐ } 1.
Part. P. Pa.	**Imperat. Pe.**	**Infin. Aph.**	**Pret. Ethpe.**	
ܡ**ܘ	ܘ***	ܡ**ܘܘ	ܐܬ**ܘ	ܝ
3Pl.f.Fu.Pe.	**2 Pl. f. Imp. Pe.**	**3 f. S. Pr. Pa.**	**3 f. S. Pr. Pe.**	**2. A.**
ܢ**ܘܢ	**ܘܝ	**ܘܬ	**ܘܬ	a.
2 S.f.Pr.Pa.	**2 Pl. f. Pr. Pe.**	**2 m.S. Pr.Pe.**	**1 S. Pr. Pe.**	
**ܘܬܝ	**ܘܬܝ	**ܘܬ	**ܘܬ	b.
3Pl.m.Fu.Pe	**2 S. f. Fut. Pa.**	**3 m.Pl.Pr.Pe.**	**3 f.S. Pr. Pe.**	**2.B.**
ܢ**ܘܢ	ܬ**ܘܝ	**ܘ	S. A. a.	

VERBS ܟܐ ;

Pret. Aph.	Imp. Pe.
ܐ***	***
Part. Pass.	**Imperat.**
ܡܬ***	ܐܬ***
Fut. Ethpa.	**Pr. Ethpe.**
ܢܬ***	ܐܬ***

VERBS ܟܗ and ܟܝ;

Par. Act. Pe.	Pret. Pa.
ܐ ܘ	* ܘ*
Pr. Ethta.	**2 S.m.Fut.**
ܐܬܬ*ܘ*	ܬܬ*ܘ*
Part. Pass.	**Infinit.**
ܡ*ܘ*	ܡ*ܘ*ܘ

VERBS ܟܟ ;

Par. Act. Pe.	Pr. Ethta.
ܐ	(*) ܐܬܬ**
Pr. Ethpa.	**Pret. Pa.**
ܐܬ***	***

ܐܬܐ. § 30.			Verbs ܦܐ ; ܐܟܠ. § 28.				
Fut. Pe.	Pret. Pe.		Pret. Ethpe.	Fut. Pa.	Imperat. Pe.	Pret. Pe.	
***ܢ	***	1.	***ܐܬ	***ܢ	*ܘ**	***	1.
Future.	Pr. Ethpe.		Infin. Pa.	Fut. Pa.	(2m.Fu.Pe.)	1.S.Fut.Pe.	
***ܢܐ	***ܐܬ	2.	ܘ**ܘܡ	**ܘܢ	(*ܘ*ܘܬ)	*ܘ*ܘ	2.
Fut. Pa.	Pret. Pa.		Pret. Esht.	Pret.Shaph.	Pret. Ethtap.	Pret.Aph.	
***ܢ	***	3.	**ܘܐܫܬ	**ܘܫ	**ܘܐܬܬ	**ܘܐ	3.

ܣܠܩ, ܣܩ. § 31.			Verbs ܦܢ ; ܢܦܩ. § 29.				
Part. P.Pe.	Pret. Pe.		3f. S. Pr. Pe.	Pret. Ethpe.	Imperat. Pe.	Pret. Pe.	
ܘ	*ܘ*	1.	ܬ***	***ܐܬ	***	***	1.
Future.	Pr. Ethpe.		Imperat. Pe.	1 S. Fut. Pe.	Infin. Pe.	Fut. Pe.	
*ܘ*ܬܢ	*ܘ*ܬܐܬ	2.	S. I.	**ܘܐ	**ܘܡ	**ܘܢ	2.
Fut. Aph.	Pret. Aph.		Pret. Esht.	Pret.Shaph.	Pret. Ethta.	Pret.Aph.	
*ܘ*ܢ	*ܘ*ܐ	3.	**ܘܐܫܬ	**ܘܫ	**ܘܐܬܬ	**ܘܐ	3

ܙܗܡ. § 34.			Verbs ܦܝ ; ܝܠܕ. § 33.				
Pret. Aph.	Pret. Pe.		Fut. Aph.	Pret. Aph.	Infin. Pe.	Fut. Pe.	
(*) **ܐ	(*) **	1.	**ܘܢ	**ܘܐ	**ܘܡ	*ܘ*ܘܢ	
Pr.Ethpe.	Part. P. Pe.						
***ܐܬ	*ܐ**	2.					

A. Quiescent Verbs.

§ 28. *Verbs 1 rad. Olaph quiescent* (ܦܐ) ܐܟܠ *to eat.*

The following are the irregularities of these verbs.

1. In the Pret. Peal, where, in the regular verb, the first radical has no vowel, ܐ takes ܰ, but in the imperat. and part. pass., it takes ܶ; e. g. ܐܟܘܠ, ܐܟܝܠ. If the preformative or characteristic consonant of the conjugation be without a vowel, the vowel of ܐ falls back upon it; e. g. fut. Pa. ܢܐܟܠ; pret. Ethpe. ܐܬܐܟܠ.

Rem.—In the fut. and infinit. Pe. the preformative takes ܰ, in the verbs ܐܡܪ, ܐܟܠ, ܐܙܠ, ܐܠܦ, ܐܣܪ, ܐܘܕ, ܐܚܕ, ܐܪܙ; e.g. ܢܐܟܘܠ, ܡܐܟܠ. But ܶ is used in the verbs ܐܚܕ, ܐܙܠ, ܐܠܦ, ܐܡܢ, ܐܣܪ, ܐܪܟ; e. g. ܢܐܣܪ, ܡܐܣܪ. Both of these forms are found in ܐܬܐ. It should further be remarked that the first class of verbs mentioned above, form the fut. and imperat. Pe. like transitives with ܘ, excepting Verbs 3 rad. Gutt. or ܪ, and the second class form them like intransitives with ܰ. Lud. de Dieu (p. 265), rightly doubts the correctness of the double form of the infinit. and fut. Pe. with ܰ and ܶ, although the form ܠܡܐܟܠ is found in I Cor. x. 27; but the fut. of it is not found with ܘ. Also the correctness of ܬܐܟܠܘܢ in 1 Cor. x. 28, is suspected. The forms of the 3 plur. fem. pret. ܐܟܠܝܢ and ܐܟܠܝܢ are not approved. The vowel ܶ is sometimes found in the part. pass. Pe. of the regular verb (§20.1.Rem.). In the passives Ethpe. and Ethpa. of the Verb ܐܡܪ, ܐ is assimilated to the preceding ܬ; e. g. ܐܬܬܡܪ. This formation is also found in some other verbs varying little from regular verbs; e. g. ܐܬܬܟܠ and ܐܬܐܟܠ.

2. The radical ܐ usually falls away in the 1 sing. fut. Pe.; e. g. ܐܟܘܠ *I will eat,* ܐܡܪ *I will speak.* ܐ does not so often fall away in the other persons. The same peculiarity exists in the infinit. fut. and part. Pa., and the vowel is thrown back upon the preformative; e. g. ܢܟܠ and ܢܐܟܠ.

Rem.—The Verbs ܐܙܠ *to go away* and ܐܬܐ *to come*, lose ܐ in the imperat., and form;

ܙܠ، ܙܠܝ، ܙܠܘ، ܙܠܝܢ

ܬܐ، ܬܝ، ܬܘ، ܬܝܢ.

3. In Aphel and Shaphel with their passives, ܐ is changed into ܘ, and, with the preceding ܰ, forms *au*; e. g. ܐܘܟܠ, ܡܘܟܠ.

Rem.—In two verbs ܐ is changed into ܝ, viz: ܐܬܐ, Aph. ܐܝܬܝ, imperat. ܐܝܬܐ, fut. ܢܝܬܐ, infinit. ܡܝܬܝܘ, part. ܡܝܬܐ. (ܐܡܢ, Aph. ܗܝܡܢ = הֶאֱמִין). For this reason ܐܠܦ and ܝܠܦ *to learn*, are sometimes found together.

General Remarks.

The Verb ܐܙܠ (according. to § 12.1; § 15.2) should be noticed in the following persons; pret. 3 fem. and 1 sing. ܐܙܠܬ, ܐܙܠܬ; fut. 2 fem.sing. and 2 and 3 plur. ܬܐܙܠܝܢ, ܬܐܙܠܘܢ, etc.; part.fem.sing. ܐܙܠܐ and plur.masc. and fem. ܐܙܠܝܢ, ܐܙܠܢ. In the signification, *to be of use, to profit*, it is formed regularly. Verbs which commence with ܗ, like Verbs ܦܐ, assume the vowel and throw it back upon ܢ, but do not, like those, reject or change it, although this latter occurs in the Galilean dialect, which had but a single character for the two gutturals (comp. § 1. Rem. 1).

---

§ 29. *Verbs with* 1 *Rad. Yud* (ܦܝ) ܝܠܕ *to bring forth.*

In respect to these verbs it should be observed:

1. That in the pret. Pe. even when transitive, they take ܰ in the ultimate syllable (excepting Verbs 3 Rad. Gutt.);

e. g. ܝܺܬܶܒ (ܝܺܪܶܬ). If ܝ, the first radical, be without a vowel, as is usually the case (in pret., imperat., part. pass. Pe.), it quiesces in ◌ܺ. In the fut. and infinit. Pe. the vowel ◌ܺ falls back upon the vowelless preformative; e. g. ܢܺܕܰܥ, ܡܶܕܰܥ. So too in Ethpe., ◌ܺ falls back upon ܬ; e. g. ܐܶܬܺܝܕܰܥ. But where, in the regular verb, the first radical takes a vowel, these verbs are regularly inflected; e.g. ܝܶܕܥܰܬ.

Rem.—In the part. pass. Pe., besides the regular form, one with ◌ܰ appears; e. g. ܝܰܕܺܝܥ. Only ܝܗܰܒ takes ◌ܰ; but where the regular verb takes ◌ over the first radical, ◌ܰ, with Linea occultans under ܗ, falls away; e.g. ܝܗܰܒܬ. Lin. occultans with ◌ܰ appears in the 3 fem. and 1 sing. pret. with a suffix attached; e.g. ܝܰܗ̱ܒܬܶܗ *she has given him* (ܝܶܗܒܰܬ). In 3 plur. masc. and fem. under similar circumstances, Lin. occult. falls away; e. g. ܝܰܗ̱ܒܽܘܗ̱ܝ *they have given him* (ܝܗܰܒܘ).

2. In the fut.and imperat.Pe.the second syllable takes ◌ܰ. In the fut. and infinit. Pe. this class of verbs is similar to Verbs ܦܐ, and changes ܝ into ܐ which quiesces in ◌ܺ (vid. 1. above). But in the 1 sing. fut. ܝ falls away; e. g. ܐܺܕܰܥ. The imperat. on the contrary retains ܝ; e. g. ܝܺܕܰܥ.

Rem.—ܝܺܪܶܬ and ܝܺܬܶܒ follow the inflection of Verbs ܦܢ (§ 33); e. g. imperat. ܪܰܬ and ܬܶܒ, fut. ܢܺܐܪܰܬ and ܢܺܬܶܒ, infinit. ܡܶܐܪܰܬ and ܡܶܬܰܒ. In like manner ܗܰܒ imperat. from ܝܗܰܒ follows the same rule.

3. In Aph. and Shaph. with their passives ܝ is changed into ܘ (vid. Verbs ܦܐ, § 28. 3); e.g. ܐܰܘܕܰܥ, ܡܰܘܪܰܬ.

Rem.—ܝ is retained in ܐܰܝܠܶܠ and ܐܰܝܢܶܩ; still it should scarcely be considered as an irregularity, since from ܝܕܥ appear Pa. ܘܰܕܰܥ, Ethpa. ܐܶܬܘܰܕܰܥ.

§ 30. *Verbs Med. Olaph quiescent* (ܫܐܠ) ܫܐܶܠ *to ask.*

The irregularities of these verbs occur only in Pe., Ethpe., and Pa. with its passive.

1. Peal. In the pret. ܐ quiesces in ܰ and the latter falls back from ܐ upon the first radical; e. g. ܫܶܐܠ; but when ܝ is the third radical, it quiesces in ܳ standing before ܐ; e. g. ܠܳܐܝ. The vowel ܶ appears in Aph.; e.g. ܐܰܫܐܶܠ. In the imperat. and fut. Pe. ܐ quiesces in ܰ; e.g. ܫܰܐܠ, ܢܶܫܰܐܠ.

2. In Ethpe., besides the regular form ܐܶܬܫܐܶܠ, ܰ is sometimes inserted after ܬ; e. g. ܐܶܬܫܰܐܶܠ.

Rem.—In both cases metathesis of ܐ takes place; also a duplication of it; e.g. ܬܶܐܟܰܠ, ܬܐܟܽܠ and ܬܐܟܰܠ; Ethpe. ܐܶܬܬܰܐܡܰܪ and ܐܶܬܬܐܶܡܰܪ.

3. In Pa. and Ethpa. ܐ is generally changed into ܝ; e.g., ܒܰܝܶܫ and ܐܶܬܒܰܝܰܫ. The other verbs retain ܐ; e. g. ܐܰܬܠܐܶܒ.

Rem.——Both forms are found from ܙܐܐ (ܐܶܙܕܰܐܰܐ and ܐܶܙܕܰܝܰܐ).

---

§ 31. *Verbs Med. Rad. Vau and Yud quiescent*

(ܩܘܡ *and* ܕܝܢ) ܩܳܡ (ܩܘܡ) *to stand up,* ܡܺܝܬ *to die.*

The verbs whose middle radical letter is ܘ or ܝ, and whose grammatical structure generally agrees with that of the regular verb, differ from the same in the following cases:

1. In the pret. and infinit. Pe. of Verbs ܩܘܡ, the vowel ܳ appears in place of ܘ, which is dropped; e. g. ܩܳܡ, ܡܶܩܳܡ. In the part. pass. Pe., and in the other conjugations generally, ܘ is changed into ܝ, and quiesces in ܺ in the part. P., Pe., Ethpe., Aph. and Ethtaph.; e. g. ܩܺܝܡ, ܐܶܬܩܺܝܡ, ܐܰܩܺܝܡ.

On the contrary, ܝ is movable in Pa. and Ethpa; e. g. ܩܰܝܶܡ, ܐܶܬ݂ܩܰܝܰܡ. In the part.act. masc. of Pe., ܐ (=y, vid. §1. Rem. 4), which has arisen from ܘ, goes over in the other inflections into ܝ; e. g. ܩܳܐܶܡ masc., ܩܳܝܡܳܐ fem. Only in the imperat. and fut. Pe., ܘ remains and quiesces in ܽ; e.g. ܢܩܽܘܡ, in which cases, as well as in the pret. (in Verbs ܥܝ), ܝ appears and quiesces in ܺ; e. g. ܣܺܝܡ, ܢܣܺܝܡ. Finally the preformatives of the fut. Pe. have no vowel, except the 1 sing., which takes ܶ over ܐ; e. g. ܐܶܩܽܘܡ.

Rem.—In Pe., Ethpe., Aph., and Eshta., verbs of this class, which are at the same time ܠܐ (§ 32), as ܠܘܳܐ and some others which can be referred to no particular species, as ܙܘܰܥ, ܩܘܳܐ, retain ܘ movable. Some are inflected in both ways, but with a different signification; e. g. ܚܘܰܢ *to take a handful*, Aph. ܐܰܙܺܝܚ *to deviate from the way.* TheVerb ܡܳܬ, contrary to the rule, takes ܝ in the fut. and imperat. But ܣܺܝܡ follows the inflection of ܥܘ Verbs; e.g. fut. ܢܣܽܘܡ. The imperat. of ܚܘܣ *to spare*, takes ܳ (ܚܳܣ), with the signification, *far be it.* In some manuscripts ܶ is found in the preformatives of the fut. and in the infinit. Pe., which manner of writing was received by the ancient grammarians, and which, as is testified by Amira, p. 311, the Mandæans used on account of metre (vid. *Lud. de Dieu* p. 292).

2. In Ethpe. ܬ of the formative syllable ܐܬ is doubled; e. g. ܐܶܬ݁ܬ݁ܩܺܝܡ. By this, the transposition of the sibilants does not occur; e. g. ܐܶܬ݁ܬ݁ܙܺܝܥ. When three ܬ come together in the 3 sing. fem. and 2 sing. and plur. masc. and fem. fut., one ܬ is omitted; e. g. ܬܶܬ݁ܩܺܝܡ. The occurrence of three ܬ together is unavoidable only when the verb itself begins with ܬ, in which case four ܬ would properly come in succession; e. g. ܬܬܬܟܰܠܽܘܢ Ps. lxii. 10, from ܬܟܰܠ. Ethtaph. differs from Ethpe. merely in signification; e. g. ܐܶܬ݁ܬ݁ܪܺܝܡ Ethpe. *to raise one's self*, Ethtaph. *to be taken away.*

Rem.—ܐܶܬ݁ܬ݁ܦܺܝܣ *to be convinced*, Ethtaph.. from ܐܰܦܺܝܣ, is usually written ܐܶܬ݁ܛܦܺܝܣ.

3. In Aph. the preformatives of the fut., infinit., and part., lose the characteristic ܰ, excepting the 1 sing. fut.; e. g. ܐܰܩܛܶܠ. The part. pass., contrary to the analogy of other part. passives, changes ܶ into ܳ; e.g. ܡܩܳܛܰܠ, to distinguish it from the active form ܡܰܩܛܶܠ.

Rem.—No example is found of Shaphel.

---

§ 32. *Verbs 3 rad. Olaph Quiescent* (ܠܐ) ܓܠܳܐ *to disclose.*

These verbs, which include the Hebrew לא and לה Verbs, are different from the regular verbs in the following cases.

1. The third radical ܐ either quiesces or is changed into ܝ. Here it should be remarked that the pret. Pe. ends in ܳܐ; e. g. ܓܠܳܐ, the other preterits in ܺܝ; e. g. Ethpe. ܐܶܬ݂ܓܠܺܝ. The futures of all the conjugations end in ܶܐ; e. g. Pe. ܢܶܓܠܶܐ, the imperat. Pe. in ܺܝ; e.g. ܓܠܺܝ, imperat. Ethpe. in ܰܝ; e.g. ܐܶܬ݂ܓܠܰܝ; the other conjugations in ܳܐ; e.g. Pa. ܓܰܠܳܐ. The termination of the infinit. Pe. is the same; e.g ܡܶܓܠܳܐ. The other conjugations in the infinit. end with ܳܝܽܘ; e. g. Aph. ܡܰܓܠܳܝܽܘ, the participles generally with ܶܐ; e. g. Pe. ܓܳܠܶܐ. Only the part. pass. of Pa., Aph., and Shaph., ends with ܰܝ; e. g. Pa. ܡܓܰܠܰܝ.

Rem.—Some verbs with ܺܝ (ܺܝ) in the pret. Pe. are inflected like the other preterits. Here belong mostly intransitives, or Verbs Med. E.; e. g. ܪܒܺܝ *to be great.* Both forms are found in the Verbs ܝܰܡܳܐ and ܝܡܺܝ *to swear.* The imperatives of this kind of verbs, take ܰܝ at the end. Some verbs with 3 rad. He., seem to belong here; e.g. ܫܡܰܗ *to name,* Pa. ܫܰܡܺܝ. Some grammarians, without proof, derive from the imperat. Ethpe. the forms ܐܬܓܠܐ and ܐܬܓܠܐ. The Verb ܗܘܐ has two forms of the future; e. g. ܢܗܘܐ and ܢܗܘܐ. In the formation of the present tense in connection with the pronoun, the part. takes ܝ quiescent, instead of ܐ; e. g. ܡܫܪܝܢܐ for ܡܫܪܐ ܐܢܐ. From ܣܢܐ *to hate* appears a double form of the part. pass.; e. g. ܣܢܐ and ܣܢܝܐ. The former refers more particularly to things, and the latter to persons.

2. When a letter or syllable is added, ܐ is either changed into ܝ or falls entirely away.

A. In the first case, ܝ is *a*) *movable* in the pret. 3 sing. fem. of all the conjugations excepting Pe. of verbs ending in ܐ; e.g. Ethpe. ܐܬܓܠܝܬ (Pe. ܓܠܬ); in the second form of 3 plur. fem.; e. g. Pa. ܓܠܝܢ; in the 2 plur. fem. of all the imperatives; e. g. Pe. ܓܠܝܢ; in the 2 and 3 plur. fem. of all the futures; e. g. Ethpe. ܢܬܓܠܝܢ; in the fem. sing. and plur. of all the participles; e. g. Pe. ܓܠܝܐ; and finally in all the infinitives except that of Pe.; e. g. Aph. ܡܓܠܝܘ (Pe. ܡܓܠܐ); *b*) ܝ is *quiescent* in the 1 and 2 masc. and fem. of both numbers of all the preterits, and in such a manner that ܝ in Pe. (excepting the 1 sing. ܓܠܝܬ) quiesces in ܺ; e.g. ܓܠܝܬ, ܓܠܝܬܘܢ. In other cases ܝ quiesces in ܺ; e.g. Ethpe. ܐܬܓܠܝܬ, ܐܬܓܠܝܬܘܢ.

B. ܐ *falls away* in the 3 sing. fem. pret. Pe. of Verbs ending in ܐ with ܰ retained; e. g. ܓܠܬ; in the 3 plur. masc. and fem. pret. Pe., and in the 3 plur. fem. (in the 3 plur. masc. Pe. of Verbs ܝ and of other preterits, ܝ remains) of all the preterits; e. g. Pe. ܓܠܘ; in the fut. throughout in the 2 sing. fem., while the regular form ܝܢ is changed into ܝܢ; e. g. Pa. ܬܓܠܝܢ, and in the 2 and 3 plur. masc.; e.g. Pe. ܢܶܓܠܽܘܢ; also in the 2 sing. fem. imperat., where ܝ quiesces in —; e.g. Pa. ܓܰܠܳܝ; also in the 2 plur. masc. imperat., where ܘ quiesces in —; e.g. Aph. ܐܰܓܠܰܘ; finally in the plur. masc. of the part., where the regular form ܝܺܢ is exchanged with ܶܝܢ; e.g. Pe. ܓܳܠܶܝܢ.

Rem.—Instead of Pa. and Ethpa., sometimes the quadriliteral form ܓܰܠܘܺܝ appears. The 3 plur. masc. pret. ܓܠܰܘ (with paragog. Nun ܓܠܰܘܢ) occurs, sometimes with ܐ retained; e. g. Acts xxviii. 2. ܚܙܳܐܘܢ. But the form ܓܠܘ which Buxtorf adduces, is neither confirmed by examples nor found in Amira. In all the conjugations excepting Pe., the 3 plur. fem. pret. differs from the 3 sing. masc. only by taking Ribui (vid. § 6), for which Amira (p. 266) in verbs ending with ܺܝ, and in Pa. of verbs ending with ܝܳܐ, writes a double ܝ; e. g. ܓܰܠܺܝܝ. In the imperat. Ethpe., besides the form given in the paradigm, occurs the 2 plur. fem. ܐܶܬܓܠܺܝܶܝܢ.

General Remark.—Verbs ܠܐ or ܠܝ, which are at the same time ܦܐ (comp. § 30. 1), are inflected like Verbs ܦܐ; e. g. pret. Pe. ܐܶܬܳܐ. ܐܶܬܳܬ, ܐܶܬܰܬ, ܐܶܬܰܝܬ, plur. ܐܶܬܰܘ, etc., infinit. ܡܶܐܬܳܐ, imperat. ܬܳܐ, ܬܳܝ, etc., fut. ܢܺܐܬܶܐ, plur. ܢܺܐܬܽܘܢ, etc., part. act. ܐܳܬܶܐ, pass. ܐܬܶܐ, Aph. pret. ܐܰܝܬܺܝ and ܐܰܝܬܺܝ, infinit. ܡܰܝܬܳܝܘ, imperat. ܐܰܝܬܺܝ, fut. ܢܰܝܬܶܐ, part. ܡܰܝܬܶܐ.

APPENDIX TO § 32.

Inflection of the Verb ܚܝܳܐ *to live.*

In the Verb ܚܝܳܐ with ܝ movable, ܝ is rejected when the first radical and the preformative are without a vowel; e. g. infinit. Pe. ܡܶܚܳܐ for ܡܶܚܝܳܐ. Sometimes this verb takes ܐ between the preformatives and the first radical; e. g.

ܡܚܐܝܐ (better perhaps ܡܚܐܝܐ), fut. ܢܚܶܐ for ܢܚܝܶܐ and with ܐ inserted ܢܐܚܘܢ, Aph. pret. ܐܚܝ, infinit. ܡܚܝܘ or ܡܐܚܝܘ, fut. ܢܚܶܐ and ܢܐܚܐ, imperat. ܐܚܐ, part. ܡܚܐ and ܡܐܚܐ. ܝ also falls away when no preformative precedes, and its vowel falls back upon the first vacant radical; e.g. imperat. Pe. ܚܰܝ for ܚܝܰܝ, part. fem. ܚܝܳܐ for ܚܝܝܳܐ. The form ܚܳܝܶܝܢ (Matt. xv. 27) is found in the part. plur. masc.

B. Defective Verbs.

§ 33. *Verbs with the first radical Nun* (ܦܢ) ܢܦܰܩ *to go out.*

The irregularities of these verbs are the following :—

In the fut., imperat., and infinit. Pe., and in all forms of Aph., the first rad. ܢ falls away; e. g. ܢܶܦܽܘܩ, ܦܽܘܩ, ܡܶܦܰܩ, ܐܰܦܶܩ. The fut. and imperat. Pe. sometimes take ܰ and ܶ; e. g. ܢܶܣܰܒ, ܢܶܬܶܠ.

Rem. — The exceptions to this rule are; *a*) Verbs Med. Rad. doubled (§ 34); e. g. ܢܶܪ; *b*) Verbs Med. Rad. Quiescent; e. g. ܢܽܘܚ; *c*) Verbs Med. Rad. ܗ; e. g. ܢܗܰܪ, fut. ܢܶܢܗܰܪ. Those verbs whose third radical is ܝ or ܬ, are not changed by assimilation, as in Hebrew; e.g. ܗܰܝܡܶܢܢ *we have believed,* ܢܚܶܬܬܘܢ *ye have descended.* The Verb ܢܣܶܩ *to mount up,* takes its pret. and part. Pe. from ܣܠܶܩ (vid. § 35.2). Upon retaining the characteristic ܐ in Aph.; e.g. ܬܐܦܶܩ for ܬܦܶܩ. Comp., § 23. 1. Rem.

---

§ 34. *Verbs with Med. Rad. doubled* (ܥܥ) ܪܣܰܣ *to sprinkle.*

In respect to these verbs it should be remarked :—

1. That the middle radical falls away in the pret., infinit.,

imperat., and fut. (having ܽ over the preformative) Pe.; e. g. pret. ܩܳܡ, infinit. ܡܶܩܳܡ, fut. ܢܩܽܘܡ, imperat., ܩܽܘܡ. Also Aph. and Shaph. with their passives; e. g. ܐܰܩܺܝܡ, ܐܶܬܬܩܺܝܡ. The part. act. Pe. takes ܐ in place of the middle radical, which has fallen away; e. g. ܩܳܐܶܡ; but ܐ falls away again when a syllable is added; e. g. plur. ܩܳܝܡܺܝܢ.

Rem.—Those verbs whose 2 and 3 rad. is ܐ, are exceptions, and are inflected according to the rules for quiescent verbs (§ 35. 1. d). In the fut. and imperat. Pe. forms with ܰ (not ܽ) appear; e. g. ܢܣܰܥ, ܚܰܝ. The part. act. Pe. has ܥܳܐܠܺܝܢ in the plur. from the Verb ܥܰܠ *to go in.* In the part. Aph. sometimes the middle radical appears again, but it is marked by Linea occultans; e. g. Heb. ix. 5, ܡܛܰܠܠܺܝܢ. In Aph. the characteristic ܐ sometimes remains after the preformative; e. g. ܠܡܰܐܢܳܚܽܘܬܗ from ܢܚܚ (Comp. § 23. 1. Rem.).

2. The part. pass. Pe. ܩܺܝܡ, Ethpe., Pa. and Ethpa.; e. g. ܐܶܬܩܰܘܰܡ, ܩܰܘܶܡ, are regularly inflected, with the retention of the middle radical. Instead of the last two forms, however, Palpel. and Ethpalp. (§ 25. D) are more in use; e. g. ܩܰܡܩܶܡ, ܐܶܬܩܰܡܩܰܡ.

Rem.—The last remark holds good also of Shaphel, which occurs more rarely (Comp. 1. above).

---

§ 35. *Doubly Irregular and Defective Verbs.*

1. By Doubly Irregular Verbs are understood those in which occur two of those letters which usually give rise to irregularities. In the inflection of these verbs, either one or both of those letters may retain their peculiarities. This class of verbs consists of (vid. Lud. de Dieu, p. 340, sq.); a) Verbs ܦ̈ܢ and ܠ̈ܐ; e. g. ܢܦܳܐ, Aph. ܐܰܦܺܝ *to approve;* b) Verbs ܦ̈ܐ and ܠ̈ܐ; e. g. ܐܶܬܳܐ *to come,* Aph. ܐܰܝܬܺܝ, ܐܳܣܳܐ *to heal,* Pa. ܐܰܣܺܝ, ܐܳܦܳܐ *to boil,* Ethpe. ܐܶܬܐܰܦܺܝ; c) Verbs ܥ̈ܘ and ܠ̈ܐ,

e. g. ܝܡܐ *to swear*, imperat. ܝܡܝ, fut. ܢܐܡܐ, infinit. ܡܐܡܐ, Aph. ܐܘܡܝ; ܢܒܐ *to sprout*, imperat. ܢܒܝ, Aph. ܐܘܒܝ and ܐܢܒܝ; d) Verbs ܠܐ̈ and ܥܥ̈; e. g. ܟܐܐ *to chide*, imperat. ܟܐܝ, infinit. ܡܟܐܐ; ܥܐܝ *to be displeased*, Aph. ܐܥܝ.

2. To Defective verbs (see Lud. de Dieu, p. 344) belong the following, in so far as they occur in the language, either in individual forms only, or have borrowed their defective forms from synonymous verbs, or, finally, vary from the regular verb in inflection and interpunction. a) Impersonal Verbs. From ܘܙܢ *to be fit*, occurs only the part. act. ܘܙܢ *it befits*. From ܡܐܟܪ appear the 3 sing. fem. pret. ܡܐܟܪܬ *it is disagreeable*, the part. act. fem. ܡܐܟܪܐ and the 3 sing. fem. fut. ܬܡܐܟܪ; and from ܦܐ and ܝܐ appear the act. part. ܦܐܐ and ܝܐܐ *it is suitable*.

b) The following defective verbs are completed from others which are synonymous: ܣܠܩ *to mount up*, part. act. ܣܠܩ; the other tenses of this verb are formed from ܢܣܩ, imperat. ܣܩ, fut. ܢܣܩ, infinit. ܡܣܩ, Aph. ܐܣܩ, part. ܡܣܩ, Ethpa. ܐܬܣܠܩ. A similar complement is found in ܝܗܒ *to give* (see § 29. 1. Rem.), imperat. ܗܒ, infinit. ܡܬܠ, fut. ܢܬܠ from ܢܬܠ, Ethpe. ܐܬܝܗܒ.

c) Those which differ in form and inflection are ܪܗܛ, *to run*, imperat. ܪܗܘܛ; ܐܙܠ *to go away* and ܐܬܐ *to come* (see § 28. 2. 3. Rem.); also ܗܘܐ *to be* (see § 32. 1. Rem. and § 38), fut. ܢܗܘܐ and ܢܗܘܐ; also from ܗܘܐ is found a fut. apocopate ܢܗܘ, ܬܗܘ, plur. ܢܗܘܘܢ, etc., having the signification of the conjunctive as well as of the usual future (comp. Agrell. Otiola Syr. p. 46); ܫܬܐ *to drink*, with ܐ prosthet. ܐܫܬܝ, imperat. ܐܫܬܝ, part. ܫܬܐ, fut. ܢܫܬܐ, infinit. ܡܫܬܐ; ܐܫܬܝ, Aph. ܗܝܡܢ *to believe;* ܚܝܐ (see App. to § 32), *to live.* Finally, in four verbs 3 rad. Olaph.; e. g. ܚܛܐ, ܛܡܐ, ܕܐܐ, ܐܬܡܐ (ܐܬܕܐ), which merely occur in Pa. and its passive, the second syllable quiesces in ـܶ, as in Verbs 3 Gutt. (see § 13. 1. Rem.), and ܐ is retained in all of the tenses and moods, while its vowel falls back upon the preceding vacant consonant; e. g. 3 sing. fem. pret. ܦܰܢܳܐܬ. The formation is as follows; pret. Pa. ܦܰܢܺܐ, part. ܡܦܰܢܶܐ, infinit. ܡܦܰܢܳܐܘ, imperat. ܦܰܢܺܐ, fut. ܢܦܰܢܶܐ, Ethpa. ܐܶܬܦܰܢܺܐ, part. ܡܶܬܦܰܢܶܐ, infinit. ܡܶܬܦܰܢܳܐܘ, fut. ܢܶܬܦܰܢܶܐ.

The Regular Verb.

	Peal.		Ethpeel.	Pael.	Ethpaal.	Aphel.	Ethtaphal.	Shaphel.	Eshtaph.
Pret. 3 m.	ܩܛܰܠ	ܕܚܶܠ	ܐܶܬܩܛܶܠ	ܩܰܛܶܠ	ܐܶܬܩܰܛܰܠ	ܐܰܩܛܶܠ	ܐܶܬܬܰܩܛܰܠ	ܫܰܩܛܶܠ	ܐܶܫܬܰܩܛܰܠ
3 f.	ܩܶܛܠܰܬ	ܕܶܚܠܰܬ	ܐܶܬܩܰܛܠܰܬ	ܩܰܛܠܰܬ	ܐܶܬܩܰܛܠܰܬ	ܐܰܩܛܠܰܬ	ܐܶܬܬܰܩܛܠܰܬ	like Aphel.	like Ethtaphal.
2 m.	ܩܛܰܠܬ	ܕܚܶܠܬ	ܐܶܬܩܛܶܠܬ	ܩܰܛܶܠܬ	ܐܶܬܩܰܛܰܠܬ	ܐܰܩܛܶܠܬ	ܐܶܬܬܰܩܛܰܠܬ		
2 f.	ܩܛܰܠܬܝ	ܕܚܶܠܬܝ	ܐܶܬܩܛܶܠܬܝ	ܩܰܛܶܠܬܝ	ܐܶܬܩܰܛܰܠܬܝ	ܐܰܩܛܶܠܬܝ	ܐܶܬܬܰܩܛܰܠܬܝ		
1 c.	ܩܶܛܠܶܬ	ܕܶܚܠܶܬ	ܐܶܬܩܰܛܠܶܬ	ܩܰܛܠܶܬ	ܐܶܬܩܰܛܠܶܬ	ܐܰܩܛܠܶܬ	ܐܶܬܬܰܩܛܠܶܬ		
Plur. 3 m.	ܩܛܰܠܘ	ܕܚܶܠܘ	ܐܶܬܩܛܶܠܘ	ܩܰܛܶܠܘ	ܐܶܬܩܰܛܰܠܘ	ܐܰܩܛܶܠܘ	ܐܶܬܬܰܩܛܰܠܘ		
3 f.	ܩܛܰܠ̈, ܝܢ̈	ܕܚܶܠ̈	ܐܶܬܩܛܶܠ̈, ܝܢ̈	ܩܰܛܶܠ̈, ܝܢ̈	ܐܶܬܩܰܛܰܠ̈, ܝܢ̈	ܐܰܩܛܶܠ̈, ܝܢ̈	ܐܶܬܬܰܩܛܰܠ̈, ܝܢ̈		
2 m.	ܩܛܰܠܬܘܢ	ܕܚܶܠܬܘܢ	ܐܶܬܩܛܶܠܬܘܢ	ܩܰܛܶܠܬܘܢ	ܐܶܬܩܰܛܰܠܬܘܢ	ܐܰܩܛܶܠܬܘܢ	ܐܶܬܬܰܩܛܰܠܬܘܢ		
2 f.	ܩܛܰܠܬܶܝܢ	ܕܚܶܠܬܶܝܢ	ܐܶܬܩܛܶܠܬܶܝܢ	ܩܰܛܶܠܬܶܝܢ	ܐܶܬܩܰܛܰܠܬܶܝܢ	ܐܰܩܛܶܠܬܶܝܢ	ܐܶܬܬܰܩܛܰܠܬܶܝܢ		
1 c.	ܩܛܰܠܢ, ܢܰܢ	ܕܚܶܠܢ	ܐܶܬܩܛܶܠܢ, ܢܰܢ	ܩܰܛܶܠܢ, ܢܰܢ	ܐܶܬܩܰܛܰܠܢ, ܢܰܢ	ܐܰܩܛܶܠܢ, ܢܰܢ	ܐܶܬܬܰܩܛܰܠܢ, ܢܰܢ		
Infin.	ܡܶܩܛܰܠ (ܡܶܕܚܰܠ)		ܡܶܬܩܛܳܠܘ	ܡܩܰܛܳܠܘ	ܡܶܬܩܰܛܳܠܘ	ܡܰܩܛܳܠܘ	ܡܶܬܬܰܩܛܳܠܘ	ܡܫܰܩܛܳܠܘ	ܡܶܫܬܰܩܛܳܠܘ
Imp. 2 m.	ܩܛܘܿܠ	ܕܚܰܠ	ܐܶܬܩܛܶܠ	ܩܰܛܶܠ	ܐܶܬܩܰܛܰܠ	ܐܰܩܛܶܠ	ܐܶܬܬܰܩܛܰܠ (ܩܛܶܠ)	ܫܰܩܛܶܠ	ܐܶܫܬܰܩܛܰܠ
2 f.	ܩܛܘܿܠܝ	ܕܚܰܠܝ	ܐܶܬܩܛܶܠܝ	ܩܰܛܶܠܝ	ܐܶܬܩܰܛܶܠܝ	ܐܰܩܛܶܠܝ	ܐܶܬܬܰܩܛܰܠܝ		(ܐܶܫܬܰܩܛܶܠ)

Plur. 2 m.	ܩܛܘܠܘ	ܕܚܠܘ	ܐܬܩܛܠܘ	ܩܛܠܘ	ܐܬܩܛܠܘ	ܐܩܛܠܘ	ܐܬܬܩܛܠܘ		
2 f.	ܩܛܘܠܝܢ	ܕܚܠܝܢ	ܐܬܩܛܠܝܢ	ܩܛܠܝܢ	ܐܬܩܛܠܝܢ	ܐܩܛܠܝܢ	ܐܬܬܩܛܠܝܢ		
Fut. 3 m.	ܢܩܛܘܠ	ܢܕܚܠ	ܢܬܩܛܠ	ܢܩܛܠ	ܢܬܩܛܠ	ܢܩܛܠ	ܢܬܬܩܛܠ	ܢܫܩܛܠ	ܢܫܬܩܛܠ
3 f.	ܬܩܛܘܠ, ܟܕ	ܬܕܚܠ	ܬܬܩܛܠ, ܟܕ	ܬܩܛܠ, ܟܕ	ܬܬܩܛܠ, ܟܕ	ܬܩܛܠ, ܟܕ	ܬܬܬܩܛܠ, ܟܕ		
2 m.	ܬܩܛܘܠ	ܬܕܚܠ	ܬܬܩܛܠ	ܬܩܛܠ	ܬܬܩܛܠ	ܬܩܛܠ	ܬܬܬܩܛܠ		
2 f.	ܬܩܛܠܝܢ	ܬܕܚܠܝܢ	ܬܬܩܛܠܝܢ	ܬܩܛܠܝܢ	ܬܬܩܛܠܝܢ	ܬܩܛܠܝܢ	ܬܬܬܩܛܠܝܢ		
1 c.	ܐܩܛܘܠ	ܐܕܚܠ	ܐܬܩܛܠ	ܐܩܛܠ	ܐܬܩܛܠ	ܐܩܛܠ	ܐܬܬܩܛܠ		
Plur. 3 m.	ܢܩܛܠܘܢ		ܢܬܩܛܠܘܢ	ܢܩܛܠܘܢ	ܢܬܩܛܠܘܢ	ܢܩܛܠܘܢ	ܢܬܬܩܛܠܘܢ		
3 f.	ܢܩܛܠܢ		ܢܬܩܛܠܢ	ܢܩܛܠܢ	ܢܬܩܛܠܢ	ܢܩܛܠܢ	ܢܬܬܩܛܠܢ		
2 m.	ܬܩܛܠܘܢ		ܬܬܩܛܠܘܢ	ܬܩܛܠܘܢ	ܬܬܩܛܠܘܢ	ܬܩܛܠܘܢ	ܬܬܬܩܛܠܘܢ		
2 f.	ܬܩܛܠܢ		ܬܬܩܛܠܢ	ܬܩܛܠܢ	ܬܬܩܛܠܢ	ܬܩܛܠܢ	ܬܬܬܩܛܠܢ		
1 c.	ܢܩܛܘܠ		ܢܬܩܛܠ	ܢܩܛܠ	ܢܬܩܛܠ	ܢܩܛܠ	ܢܬܬܩܛܠ		
Part. act. m.	ܩܛܠ			ܡܩܛܠ		ܡܩܛܠ		ܡܫܩܛܠ	
f.	ܩܛܠܐ			ܡܩܛܠܐ		ܡܩܛܠܐ		ܡܫܩܛܠܐ	
Part. P. m.	ܩܛܝܠ		ܡܬܩܛܠ	ܡܩܛܠ	ܡܬܩܛܠ	ܡܩܛܠ	ܡܬܬܩܛܠ	ܡܫܩܛܠ	ܡܫܬܩܛܠ
f.	ܩܛܝܠܐ		ܡܬܩܛܠܐ	ܡܩܛܠܐ	ܡܬܩܛܠܐ	ܡܩܛܠܐ	ܡܬܬܩܛܠܐ	ܡܫܩܛܠܐ	ܡܫܬܩܛܠܐ

Verb First Rad. Olaph Quiescent (ܦܩܐ § 28).

	Peal.		Ethpeel.	Pael.	Ethpaal.	Aphel.	Ethtaphal.	Shaphel.	Eshtaph.
Pret. 3 m.	ܐܟܠ		ܐܬܐܟܠ } ܐܬܬܟܝܠ	ܐܟܠ	ܐܬܐܟܠ } ܐܬܬܟܠ	ܐܘܟܠ	ܐܬܬܘܟܠ	ܫܘܟܠ	ܐܫܬܘܟܠ
3 f.	ܐܟܠܬ		ܐܬܐܟܠܬ	ܐܟܠܬ	ܐܬܐܟܠܬ	ܐܘܟܠܬ	ܐܬܬܘܟܠܬ		
2 m.	ܐܟܠܬ		ܐܬܐܟܠܬ	ܐܟܠܬ	ܐܬܐܟܠܬ	ܐܘܟܠܬ	ܐܬܬܘܟܠܬ		
2 f.	ܐܟܠܬܝ		ܐܬܐܟܠܬܝ	ܐܟܠܬܝ	ܐܬܐܟܠܬܝ	ܐܘܟܠܬܝ	ܐܬܬܘܟܠܬܝ		
1 c.	ܐܟܠܬ		ܐܬܐܟܠܬ	ܐܟܠܬ	ܐܬܐܟܠܬ	ܐܘܟܠܬ	ܐܬܬܘܟܠܬ		
Plur. 3 m.	ܐܟܠܘ		ܐܬܐܟܠܘ	ܐܟܠܘ	ܐܬܐܟܠܘ	ܐܘܟܠܘ	ܐܬܬܘܟܠܘ		
3 f.	ܐܟܠܝ̈, ܢ		ܐܬܐܟܠܝ̈, ܢ	ܐܟܠܝ̈, ܢ	ܐܬܐܟܠܝ̈, ܢ	ܐܘܟܠܝ̈, ܢ	ܐܬܬܘܟܠܝ̈, ܢ		
2 m.	ܐܟܠܬܘܢ		ܐܬܐܟܠܬܘܢ	ܐܟܠܬܘܢ	ܐܬܐܟܠܬܘܢ	ܐܘܟܠܬܘܢ	ܐܬܬܘܟܠܬܘܢ		
2 f.	ܐܟܠܬܝܢ		ܐܬܐܟܠܬܝܢ	ܐܟܠܬܝܢ	ܐܬܐܟܠܬܝܢ	ܐܘܟܠܬܝܢ	ܐܬܬܘܟܠܬܝܢ		
1 c.	ܐܟܠܢ, ܢ		ܐܬܐܟܠܢ, ܢ	ܐܟܠܢ, ܢ	ܐܬܐܟܠܢ, ܢ	ܐܘܟܠܢ, ܢ	ܐܬܬܘܟܠܢ, ܢ		
Infin.	ܡܐܟܠ	ܡܐܡܪ	ܡܬܐܟܠܘ } ܡܬܬܟܝܪܘ	ܡܐܟܠܘ ܡܟܠܚܘ	ܡܬܐܟܠܘ } ܡܬܬܟܠܘ	ܡܘܟܠܘ	ܡܬܬܘܟܠܘ	ܡܫܘܟܠܘ	ܡܫܬܘܟܠܘ
Imp. 2 m.	ܐܟܘܠ	ܐܡܪ	ܐܬܐܟܠ } ܐܬܬܟܝܠ	ܐܟܠ	ܐܬܐܟܠ } ܐܬܬܟܠ	ܐܘܟܠ	ܐܬܬܘܟܠ (ܘܟܠ)	ܫܘܟܠ	ܐܫܬܘܟܠ
2 f.	ܐܟܘܠܝ	ܐܡܪܝ	ܐܬܐܟܠܝ	ܐܟܠܝ	ܐܬܐܟܠܝ	ܐܘܟܠܝ	ܐܬܬܘܟܠܝ		(ܐܫܬܘܟܠܝ)

Plur. 2 m.	ܐܟܘܠܘ	ܐܡܘܪܘ	ܐܬܐܟܠܘ	ܐܟܠܘ	ܐܬܐܟܠܘ	ܐܘܟܠܘ	ܐܬܬܘܟܠܘ		
2 f.	ܐܟܘܠܝܢ	ܐܡܘܪܝܢ	ܐܬܐܟܠܝܢ	ܐܟܠܝܢ	ܐܬܐܟܠܝܢ	ܐܘܟܠܝܢ	ܐܬܬܘܟܠܝܢ		
Fut. 3 m.	ܢܐܟܘܠ	ܢܐܡܪ	{ ܢܬܐܟܠ ܢܬܬܟܝܠ	{ ܢܐܟܠ ܢܟܠ	{ ܢܬܐܟܠ ܢܬܬܟܠ	ܢܘܟܠ	ܢܬܬܘܟܠ	ܢܫܘܟܠ	ܢܫܬܘܟܠ
3 f.	ܬܐܟܘܠ ܠܗ	ܬܐܡܪ	ܬܬܐܟܠ ܠܗ	ܬܐܟܠ ܠܗ	ܬܬܐܟܠ ܠܗ	ܬܘܟܠ ܠܗ	ܬܬܬܘܟܠ ܠܗ		
2 m.	ܬܐܟܘܠ	ܬܐܡܪ	ܬܬܐܟܠ	ܬܐܟܠ	ܬܬܐܟܠ	ܬܘܟܠ	ܬܬܬܘܟܠ		
2 f.	ܬܐܟܠܝܢ	ܬܐܡܪܝܢ	ܬܬܐܟܠܝܢ	ܬܐܟܠܝܢ	ܬܬܐܟܠܝܢ	ܬܘܟܠܝܢ	ܬܬܬܘܟܠܝܢ		
1 c.	ܐܟܘܠ	ܐܡܪ	ܐܬܐܟܠ	ܐܟܠ	ܐܬܐܟܠ	ܐܘܟܠ	ܐܬܬܘܟܠ		
Plur. 3 m.	ܢܐܟܠܘܢ	ܢܐܡܪܘܢ	ܢܬܐܟܠܘܢ	ܢܐܟܠܘܢ	ܢܬܐܟܠܘܢ	ܢܘܟܠܘܢ	ܢܬܬܘܟܠܘܢ		
3 f.	ܢܐܟܠܢ	ܢܐܡܪܢ	ܢܬܐܟܠܢ	ܢܐܟܠܢ	ܢܬܐܟܠܢ	ܢܘܟܠܢ	ܢܬܬܘܟܠܢ		
2 m.	ܬܐܟܠܘܢ	ܬܐܡܪܘܢ	ܬܬܐܟܠܘܢ	ܬܐܟܠܘܢ	ܬܬܐܟܠܘܢ	ܬܘܟܠܘܢ	ܬܬܬܘܟܠܘܢ		
2 f.	ܬܐܟܠܢ	ܬܐܡܪܢ	ܬܬܐܟܠܢ	ܬܐܟܠܢ	ܬܬܐܟܠܢ	ܬܘܟܠܢ	ܬܬܬܘܟܠܢ		
1 c.	ܢܐܟܘܠ	ܢܐܡܪ	ܢܬܐܟܠ	ܢܐܟܠ	ܢܬܐܟܠ	ܢܘܟܠ	ܢܬܬܘܟܠ		
Part. act. m.	ܐܟܠ			{ ܡܐܟܠ ܡܟܠ		ܡܘܟܠ		ܡܫܘܟܠ	
f.	ܐܟܠܐ			ܡܐܟܠܐ		ܡܘܟܠܐ			
Part. P. m.	ܐܟܝܠ		{ ܡܬܐܟܠ ܡܬܬܟܝܠ	{ ܡܐܟܠ ܡܟܠ	{ ܡܬܐܟܠ ܡܬܬܟܠ	ܡܘܟܠ	ܡܬܬܘ ܟܠ	ܡܫܘܟܠ	ܡܫܬܘܟܠ
f.	ܐܟܝܠܐ		ܡܬܐܟܠܐ	ܡܐܟܠܐ	ܡܬܐܟܠܐ	ܡܘܟܠܐ	ܡܬܬܘ ܟܠܐ		

Verbs First Rad. Jud (ܝܕܰܥ § 29).

	Peal.	*Ethpeel.*	*Pael.*	*Ethpaal.*	*Aphel.*	*Ethtaphal.*	*Shaphel.*	*Eshtaph.*
Pret. 3 m.	ܝܺܕܰܥ	ܐܶܬܝܺܕܰܥ	ܝܰܕܰܥ	ܐܶܬܝܰܕܰܥ	ܐܰܘܕܰܥ	ܐܶܬܬܰܘܕܰܥ	ܫܰܘܕܰܥ	ܐܶܫܬܰܘܕܰܥ
3 f.	ܝܶܕܥܰܬ	ܐܶܬܝܰܕܥܰܬ	ܝܰܕܥܰܬ	ܐܶܬܝܰܕܥܰܬ	ܐܰܘܕܥܰܬ	ܐܶܬܬܰܘܕܥܰܬ		
2 m.	ܝܺܕܰܥܬ	ܐܶܬܝܺܕܰܥܬ	ܝܰܕܰܥܬ	ܐܶܬܝܰܕܰܥܬ	ܐܰܘܕܰܥܬ	ܐܶܬܬܰܘܕܰܥܬ		
2 f.	ܝܺܕܰܥܬܝ	ܐܶܬܝܺܕܰܥܬܝ	ܝܰܕܰܥܬܝ	ܐܶܬܝܰܕܰܥܬܝ	ܐܰܘܕܰܥܬܝ	ܐܶܬܬܰܘܕܰܥܬܝ		
1 c.	ܝܶܕܥܶܬ	ܐܶܬܝܰܕܥܶܬ	ܝܰܕܥܶܬ	ܐܶܬܝܰܕܥܶܬ	ܐܰܘܕܥܶܬ	ܐܶܬܬܰܘܕܥܶܬ		
Plur. 3 m.	ܝܺܕܰܥܘ	ܐܶܬܝܺܕܰܥܘ	ܝܰܕܰܥܘ	ܐܶܬܝܰܕܰܥܘ	ܐܰܘܕܰܥܘ	ܐܶܬܬܰܘܕܰܥܘ		
3 f.	ܝܺܕܰ̈ܥܝ, ܝܺܕܰ̈ܥܶܝܢ	ܐܶܬܝܺܕܰ̈ܥܝ, ܐܶܬܝܺܕܰ̈ܥܶܝܢ	ܝܰܕܰ̈ܥܝ, ܝܰܕܰ̈ܥܶܝܢ	ܐܶܬܝܰܕܰ̈ܥܝ, ܐܶܬܝܰܕܰ̈ܥܶܝܢ	ܐܰܘܕܰ̈ܥܝ, ܐܰܘܕܰ̈ܥܶܝܢ	ܐܶܬܬܰܘܕܰ̈ܥܝ, ܐܶܬܬܰܘܕܰ̈ܥܶܝܢ		
2 m.	ܝܺܕܰܥܬܽܘܢ	ܐܶܬܝܺܕܰܥܬܽܘܢ	ܝܰܕܰܥܬܽܘܢ	ܐܶܬܝܰܕܰܥܬܽܘܢ	ܐܰܘܕܰܥܬܽܘܢ	ܐܶܬܬܰܘܕܰܥܬܽܘܢ		
2 f.	ܝܺܕܰܥܬܶܝܢ	ܐܶܬܝܺܕܰܥܬܶܝܢ	ܝܰܕܰܥܬܶܝܢ	ܐܶܬܝܰܕܰܥܬܶܝܢ	ܐܰܘܕܰܥܬܶܝܢ	ܐܶܬܬܰܘܕܰܥܬܶܝܢ		
1 c.	ܝܺܕܰܥܢ, ܝܺܕܰܥܢܰܢ	ܐܶܬܝܺܕܰܥܢ, ܐܶܬܝܺܕܰܥܢܰܢ	ܝܰܕܰܥܢ, ܝܰܕܰܥܢܰܢ	ܐܶܬܝܰܕܰܥܢ, ܐܶܬܝܰܕܰܥܢܰܢ	ܐܰܘܕܰܥܢ, ܐܰܘܕܰܥܢܰܢ	ܐܶܬܬܰܘܕܰܥܢ, ܐܶܬܬܰܘܕܰܥܢܰܢ		
Infin.	ܡܶܕܰܥ	ܡܶܬܝܺܕܳܥܽܘ	ܡܝܰܕܳܥܽܘ	ܡܶܬܝܰܕܳܥܽܘ	ܡܰܘܕܳܥܽܘ	ܡܶܬܬܰܘܕܳܥܽܘ	ܡܫܰܘܕܳܥܽܘ	ܡܶܫܬܰܘܕܳܥܽܘ
Imp. 2 m.	ܝܺܕܰܥ	ܐܶܬܝܰܕܰܥ	ܝܰܕܰܥ	ܐܶܬܝܰܕܰܥ	ܐܰܘܕܰܥ	ܐܶܬܬܰܘܕܰܥ (ܘܕܰܥ)	ܫܰܘܕܰܥ	ܐܶܫܬܰܘܕܰܥ
2 f.	ܝܺܕܰܥܝ	ܐܶܬܝܰܕܰܥܝ	ܝܰܕܰܥܝ	ܐܶܬܝܰܕܰܥܝ	ܐܰܘܕܰܥܝ	ܐܶܬܬܰܘܕܰܥܝ		(ܐܶܫܬܰܘܕܰܥܝ)

Plur. 2 m.	ܝܠܕܘ	ܐܬܝܠܕܘ	ܝܠܕܘ	ܐܬܝܠܕܘ	ܐܘܠܕܘ	ܐܬܬܘܠܕܘ		
2 f.	ܝܠܕܝܢ	ܐܬܝܠܕܝܢ	ܝܠܕܝܢ	ܐܬܝܠܕܝܢ	ܐܘܠܕܝܢ	ܐܬܬܘܠܕܝܢ		
Fut. 3 m.	ܢܐܠܕ	ܢܬܝܠܕ	ܢܝܠܕ	ܢܬܝܠܕ	ܢܘܠܕ	ܢܬܬܘܠܕ	ܢܫܘܠܕ	ܢܫܬܘܠܕ
3 f.	ܬܐܠܕ	ܬܬܝܠܕ	ܬܝܠܕ	ܬܬܝܠܕ	ܬܘܠܕ	ܬܬܬܘܠܕ		
2 m.	ܬܐܠܕ	ܬܬܝܠܕ	ܬܝܠܕ	ܬܬܝܠܕ	ܬܘܠܕ	ܬܬܬܘܠܕ		
2 f.	ܬܐܠܕܝܢ	ܬܬܝܠܕܝܢ	ܬܝܠܕܝܢ	ܬܬܝܠܕܝܢ	ܬܘܠܕܝܢ	ܬܬܬܘܠܕܝܢ		
1 c.	ܐܐܠܕ	ܐܬܝܠܕ	ܐܝܠܕ	ܐܬܝܠܕ	ܐܘܠܕ	ܐܬܬܘܠܕ		
Plur. 3 m.	ܢܐܠܕܘܢ	ܢܬܝܠܕܘܢ	ܢܝܠܕܘܢ	ܢܬܝܠܕܘܢ	ܢܘܠܕܘܢ	ܢܬܬܘܠܕܘܢ		
3 f.	ܢܐܠܕܢ	ܢܬܝܠܕܢ	ܢܝܠܕܢ	ܢܬܝܠܕܢ	ܢܘܠܕܢ	ܢܬܬܘܠܕܢ		
2 m.	ܬܐܠܕܘܢ	ܬܬܝܠܕܘܢ	ܬܝܠܕܘܢ	ܬܬܝܠܕܘܢ	ܬܘܠܕܘܢ	ܬܬܬܘܠܕܘܢ		
2 f.	ܬܐܠܕܢ	ܬܬܝܠܕܢ	ܬܝܠܕܢ	ܬܬܝܠܕܢ	ܬܘܠܕܢ	ܬܬܬܘܠܕܢ		
1 c.	ܢܐܠܕ	ܢܬܝܠܕ	ܢܝܠܕ	ܢܬܝܠܕ	ܢܘܠܕ	ܢܬܬܘܠܕ		
Part. act. m.	ܝܠܕ		ܡܝܠܕ		ܡܘܠܕ		ܡܫܘܠܕ	
f.	ܝܠܕܐ		ܡܝܠܕܐ		ܡܘܠܕܐ		ܡܫܘܠܕܐ	
Part. P. m.	ܝܠܝܕ	ܡܬܝܠܕ	ܡܝܠܕ	ܡܬܝܠܕ	ܡܘܠܕ	ܡܬܬܘܠܕ	ܡܫܘܠܕ	ܡܫܬܘܠܕ
f.	ܝܠܝܕܐ	ܡܬܝܠܕܐ	ܡܝܠܕܐ	ܡܬܝܠܕܐ	ܡܘܠܕܐ	ܡܬܬܘܠܕܐ	ܡܫܘܠܕܐ	ܡܫܬܘܠܕܐ

Verbs Mid. Rad. Olaph Quiescent (ܫܐܠ § 30).

	Peal.	Ethpeel.	Pael.		Ethpaal.		Aphel.	Ethtaphal.
Pret. 3 m.	ܫܐܠ	ܐܬܫܐܠ	ܫܐܠ	ܫܝܠ	ܐܬܫܐܠ	ܐܬܫܝܠ	ܐܫܐܠ	ܐܬܬܫܐܠ
3 f.	ܫܐܠܬ	ܐܬܫܐܠܬ	ܫܐܠܬ	ܫܝܠܬ	ܐܬܫܐܠܬ	ܐܬܫܝܠܬ	ܐܫܐܠܬ	ܐܬܬܫܐܠܬ
2 m.	ܫܐܠܬ	ܐܬܫܐܠܬ	ܫܐܠܬ	ܫܝܠܬ	ܐܬܫܐܠܬ	ܐܬܫܝܠܬ	ܐܫܐܠܬ	ܐܬܬܫܐܠܬ
2 f.	ܫܐܠܬܝ	ܐܬܫܐܠܬܝ	ܫܐܠܬܝ	ܫܝܠܬܝ	ܐܬܫܐܠܬܝ	ܐܬܫܝܠܬܝ	ܐܫܐܠܬܝ	ܐܬܬܫܐܠܬܝ
1 c.	ܫܐܠܬ	ܐܬܫܐܠܬ	ܫܐܠܬ	ܫܝܠܬ	ܐܬܫܐܠܬ	ܐܬܫܝܠܬ	ܐܫܐܠܬ	ܐܬܬܫܐܠܬ
Plur. 3 m.	ܫܐܠܘ	ܐܬܫܐܠܘ	ܫܐܠܘ	ܫܝܠܘ	ܐܬܫܐܠܘ	ܐܬܫܝܠܘ	ܐܫܐܠܘ	ܐܬܬܫܐܠܘ
3 f.	ܫܐܠܝ̈,ܢ	ܐܬܫܐܠܝ̈,ܢ	ܫܐܠܝ̈,ܢ	ܫܝܠܝ̈,ܢ	ܐܬܫܐܠܝ̈,ܢ	ܐܬܫܝܠܝ̈,ܢ	ܐܫܐܠܝ̈,ܢ	ܐܬܬܫܐܠܝ̈,ܢ
2 m.	ܫܐܠܬܘܢ	ܐܬܫܐܠܬܘܢ	ܫܐܠܬܘܢ	ܫܝܠܬܘܢ	ܐܬܫܐܠܬܘܢ	ܐܬܫܝܠܬܘܢ	ܐܫܐܠܬܘܢ	ܐܬܬܫܐܠܬܘܢ
2 f.	ܫܐܠܬܝܢ	ܐܬܫܐܠܬܝܢ	ܫܐܠܬܝܢ	ܫܝܠܬܝܢ	ܐܬܫܐܠܬܝܢ	ܐܬܫܝܠܬܝܢ	ܐܫܐܠܬܝܢ	ܐܬܬܫܐܠܬܝܢ
1 c.	ܫܐܠܢ,ܢ	ܐܬܫܐܠܢ,ܢ	ܫܐܠܢ,ܢ	ܫܝܠܢ,ܢ	ܐܬܫܐܠܢ,ܢ	ܐܬܫܝܠܢ,ܢ	ܐܫܐܠܢ,ܢ	ܐܬܬܫܐܠܢ,ܢ
Infin.	ܡܫܐܠ	ܡܬܫܐܠܘ	ܡܫܐܠܘ	ܡܫܝܠܘ	ܡܬܫܐܠܘ	ܡܬܫܝܠܘ	ܡܫܐܠܘ	ܡܬܬܫܐܠܘ
Imp. 2 m.	ܫܐܠ	ܐܬܫܐܠ	ܫܐܠ	ܫܝܠ	ܐܬܫܐܠ	ܐܬܫܝܠ	ܐܫܐܠ	ܐܬܬܫܐܠ
2 f.	ܫܐܠܝ	ܐܬܫܐܠܝ	ܫܐܠܝ	ܫܝܠܝ	ܐܬܫܐܠܝ	ܐܬܫܝܠܝ	ܐܫܐܠܝ	ܐܬܬܫܐܠܝ

Plur. 2 m.	ܒܐܫܘ	ܐܬܒܐܫܘ	ܒܐܫܘ	ܛܝܒܘ	ܐܬܒܐܫܘ	ܐܬܛܝܒܘ	ܐܒܐܫܘ	ܐܬܬܒܐܫܘ
2 f.	ܒܐܫܝܢ	ܐܬܒܐܫܝܢ	ܒܐܫܝܢ	ܛܝܒܝܢ	ܐܬܒܐܫܝܢ	ܐܬܛܝܒܝܢ	ܐܒܐܫܝܢ	ܐܬܬܒܐܫܝܢ
Fut. 3 m.	ܢܒܐܫ	ܢܬܒܐܫ	ܢܒܐܫ	ܢܛܝܒ	ܢܬܒܐܫ	ܢܬܛܝܒ	ܢܒܐܫ	ܢܬܬܒܐܫ
3 f.	ܬܒܐܫ, ܗܝ	ܬܬܒܐܫ, ܗܝ	ܬܒܐܫ, ܗܝ	ܬܛܝܒ, ܗܝ	ܬܬܒܐܫ, ܗܝ	ܬܬܛܝܒ, ܗܝ	ܬܒܐܫ, ܗܝ	ܬܬܬܒܐܫ, ܗܝ
2 m.	ܬܒܐܫ	ܬܬܒܐܫ	ܬܒܐܫ	ܬܛܝܒ	ܬܬܒܐܫ	ܬܬܛܝܒ	ܬܒܐܫ	ܬܬܬܒܐܫ
2 f.	ܬܒܐܫܝܢ	ܬܬܒܐܫܝܢ	ܬܒܐܫܝܢ	ܬܛܝܒܝܢ	ܬܬܒܐܫܝܢ	ܬܬܛܝܒܝܢ	ܬܒܐܫܝܢ	ܬܬܬܒܐܫܝܢ
1 c.	ܐܒܐܫ	ܐܬܒܐܫ	ܐܒܐܫ	ܐܛܝܒ	ܐܬܒܐܫ	ܐܬܛܝܒ	ܐܒܐܫ	ܐܬܬܒܐܫ
Plur. 3 m.	ܢܒܐܫܘܢ	ܢܬܒܐܫܘܢ	ܢܒܐܫܘܢ	ܢܛܝܒܘܢ	ܢܬܒܐܫܘܢ	ܢܬܛܝܒܘܢ	ܢܒܐܫܘܢ	ܢܬܬܒܐܫܘܢ
3 f.	ܢܒܐܫܢ	ܢܬܒܐܫܢ	ܢܒܐܫܢ	ܢܛܝܒܢ	ܢܬܒܐܫܢ	ܢܬܛܝܒܢ	ܢܒܐܫܢ	ܢܬܬܒܐܫܢ
2 m.	ܬܒܐܫܘܢ	ܬܬܒܐܫܘܢ	ܬܒܐܫܘܢ	ܬܛܝܒܘܢ	ܬܬܒܐܫܘܢ	ܬܬܛܝܒܘܢ	ܬܒܐܫܘܢ	ܬܬܬܒܐܫܘܢ
2 f.	ܬܒܐܫܢ	ܬܬܒܐܫܢ	ܬܒܐܫܢ	ܬܛܝܒܢ	ܬܬܒܐܫܢ	ܬܬܛܝܒܢ	ܬܒܐܫܢ	ܬܬܬܒܐܫܢ
1 c.	ܢܒܐܫ	ܢܬܒܐܫ	ܢܒܐܫ	ܢܛܝܒ	ܢܬܒܐܫ	ܢܬܛܝܒ	ܢܒܐܫ	ܢܬܬܒܐܫ
Part. act. m.	ܒܐܫ		ܡܒܐܫ	ܡܛܝܒ			ܡܒܐܫ	
f.	ܒܐܫܐ		ܡܒܐܫܐ	ܡܛܝܒܐ			ܡܒܐܫܐ	
Part. P. m.	ܒܝܫ	ܡܬܒܐܫ	ܡܒܐܫ	ܡܛܝܒ	ܡܬܒܐܫ	ܡܬܛܝܒ	ܡܒܐܫ	ܡܬܬܒܐܫ
f.	ܒܝܫܐ	ܡܬܒܐܫܐ	ܡܒܐܫܐ	ܡܛܝܒܐ	ܡܬܒܐܫܐ	ܡܬܛܝܒܐ	ܡܒܐܫܐ	ܡܬܬܒܐܫܐ

Verbs Mid. Rad. Vau and Jud (ܥ̈ܘ, ܥ̈ܝ § 31).

	Peal.		Ethpeel.	Pael.	Ethpaal.	Aphel.	Ethtaphal.
Pret. 3 m.	ܩܳܡ	ܣܺܝܡ	ܐܶܬܬܩܺܝܡ	ܩܰܝܶܡ	ܐܶܬܩܰܝܰܡ	ܐܰܩܺܝܡ	ܐܶܬܬܩܺܝܡ
3 f.	ܩܳܡܰܬ	ܣܺܝܡܰܬ	ܐܶܬܬܩܺܝܡܰܬ	ܩܰܝܡܰܬ	ܐܶܬܩܰܝܡܰܬ	ܐܰܩܺܝܡܰܬ	ܐܶܬܬܩܺܝܡܰܬ
2 m.	ܩܳܡܬ	ܣܺܝܡܬ	ܐܶܬܬܩܺܝܡܬ	ܩܰܝܶܡܬ	ܐܶܬܩܰܝܰܡܬ	ܐܰܩܺܝܡܬ	ܐܶܬܬܩܺܝܡܬ
2 f.	ܩܳܡܬܝ	ܣܺܝܡܬܝ	ܐܶܬܬܩܺܝܡܬܝ	ܩܰܝܶܡܬܝ	ܐܶܬܩܰܝܰܡܬܝ	ܐܰܩܺܝܡܬܝ	ܐܶܬܬܩܺܝܡܬܝ
1 c.	ܩܳܡܶܬ	ܣܺܝܡܶܬ	ܐܶܬܬܩܺܝܡܶܬ	ܩܰܝܡܶܬ	ܐܶܬܩܰܝܡܶܬ	ܐܰܩܺܝܡܶܬ	ܐܶܬܬܩܺܝܡܶܬ
Plur. 3 m.	ܩܳܡܘ	ܣܺܝܡܘ	ܐܶܬܬܩܺܝܡܘ	ܩܰܝܶܡܘ	ܐܶܬܩܰܝܰܡܘ	ܐܰܩܺܝܡܘ	ܐܶܬܬܩܺܝܡܘ
3 f.	ܩܳܡ̈ܝ, ̈ܝܢ	ܣܺܝܡ̈ܝ	ܐܶܬܬܩܺܝܡ̈ܝ, ̈ܝܢ	ܩܰܝܶܡ̈ܝ, ̈ܝܢ	ܐܶܬܩܰܝܰܡ̈ܝ, ̈ܝܢ	ܐܰܩܺܝܡ̈ܝ, ̈ܝܢ	ܐܶܬܬܩܺܝܡ̈ܝ, ̈ܝܢ
2 m.	ܩܳܡܬܘܢ	ܣܺܝܡܬܘܢ	ܐܶܬܬܩܺܝܡܬܘܢ	ܩܰܝܶܡܬܘܢ	ܐܶܬܩܰܝܰܡܬܘܢ	ܐܰܩܺܝܡܬܘܢ	ܐܶܬܬܩܺܝܡܬܘܢ
2 f.	ܩܳܡܬܶܝܢ	ܣܺܝܡܬܶܝܢ	ܐܶܬܬܩܺܝܡܬܶܝܢ	ܩܰܝܶܡܬܶܝܢ	ܐܶܬܩܰܝܰܡܬܶܝܢ	ܐܰܩܺܝܡܬܶܝܢ	ܐܶܬܬܩܺܝܡܬܶܝܢ
1 c.	ܩܳܡܢ, ܢܰܢ	ܣܺܝܡܢ	ܐܶܬܬܩܺܝܡܢ, ܢܰܢ	ܩܰܝܶܡܢ, ܢܰܢ	ܐܶܬܩܰܝܰܡܢ, ܢܰܢ	ܐܰܩܺܝܡܢ, ܢܰܢ	ܐܶܬܬܩܺܝܡܢ, ܢܰܢ
Infin.	ܡܩܳܡ	ܡܣܺܝܡ	ܡܶܬܬܩܳܡܘ	ܡܩܰܝܳܡܘ	ܡܶܬܩܰܝܳܡܘ	ܡܩܳܡܘ	ܡܶܬܬܩܳܡܘ
Imp. 2 m.	ܩܘܡ	ܣܺܝܡ	ܐܶܬܬܩܺܝܡ	ܩܰܝܶܡ	ܐܶܬܩܰܝܰܡ	ܐܰܩܺܝܡ	ܐܶܬܬܩܺܝܡ
2 f.	ܩܘܡܝ	ܣܺܝܡܝ	ܐܶܬܬܩܺܝܡܝ	ܩܰܝܶܡܝ	ܐܶܬܩܰܝܰܡܝ	ܐܰܩܺܝܡܝ	ܐܶܬܬܩܺܝܡܝ

Plur. 2 m.	ܩܡܬܘܢ	ܣܡܬܘܢ	ܐܬܬܩܝܡܬܘܢ	ܩܝܡܬܘܢ	ܐܬܩܝܡܬܘܢ	ܐܩܝܡܬܘܢ	ܐܬܬܩܝܡܬܘܢ
2 f.	ܩܡܬܝܢ	ܣܡܬܝܢ	ܐܬܬܩܝܡܬܝܢ	ܩܝܡܬܝܢ	ܐܬܩܝܡܬܝܢ	ܐܩܝܡܬܝܢ	ܐܬܬܩܝܡܬܝܢ
Fut. 3 m.	ܢܩܘܡ	ܢܣܝܡ	ܢܬܬܩܝܡ	ܢܩܝܡ	ܢܬܩܝܡ	ܢܩܝܡ	ܢܬܬܩܝܡ
3 f.	ܬܩܘܡ, ܘܟܒ	ܬܣܝܡ	ܬܬܬܩܝܡ, ܘܟܒ	ܬܩܝܡ, ܘܟܒ	ܬܬܩܝܡ, ܘܟܒ	ܬܩܝܡ, ܘܟܒ	ܬܬܬܩܝܡ, ܘܟܒ
2 m.	ܬܩܘܡ	ܬܣܝܡ	ܬܬܬܩܝܡ	ܬܩܝܡ	ܬܬܩܝܡ	ܬܩܝܡ	ܬܬܬܩܝܡ
2 f.	ܬܩܘܡܝܢ	ܬܣܝܡܝܢ	ܬܬܬܩܝܡܝܢ	ܬܩܝܡܝܢ	ܬܬܩܝܡܝܢ	ܬܩܝܡܝܢ	ܬܬܬܩܝܡܝܢ
1 c.	ܐܩܘܡ	ܐܣܝܡ	ܐܬܬܩܝܡ	ܐܩܝܡ	ܐܬܩܝܡ	ܐܩܝܡ	ܐܬܬܩܝܡ
Plur. 3 m.	ܢܩܘܡܘܢ	ܢܣܝܡܘܢ	ܢܬܬܩܝܡܘܢ	ܢܩܝܡܘܢ	ܢܬܩܝܡܘܢ	ܢܩܝܡܘܢ	ܢܬܬܩܝܡܘܢ
3 f.	ܢܩܘܡܢ	ܢܣܝܡܢ	ܢܬܬܩܝܡܢ	ܢܩܝܡܢ	ܢܬܩܝܡܢ	ܢܩܝܡܢ	ܢܬܬܩܝܡܢ
2 m.	ܬܩܘܡܘܢ	ܬܣܝܡܘܢ	ܬܬܬܩܝܡܘܢ	ܬܩܝܡܘܢ	ܬܬܩܝܡܘܢ	ܬܩܝܡܘܢ	ܬܬܬܩܝܡܘܢ
2 f.	ܬܩܘܡܢ	ܬܣܝܡܢ	ܬܬܬܩܝܡܢ	ܬܩܝܡܢ	ܬܬܩܝܡܢ	ܬܩܝܡܢ	ܬܬܬܩܝܡܢ
1 c.	ܢܩܘܡ	ܢܣܝܡ	ܢܬܬܩܝܡ	ܢܩܝܡ	ܢܬܩܝܡ	ܢܩܝܡ	ܢܬܬܩܝܡ
Part. act. m.	ܩܐܡ			ܡܩܝܡ		ܡܩܝܡ	
f.	ܩܝܡܐ			ܡܩܝܡܐ		ܡܩܝܡܐ	
Part. P. m.	ܣܝܡ		ܡܬܬܩܝܡ	ܡܩܝܡ	ܡܬܩܝܡ	ܡܩܝܡ	ܡܬܬܩܝܡ
f.	ܣܝܡܐ		ܡܬܬܩܝܡܐ	ܡܩܝܡܐ	ܡܬܩܝܡܐ	ܡܩܝܡܐ	ܡܬܬܩܝܡܐ

Verbs Third Rad. Olaph (ܠܐ § 32).

	Peal.		Ethpeel.	Pael.	Ethpaal.	Aphel.	Ethtaphal.	Shaphel.	Eshtaph.
Pret. 3 m.	ܓܠܐ	ܚܕܝ	ܐܬܓܠܝ	ܓܠܝ	ܐܬܓܠܝ	ܐܓܠܝ	ܐܬܬܓܠܝ	ܫܓܠܝ	ܐܫܬܓܠܝ
3 f.	ܓܠܬ	ܚܕܝܬ	ܐܬܓܠܝܬ	ܓܠܝܬ	ܐܬܓܠܝܬ	ܐܓܠܝܬ	ܐܬܬܓܠܝܬ		
2 m.	ܓܠܝܬ	ܚܕܝܬ	ܐܬܓܠܝܬ	ܓܠܝܬ	ܐܬܓܠܝܬ	ܐܓܠܝܬ	ܐܬܬܓܠܝܬ		
2 f.	ܓܠܝܬܝ	ܚܕܝܬܝ	ܐܬܓܠܝܬܝ	ܓܠܝܬܝ	ܐܬܓܠܝܬܝ	ܐܓܠܝܬܝ	ܐܬܬܓܠܝܬܝ		
1 c.	ܓܠܝܬ	ܚܕܝܬ	ܐܬܓܠܝܬ	ܓܠܝܬ	ܐܬܓܠܝܬ	ܐܓܠܝܬ	ܐܬܬܓܠܝܬ		
Plur. 3 m.	ܓܠܘ	ܚܕܝܘ	ܐܬܓܠܝܘ	ܓܠܝܘ	ܐܬܓܠܝܘ	ܐܓܠܝܘ	ܐܬܬܓܠܝܘ		
3 f.	ܓܠܝ̈, ܢܝ	ܚܕܝ̈	ܐܬܓܠܝ̈, ܢܝ	ܓܠܝ̈, ܢܝ	ܐܬܓܠܝ̈, ܢܝ	ܐܓܠܝ̈, ܢܝ	ܐܬܬܓܠܝ̈, ܢܝ		
2 m.	ܓܠܝܬܘܢ	ܚܕܝܬܘܢ	ܐܬܓܠܝܬܘܢ	ܓܠܝܬܘܢ	ܐܬܓܠܝܬܘܢ	ܐܓܠܝܬܘܢ	ܐܬܬܓܠܝܬܘܢ		
2 f.	ܓܠܝܬܝܢ	ܚܕܝܬܝܢ	ܐܬܓܠܝܬܝܢ	ܓܠܝܬܝܢ	ܐܬܓܠܝܬܝܢ	ܐܓܠܝܬܝܢ	ܐܬܬܓܠܝܬܝܢ		
1 c.	ܓܠܝܢ, ܢ	ܚܕܝܢ	ܐܬܓܠܝܢ, ܢ	ܓܠܝܢ, ܢ	ܐܬܓܠܝܢ, ܢ	ܐܓܠܝܢ, ܢ	ܐܬܬܓܠܝܢ, ܢ		
Infin.	ܡܓܠܐ		ܡܬܓܠܝܘ	ܡܓܠܝܘ	ܡܬܓܠܝܘ	ܡܓܠܝܘ	ܡܬܬܓܠܝܘ	ܡܫܓܠܝܘ	ܡܫܬܓܠܝܘ
Imp. 2 m.	ܓܠܝ		ܐܬܓܠܝ	ܓܠܐ	ܐܬܓܠܐ	ܐܓܠܐ	ܐܬܬܓܠܐ	ܫܓܠܐ	ܐܫܬܓܠܐ
2 f.	ܓܠܝ		ܐܬܓܠܝ	ܓܠܝ	ܐܬܓܠܝ	ܐܓܠܝ	ܐܬܬܓܠܝ		

	Peal	Ethpeel	Pael	Ethpaal	Aphel	Ettaphal	Shaphel	Eshtaphal
Plur. 2 m.	ܓܠܘ	ܐܬܓܠܘ	ܓܠܘ	ܐܬܓܠܘ	ܐܓܠܘ	ܐܬܬܓܠܘ		
2 f.	ܓܠܝܝܢ	ܐܬܓܠܝܝܢ	ܓܠܝܝܢ	ܐܬܓܠܝܝܢ	ܐܓܠܝܝܢ	ܐܬܬܓܠܝܝܢ		
Futr. 3 m.	ܢܓܠܐ	ܢܬܓܠܐ	ܢܓܠܐ	ܢܬܓܠܐ	ܢܓܠܐ	ܢܬܬܓܠܐ	ܢܫܓܠܐ	ܢܫܬܓܠܐ
3 f.	ܬܓܠܐ	ܬܬܓܠܐ	ܬܓܠܐ	ܬܬܓܠܐ	ܬܓܠܐ	ܬܬܬܓܠܐ		
2 m.	ܬܓܠܐ	ܬܬܓܠܐ	ܬܓܠܐ	ܬܬܓܠܐ	ܬܓܠܐ	ܬܬܬܓܠܐ		
2 f.	ܬܓܠܝܢ	ܬܬܓܠܝܢ	ܬܓܠܝܢ	ܬܬܓܠܝܢ	ܬܓܠܝܢ	ܬܬܬܓܠܝܢ		
1 c.	ܐܓܠܐ	ܐܬܓܠܐ	ܐܓܠܐ	ܐܬܓܠܐ	ܐܓܠܐ	ܐܬܬܓܠܐ		
Plur. 3 m.	ܢܓܠܘܢ	ܢܬܓܠܘܢ	ܢܓܠܘܢ	ܢܬܓܠܘܢ	ܢܓܠܘܢ	ܢܬܬܓܠܘܢ		
3 f.	ܢܓܠܝܢ	ܢܬܓܠܝܢ	ܢܓܠܝܢ	ܢܬܓܠܝܢ	ܢܓܠܝܢ	ܢܬܬܓܠܝܢ		
2 m.	ܬܓܠܘܢ	ܬܬܓܠܘܢ	ܬܓܠܘܢ	ܬܬܓܠܘܢ	ܬܓܠܘܢ	ܬܬܬܓܠܘܢ		
2 f.	ܬܓܠܝܢ	ܬܬܓܠܝܢ	ܬܓܠܝܢ	ܬܬܓܠܝܢ	ܬܓܠܝܢ	ܬܬܬܓܠܝܢ		
1 c.	ܢܓܠܐ	ܢܬܓܠܐ	ܢܓܠܐ	ܢܬܓܠܐ	ܢܓܠܐ	ܢܬܬܓܠܐ		
Part. act. m.	ܓܠܐ		ܡܓܠܐ		ܡܓܠܐ		ܡܫܓܠܐ	
f.	ܓܠܝܐ		ܡܓܠܝܐ		ܡܓܠܝܐ		ܡܫܓܠܝܐ	
Part. P. m.	ܓܠܐ	ܡܬܓܠܐ	ܡܓܠܝ	ܡܬܓܠܐ	ܡܓܠܝ	ܡܬܬܓܠܐ	ܡܫܓܠܝ	ܡܫܬܓܠܐ
f.	ܓܠܝܐ	ܡܬܓܠܝܐ	ܡܓܠܝܐ	ܡܬܓܠܝܐ	ܡܓܠܝܐ	ܡܬܬܓܠܝܐ	ܡܫܓܠܝܐ	ܡܫܬܓܠܝܐ

Verbs First Rad. Nun (ܢܦܰܩ § 33).

	Peal.	Ethpeel.	Pael.	Ethpaal.	Aphel.	Ethtaphal.	Shaphel.	Eshtaph.
Pret. 3 m.	ܢܦܰܩ	ܐܶܬܢܦܶܩ	ܢܰܦܶܩ	ܐܶܬܢܰܦܰܩ	ܐܰܦܶܩ	ܐܶܬܬܰܦܰܩ	(ܫܰܦܶܩ)	(ܐܶܫܬܰܦܰܩ)
3 f.	ܢܶܦܩܰܬ	ܐܶܬܢܰܦܩܰܬ	ܢܰܦܩܰܬ	ܐܶܬܢܰܦܩܰܬ	ܐܰܦܩܰܬ	ܐܶܬܬܰܦܩܰܬ		
2 m.	ܢܦܰܩܬ	ܐܶܬܢܦܶܩܬ	ܢܰܦܶܩܬ	ܐܶܬܢܰܦܰܩܬ	ܐܰܦܶܩܬ	ܐܶܬܬܰܦܰܩܬ		
2 f.	ܢܦܰܩܬܝ	ܐܶܬܢܦܶܩܬܝ	ܢܰܦܶܩܬܝ	ܐܶܬܢܰܦܰܩܬܝ	ܐܰܦܶܩܬܝ	ܐܶܬܬܰܦܰܩܬܝ		
1 c.	ܢܶܦܩܶܬ	ܐܶܬܢܰܦܩܶܬ	ܢܰܦܩܶܬ	ܐܶܬܢܰܦܩܶܬ	ܐܰܦܩܶܬ	ܐܶܬܬܰܦܩܶܬ		
Plur. 3 m.	ܢܦܰܩܘ	ܐܶܬܢܦܶܩܘ	ܢܰܦܶܩܘ	ܐܶܬܢܰܦܰܩܘ	ܐܰܦܶܩܘ	ܐܶܬܬܰܦܰܩܘ		
3 f.	ܢܦܰܩ̈ܝܢ	ܐܶܬܢܦܶܩ̈ܝܢ	ܢܰܦܶܩ̈ܝܢ	ܐܶܬܢܰܦܰܩ̈ܝܢ	ܐܰܦܶܩ̈ܝܢ	ܐܶܬܬܰܦܰܩ̈ܝܢ		
2 m.	ܢܦܰܩܬܘܢ	ܐܶܬܢܦܶܩܬܘܢ	ܢܰܦܶܩܬܘܢ	ܐܶܬܢܰܦܰܩܬܘܢ	ܐܰܦܶܩܬܘܢ	ܐܶܬܬܰܦܰܩܬܘܢ		
2 f.	ܢܦܰܩܬܝܢ	ܐܶܬܢܦܶܩܬܝܢ	ܢܰܦܶܩܬܝܢ	ܐܶܬܢܰܦܰܩܬܝܢ	ܐܰܦܶܩܬܝܢ	ܐܶܬܬܰܦܰܩܬܝܢ		
1 c.	ܢܦܰܩܢܢ	ܐܶܬܢܦܶܩܢܢ	ܢܰܦܶܩܢܢ	ܐܶܬܢܰܦܰܩܢܢ	ܐܰܦܶܩܢܢ	ܐܶܬܬܰܦܰܩܢܢ		
Infin.	ܡܶܦܰܩ	ܡܶܬܢܦܳܩܘ	ܡܢܰܦܳܩܘ	ܡܶܬܢܰܦܳܩܘ	ܡܰܦܳܩܘ	ܡܶܬܬܰܦܳܩܘ	(ܡܫܰܦܳܩܘ)	(ܡܶܫܬܰܦܳܩܘ)
Imp. 2 m.	ܦܘܩ	ܐܶܬܢܦܶܩ	ܢܰܦܶܩ	ܐܶܬܢܰܦܰܩ	ܐܰܦܶܩ	ܐܶܬܬܰܦܰܩ (ܦܶܩ)	(ܫܰܦܶܩ)	(ܐܶܫܬܰܦܰܩ)
2 f.	ܦܘܩܝ	ܐܶܬܢܦܶܩܝ	ܢܰܦܶܩܝ	ܐܶܬܢܰܦܰܩܝ	ܐܰܦܶܩܝ	ܐܶܬܬܰܦܰܩܝ		(ܐܶܫܬܰܦܰܩܝ)

Plur. 2 m.	ܦܩܘ	ܐܬܢܦܩܘ	ܢܦܩܘ	ܐܬܢܦܩܘ	ܐܦܩܘ	ܐܬܬܦܩܘ		
2 f.	ܦܩܝܢ	ܐܬܢܦܩܝܢ	ܢܦܩܝܢ	ܐܬܢܦܩܝܢ	ܐܦܩܝܢ	ܐܬܬܦܩܝܢ		
Fut. 3 m.	ܢܦܘܩ	ܢܬܢܦܩ	ܢܢܦܩ	ܢܬܢܦܩ	ܢܦܩ	ܢܬܬܦܩ	(ܢܫܦܩ)	(ܢܫܬܦܩ)
3 f.	ܬܦܘܩ, ܡܢ	ܬܬܢܦܩ, ܡܢ	ܬܢܦܩ, ܡܢ	ܬܬܢܦܩ, ܡܢ	ܬܦܩ, ܡܢ	ܬܬܬܦܩ, ܡܢ		
2 m.	ܬܦܘܩ	ܬܬܢܦܩ	ܬܢܦܩ	ܬܬܢܦܩ	ܬܦܩ	ܬܬܬܦܩ		
2 f.	ܬܦܩܝܢ	ܬܬܢܦܩܝܢ	ܬܢܦܩܝܢ	ܬܬܢܦܩܝܢ	ܬܦܩܝܢ	ܬܬܬܦܩܝܢ		
1 c.	ܐܦܘܩ	ܐܬܢܦܩ	ܐܢܦܩ	ܐܬܢܦܩ	ܐܦܩ	ܐܬܬܦܩ		
Plur. 3 m.	ܢܦܩܘܢ	ܢܬܢܦܩܘܢ	ܢܢܦܩܘܢ	ܢܬܢܦܩܘܢ	ܢܦܩܘܢ	ܢܬܬܦܩܘܢ		
3 f.	ܢܦܩܢ	ܢܬܢܦܩܢ	ܢܢܦܩܢ	ܢܬܢܦܩܢ	ܢܦܩܢ	ܢܬܬܦܩܢ		
2 m.	ܬܦܩܘܢ	ܬܬܢܦܩܘܢ	ܬܢܦܩܘܢ	ܬܬܢܦܩܘܢ	ܬܦܩܘܢ	ܬܬܬܦܩܘܢ		
2 f.	ܬܦܩܢ	ܬܬܢܦܩܢ	ܬܢܦܩܢ	ܬܬܢܦܩܢ	ܬܦܩܢ	ܬܬܬܦܩܢ		
1 c.	ܢܦܘܩ	ܢܬܢܦܩ	ܢܢܦܩ	ܢܬܢܦܩ	ܢܦܩ	ܢܬܬܦܩ		
Part. act. m.	ܢܦܩ		ܡܢܦܩ		ܡܦܩ		(ܡܫܦܩ)	
f.	ܢܦܩܐ		ܡܢܦܩܐ		ܡܦܩܐ			
Part. P. m.	ܢܦܝܩ	ܡܬܢܦܩ	ܡܢܦܩ	ܡܬܢܦܩ	ܡܦܩ	ܡܬܬܦܩ	(ܡܫܦܩ)	(ܡܫܬܦܩ)
f.	ܢܦܝܩܐ	ܡܬܢܦܩܐ	ܡܢܦܩܐ	ܡܬܢܦܩܐ	ܡܦܩܐ	ܡܬܬܦܩܐ		

Verbs Middle Rad. Doubled (ܥܥ § 34).

	Peal.	Ethpeel.	Pael.	Ethpaal.	Aphel.	Ethtaphal.	Shaphel.	Eshtaph.
Pret. 3 m.	ܪܣ	ܐܬܪܣܣ	ܪܣܣ	ܐܬܪܣܣ	ܐܪܣ	ܐܬܬܪܣ	ܫܪܣ	ܐܫܬܪܣ
3 f.	ܪܣܬ	ܐܬܪܣܣܬ	ܪܣܣܬ	ܐܬܪܣܣܬ	ܐܪܣܬ	ܐܬܬܪܣܬ		
2 m.	ܪܣܬ	ܐܬܪܣܣܬ	ܪܣܣܬ	ܐܬܪܣܣܬ	ܐܪܣܬ	ܐܬܬܪܣܬ		
2 f.	ܪܣܬܝ	ܐܬܪܣܣܬܝ	ܪܣܣܬܝ	ܐܬܪܣܣܬܝ	ܐܪܣܬܝ	ܐܬܬܪܣܬܝ		
1 c.	ܪܣܬ	ܐܬܪܣܣܬ	ܪܣܣܬ	ܐܬܪܣܣܬ	ܐܪܣܬ	ܐܬܬܪܣܬ		
Plur. 3 m.	ܪܣܘ	ܐܬܪܣܣܘ	ܪܣܣܘ	ܐܬܪܣܣܘ	ܐܪܣܘ	ܐܬܬܪܣܘ		
3 f.	ܪܣܝ̈, ܝ̈ܢ	ܐܬܪܣܣܝ̈, ܝ̈ܢ	ܪܣܣܝ̈, ܝ̈ܢ	ܐܬܪܣܣܝ̈, ܝ̈ܢ	ܐܪܣܝ̈, ܝ̈ܢ	ܐܬܬܪܣܝ̈, ܝ̈ܢ		
2 m.	ܪܣܬܘܢ	ܐܬܪܣܣܬܘܢ	ܪܣܣܬܘܢ	ܐܬܪܣܣܬܘܢ	ܐܪܣܬܘܢ	ܐܬܬܪܣܬܘܢ		
2 f.	ܪܣܬܝܢ	ܐܬܪܣܣܬܝܢ	ܪܣܣܬܝܢ	ܐܬܪܣܣܬܝܢ	ܐܪܣܬܝܢ	ܐܬܬܪܣܬܝܢ		
1 c.	ܪܣܢ, ܢ	ܐܬܪܣܣܢ, ܢ	ܪܣܣܢ, ܢ	ܐܬܪܣܣܢ, ܢ	ܐܪܣܢ, ܢ	ܐܬܬܪܣܢ, ܢ		
Infin.	ܡܪܣ	ܡܬܪܣܣܘ	ܡܪܣܣܘ	ܡܬܪܣܣܘ	ܡܪܣܘ	ܡܬܬܪܣܘ	ܡܫܪܣܘ	ܡܫܬܪܣܘ
Imp. 2 m.	ܪܘܣ	ܐܬܪܣܣ	ܪܣܣ	ܐܬܪܣܣ	ܐܪܣ	ܐܬܬܪܣ (ܪܣ)	ܫܪܣ	ܐܫܬܪܣ
2 f.	ܪܘܣܝ	ܐܬܪܣܣܝ	ܪܣܣܝ	ܐܬܪܣܣܝ	ܐܪܣܝ	ܐܬܬܪܣܝ		(ܐܫܬܪܣܝ)

Plur. 2 m.	ܕܘܫܬܘܢ	ܐܬܕܫܬܘܢ	ܕܫܫܬܘܢ	ܐܬܕܫܫܬܘܢ	ܐܕܫܬܘܢ	ܐܬܬܕܫܬܘܢ		
2 f.	ܕܘܫܬܝܢ	ܐܬܕܫܬܝܢ	ܕܫܫܬܝܢ	ܐܬܕܫܫܬܝܢ	ܐܕܫܬܝܢ	ܐܬܬܕܫܬܝܢ		
Fut. 3 m.	ܢܕܘܫ	ܢܬܕܫ	ܢܕܫܫ	ܢܬܕܫܫ	ܢܕܫ	ܢܬܬܕܫ	ܢܫܕܫ	ܢܫܬܕܫ
3 f.	ܬܕܘܫ, ܗܝ	ܬܬܕܫ, ܗܝ	ܬܕܫܫ, ܗܝ	ܬܬܕܫܫ, ܗܝ	ܬܕܫ, ܗܝ	ܬܬܬܕܫ , ܗܝ		
2 m.	ܬܕܘܫ	ܬܬܕܫ	ܬܕܫܫ	ܬܬܕܫܫ	ܬܕܫ	ܬܬܬܕܫ		
2 f.	ܬܕܘܫܝܢ	ܬܬܕܫܝܢ	ܬܕܫܫܝܢ	ܬܬܕܫܫܝܢ	ܬܕܫܝܢ	ܬܬܬܕܫܝܢ		
1 c.	ܐܕܘܫ	ܐܬܕܫ	ܐܕܫܫ	ܐܬܕܫܫ	ܐܕܫ	ܐܬܬܕܫ		
Plur. 3 m.	ܢܕܘܫܘܢ	ܢܬܕܫܘܢ	ܢܕܫܫܘܢ	ܢܬܕܫܫܘܢ	ܢܕܫܘܢ	ܢܬܬܕܫܘܢ		
3 f.	ܢܕܘܫܢ	ܢܬܕܫܢ	ܢܕܫܫܢ	ܢܬܕܫܫܢ	ܢܕܫܢ	ܢܬܬܕܫܢ		
2 m.	ܬܕܘܫܘܢ	ܬܬܕܫܘܢ	ܬܕܫܫܘܢ	ܬܬܕܫܫܘܢ	ܬܕܫܘܢ	ܬܬܬܕܫܘܢ		
2 f.	ܬܕܘܫܢ	ܬܬܕܫܢ	ܬܕܫܫܢ	ܬܬܕܫܫܢ	ܬܕܫܢ	ܬܬܬܕܫܢ		
1 c.	ܢܕܘܫ	ܢܬܕܫ	ܢܕܫܫ	ܢܬܕܫܫ	ܢܕܫ	ܢܬܬܕܫ		
Part. act. m.	ܕܐܫ		ܡܕܫܫ		ܡܕܫ		ܡܫܕܫ	
f.	ܕܝܫܐ		ܡܕܫܫܐ		ܡܕܫܐ		ܡܫܕܫܐ	
Part. P. m.	ܕܝܫ	ܡܬܕܫ	ܡܕܫܫ	ܡܬܕܫܫ	ܡܕܫ	ܡܬܬܕܫ	ܡܫܕܫ	ܡܫܬܕܫ
f.	ܕܝܫܐ	ܡܬܕܫܐ	ܡܕܫܫܐ	ܡܬܕܫܫܐ	ܡܕܫܐ	ܡܬܬܕܫܐ	ܡܫܕܫܐ	ܡܫܬܕܫܐ

PARADIGM OF THE VERB WITH DIACRITICAL POINTS.

(*Compare* § 4. *Rem.*).

	3 *m.*	3 *f.*	2 *m.*	1 *c.*
Preter. Sing.	ܩܛܠ ܩ̇ܛܠ ܩܛܠ̣	ܩܛܠܬ ܩܛܠܬ̇ ܩܛܠܬ ܩܛܠ̇ܬ ܩ̇ܛܠܬ	ܩܛܠܬ ܩ̇ܛܠܬ ܩܛܠܬ̣	ܩ̇ܛܠܬ ܩ̇ܛܠܬ ܩܛܠܬ
Plur.	ܩܛܠܘ ܩܛܠܘ ܩ̇ܛܠܘ ܩ̇ܛܠܘ	*	*	ܩܛܠܢ ܩ̇ܛܠܢ
Fut. Sing.	ܢܩܛܘܠ ܢܩ̇ܛܘܠ ܢܩܛ̇ܘܠ	ܬܩܛܘܠ ܬܩ̇ܛܘܠ ܬܩܛ̇ܘܠ	ܬܩܛܘܠ ܬܩ̇ܛܘܠ ܬܩܛ̇ܘܠ	ܐܩ̇ܛܘܠ ܐܩ̇ܛܘܠ (ܐܬܩܛ̇ܠ)
Plur.	ܢܩܛܠܘܢ، ܢܩܛܠܘܢ ܢܩܛܠܘܢ، ܢܩ̇ܛܠܘܢ ܢܩܛܠ̇ܘܢ	*	ܬܩܛܠܘܢ ܬܩ̇ܛܠܘܢ ܬܩܛܠ̇ܘܢ	ܢܩܛܘܠ ܢܩ̇ܛܘܠ ܢܩܛ̇ܘܠ
Imper.Sing. m.	ܩܛܘܠ ܩܛܘܠ ܩܛܘܠ	Plur. m.	ܩܛܘܠܘ ܩܛܘܠܘ ܩ̇ܛܘܠܘ ܩܛܘܠܘ	
Infin.	ܡܩܛܠ ܡܩܛܠ ܡܩܛܠ ܡܩܛܠ ܡܩܛܠܘ etc.			
Part. Act.	ܩ̇ܛܠ m. ܩ̇ܛܠܐ f. ܡܩ̇ܛܠ	Passive	ܩܛܝܠ ܩܛܝܠ ܩܛܝܠ ܡܬܩ̇ܛܠ ܡܬܩܛܠ ܡܬܩ̇ܛܠ	

Rem.—The forms of the verb which are omitted in the foregoing Table, are not marked with diacritical points, since they may easily be recognized from their formation.

§ 36. *Verbs with Suffixes.*

The union of verbal forms with suffixes is much more simple in Syriac than in Hebrew. It should be remarked in general that the vowel of the first or second syllable either falls away; e. g. ◌ܲ in the 3 fem. and 1 sing. pret. and ܘܳ in the fut.; or the vowel of the second syllable falls back upon the preceding consonant; e. g. in the same persons of pret. Pe. in which ◌ܲ of the first syllable falls away. The verbal endings ܝ and ܘ quiesce in ◌ܺ and ◌ܽ. Verbal forms, unless they terminate with ܝܺ and ܘܽ, remain unchanged before the suffixes ܟ݁ܽܘܢ, ܟ݁ܶܝܢ. Also the characteristic vowel of the first syllable of Pa. and Aph. remains unchanged, and the suffixes of the 3 plur. are attached to verbs in the form of separate pronouns. In respect to the particular persons the following should be remarked (see Table of the pronouns, § 16. and table of the verbs, with suffixes, § 36).

A. Preterit with Suffixes.

3 sing. masc. ܩܛܰܠ before the suffixes ܟ݁ܽܘܢ, ܟ݁ܶܝܢ in the 2 plur. masc. and fem. The other persons ܩܰܛܠ with suff. a. 1.

3 sing. fem. ܩܶܛܠܰܬ݂ before ܟ݁ܽܘܢ, ܟ݁ܶܝܢ. The others ܩܛܰܠܬ݂ with suff. a. 1.

2 sing. masc. ܩܛܰܠܬ݁ unchanged, and by way of exception with suff. c.

2 sing. fem. ܩܛܰܠܬ݁ܝ is changed into ܩܛܰܠܬ݁ܺܝ with suff. b.

1 sing. com. ܩܶܛܠܶܬ݂ forms ܩܛܰܠܬ݂ with suff. a. 1.

3 plur. masc. ܩܛܰܠܘ becomes ܩܛܰܠܽܘܗ with suff. b. or with ܢ parag., excepting before ܟ݁ܽܘܢ, ܟ݁ܶܝܢ.

3 plur. fem. ܩܛܰܠ̈ܝ either ܩܛܰܠ̈ with suff. c. or with ܢ parag. ܩܛܰܠܶܝܢ.

2 plur. masc. and fem. and 1 com. retain the forms ܩܛܰܠܬܽܘܢ, ܩܛܰܠܬܶܝܢ, ܩܛܰܠܢ with suff. c.

Rem.—The 3 fem. 2 masc. and 1 com. sing. in some forms with suffixes are only distinguished from each other by the diacritical point, which, in the first person, stands over the consonant (vid. § 4). Verbs Med. E. with suff. follow the form of Verbs Med. A., and retain ܳ where the latter retain ܰ; e. g. 3 sing. fem. ܩܶܛܠܰܬ with suff. ܩܶܛܠܳܬܶܗ. Yet the form ܢܶܛܪܰܬܶܗ occurs in Ps. cxviii. 167, instead of which, since no similar example occurs, the punctuation should perhaps be ܳ. The same is the case even in Verbs Med. Olaph. Quies. So the vowel ܳ belonging to ܫܶܐܠܳܬ is changed into ܰ over ܫܶܐܠܰܬܶܗ; but in the 1 sing., ܳ remains; e. g. ܫܶܐܠܳܬܟ݂. In respect to verbs 1 rad. ܐ and ܝ quiescent, it should be remarked, that where, in the regular verb, the first radical is without a vowel, ܐ retains its ܳ and ܝ its ܶ; e. g. ܐܳܟ݂ܠܳܬܶܗ. But where, in the regular verb, ܰ stands over the first radical, this class of verbs retains it in the same manner; e. g. ܐܰܡܪܶܬ with suff. ܐܰܡܪܬܶܗ, ܝܶܠܕܶܬ with suff. ܝܰܠܕܬܳܢܝ. Defective verbs, or those with Med. Rad. doubled, retain ܰ in the pret. unchanged, like the form ܩܛܰܠ. The 3 fem. and 1 sing. change ܳ into ܰ; e. g. ܪܡܳܬ with suff. ܪܡܰܬܶܗ; but they remain unchanged before ܟ݂ܽܘܢ and ܟ݂ܶܝܢ; e. g. ܪܡܳܬܟ݂ܽܘܢ. Pa. and Aph. retain the vowel of the first syllable unchanged. In respect to ܳ of the second syllable, it should be observed that where Pe. retains ܰ, Pa. retains ܳ; but where ܰ falls away or falls back upon the first syllable, ܳ is lost. The 3 sing. masc. and 3 plur. masc. and fem. in Pe. and Pa. with suff., are hence all similar, and can only be distinguished from each other by their signification in the context; e. g. ܩܰܛܠܶܗ (from ܩܛܰܠ or ܩܰܛܶܠ). But these forms are exceptions to this rule when standing before ܟ݂ܽܘܢ and ܟ݂ܶܝܢ.

B. Future with Suffixes.

Throughout the sing. and in the 1 plur., ܽ, which has been inserted, remains unchanged before the suffixes ܟ݂ܽܘܢ and

ܩܛܠܝ. Before the other suffixes it falls away, and the form ܢܩܛܘܠ takes the suff. a. 1.; but if the suff. is in the 3 person, only the suffix. a. 2. is used. The other persons are treated according to the rule laid down. In the plur. the 2 and 3 masc. and fem. remain unchanged with suff. c.

Rem.—ܝ parag. of the 3 sing. fem. falls away, and is connected with the suff. after the form ܬܩܛܘܠ. What is true of ܘ in Pe. is also true in Pa. in respect to the falling away of the vowel of the last syllable, excepting before ܟܘܢ and ܟܝܢ. In the 3 sing. masc. with suff. of 3 person masc.; e. g. ܢܩܛܠܝܘܗܝ, ܳ appears sometimes over ܘ. But this form is neither mentioned by Amira nor by Sionita. The 2 sing. sometimes takes ܝ before the suff. of the 1 sing. and plur. The same is true in respect to the imperat.; e. g. ܠܐ ܬܒܗܬܢܝ *put me not to shame.* In Verbs Med. E. the middle radical retains ܶ, and in Verbs 3 Gutt., ܰ. This peculiarity, Amira, p. 389, refers exclusively to quadriliterals, i. e. to Aph.; but examples are also found in Pe.; e. g. Ps. lxxi. 9. ed. Erpen. ܠܐ ܬܫܒܘܩܝܢܝ, ed. Paris. ܬܫܒܘܩܢܝ, and in Pa. Ps. cxviii. 172, ܬܠܦܝܢܝ. Amira adds that this form is found particularly in prohibitory negations, which remark is likewise confirmed by the examples given. The persons of the fut. with ܢ remain unchanged. But it should be remarked that if the form ܢܩܛܠܘܢ takes the suff. of the 3 per. sing. masc.; e. g. ܢܩܛܠܘܢܝܗܝ, sometimes ܢ falls away; e. g. Matt. viii. 25, ܘܢܟܣܪܘܗܝ.

C. Imperative with Suffixes.

The 2 sing. masc. ܩܛܘܠ remains unchanged with suff. a. 2. of the 1 per. sing. and plur., and of the 3 sing. fem. When the suff. is in the 3 sing. masc. the form of suff. c. is used.

In the 2 sing. fem. of the form ܩܛܘܠܝ with suff. b. ܝ quiesces in ܺ.

In the 2 plur. masc. ܩܛܘܠܘ passes into ܩܛܠܘ with suff. b.

The 2 plur. fem. is rare, and omits ܝ before the suffix.

Rem.—The imperative with ܰ and ܽ in Pe. and in the other conjugations, retains its vowel unchanged; e. g. ܫܡܰܥܝܢܝ *hear me*, ܩܰܒܠܽܘܗܝ *receive him*. The forms of the imperat. pass., with an active signification, also remain unchanged; e. g. ܐܶܬܕܟܰܪ *be reminded*, with suff. ܐܶܬܕܰܟܪܰܝܢܝ. In respect to the transposition of ܘ in the plur. it should be remarked that ܐ of Verbs ܦܐ (§ 28. 1) loses its vowel ܶ. But in those ܦܐ Verbs whose imperat. does not take ܘ, this vowel is inserted after the first radical; e. g. ܐܶܚܘܽܕ with suff. ܐܽܘܚܕܽܘܗܝ. Yet this transposition of ܘ does not always take place, as the form ܦܩܽܘܕܽܘܢܝ sometimes occurs. In Pa. and Aph. ܶ, in Verbs 3 Gutt., ܰ, falls away; e. g. ܫܰܒܰܚ with suff. ܫܰܒܚܽܘܗܝ *praise him*, ܐܰܩܪܶܒ with suff. ܐܰܩܪܒܽܘܗܝ *lead him hither*. Verbs ܠܐ are an exception, as they retain ܶ; e. g. ܐܰܛܶܒܽܘܢܝ *do me good*. Also a form with ܝ parag. sometimes occurs; e. g. ܦܩܽܘܕܝ with suff. ܦܩܽܘܕܝܢܳܝܗܝ. In the fem. plur. the paragogic form is the more usual; but in Pa. and Aph. both forms occur together.

D. Infinitive with Suffixes.

The infinitive Pe. ܡܶܦܩܰܕ with suff. a. 1. remains unchanged before the suff. of the 2 per. plur. The suffixes of the other persons are attached to the form ܡܶܦܩܕ. But the infinitives of the remaining conjugations with ܘ are treated as feminine substantives, the feminine suffixes of which (those of the 3 plur. excepted, which are attached separately to the form with ܘ) they take, attached to the termination ܘܬ (Compare § 45. 2. and § 48. B. feminines, declension 1).

Rem.—In Pe., where ܰ of the second syllable falls away, some grammarians insert, in its place, ܳ; e. g. ܠܡܶܦܩܳܕܶܗ. Buxtorf adds yet two other forms with ܘ and ܘ inserted after the third radical; e. g.

ܡܩܛܠܢܘܗܝ and ܡܩܛܠܢܘܗܝ. If the vowel be ܶ, as in Verbs ܠܗ, it remains unchanged; e. g. ܠܡܦܩܢܗ.

E. Participle with Suffixes.

Participles, which are considered as nouns, take *their* suffixes. This occurs, however, more rarely in the part. act., where either prepositions are used; e. g. ܠܟ, ܒܥܝܢ *who seek thee*, or a noun formed from the participle is joined with the suffix; e. g. ܥܕܪ *supporting*, ܥܕܘܪܗ *his helper*. On the contrary participles with separate pronouns (vid. § 18. 4. Rem.), or with afformatives (§ 20) form the present tense.

Proper Form.		Sing. 1 c.	2 m.	2 f.
Pret. Pe. Sing. 3 m.	ܩܛܠ	ܩܛܠܢܝ	ܩܛܠܟ	ܩܛܠܟܝ
3 f.	ܩܛܠܬ	ܩܛܠܬܢܝ	ܩܛܠܬܟ	ܩܛܠܬܟܝ
2 m.	ܩܛܠܬ	ܩܛܠܬܢܝ	*	*
2 f.	ܩܛܠܬܝ	ܩܛܠܬܝܢܝ	*	*
1 c.	ܩܛܠܬ	*	ܩܛܠܬܟ	ܩܛܠܬܟܝ
Plur. 3 m.	ܩܛܠܘ	ܩܛܠܘܢܝ ܩܛܠܘܢܢܝ	ܩܛܠܘܟ ܩܛܠܘܢܟ	ܩܛܠܘܟܝ ܩܛܠܘܢܟܝ
3 f.	ܩܛܠܝ ܩܛܠܝܢ	ܩܛܠܝܢܝ ܩܛܠܝܢܢܝ	ܩܛܠܝܟ ܩܛܠܝܢܟ	ܩܛܠܝܟܝ ܩܛܠܝܢܟܝ
2 m.	ܩܛܠܬܘܢ	ܩܛܠܬܘܢܢܝ	*	*
2 f.	ܩܛܠܬܝܢ	ܩܛܠܬܝܢܢܝ	*	*
1 c.	ܩܛܠܢ	*	ܩܛܠܢܟ	ܩܛܠܢܟܝ
Infinit.	ܡܩܛܠ	ܡܩܛܠܢܝ	ܡܩܛܠܟ	ܡܩܛܠܟܝ
Imp. sing. 2 m.	ܩܛܘܠ	ܩܛܘܠܝܢܝ	*	*
2 f.	ܩܛܘܠܝ	ܩܛܘܠܝܢܝ	*	*
Plur. 2 m.	ܩܛܘܠܘ	ܩܛܘܠܘܢܝ	*	*
2 f.	ܩܛܘܠܝܢ	ܩܛܘܠܝܢܝ ܩܛܘܠܝܢܢܝ	*	*
Fut. sing. 3 m.	ܢܩܛܘܠ	ܢܩܛܠܢܝ	ܢܩܛܠܟ	ܢܩܛܠܟܝ
Plur. 3 m.	ܢܩܛܠܘܢ	ܢܩܛܠܘܢܢܝ	ܢܩܛܠܘܢܟ	ܢܩܛܠܘܢܟܝ
Pret. Pa.	ܩܛܠ	ܩܛܠܢܝ	ܩܛܠܟ	ܩܛܠܟܝ
Infin. Pa.	ܡܩܛܠܘ	ܡܩܛܠܘܬܢܝ	ܡܩܛܠܘܬܟ	ܡܩܛܠܘܬܟܝ

3 m.	3 f.	Plur. 1 c.	2 m.	2 f.
ܩܛܠܗ	ܩܛܠܗ̇	ܩܛܠܢ	ܩܛܠܟ	ܩܛܠܟܝ
ܩܛܠܬܗ	ܩܛܠܬܗ̇	ܩܛܠܬܢ	ܩܛܠܬܟ	ܩܛܠܬܟܝ
ܩܛܠܬܝܗܝ	ܩܛܠܬܗ̇	ܩܛܠܬܢ	*	*
ܩܛܠܬܝܘܗܝ	ܩܛܠܬܝܗ̇	ܩܛܠܬܝܢ	*	*
ܩܛܠܬܗ	ܩܛܠܬܗ̇	*	ܩܛܠܬܟ	ܩܛܠܬܟܝ
ܩܛܠܘܗܝ ܩܛܠܘܢܝܗܝ	ܩܛܠܘܗ̇ ܩܛܠܘܢܗ̇	ܩܛܠܘܢ ܩܛܠܘܢܢ	ܩܛܠܘܟ ܩܛܠܘܢܟ	ܩܛܠܘܟܝ ܩܛܠܘܢܟܝ
ܩܛ̈ܠܝܗܝ ܩܛ̈ܠܝܢܝܗܝ	ܩܛ̈ܠܗ̇ ܩܛ̈ܠܝܢܗ̇	ܩܛ̈ܠܢ ܩܛ̈ܠܝܢܢ	ܩܛܠܟ ܩܛ̈ܠܝܢܟ	ܩܛܠܟܝ ܩܛ̈ܠܝܢܟܝ
ܩܛܠܬܘܢܝܗܝ	ܩܛܠܬܘܢܗ̇	ܩܛܠܬܘܢܢ	*	*
ܩܛܠܬܝ̈ܢܝܗܝ	ܩܛܠܬܝ̈ܢܗ̇	ܩܛܠܬܝ̈ܢܢ	*	*
ܩܛܠܢܝܗܝ	ܩܛܠܢܗ̇	*	ܩܛܠܢܟ	ܩܛܠܢܟܝ
ܢܩܛܠܗ	ܢܩܛܠܗ̇	ܢܩܛܠܢ	ܢܩܛܠܟ	ܢܩܛܠܟܝ
ܩܛܘܠܝܗܝ	ܩܛܘܠܝܗ̇	ܩܛܘܠܝܢ	*	*
ܩܛܘܠܝܘܗܝ	ܩܛܘܠܝܗ̇	ܩܛܘܠܝܢ	*	*
ܩܛܘܠܘܗܝ	ܩܛܘܠܘܗ̇	ܩܛܘܠܘܢ	*	*
ܩܛܘܠ̈ܝܗܝ ܩܛܘܠ̈ܝܢܝܗܝ	ܩܛܘܠ̈ܝܗ̇ ܩܛܘܠ̈ܝܢܗ̇	ܩܛܘܠ̈ܝܢ ܩܛܘܠ̈ܝܢܢ	*	*
ܢܩܛܘܠܝܘܗܝ	ܢܩܛܘܠܝܗ̇	ܢܩܛܘܠܢ	ܢܩܛܘܠܟ	ܢܩܛܘܠܟܝ
ܢܩܛܠܘܢܝܗܝ	ܢܩܛܠܘܢܗ̇	ܢܩܛܠܘܢܢ	ܢܩܛܠܘܢܟ	ܢܩܛܠܘܢܟܝ
ܩܛܠܗ	ܩܛܠܗ̇	ܩܛܠܢ	ܩܛܠܟ	ܩܛܠܟܝ
ܡܩܛܠܘܬܗ	ܡܩܛܠܘܬܗ̇	ܡܩܛܠܘܬܢ	ܡܩܛܠܘܬܟ	ܡܩܛܠܘܬܟܝ

§ 37. *Suffixes to Verbs with third Radical Olaph Quiescent* (ܠ̈ܐ).

Verbs ܠ̈ܐ (§ 32) differ so widely in their mode of connection with suffixes, from regular verbs, as to demand a separate treatment. It may be remarked in general:

1. That the termination ܳܐ either loses ܐ, as in the 3 sing. masc. pret. Pe., or in the sing. masc. of the imperat. Pa., Aph., Shaph. with suff. c; or ܐ is changed into ܝ movable, as in the infinit. Pe. with suff. a. 1, excepting before ܟܽܘܢ, ܟܶܝܢ, where the ܝ which has arisen from ܐ also falls away, according to some. So the termination of the fut. ܶܐ is changed into ܶܝ with suff. b.

2. Forms which end in ܺܝ either omit ܺ entirely, and connect the suff. a. 1, with ܝ movable, as 3 sing. masc. pret. Pa. and Aph. (and sometimes Pe. with ܺܝ final), or ܺ remains with suff. b, as 2 sing. masc. imperat. Pe., and, without exception, ܺ remains also in the first case before ܟܽܘܢ, ܟܶܝܢ. The terminations of the imperat. fem. ܝ̣, ܝ̈ܶܢ are changed into ܺܝ (or ܺܐܝ) with suff. b, and into ܰܝ̈ܢ with suff. c.

3. The forms which end with ܘ otiant., take for ܘ the forms ܽܘܗ (and ܽܘܐ); and for ܺܘ the form ܘ unchanged in all the preceding cases with suff. b; e. g. 3 plur. masc. pret. of all the conjugations excepting Peal.

In respect to individual persons of this class of verbs with suffixes, the following should be remarked:

A. Preter. with Suffixes.

(*Comp. Table of Verbs* ܠ̈ܐ *with Suffixes.*

The 3 sing. masc. ܓܠܳܐ loses ܐ and appends suff b, and suff. ܘܗܝ of the 3 sing. masc. to the form ܓܠܳܝ.

The 3 sing. fem. ܓܠܳܬ takes, unchanged, suff. a. 1. The same is true of the 1 sing. ܓܠܺܝܬ.

2 sing. masc. ܓܠܰܝܬ takes, unchanged, suff. c.

2 sing. fem. ܓܠܰܝܬܝ attaches suff. b. to the form ܓܠܰܝܬܺܝ.

3 plur. masc. ܓܠܰܘ is changed into ܓܠܰܘܗ̄ (and ܓܠܰܐܘܗ̄) with suff. b.

3 plur. fem. ܓܠܰܝ̈ remains unchanged with suff. c.

2 masc. and fem. and 1 plur. take, unchanged, suff. c.

Rem. Verbs 3 rad. ܝ, as they are mostly intransitives, take no suffixes in Peal. But Pa. and Aph. of these verbs with a transitive signification, as well as of Verbs ܐ̈ with the same ending, take suff. a. 1, with the falling away of ܺ, excepting before ܗ̇ܝ, ܗܽܘܢ, where ܺ remains. The 3 sing. fem. remains unchanged in Pa. ܓܰܠܝܰܬ and Aph. ܐܰܓܠܝܰܬ. The same is true also of the 1 sing. in both conjugations. The 3 plur. masc. occurs mostly before the suff., with ܘ doubled (see *Amira*, p. 372); e. g. Ps. liv. 3, *ed. Erpen.*, ܒܥܰܘܘܗܝ *they have sought them.* Sometimes the original ܐ appears before both ܘܘ; e. g. Ps. lxxvii. 16, ܚܙܰܐܘܽܘܟ *they have seen thee.* In Pa. ܓܰܠܺܝܘ and Aph. ܐܰܓܠܺܝܘ, ܺ falls away before the suff., and ܝ becomes movable; but ܘ quiesces in ܽ; e. g. ܢܰܣܺܝܘ with suff. ܢܰܣܝܽܘܟ; ܐܰܠܦܺܝܘ with suff. ܐܰܠܦܽܘܟܽܘܢ. The 3 plur. fem. in Pa. and Aph. in the simple form, takes the suff. given in the tab. with the falling away of ܺ over ܝ; e. g. ܐܰܓܠܝܳܢܶܝܗ. The paragogic form of these two conjugations takes suff. c. given in the table, without change.

B. Future with Suffixes.

The 3 sing. masc. ܢܶܓܠܶܐ and all the persons which terminate with ܶܐ, affix to the form ܢܶܓܠܶܝ suff. b. The 2 and 3 plur. masc. and fem. remain unchanged, and are connected, as in the regular verb, with suff. c.

Rem. This mode of formation also occurs in Pa. and Aph. Sometimes also ܶ takes the place of ܰ in the suff. 3 sing. fem.; e. g. Matt. i. 19, ܢܫܪܝܗ *that he should dismiss her*, or in Pa.; e. g. Luke xiii. 18, 20, ܐܕܡܝܗ *I shall liken it.* And with the falling away of ܝ; e. g. ܐܚܘܟܘܢ *I will show you*, the correctness of which *Lud. de Dieu*, p. 398, doubts.

C. Imperative with Suffixes.

2 sing. masc. ܓܠܝ is unchanged with suff. b.

2 sing. fem. ܓܠܝ is changed into ܓܠܝܝ with suff. b.

2 plur. masc. ܓܠܘ is changed into ܓܠܐܘ (and ܓܠܘ) with suff. b.

2 plur. fem. ܓܠܝܝܢ affixes suff. c. to the form ܓܠܝܝܢܐ.

Rem. The imperat. Pa. ܓܠܐ and Aph. ܐܓܠܐ take the suffixes of the pret. in connection with the 3 or 1 person; e. g. ܐܣܝܗ *heal her*. The same is true in the plur. masc. of the same conjugations. In the fem., the paragogic form with suff. c. is the usual one. (Compare 2, above.)

D. Infinitive with Suffixes.

In the infinit. Pe. ܡܓܠܐ, in place of ܐ, ܝ without a vowel is inserted with suff. a. 1. In respect to the falling away of ܝ before ܟܘܢ, ܟܝܢ, (see 1. above,) *Lud. de Dieu*, p. 395, doubts. The infinitives of the other conjugations are treated as in the regular verb. (Compare § 36, D.)

E. Participle with Suffixes.

(Compare § 20 and § 36, E.)

Passive. Plur.	*Passive.* Sing.	*Active.* Plur.	*Active.* Sing.		
ܓܠܝܬܘܢ	ܓܠܝܬ	ܓܠܝܬܘܢ	ܓܠܝܬ	m.	2.
ܓܠܝܬܝܢ	ܓܠܝܬܝ	ܓܠܝܬܝܢ	ܓܠܝܬܝ	f.	2.
ܓܠܝܢܢ	ܓܠܐ ܐܢܐ	ܓܠܝܢܢ	ܓܠܐ ܐܢܐ	m.	1.
	ܓܠܝܐ ܐܢܐ		ܓܠܝܐ ܐܢܐ	f.	1.

The participles of the other conjugations are inflected in a similar manner, retaining the characteristic vowels; e. g. Pa. act. ܡܫܰܐܠܺܝܬܽܘܢ *ye ask*, Aph. ܡܰܘܕܶܝܢܰܢ *we thank*, Ethpe. ܡܶܬܗܦܶܟܺܝܢܰܢ *we turn about.*

General Remark.

Verbs of the form of ܒܰܝܺܐ *to console*, never lose the third radical letter ܐ when taking a suffix, but throw back its vowel upon the middle radical, which, according to § 36, usually stands vacant; e. g. pret. 3 sing. masc. ܒܰܝܰܐܢܝ, ܒܰܝܳܐܟ, 3 pl. masc. ܒܰܝܺܐܘܢܝ, ܒܰܝܺܐܘܟ, fem. ܒܰܝܳܐܬܢܝ, ܒܰܝܳܐܬܶܗ, fut. 3 sing. masc. ܢܒܰܝܶܐܢܝ, ܢܒܰܝܶܐܟ, imperat. 2 sing. masc. ܒܰܝܰܐܝܢܝ, ܒܰܝܰܐܝܗܝ, fem. ܒܰܝܰܐܝܢܝ, ܒܰܝܰܐܝܘܗܝ, 2 plur. masc. ܒܰܝܰܐܘܢ, fem. ܒܰܝܳܐܢܝ, ܒܰܝܳܐܝܗ.

Verb ܠܐ

Proper Form.		Sing. 1 c.	2 m.	2 f.
Pret. Sing. Pe.	ܪܡܐ	ܪܡܢܝ	ܪܡܟ	ܪܡܟܝ
3 *m.* *Pa.*	ܢܣܝ	ܢܣܝܢܝ	ܢܣܝܟ	ܢܣܝܟܝ
3 *f.* *Pe.*	ܪܡܬ	ܪܡܬܢܝ	ܪܡܬܟ	ܪܡܬܟܝ
Pa.	ܢܣܝܬ	ܢܣܝܬܢܝ	ܢܣܝܬܟ	ܢܣܝܬܟܝ
1 *c.*	ܪܡܝܬ	*	ܪܡܝܬܟ	ܪܡܝܬܟܝ
Peal.	ܪܡܘ	ܪܡܘܢܝ	ܪܡܘܟ	ܪܡܘܟܝ
Plur. 3 *m.*		ܪܡܐܘܢܝ	ܪܡܐܘܟ	ܪܡܐܘܟܝ
Pael.	ܢܣܝܘ	ܢܣܝܘܢܝ	ܢܣܝܘܟ	ܢܣܝܘܟܝ
3 *f.*	ܪܡܝ̈	ܪܡܝ̈ܢܝ	ܪܡܝ̈ܟ	ܪܡܝ̈ܟܝ
	ܪܡܝ̈ܝ	ܪܡܝ̈ܝܢܝ	ܪܡܝ̈ܝܟ	ܪܡܝ̈ܝܟܝ
Infin.	ܡܪܡܐ	ܡܪܡܝܢܝ	ܡܪܡܝܟ	ܡܪܡܝܟܝ
Imp. 2 *m.* *Pe.*	ܪܡܝ	ܪܡܝܢܝ	*	*
Pa.	ܪܡܐ	ܪܡܢܝ		
2 *f.*	ܪܡܝ	ܪܡܝܢܝ ܪܡܝܢܢܝ	*	*
Plur. 2 *m.*	ܪܡܘ	ܪܡܘܢܝ ܪܡܐܘܢܝ	*	*
2 *f.*	ܪ̈ܡܝܢ	ܪ̈ܡܝܢܢܝ	*	*
Futur. 3 *m.*	ܢܪܡܐ	ܢܪܡܝܢܝ	ܢܪܡܝܟ	ܢܪܡܝܟܝ

3 m.	3 f.	Plur. 1 c.	2 m.	2 f.
ܩܪܝܗܝ ܚܙܝܗ	ܩܪܝܗ ܚܙܝܗ	ܩܪܢ ܚܙܢ	ܩܪܟܘܢ ܚܙܝܟܘܢ	ܩܪܟܝܢ ܚܙܝܟܝܢ
ܩܪܬܗ ܚܙܝܬܗ	ܩܪܬܗ ܚܙܝܬܗ	ܩܪܬܢ ܚܙܝܬܢ	ܩܪܬܟܘܢ ܚܙܝܬܟܘܢ	ܩܪܬܟܝܢ ܚܙܝܬܟܝܢ
ܩܪܝܬܗ	ܩܪܝܬܗ	*	ܩܪܝܬܟܘܢ	ܩܪܝܬܟܝܢ
ܩܪܘܗܝ ܩܪܐܘܗܝ ܚܙܘܗܝ	ܩܪܘܗ ܩܪܐܘܗ ܚܙܘܗ	ܩܪܘܢ ܩܪܐܘܢ ܚܙܘܢ	ܩܪܘܟܘܢ ܩܪܐܘܟܘܢ ܚܙܘܟܘܢ	ܩܪܘܟܝܢ ܩܪܐܘܟܝܢ ܚܙܘܟܝܢ
ܩܪܝܬܝܗܝ ܩܪܝܢܝܗܝ	ܩܪܝܬܗ ܩܪܝܢܗ	ܩܪܝܬܢ ܩܪܝܢܢ	ܩܪܝܬܟܘܢ ܩܪܝܢܟܘܢ	ܩܪܝܬܟܝܢ ܩܪܝܢܟܝܢ
ܢܩܪܝܗ	ܢܩܪܝܗ	ܢܩܪܝܢ	ܢܩܪܝܟܘܢ ܢܩܪܝܢܟܘܢ	ܢܩܪܝܟܝܢ ܢܩܪܝܢܟܝܢ
ܩܪܝܗܝ ܩܪܝܗܝ	ܩܪܝܗ ܩܪܝܗ	ܩܪܝܢ ܩܪܢ	*	*
ܩܪܝܝܗܝ	ܩܪܝܗ	ܩܪܝܢ ܩܪܝܢܝ	*	*
ܩܪܘܗܝ ܩܪܐܘܗܝ	ܩܪܘܗ ܩܪܐܘܗ	ܩܪܘܢ ܩܪܐܘܢ	*	*
ܩܪܝܢܝܗܝ	ܩܪܝܢܗ	ܩܪܝܢܝ	*	*
ܡܩܪܝܗܝ	ܡܩܪܝܗ	ܡܩܪܝܢ	ܡܩܪܝܟܘܢ	ܡܩܪܝܟܝܢ

§ 38. *Auxiliary Verbs, or Verbs Substantive.*

1. There are in Syriac two auxiliary verbs (verbs substantive). One of these, ܗܘܐ *to be*, which, in Hebrew, exists as *Vau* conversive, is used to form the moods and tenses which are wanting (see § 18. 4. *Rem.*). The other, which is properly a noun, ܝܬ *being*, *substance*, *essence* (*essentia*), with Olaph prosthetic ܐܝܬ, takes the place of the auxiliary verb *to be*. The former of these, ܗܘܐ, belongs to Verbs ܠ̈ܐ, like which it is inflected, but in respect to which it is to be particularly observed, that, when connected with the participle, preter. or future, the ܗ (with *Linea occultans*) is not pronounced; this is also the case when the verb is added merely for the sake of emphasis; e. g. ܫܪܝ ܗܘܐ *he has begun*. Upon the double formation of the fut. ܢܗܘܐ and ܢܗܘܐ, see § 35. 2, c. The inflection of ܐܝܬ is as follows:

Plur. F.	Plur. C.	Plur. M.	Sing. F.	Sing. C.	Sing. M.	
	ܐܝܬܝܢ (*we are*)			ܐܝܬܝ (*I am*)		1.
ܐܝܬܝܟܝܢ	(*ye are*)	ܐܝܬܝܟܘܢ	ܐܝܬܝܟܝ	(*thou art*)	ܐܝܬܝܟ	2.
ܐܝܬܝܗܝܢ	(*they are*)	ܐܝܬܝܗܘܢ	ܐܝܬܝܗ	(*he, she is*)	ܐܝܬܘܗܝ	3.

2. In connection with ܠܐ is formed ܠܝܬ, which is inflected similarly to ܐܝܬ; e. g. ܠܝܬܝ *I am not*. ܐܝܬ in connection with ܗܘܐ forms the imperfect; e. g. ܐܝܬ ܗܘܐ or ܐܝܬܘܗܝ ܗܘܐ *he was*. The same tense is also expressed by ܗܘܐ ܗܘܐ. ܗܘܐ doubled marks the pluperfect; e. g. ܗܘܝܬ ܗܘܝܬ *I had been*.

CHAPTER III.

The Noun.

§ 39. *Derivation of Nouns.*

1. Nouns, as in Hebrew and Chaldee, are primitive, derivative, and sometimes compounded. To primitives belong nouns of one and two syllables, which indicate animals, plants, metals, numbers, members of the bodies of animals, etc. (See *Gesenius*, *Lehrgeb.* p. 478, sq.). Inasmuch as they coincide with simple verbal forms, they are always recognized as nouns by the nature of the object which they designate; e. g. ܒܣܪ *flesh*, ܕܗܒ *gold*, ܟܣܦ *silver*. The derivatives, which are by far the most numerous, are formed partly from verbs (verbals), and partly from nouns (denominatives).

2. The derivation of nouns is effected; *a*) without any change of the original word; e. g. ܡܠܟ *counsel*, from ܡܠܟ *to counsel*; ܐܒܠ *mourning*, from ܐܒܠ *to mourn*; or by a mere change of the vowel; e. g. ܡܠܟ *king*, ܐܣܘܪ *fetter*; *b*) by the falling away of the radical letter; e. g. ܫܢܬܐ *sleep*, from ܝܫܢ; ܨܦܬܐ *care*, from ܝܨܦ; ܠܒܐ *the heart*, from ܠܒܒ; but especially *c*) by the addition of formative letters or of entire syllables. Those letters, if initial, are ܐ, ܡ, ܢ, ܬ, ܫ; if medial, they are ܝ and ܘ; final, ܐ, ܢ, ܬ. Several of these formative letters are sometimes found in the same noun; e. g. ܬܠܡܝܕ *scholar*, ܫܘܠܛܢܐ *dominion*, ܡܪܚܡܢܘܬܐ *compassion*, ܫܠܗܒܝܬܐ *flame*.

§ 40. *Nouns derived from Verbs.*

Verbal nouns are kindred either to participles, and denote the subject or object of the action (Concrete Nouns), or they are kindred to the infinitive, and receive the signification of the action or quality itself (Abstract Nouns). But frequently in the formation of these nouns, rare or obsolete forms of the infinitives and participles are chosen. The following tables present a collective view of the modes of formation.

TABULAR VIEW
OF
NOUNS DERIVED FROM REGULAR AND IRREGULAR VERBS.

I. PARTICIPIAL FORMS.

A. Of PEAL.

a. *The simple but unusual Participial Forms, which are mostly Adjectives.*

Absolute state,	ܩܛܠ		ܩܛܠ
Emphat. state.,	ܩܛܠܐ		ܩܛܠܐ
ܓܒܪ	*a man.*	ܣܟܠܐ	*foolish.*
ܚܒܪ	*an associate.*	ܫܠܝܐ	*rural, quiet.*
ܓܪܒܐ	*leprous.*	ܟܪܝܗ	*sick.*
ܘܗ̈ and ܟܒ		ܦܐ	
ܟܡܝܪܐ	*mournful*	ܢܟܦܐ	*pure.*

ܐ and ܟܒ

ܫܘܐ, ܫܘܝܐ	*equal.*	ܩܫܐ	*hard.*

ܛܢܦܐ *impure ;* ܣܓܝ *much.*

From these are derived Abstract Nouns ; e. g. ܩܫܝܘܬܐ *hardness;* ܣܓܝܐܘܬܐ *multitude.*

b. *Usual Participial Forms of Peal.*

a. Active.	*β.* Passive.	
Absolute state, ܩܳܛܶܠ	ܩܛܺܝܠ	ܩܛܺܠ
Emphat. state, ܩܳܛܠܳܐ	ܩܛܺܝܠܳܐ	ܩܛܺܠܳܐ
ܣܳܗܶܕ *a witness.*	ܚܠܺܝܡ *sound.*	ܙܕܺܝܩ *righteous.*
ܩܳܐ	ܩܛܺܝ	ܩܳܐ
ܐܽܘܟܳܡ *black.*	ܝܗܺܝܒܳܐ *given.*	ܐܰܓܺܝܪܳܐ *a hireling.*
ܩܛܺܝ	ܩܛܽܘ and ܩܛܺܝ	ܩܛܺܝ
ܝܳܬܒܳܐ *an inhabitant.*	ܠܺܝܛ *cursed.*	ܝܰܒܺܝܫܳܐ *dry.*
ܩܰܛ	ܪܰܟܺܝܟܳܐ *soft.*	ܩܰܛ
ܪܳܥܝܳܐ *a herdsman.*	ܥܘܺܝܪ *blind.*	ܢܓܺܝܪܳܐ *long-suffering.*
ܩܽܘ and ܩܛܺܝ	ܩܛܠ	ܩܛܠ
ܓܰܕܽܘܦܳܐ *reviling.*	ܝܰܕܺܝܥܳܐ *renowned.*	ܚܰܒܺܝܒܳܐ *beloved.*
ܠܳܐ	ܚܺܐܪܳܐ *free.*	ܝܰܩܺܝܪܳܐ *rare.*
ܪܳܥܝܳܐ *a herdsman.*	ܠܳܐ	
ܡܳܪܳܐ *a landlord.*	ܟܣܶܐ *concealed.*	
ܠܳܐ and ܩܳܐ	ܠܳܐ and ܟܳܐ	
ܐܳܣܝܳܐ *a physician.*	ܫܰܦܺܝܪ m. ܫܰܦܺܝܪܬܳܐ f. *beautiful.*	
ܠܳܐ and ܟܳܐ		
ܢܳܐܶܐ *beautiful.*	ܠܳܐ and ܩܶܐ	

ܢܒܺܝܳܐ *prophet,* ܢܒܺܝܬܳܐ *prophetess.*

Here belong also AbstractNouns, as ܐܳܣܝܽܘܬܳܐ *healing,* ܡܰܟܪܙܽܘܬܳܐ *publication,* ܚܺܐܪܽܘܬܳܐ *freedom,* ܙܕܺܝܩܽܘ and ܙܕܺܝܩܽܘܬܳܐ *righteousness,* ܝܰܒܺܝܫܽܘܬܳܐ *dryness.*

c. *With Immutable Vowels.*

Ab. stat.,	ܩܛܠ	ܩܛܘܠ,	ܩܛܝܠ	ܩܛܘܠ	ܩܛܘܠ & with ܝ
Emph. ,	ܩܛܠܐ	ܩܛܘܠܐ	ܩܛܝܠܐ	ܩܛܘܠܐ	ܩܛܘܠܐ ܝܐ

ܦܠܚܐ *a ploughman.*	ܙܥܘܪ *small.*	ܡܓܕܦܢܐ *a blasphemer.*	ܣܘܡܩܐ *a red (color).*	
ܡܚܝܠܐ *weak.*	ܫܟܘܠܬܐ *a mob, a rabble.*	ܙܪܘܥܐ *a sower.*	ܪܚܡܬܐ *a friend.*	
ܢܓܪܐ *a carpenter.*	ܟܪܘܙܐ *a preacher.*	ܐܪܙܦܐ *a hammerer.*	ܐܘܟܡܐ *black.*	
ܡܦܩܢܐ *a spendthrift.*	ܪܛܝܒܐ *damp.*	ܡܘܗܒܢܐ *a giver.*	ܐܡܘܪܢܐ *a possessor.*	
ܕܝܢܐ *a judge.*	ܚܒܘܠܐ *a destroyer.*	ܡܝܘܬܘܬܐ *mortal.*	ܓܕܝܫܐ *fortunate.*	
ܩܪܒܐ *a combatant.*	ܥܠܝܡܐ *a youth.*	ܓܠܘܒܐ *a barber.*	ܫܘܒܩܐ *a bill of divorce.*	
ܡܠܠܐ *an orator.*		ܓܫܘܫܐ *a spy.*	ܦܨܝܠܐ *a cleft.*	
ܚܙܝܐ *a seer.*	ܟܡܝܪܐ *mournful.*	ܒܪܘܝܐ *creator.*		
ܡܫܝܢܐ *quiet.*		ܓܚܘܟܐ *a mocker.*		
ܐܦܝܐ *a baker.*				

From these are formed Abstract Nouns, like ܫܟܝܚܘܬܐ *rejection,* ܙܥܘܪܘܬܐ *littleness,* ܦܘܪܫܢܘܬܐ *division,* ܡܘܗܒܘܬܐ *giving,* etc.

B. PARTICIPIAL FORMS.

a. *Of the other Active Conjugations.*

Paël.	Aphel.	Shaphel.
It takes the usual form, and the form with ܳܢܳܐ and the form ܡܩܰܛܠܳܢܳܐ	Usual form and ܡܰܩܛܘܠܳܐ, ܡܰܩܛܠܳܐ	Usual form and ܫܰܩܛܠܳܐ
ܡܕܰܒܪܳܢܳܐ *a leader.*	ܡܰܥܡܪܳܐ *a dwelling.*	ܡܥܰܬܪܳܢܳܐ *rich.*
ܡܣܰܟܢܳܐ *poor.*	ܡܰܠܩܛܳܐ *pincers.*	ܡܫܰܥܒܕܳܐ *a slave.*
ܦܐ	ܡܰܟܫܘܠܳܐ *an offense.*	ܫܰܚܠܦܳܐ *changing.*
ܡܰܠܦܳܢܳܐ *a teacher.*	ܦܐ	ܦܝ
ܦܝ	ܡܗܰܝܡܢܳܐ *true.*	ܫܰܘܙܒܳܢܳܐ *a deliverer.*
ܡܫܰܢܩܳܢܳܐ *a torturer.*	ܦܝ	ܠܐ and ܥܝ
ܥܘ and ܥܝ	ܡܰܘܐܫܳܐ *despairing.*	ܡܫܰܥܒܕܳܢܳܐ *proud.*
ܡܚܰܝܕܳܐ *united.*	ܦܢ	Part. pass.
ܡܪܰܘܡܳܐ *high.*	ܡܰܚܣܪܳܢܳܐ *injurious.*	ܡܫܰܡܠܰܠ *completed.*
ܠܐ and ܥܥ	ܥܘ and ܥܝ	
ܡܫܰܓܫܳܢܳܐ *seditious.*	ܡܪܺܝܡ *high.*	
ܡܕܰܒܪܳܢܳܐ *a leader.*	ܠܐ and ܥܥ	
ܠܐ and ܦܐ	ܡܰܓܕܠܳܐ *a watch-tower.*	
ܡܐܰܣܝܳܢܳܐ *a physician.*	ܡܰܓܙܪܳܐ *a sickle.*	
ܠܐ and ܥܐ	ܠܐ and ܦܝ	
ܡܒܰܝܳܐܢܳܐ *a comforter.*	ܡܰܘܕܝܳܢܳܐ *a confessor.*	

From these are derived Abstract Nouns, as ܡܕܰܒܪܳܢܘܬܳܐ *direction,* ܡܰܠܦܳܢܘܬܳܐ *doctrine,* ܡܐܰܣܝܳܢܘܬܳܐ *healing,* &c.

b. *Of the Passive Conjugations.*

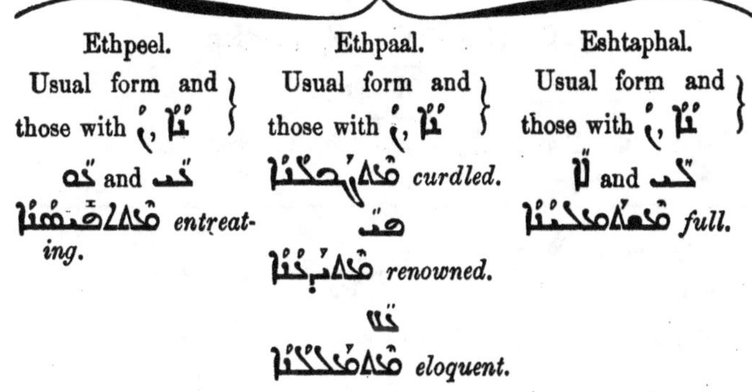

C. PARTICIPIAL FORMS OF LESS FREQUENT CONJUGATIONS.

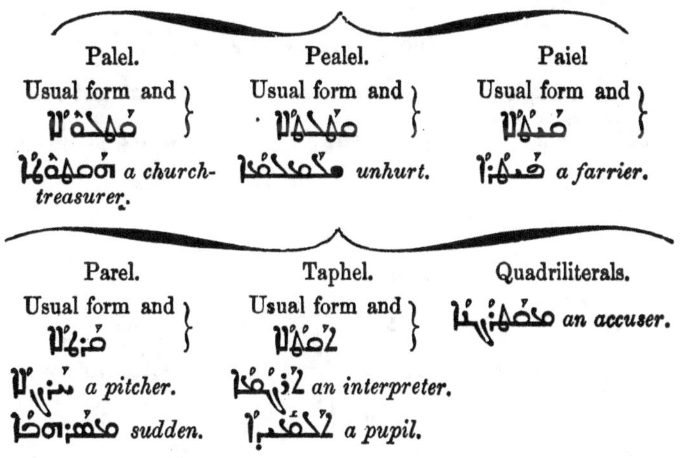

II. INFINITIVE FORMS.

A. OF PEAL.

a. *Simple Infinitive Forms—Segholates.*

Absolute state, ܩܛܠ Emphat. state, ܩܛܠܐ	ܩܛܠ ܩܛܠܐ	ܩܘܛܠ ܩܘܛܠܐ
ܢܦܫܐ *the soul.*	ܡܛܪܐ *rain.*	ܩܘܕܫܐ *holiness.*
ܠܚܡܐ *bread.*	ܨܦܪܐ *morning.*	ܒܘܪܟܐ *the knee.*
ܦܥ	ܦܐ	ܦܐ
ܥܒܠܐ *sea-grass.*	ܐܡܪܐ *a lamb.*	ܐܘܪܚܐ *a way.*
ܥܣܒܐ *herbage.*	ܦܥ	
ܛܠܝܐ *a child.*	ܙܗܝܬܐ *diligence,* (for ܙܗܝܪܘܬܐ).	
ܥܘ and ܥܝ	ܥܘ and ܥܝ	ܥܘ and ܥܝ
ܡܘܬܐ *death.*	ܫܝܢܐ *peace.*	ܛܘܒܐ *goodness.*
ܢܝܪܐ *a yoke.*	ܕܝܪܐ *a dwelling.*	ܣܘܦܐ *an end.*
ܠܐ and ܠܝ	ܠܐ and ܠܝ	
ܚܕܘܬܐ *joy.*	ܢܝܚܐ *rest.*	
ܥܥ	ܥܥ	ܥܥ
ܓܙܐ *a treasure.*	ܠܒܐ *the heart.*	ܩܘܪܐ *coldness.*
ܐ and ܠܐ	ܐ and ܠܐ	ܐ and ܦܥ
ܐܦܬܐ *countenance.*	ܠܐܘܬܐ *labor,*	ܐܘܠܨܬܐ *anguish.*

It is seldom that all three forms are found derived from one original; e. g. ܚܒܠܐ *a rope,* ܚܒܠܐ *a pestilence,* ܚܘܒܠܐ *guilt;* oftener two forms, as ܐܠܐ *an oak,* ܐܠܐ *a storm* (from ܐܠܠ).

D. *Infinitive Forms with Immutable Vowels.*

Abs. stat.	ܩܛܠ	ܩܘܛܠ	ܩܘܛܠܢ	ܩܛܠܘ
Em. stat.	ܩܛܠܐ	ܩܘܛܠܐ	ܩܘܛܠܢܐ	ܩܛܠܘܬܐ

ܪܡܟܐ *a herd.*
ܥܒܕܐ *a work.*
ܦܐ
ܐܣܪܐ *a girdle.*
ܦܢ
ܐܡܪܐ *renown.*
ܠܐ
ܡܐܢܐ *a vessel.*
ܥܘ and ܥܝ
ܟܝܢܐ *nature.*
ܪܝܕܐ *a flowing.*
ܠܐ and ܥܝ
ܗܓܝܐ *meditation.*
ܩܪܝܬܐ *reading.*
ܥܥ
ܢܝܚܐ *rest.*
ܠܐ and ܦܢ
ܢܒܬܐ *a sprout.*

ܢܘܩܙܐ *a puncture.*
ܠܘܩܛܐ *gleaning.*
ܦܐ (and ܠܐ)
ܐܘܠܝܬܐ *a howling.*
ܦܢ
ܡܘܠܠܐ *tradition.*
ܠܐ
ܫܘܐܠܐ *a question.*
ܥܘ and ܥܝ
ܒܘܣܡܐ *perfume.*
ܕܘܝܪܐ *a dwelling.*
ܠܐ and ܥܝ
ܡܘܛܝܐ *arrival.*
ܡܘܠܝܐ *fullness.*
ܥܥ
ܬܘܟܠܐ *confidence.*
ܠܐ and ܦܢ
ܛܘܥܝܐ *error.*

ܠܒܘܟܝܐ *seizure.*
ܡܟܘܪܝܐ *affiance.*
ܦܐ
ܐܣܘܪܝܐ *a fetter.*
ܥܘ and ܥܝ
ܡܠܘܠܐ *talkativeness.*

ܣܟܠܘ *folly.*
ܡܠܟܘܬܐ *a kingdom.*
ܥܘ and ܥܝ
ܛܝܒܘ *favor.*
ܠܐ and ܥܝ
ܐܣܝܘܬܐ *indecency.*
ܚܙܝܘܬܐ *appearance.*
ܩܢܝܘܬܐ *possession.*
ܠܐ and ܥܥ
ܨܒܝܘܬܐ *ornament.*

B. USUAL INFINITIVE FORMS OF PEAL AND OF THE OTHER CONJUGATIONS.

Peal	Pael.	Aphel.	Shaphel.
	Usual form and	Usual form and	Usual form and
ܡܶܩܛܳܠ, ܡܶܩܛܰܠ, ܡܶܩܛܽܘܠ	ܬܰܩܛܳܠܽܘ or ܬܰܩܛܽܘܠ	ܡܰܩܛܳܠܽܘ ܡܰܚܫܰܒܬܳܐ *thought.*	ܫܽܘܩܛܳܠܽܘ ܫܽܘܚܠܳܦܳܐ *change.*
ܡܰܫܟܒܳܐ *a bed.*	ܬܰܡܠܝܩܳܐ *flattery.*		ܫܽܘܥܒܳܕܳܐ *slavery.*
ܡܰܕܒܪܳܐ *a desert.*	ܬܰܥܕܽܘܪܳܐ *help.*	ܡܰܚܒܛܳܐ *a concussion.*	
ܡܰܕܩܢܽܘܬܳܐ *a thrust.*	ܬܰܟܬܽܘܫܳܐ *combat.*		ܫܽܘܘܚܳܪܳܐ *delay.*
ܦܐ	ܦܐ	ܦܐ	ܦܐ
ܡܐܡܪܳܐ *a speech.*	ܬܰܐܓܽܘܪܬܳܐ *merchandise.*	ܡܰܘܒܕܳܢܽܘܬܳܐ *destruction.*	
ܦܝ	ܦܝ	ܦܝ	ܦܝ
ܡܰܕܥ *insight.*	ܬܽܘܚܳܠܬܳܐ *despair.*	ܡܰܘܗܰܒܬܳܐ *a gift.*	ܫܽܘܘܙܳܒܳܐ *deliverance.*
ܦܢ	ܥܘ and ܥܝ	ܦܢ	
ܡܰܦܩܳܢܳܐ *departure.*		ܡܰܣܳܪܳܐ *a saw.*	
ܡܰܦܘܚܳܐ *bellows.*	ܬܰܦܠܽܘܬܳܐ *rubbish.*	ܡܰܪܳܐ *a hoe.*	
ܥܘ and ܥܝ	ܠܐ and ܥܥ	ܠܐ (and ܦܐ)	ܠܐ and ܥܥ
ܡܫܡܥܬܳܐ *harkening.*	ܬܰܥܛܦܬܳܐ *a mantle.*	ܡܰܟܢܫܬܳܐ *an assembly.*	ܫܽܘܡܠܳܝܳܐ *conclusion.*
ܠܐ and ܥܥ	ܠܐ and ܦܝ	ܠܐ and ܦܝ	ܠܐ and ܦܝ
ܡܰܠܝܳܐ *a drawing off* (of water).	ܬܰܘܪܝܬܳܐ *doctrine.*	ܡܰܘܣܥܢܽܘܬܳܐ *conclusion.*	ܫܽܘܘܕܳܝܳܐ *a promise.*
ܠܐ and ܦܐ			
ܡܐܬܝܬܳܐ *arrival.*			

C. INFINITIVE FORMS OF THE LESS FREQUENT CONJUGATIONS.

Palel and Palpel.	Pealel.	Pavel and Paiel.
ܙܗܪܝܪܐ *splendor.*	ܡܟܡܟܡܘܬܐ *innocence.*	ܬܘܠܥܐ *a worm.*
ܙܥ and ܙܘܥ		ܠܐ and ܠܝ
ܙܘܥܙܥܐ *motion.*		ܛܝܡܢܬܐ *a mystery.*
ܢܕ		Pali.
ܛܘܠܫܐ *contamination.*		ܬܘܗܝܐ *astonishment.*

Parel.	Pamel.	Taphel.
ܣܘܪܗܒܐ *swiftness.*	ܢܘܡܟܪܐ *shame.*	ܬܘܠܡܕܐ *doctrine.*

§ 41. *Denominative Nouns.*

Here belong :

1. Nouns ; *a*) without any formative additions, derived from some other nouns, which may be either primitives or derivatives of verbs ; e. g. ܓܰܢܳܢܳܐ *a gardener*, from ܓܰܢܬܳܐ *a garden ;* ܡܰܠܳܚܳܐ *a seaman*, from ܡܶܠܚܳܐ *salt ;* *b*) with the formative syllables ܳܝܳܐ masc., ܳܝܬܳܐ fem., (Patronymics or Gentile Nouns) ; e.g. ܪܗܘܡܳܝܳܐ *Roman*, ܐܺܝܣܪܳܝܶܠܳܝܬܳܐ *Israelitess ;* with the falling away of the syllable ܘܣ in names of towns ; e. g. ܐܶܦܶܣܳܝܳܐ *an Ephesian*, from ܐܶܦܶܣܘܣ ; or Feminine Abstract Nouns, terminating in ܘܬܳܐ and ܺܝܬܳܐ ; e.g. ܛܠܳܝܘܬܳܐ *youthfulness*, from ܛܠܳܝܳܐ *a youth ;* ܥܘܺܝܪܘܬܳܐ *blindness*, from ܥܘܺܝܪ *blind ;* ܪܺܫܳܝܬܳܐ *beginning*, from ܪܺܫ *the head, principal ;* *c*) diminutives with ܘܢ or ܘܣ masc. and ܘܢܺܝܬܳܐ fem. attached to the noun ; e. g. ܒܪܘܢܳܐ *a little son*, from ܒܪܳܐ ; ܐܰܚܘܢܳܐ *a little brother*, from ܐܰܚܳܐ ; ܒܪܬܘܢܺܝܬܳܐ *a little daughter* from ܒܪܬܳܐ ; ܟܰܠܒܘܣܳܐ *a young dog*, from ܟܰܠܒܳܐ. Sometimes we find both forms in use ; e. g. ܓܰܒܪܘܢܳܐ and ܓܰܒܪܘܣܳܐ *a manikin*, from ܓܰܒܪܳܐ. Diminutives from compound nouns also occur ; e. g. ܒܪܢܳܫܘܢܳܐ from ܒܪܢܳܫܳܐ ; also a double formation ; e. g. ܓܰܒܪܘܣܘܢܳܐ *a very little man*, ܒܪܬܘܢܬܘܢܺܝܬܳܐ *a very little daughter.*

Rem.—Amira (p. 145) mentions a form with the third radical letter doubled, and ܘ inserted between them ; e.g. ܟܢܘܫܘܫܬܳܐ *a little assembly*, from ܟܢܘܫܬܳܐ.

2. Adjectives belong here, which are formed ; *a*) by affixing the terminations ܳܢܳܐ masc. and ܳܢܺܝܬܳܐ fem. ; e. g. ܪܘܚܳܢܳܐ masc. ܪܘܚܳܢܺܝܬܳܐ fem., *spiritual*, from ܪܘܚܳܐ ; *b*) by affixing the terminations ܳܝܳܐ masc. ܳܝܬܳܐ fem. ; e. g. ܓܘܫܡܳܢܳܝܳܐ masc.

ܦܓܪܢܝܬܐ fem. *corporeal* from ܦܓܪܐ; ordinal numerals (see § 50. 3); e.g. ܬܠܝܬܝܐ *the third*, from ܬܠܬܐ; *c*) by affixing the terminations ܢܐ masc., ܢܝܬܐ fem.; e.g. ܪܘܚܢܢܐ masc., ܪܘܚܢܢܝܬܐ fem.

Rem.—In respect to the cases under *a.* and *c.* above, Amira remarks (p. 106) that the latter is rather used in metaphorical language, yet he also admits the interchange of the two forms.

---

§ 42. *Composite and Exotic Nouns.*

1. The formation of words by composition is more frequent in Syriac than in the other Semitic dialects, (see Michaelis, p. 151; Lud. de Dieu, pp. 73, 74). The words most frequently used in forming compounds are ܒܪ *son*; e.g. ܒܪܢܫܐ *man*, ܒܪܬܩܠܐ *voice*; ܒܥܠ *sir*; e.g. ܒܥܠܕܒܒܐ *enemy*; ܪܒ *much*; e.g. ܪܒ-ܒܝܬܐ *householder*; ܪܝܫ *principal*; e.g. ܪܫܥܠܠܬܐ *firstling*; ܒܝܬܐ *house*; e.g. ܒܝܬ ܦܩܣܐ *corn-house*; sometimes ܐܟܠ *eating*; e.g. ܐܟܠܩܪܨܐ *adversary*. In changing the Concrete idea into the Abstract, either the last part of the compound word only is regarded; e.g. ܒܥܠܕܒܒܘܬܐ *hostility*, or both parts are changed into the feminine; e.g. ܒܝܬܘܬܐ ܪܒܬ *house-holding*. Upon the plural inflection see § 44.

2. The Syrians have introduced many Greek words into their language, and given them either Syriac terminations or permitted them to retain, more or less, the Greek forms. The following are examples; ܐܓܝܐ ἁγια, ܐܘܢܓܠܝܘܢ εὐαγγελιον, ܐܝܣܓܘܓܝ εἰσαγωγη, ܦܘܪܓܘܣ πυργος, ܓܐܘܡܛܪܝܐ γεωμετρια, ܗܓܡܘܢܐ ἡγεμων, ܡܠܠܘܢ μαλλον, ܡܬܡܐܛܐ μαθηματα, ܣܘܠܠܘܓܝܣܡܘܣ συλλογισμος. There are some peculiarities

in the formation of these words, for which see § 12. 5. and § 44. Rem. 8. At the time of the Crusades, the Syrians introduced words also from the western languages; e. g. ܦܪ̈ܢܓܝܐ *the Franks*, ܐܠܡܐܢܝܐ *Germany*, ܐܢܓܠܛܪܐ *England*, ܦܪܢܣܐ *Prince*, ܗܢܪܝ *Henry*, etc.

---

§ 43. *Gender of Nouns.*

The Syriac language has but two genders, *masculine* and *feminine.* The latter is distinguished partly by the signification and partly by the form.

1. In respect to the signification, the gender is fixed by the same rules as in Hebrew. Masculines are the names of men, masculine offices, nations, mountains, months and rivers. Feminines are the names of female persons and animals, countries, cities, and members of human and animal bodies, which are found double although they have masculine endings in the plural; e. g. ܪ̈ܓܠܝܢ *feet* from ܪܓܠܐ, etc.

2. In respect to form, the feminine is characterized by the terminations ܬܐ (ܬܐ), ܝ, ܘ, ܬ. But the first of those final syllables, which is particularly used for the formation of feminines from masculines (e. g. ܚܒܪܬܐ *female companion* from ܚܒܪ masc.), must not be confounded with a similar sounding termination of masculines (the emphatic state, § 45, 3) usually given in the lexicons, as the only masculine form in use. To distinguish this fem. form from the masculines, it is usually given with the termination ܬܐ; e. g. ܡܠܟܬܐ *the queen.* The forms with ܘ and ܝ have arisen by apocope from ܬܐ; e. g. ܛܝܒܘ *goodness,* ܩܪܝ *beam.* The last of the above mentioned endings ܬ is seldom used; e. g. ܡܢܬ *part.*

Rem.—1. The feminine ending ܬܳܐ is generally found in adjectives; e. g. ܛܳܒ masc. ܛܳܒܬܳܐ fem. If the word ends with ܐ, this letter is changed into ܝ, and forms ܝܬܐ; e. g. ܢܩܳܐ masc. ܢܩܝܬܳܐ fem. Gentile nouns and numerals ending with ܳܝ change that termination into ܳܝܬܳܐ; e.g. ܝܗܽܘܕܳܝ masc. ܝܗܽܘܕܳܝܬܳܐ fem. Nouns with ܬܐ final are masculine when ܬ is a radical letter of the noun; e. g. ܩܶܫܬܳܐ *bow*, ܨܶܒܬܳܐ *ornament*, ܙܰܝܬܳܐ *olive*.

Rem.—2. Many nouns with a masculine ending are feminine or common. They are usually given in the emphatic state (§ 45. 3); e. g. ܐܶܠܦܳܐ *ship*, ܐܽܘܪܚܳܐ *way*, ܐܶܠܥܳܐ *rib*, ܐܰܪܥܳܐ *earth*, ܐܰܓܳܢܳܐ *pitcher*, ܒܺܐܪܳܐ *well*, ܒܩܪܳܐ *herd*, ܣܕܪܳܐ *line of battle*, ܥܶܕܳܢܳܐ com. *time*, ܙܩܳܐ *leather bottle*, ܣܰܝܦܳܐ *sword*, com., ܡܰܘܒܠܳܐ *burden*, ܟܰܟܪܳܐ *talent*, ܟܺܐܦܳܐ *stone*, ܟܰܪܣܳܐ *belly*, ܠܶܫܳܢܳܐ com. *tongue*, ܢܰܦܫܳܐ *soul*, ܢܽܘܪܳܐ *fire*, ܣܰܗܪܳܐ com. *moon*, ܬܰܪܣܳܐ *shield*, ܣܳܣܳܐ com. *moth*, ܣܽܘܟܳܐ *branch*, ܥܰܪܣܳܐ *bed*, ܪܽܘܚܳܐ com. *wind*, ܪܶܬܝܬܳܐ com. *terror*, ܪܽܩܺܝܥܳܐ com. *firmament*, ܫܝܽܘܠ *hades*, ܫܽܘܚܬܳܐ *rust*, ܫܡܰܝܳܐ com. *heaven*, ܫܶܡܫܳܐ com. *sun*, ܫܽܘܫܰܢ *lily*. Names of animals also are of the common gender; e. g. ܚܡܳܪܳܐ *an ass*, ܓܰܡܠܳܐ *a camel*; also the cardinal numbers from 20 to 100. Greek nouns retain their gender; e. g. ܣܽܘܢܗܳܕܽܘܣ σuvoδoς, ܕܺܝܰܬܺܩܺܐ διαθηκη. In general, those nouns are considered as feminine which come from the feminine of the Hebrew, ending in ָה, and all of those nouns which, in the emphatic state, end in ܬܐ (§ 45. 3).

§ 44. *Number of Nouns.*

There are two numbers in Syriac, the singular and plural. There are, indeed, four dual forms, taken from the Hebrew, ending in ـܝܢ (ܬܪܝܢ masc. *two*, ܬܪܬܝܢ fem. *two*, ܡܐܬܝܢ *two hundred*, and ܡܨܪܝܢ *Egypt*); but they cannot be considered as a special form of the language. Pairs are usually expressed by the plural, and duality by the numeral *two*.

The plural of masculines is formed by annexing the syllable ـܝܢ to the noun sing.; e. g. ܛܘܪ̈ܝܢ *mountains*, from ܛܘܪ; that of the feminine by ـܢ (instead of ܐ); e. g. ܒܬܘܠܬܐ *virgin*, plur. ܒܬܘ̈ܠܢ.

Rem. 1. Plural masculines of derivatives from Verbs ܠܐ, ending with ܝܐ and ـܝ, terminate in ـܝܢ; e. g. ܛܠܝܐ *boy*, plur. ܛܠ̈ܝܝܢ; ܡܫܪܝ *dwelling*, plur. ܡܫܪ̈ܝܢ. Feminines ending in ܘ and ܬܐ take ܘ̈ܬܐ; e. g. ܡܠܟܘܬܐ *kingdom*, plur. ܡܠܟܘ̈ܬܐ: those ending in ـܝܬܐ take ـ̈ܝܬܐ; e. g. ܒܪܝܬܐ *creature*, plur. ܒܪ̈ܝܬܐ. Nouns derived from Verbs ܥܥ, if the doubled consonant appear again in the plural, take *Linea occultans* under the first of the similar letters; e. g. ܝܡ̈ܡܝܢ from ܝܡܐ *sea*, ܥܡ̈ܡܝܢ from ܥܡܐ *people*.

Rem. 2. Some masculines form the plural in the same manner as feminines. Here belong: ܐܣܝܐ *physician*, plur. ܐܣ̈ܘܬܐ; ܐܘܪܝܐ *crib*, plur. ܐܘܪ̈ܝܘܬܐ; ܐܪܝܐ *lion*, plur. ܐܪ̈ܝܘܬܐ; ܐܬܪ *place*, plur. ܐܬܪ̈ܘܬܐ; ܚܘܝܐ *snake*, plur. ܚܘ̈ܘܬܐ; ܟܘܕܢܐ *mule*, plur. ܟܘܕ̈ܢܘܬܐ; ܟܘܪܣܝܐ *throne*, plur. ܟܘܪ̈ܣܘܬܐ; ܠܠܝܐ *night*, plur. ܠܠ̈ܘܬܐ; ܗܕܡܐ *member*, plur. ܗܕ̈ܡܘܬܐ; ܪܥܝܐ *herdsman*, plur. (as a part. ܪ̈ܥܝܢ) ܪ̈ܥܘܬܐ; ܫܩܝܐ *cup-bearer*, plur. ܫܩ̈ܝܘܬܐ, &c. (Compare *Agrell*, *Comment. de varietate generis et numeri*, p. 68; and upon the absolute and emphatic states, their form and use, see § 45. 1. 3.)

Rem.—3. The following feminines form the plural like masculines; *a*) by rejecting the feminine ending of the emphatic singular (§ 45. 3), ܐܡܬܐ *ell*, ܐܡܝܢ; (ܐܢܬܬܐ *woman*, ܢܫܐ); ܐܣܬܐ *wall*, ܐܣܐ; ܓܢܬܐ *garden*, ܓܢܐ; ܓܘܡܪܬܐ *coal*, ܓܘܡܪܐ; ܕܘܩܠܬܐ *fig-basket*, ܕܩܠܝܢ; ܕܡܥܬܐ *tear*, ܕܡܥܐ; ܚܘܛܬܐ *thorn*, ܚܘܛܐ; ܚܛܬܐ *wheat*, ܚܛܐ; ܟܘܬܐ *window*, ܟܘܐ; ܠܒܢܬܐ *tile*, ܠܒܢܐ; ܠܓܬܐ *basin*, ܠܓܐ; ܡܓܠܬܐ *leaf* (*of paper*), ܡܓܠܐ; ܡܓܠܬܐ *sickle*, ܡܓܠܐ; ܡܢܣܘܠܬܐ *sieve*, ܡܢܣܘܠܐ; ܡܠܬܐ *word*, ܡܠܐ; ܣܥܪܬܐ *hair*, ܣܥܪܐ; ܡܥܪܬܐ *cave*, ܡܥܪܐ; ܣܥܪܬܐ *barley*, ܣܥܪܐ; ܣܦܝܢܬܐ *ship*, ܣܦܝܢܐ; ܥܛܟܬܐ *cluster* (*of grapes*), ܥܛܟܐ; ܥܪܩܬܐ *thong*, ܥܪܩܐ; ܦܓܘܪܬܐ *bridle*, ܦܓܘܪܐ; ܩܠܦܬܐ *bark*, ܩܠܦܐ; ܦܘܓܬܐ *almond*, ܦܘܓܐ; ܫܢܬܐ *year*, ܫܢܝܢ; ܫܥܬܐ *hour*, ܫܥܝܢ; ܬܐܢܬܐ *fig*, ܬܐܢܐ, etc.; *b*) by retaining ܬ; e. g. ܒܙܬܐ *booty*, ܒܙܬܐ; ܓܥܬܐ *cry*, ܓܥܬܐ; ܚܙܬܐ *sight*, ܚܙܬܐ; ܠܘܬܐ *noxious means*, ܠܘܬܐ; ܣܢܝܘܬܐ *ugliness*, ܣܢܝܘܬܐ; ܨܦܬܐ *care*, ܨܦܬܐ; ܩܪܬܐ *calling*, ܩܪܬܐ; ܫܘܚܬܐ *rust*, ܫܘܚܬܐ (see *Agrell*, *passim*, p. 70. *sq.*)

Rem.—4. Some nouns form a double plural (the feminine form sometimes having a metaphorical meaning); e. g. ܐܒ *father*, ܐܒܗܝ and ܐܒܗܘܗܝ; ܚܝܠ *army*, ܚܝܠܝ and ܚܝܠܘܗܝ; ܚܕܝܐ *breast*, ܚܕܝܝ and ܚܕܘܗܝ; ܙܒܢ *time*, ܙܒܢܝ and ܙܒܢܝ (*times*, *turns in repetition*); ܐܝܕ *hand*, ܐܝܕܝ and ܐܝܕܘܗܝ (*gripe of the hand*); ܝܘܡ *day*, ܝܘܡܝ and ܝܘܡܝ; ܠܒܐ *heart*, ܠܒܝ and ܠܒܘܗܝ; ܡܪܐ *lord*, ܡܪܝ and ܡܪܘܗܝ; ܢܗܪ *stream*, ܢܗܪܝ and ܢܗܪܘܗܝ; ܥܐܕܐ *feast*, ܥܐܕܝ and ܥܐܕܝ; ܥܝܢܐ *eye*, ܥܝܢܝ and ܥܝܢܝ (*fountain*); ܥܩܒܐ *heel*, ܥܩܒܝ and ܥܩܒܝ; ܩܪܢܐ *horn*, ܩܪܢܝ and ܩܪܢܝ (*corner*); ܫܡܐ *name*, ܫܡܗܝ and ܫܡܗܘܗܝ, etc. Some *masculines* as in some of the above examples, take ܘ or ܗ between the plural ending and the last radical. Also some *feminines* in ܬܐ take ܘ and ܗ before the plural ending; e.g. ܐܘܡܬܐ *people*, ܐ̈ܘܡܘܬܐ; ܡܢܬܐ *part*, ܡ̈ܢܘܬܐ; ܢܟܣܬܐ *offering*, ܢܟ̈ܣܘܬܐ; ܐܡܐ *mother*, ܐܡ̈ܗܬܐ; ܐܡܬܐ *handmaid*, ܐܡ̈ܗܬܐ (compare § 49). Sometimes ܝ is inserted; e. g. ܕܒܘܪܝܬܐ *bee*, ܕܒܘܪ̈ܝܬܐ; ܕܘܟܬܐ *place*, ܕܘܟ̈ܝܬܐ; ܣܘܣܬܐ *mare*, ܣܘܣ̈ܝܬܐ, etc.

Rem.—5. The composites (§42.1) form the plural in such a manner that either; *a*) the last part of the composite is inflected; e.g. ܒܝܬ ܩܦܣ̈ܐ *granary*, or; *b*) the first part; e.g. ܒܢ̈ܝܢܫܐ *mankind*, or; *c*) both parts; e.g. ܒܢ̈ܬ ܩܠ̈ܐ *tattling*.

Rem. 6.—Some words only occur in the plural; e.g. ܡ̈ܝܐ *water*, ܚ̈ܝܐ *life*, ܐ̈ܦܐ *face*, ܕܡ̈ܝܐ *worth*.

Rem. 7.—Some singular names (*collectives*) take the plural mark, *Ribui* (§ 6); e. g. ܪ̈ܟܫܐ *horses*, ܒ̈ܥܝܪܐ *cattle*, ܥ̈ܢܐ *sheep*. Amira (p. 95) also places here ܦܪ̈ܚܐ *birds* and ܒ̈ܩܪܐ *draft-cattle*.

Rem. 8. Greek nouns, without regard to gender, take the Syriac plural ending of masculines in ܐ̈; e. g. ܐܦܝܣܩܘ̈ܦܐ ἐπισκοποι, ܦܠܓ̈ܐ φαλαγγες, ܕܘܓ̈ܡܐ δογματα. Less frequently do they take the plural terminations of feminines in ܬܐ; e.g. ܡܟܢ̈ܘܬܐ μηχαναι, ܐܣܛܕ̈ܘܬܐ σταδια. Letters which constitute the Greek singular terminations are commonly omitted; but in some instances retained; e. g. ܢܘܡ̈ܘܣܐ νομοι from νομος. The plural terminations δες and τες, from ις and ας, are represented by ܕ̈ܐ and ܛ̈ܐ; e. g. ܩܠܝ̈ܕܐ χλειδες from χλεις; ܐܢܕܪܝܢ̈ܛܐ ἀνδριαντες from ἀνδριας. The Syriac often retains the termination of the Greek plural and of the cases, representing the accusative ας (first declension) by ܣ, ܐܣ, ܘܣ and ܐܘܣ; e. g. ܙܘܢܐܣ ζωνας, ܦܝܠܐܣ φιαλας, ܐܬܝܢܐܣ 'Αθηνας, ܩܢܟܪܐܘܣ Κεγχρεας; οι and ους (second declension) by ܘ and

ـܘܣ; e. g. ܐܣܛܘܐܝܟܘ Στωϊχοι, ܦܝܠܝܦܦܘܣ Φιλιππους; and neuters of this declension by ܐ; e. g. ܩܦܠܐܐ κεφαλαια; the genitive by ܘܢ; e.g. ܐܪܟܝܘܢ ἀρχειων; ες and ας of the third declension are represented by ܝܣ, ܣ, ܐܣ and ܘܣ; e.g. ܩܣܪܣ Καισαρας, ܦܠܟܐܣ πλακας, ܗܠܝܢܘܣ Ἑλληνας; εις from the singular in ις is represented by ܝܣ; e. g. ܐܗܪܣܝܣ αἱρεσεις; and the neuters ending in ατα, are represented by ܛܐ and ܐܛܐ; e. g. ܕܘܓܡܛܐ and ܕܘܓܡܐܛܐ δογματα. Some of these plural endings occur in Latin nouns; e. g. ܐܢܘܢܐܣ *annonæ;* ܩܣܛܪܐܣ *castra.* The same is true in respect to Syriac words; e. g. ܓܢܣ *garden,* for ܓܢܐ from ܓܢܬܐ (comp. *Agrell Otiol. Syr. p.* 46—49).

---

§ 45. *Different Relations (States) of the Noun.*

1. Besides the absolute and construct state of the Hebrew, of which the latter marks the genitive, there is in Syriac and Chaldee, an *emphatic state.* It originally marked the noun with the definite article. It also occurs where we should not expect to find the definite article.

REM.—The indefinite article is expressed by the absolute state, or by ܚܕ *one.* There are many nouns which never, or very seldom, occur in the absolute state; e. g. ܚܘܡܐ *heat,* ܩܘܡܐ *situation,* ܬܘܪܐ *bull,* ܡܘܬܐ *death,* etc.

2. The construct state; *a*) of nouns masc. sing., does not differ from the absolute state; e. g. ܛܒ *good;* but in the

plural, the ending ـܝܢ is changed into ـܝ; e. g. ܡܠܟܝ construct state from ܡܠܟܝܢ. Nouns masc., which form the plural by ـ̈ܝܢ (§ 44. Rem. 1), change that termination into ـܝ; e.g. ܩܪ̈ܝ from ܩܪ̈ܝܢ; *b*) in the fem. sing., ـܐ of the absolute state is changed into ܬ; e. g. ܡܠܟܬ from ܡܠܟܐ. To the terminations ܘ and ـܝ only ܬ is added; e. g. ܡܠܟܘܬ from ܡܠܟܘ, ܩܪܝܬ from ܩܪܝ. In the plural, ܬ is appended instead of ܢ; e.g. ܡܠܟܬ from ܡܠܟܢ.

3. The characteristic of the emphatic state, for both genders and numbers, is final ܐ (= ה the Hebrew article). This is; *a*) attached to the sing. of nouns masc. with ـ preceding; e.g. ܥܡܐ from ܥܡ *people*. In the plural the noun masc. takes the termination ـ̈ܐ with the falling away of ـܝ; e. g. ܓܒܪ̈ܐ *the men*, (from the constr. state ܓܒܪ̈ܝ) from ܓܒܪ; *b*) in the emphatic state fem. sing. and plur. ـܐ is attached to the construct state. In the sing., ـ falls away before ܬ; e. g. ܡܠܟܘܬܐ from constr. state ܡܠܟܘܬ. In the plural, ـ is retained before ܬ; e. g. ܡܠܟܘ̈ܬܐ from ܡܠܟܘ̈ܬ.

Rem. 1.—The emphatic state plur. masc. ends in ـܝ̈ܐ in nouns which take ـ̈ܝܢ in the plural, (§ 44. Rem. 1); e. g. ܡܟܣ̈ܝܐ from ܡܟܣ̈ܝܢ. Only three nouns take ـ̈ܝܐ instead of ـܝ̈ܐ; viz. ܛܠ̈ܝܐ *boys*, ܩܨ̈ܝܐ *fragments*, and ܚܕ̈ܝܐ *breast*, from the emphat. sing. ܛܠܝܐ, ܩܨܝܐ, ܚܕܝܐ. The emphatic forms ܡܝ̈ܐ *water*, and ܫܡܝ̈ܐ *heaven*, belong here. Buxtorf cites yet a third form, with ـ̈ܝܐ; e. g. Rom. ix. 24. ܥܡ̈ܡܐ; 26. ܒܢ̈ܝܐ; Ephes. ii. 11. ܐܡ̈ܡܐ. But these forms are not recognized by Amira, and the form in ـܝ̈ܐ should perhaps be restored in these cases, as more correct. The following should be noted as irregular emphatic plural forms: ܐܚ̈ܐ

from ܦܐܪܐ *fruit*, ܪܝܚܬܐ from ܪܝܚܐ *odor*, ܚܙܘܬܐ from ܚܙܘܐ *sight*, ܒܝܬܐ from ܒܝܬܐ *house*, etc.

REM. 2.—Feminines with masculine endings (§ 43. Rem.2), form the emphatic state like masculines by attaching the termination ܐ; e.g. ܐܪܥ *earth*, emphat. state ܐܪܥܐ; ܒܘܪܟ *knee*, emphat. state ܒܘܪܟܐ. Before the ending ܬܐ of the fem. absol., ܘ is inserted and quiesces in ‑; e.g. ܚܕܘܬܐ from ܚܕܘ *joy*. Forms with ܝܐ take ܝܬܐ. Some words in the emphatic form take ܘ before the last radical; e.g. ܡܐܟܘܠܬܐ from ܡܐܟܠܐ *food*. Feminines which are formed from masculines, like ܥܒܕܬܐ from ܥܒܕ, and especially adjectives, form the emphatic state fem., by affixing the syllable ܬܐ to the masc. absol.; e.g. ܛܒܬܐ (from ܛܒ masc). Adjectives in ܝܐ change this termination into ܝ; e.g. ܛܟܝܬܐ from ܛܟܐ *dull*. Those in ܢ take ܝ after ܢ; e.g. ܡܪܚܡܢܝܬܐ from ܡܪܚܡܢ *compassionate*. In the emphat. state plur., some words change ܝ before ܬ into ܘ; e.g. ܢܩܘܬܐ from ܢܩܝܐ *sheep*. Some take ܘ; e.g. ܡܢܘܬܐ from ܡܢܬ *part*. Others insert ܝ; e.g. ܡܐܨܪܝܬܐ from ܡܐܨܪܬܐ *bundle*.

REM. 3.—The emphatic form is found even before the genitive, which is formed by ܕ; e.g. ܥܒܕܐ ܕܡܠܟܐ *servant of the king* (vid. Syntax, § 73).

Table of the Different Relations (States) of the Noun.

(§§ 45 and 48).

MASCULINES.

A. Nouns of one and two syllables with immutable vowels. (Decl. 1. § 48).

Plural.			*Singular.*		
emphat.	constr.	absol.	emphat.	constr. and absol.	
ܪܫܐ	ܪܫܝ	ܪܫܝܢ	ܪܫܐ	ܪܫ	*Head.*
ܡܐܢܐ	ܡܐܢܝ	ܡܐܢܝܢ	ܡܐܢܐ	ܡܐܢ	*Vessel.*
ܓܢܒܐ	ܓܢܒܝ	ܓܢܒܝܢ	ܓܢܒܐ	ܓܢܒ	*Thief.*
ܝܪܘܩܐ	ܝܪܘܩܝ	ܝܪܘܩܝܢ	ܝܪܘܩܐ	ܝܪܘܩ	*Herb.*
ܢܙܝܪܐ	ܢܙܝܪܝ	ܢܙܝܪܝܢ	ܢܙܝܪܐ	ܢܙܝܪ	*Nazarite.*
ܥܡܡܐ	ܥܡܡܝ	ܥܡܡܝܢ	ܥܡܐ	ܥܡ	*Nation.*

B. Nouns in which $\acute{}$ and $\hat{}$ of the ultimate syllable fall away, but the vowel of the penultimate is retained (Decl. II).

ܟܟܪܐ	ܟܟܪܝ	ܟܟܪܝܢ	ܟܟܪܐ	ܟܟܪ	*Talent.*
ܣܗܕܐ	ܣܗܕܝ	ܣܗܕܝܢ	ܣܗܕܐ	ܣܗܕ	*Witness.*
ܐܝܕܐ	ܐܝܕܝ	ܐܝܕܝܢ	ܐܝܕܐ	ܐܝܕ	*Hand.*
ܡܕܒܚܐ	ܡܕܒܚܝ	ܡܕܒܚܝܢ	ܡܕܒܚܐ }	ܡܕܒܚ	*Altar.*

C. Nouns in which ◌̄ (in gutturals ◌̄) of the ultimate syllable falls away, and the vowel ◌̄ appears over the antepenultimate radical consonant. (Decl III).

ܩܛܝܠܐ ܩܛܝܠܝ ܩܛܝܠܝܢ ܩܛܝܠܐ ܩܛܝܠ (*One dead*).

D. Segholate forms, which begin with a vacant consonant, over which the original ◌̄ or ◌̄ reappears in inflection, or ܘ is assumed in their stead (Decl. IV).

ܡܠܟܐ	ܡܠܟܝ	ܡܠܟܝܢ	ܡܠܟܐ	ܡܠܟ	*King.*
ܪܡܙܐ	ܪܡܙܝ	ܪܡܙܝܢ	ܪܡܙܐ	ܪܡܙ	*Beck.*
ܩܘܕܫܐ	ܩܘܕܫܝ	ܩܘܕܫܝܢ	ܩܘܕܫܐ	ܩܘܕܫ	*Holiness.*
ܒܥܠܐ	ܒܥܠܝ	ܒܥܠܝܢ	ܒܥܠܐ	ܒܥܠ	*Master.*
ܝܘܡܐ	ܝܘܡܝ	ܝܘܡܝܢ	ܝܘܡܐ	ܝܘܡ	*Day.*
ܥܝܢܐ	ܥܝܢܝ	ܥܝܢܝܢ	ܥܝܢܐ	ܥܝܢ	*Eye.*
ܛܡܐܐ	ܛܡܐܝ	ܛܡܐܝܢ	ܛܡܐܐ	ܛܡܐ	*Impure.*

E. Nouns derived from Verbs ܠܐ ending with ܐ, ܝ, ܝ, in which ܐ passes into ܝ and is movable as in both the other forms (Decl. V).

ܪܥܝܐ	ܪܥܝ	ܪܥܝܢ	ܪܥܝܐ	ܪܥܐ	*that grazes.*
ܪܥܘܬܐ	ܪܥܘܬ	ܪܥܘܝ	ܪܥܝܐ +	ܪܥܐ	*Herdsman.*
ܡܫܠܝܐ	ܡܫܠܝ	ܡܫܠܝܢ	ܡܫܠܝܐ	ܡܫܠܝ	*Abandoned.*
*	*	*	ܫܠܝܐ	ܫܠܝ	*Rest.*
ܫܒܝܐ	ܫܒܝ	ܫܒܝܢ	ܫܒܝܐ	ܫܒܝ	*Prisoner.*

FEMININES.

A. Nouns with immutable vowels (ܘ, ܝ, etc.) before the ending ܬܐ (Decl. I).

ܒܬܘܠܬܐ *Virgin,* ܟܠܬܐ *Bride,* ܡܕܝܢܬܐ *City.*

Plural.			*Singular.*		
emphat.	constr.	absol.	emphat.	constr.	absol.
ܒܬܘܠܬܐ	ܒܬܘܠܬ	ܒܬܘܠܢ	ܒܬܘܠܬܐ	ܒܬܘܠܬ	ܒܬܘܠܐ
ܟܠܬܐ	ܟܠܬ	ܟܠܢ	ܟܠܬܐ	ܟܠܬ	ܟܠܐ
ܡܕܝܢܬܐ	ܡܕܝܢܬ	ܡܕܝܢܢ	ܡܕܝܢܬܐ	ܡܕܝܢܬ	ܡܕܝܢܐ

B. Nouns, whose final syllable begins with two consonants, which, in the emphat. state sing. have ܶ or ܰ inserted between them (Decl. II).

ܐܪܡܠܬܐ *Widow,* ܡܪܟܒܬܐ *Chariot,* ܙܕܩܬܐ *Alms.*

ܐܪܡܠܬܐ	ܐܪܡܠܬ	ܐܪܡܠܢ	ܐܪܡܠܬܐ	ܐܪܡܠܬ	ܐܪܡܠܐ
ܡܪܟܒܬܐ	ܡܪܟܒܬ	ܡܪܟܒܢ	ܡܪܟܒܬܐ	ܡܪܟܒܬ	ܡܪܟܒܐ
ܙܕܩܬܐ	ܙܕܩܬ	ܙܕܩܢ	ܙܕܩܬܐ	ܙܕܩܬ	ܙܕܩܐ

C. Nouns, in whose emphat. state, the vowel of the first syllable is moved forward to the second vacant consonant (Decl. III).

ܚܒܪܬܐ *Partner,* ܥܓܠܬܐ *Cow.*

ܚܒܪܬܐ	ܚܒܪܬ	ܚܒܪܢ	ܚܒܪܬܐ	ܚܒܪܬ	ܚܒܪܐ
ܥܓܠܬܐ	ܥܓܠܬ	ܥܓܠܢ	ܥܓܠܬܐ	ܥܓܠܬ	ܥܓܠܐ

D. Derivatives of Verbs ܠ̈ ending in ܝܐ and ܘܐ, whose ܝ and ܘ in the emphat. state sing. quiesce in ِ and ُ (Decl. IV).

ܨܘܚܝܐ *Blame*, ܚܝܘܐ *Animal*, ܛܠܝܐ *Girl*.

ܨܘܚ̈ܝܬܐ	ܨܘܚ̈ܝܬ	ܨܘܚ̈ܝܢ	ܨܘܚܝܬܐ	ܨܘܚܝܬ	ܨܘܚܝܐ
ܚ̈ܝܘܬܐ	ܚ̈ܝܘܬ	ܚ̈ܝܘܢ	ܚܝܘܬܐ	ܚܝܘܬ	ܚܝܘܐ
ܛܠ̈ܝܬܐ	ܛܠ̈ܝܬ	ܛܠ̈ܝܢ	ܛܠܝܬܐ	ܛܠܝܬ	ܛܠܝܐ

E. Derivatives of Verbs ܠ ending in ܘ and ܝ (ܬ), beginning with two consonants, and having ܘ and ܝ movable in the plural (Decl. V).

ܨܒܘ *Thing*, ܡܚܘ *Plague*, ܒܪܝ *Creature*. ܨܠܘ *Request*, ܡܢܬ *Part*, ܡܪܘ *Dominion*.

ܨ̈ܒܘܬܐ	ܨ̈ܒܘܬ	ܨ̈ܒܘܢ	ܨܒܘܬܐ	ܨܒܘܬ	ܨܒܘ
ܡ̈ܚܘܬܐ	ܡ̈ܚܘܬ	ܡ̈ܚܘܢ	ܡܚܘܬܐ	ܡܚܘܬ	ܡܚܘ
ܒܪ̈ܝܬܐ	ܒܪ̈ܝܬ	ܒܪ̈ܝܢ	ܒܪܝܬܐ	ܒܪܝܬ	ܒܪܝ
ܨܠ̈ܘܬܐ	ܨܠ̈ܘܬ	ܨܠ̈ܘܢ	ܨܠܘܬܐ	ܨܠܘܬ	ܨܠܘ
ܡ̈ܢܘܬܐ	ܡ̈ܢܘܬ	ܡ̈ܢܘܢ	ܡܢܬܐ	ܡܢܬ	ܡܢܬ
ܡܪ̈ܘܬܐ	ܡܪ̈ܘܬ	ܡܪ̈ܘܢ	ܡܪܘܬܐ	ܡܪܘܬ	ܡܪܘ

§ 46. *Nouns with Suffixes.*

The noun, in taking suffixes (see § 16. 2. B. and table of suffixes, § 16), undergoes the following changes:

1. In masculines; *a*) the suff. in the sing., is attached to the emphatic state, with the falling away of ܐ; e. g. ܡܰܠܟܳܐ (from ܡܶܠܶܟ), with the suffix ܡܰܠܟܳܟ. In decl. I. III. IV. V. (§ 48. A) the radical vowels are not changed. In nouns of decl. II., the final vowel of the absolute state ◌ܰ or ◌ܶ, re-appears before the suffix of the 1 sing. and 2 and 3 plural; e. g. ܢܟܶܣ, emphat. ܢܶܟܣܳܐ, with suffix ܢܟܶܣܝ; ܦܽܘܗܳܪ, emphat. ܦܽܘܗܪܳܐ, with suffix ܦܽܘܗܳܪܗܽܘܢ. So also monosyllabic nouns, which lose ◌ܰ or ◌ܶ in the emphatic state, take it again before the suffix of the 1 sing. and 2 and 3 plur.; e.g. ܩܰܫܛ, emphat. ܩܶܫܛܳܐ, with suffix ܩܰܫܛܝ, ܩܶܫܛܟ (ܦܰܪܝ from ܦܰܪ), etc. In nouns, derived from Verbs ܠܐ ending in ܝܐ, emphat. state ܝܳܐ (Decl. V), ܝ before the suffix of the 1 sing., 2 and 3 plur., quiesces in ◌ܺ; e. g. ܛܰܠܝܝ, ܛܰܠܝܗܽܘܢ from ܛܠܐ, emphat. ܛܰܠܝܳܐ; but before the other suffixes ܝ is movable; e. g. ܛܰܠܝܳܟ, ܛܰܠܝܶܗ; (and according to Syriac grammarians, ܝ is movable even before the suffix 1 sing; e.g. ܛܰܠܝܝ). The same is true also of nouns ending with ◌ܶܐ (passive participles of Pa. Aph. and Shaph. of Verbs ܠܐ, §32.1, §48 masculines, Decl. V); e.g. ܡܰܫܬܝܗܽܘܢ, ܡܰܫܬܝܟ (ܡܰܫܬܝܝ) from ܡܰܫܬܝ *drink.* These nouns with suffixes of the 1, sing. are pronounced like the absol. state; e. g. ܡܰܫܬܝ *my drink,* (ܟܽܘܪܣܝܝ *my throne* from ܟܽܘܪܣܝܳܐ is an exception). Here belong all the emphatic forms ending with ܝܳܐ, having a vacant consonant preceding, excepting ܡܳܪܝܳܐ *master*, which with a suffix is as follows: ܡܳܪܝ, ܡܳܪܟ, ܡܳܪܗ, ܡܳܪܗܽܘܢ, etc. Finally, in emphatic nouns ending in ܝܳܐ, having a vowel preceding, the general rule is followed; e.g. ܗܶܓܝܳܐ *reflection,*

with suffix ܗܘܝܢ, or ܒܪܘܝܐ *creator*, with suff. ܒܪܘܝܝ, ܒܪܘܝܢ. The same is true of nouns with ܐܐ for ܝܐ; e. g. ܩܘܫܐܐ with suff. ܩܘܫܐܝ, ܩܘܫܐܟ, ܩܘܫܐܗܘܢ, etc., plur. ܩܘܫܐܝ, ܩܘܫܐܝܢ. But in cases where the termination ܐܐ does not stand for ܝܐ, as in ܡܫܐܐ, ܐ takes Lin. occul. in suff. 1 sing. and 2 and 3 plur.; e. g. ܡܫܐܝ, ܡܫܐܟܘܢ, etc. In the other suff., and in the plur. with suff., the vowel of ܐ is thrown back upon the preceding vacant consonant; e. g. ܡܫܐܗܘܢ, ܡܫܐܝܢ, plur. ܡܫܐܝ, ܡܫܐܝܢ, etc.

b) Plural suffixes in the masc. are attached to the construct form (§ 45. 2. *a*) with which the suff. 1 sing. forms a crasis; e. g. ܡܠܟܝ. In the sing. masc., however, ܝ passes into ܘ; e. g. ܡܠܟܘܗܝ (also ܘܗܝ = Germ. aü (Engl. oi, *nearly*), according to *Lud. de Dieu*, p. 160, but not according to Amira); and in the 3 fem. ܝ before ܗ passes into ܝ; e. g. ܡܠܟܝܗ (§ 16. B). Plural nouns with ܝܢ, attach the suffix to the construct form ending in ܝ; e. g. ܟܠܝܢ with suff. ܟܠܝܢ, ܟܠܝܗܘܢ. So also in the emphatic ending with ܝܐ; e.g. ܟܠܝܢ, ܟܠܝܗܘܢ (see Lud. de Dieu, p. 163). Also plurals with ܬܐ; e.g. ܐܟܠܬܐ, with suff. ܐܟܠܬܝ and ܐܟܠܬܟ, and those plurals which, with the suffix of 1 sing., differ from the sing. with the same suff. only by taking Ribui; e.g. ܡܫܬܝܐ *drink*, with suff. ܡܫܬܝ; plur. emphat. ܡܫܬܝܐ with suff. ܡܫܬܝ and ܡܫܬܝܝ *my drinks*.

Rem. 1.—Collective nouns sing. with Ribui, take the suff. sing.; e.g. ܥܢܐ with suff. ܥܢܗ, ܥܢܝ. Only ܐܢܫܐ takes the suff. plur.; e. g. ܐܢܫܘܗܝ. Amira p. 213, supposes that ܩܘܪܝܐ with both suffixes belongs here.

Rem. 2. ܐܰܒ݂ܳܐ *father*, ܐܰܚܳܐ *brother*, ܚܡܳܐ *father-in-law*, are formed anomalously. The first two, with the suff. of the 1 sing., change ܰ into ܳ; e. g. ܐܳܒ݂ܝ. The last takes ܺ; e.g. ܚܡܺܝ. Final ܐ before the other suffixes is changed into ܘ; e. g. ܐܰܒ݂ܘܟ݂, ܐܰܒ݂ܘܟ݂ܝ, ܐܰܒ݂ܘܗ̄ܝ, ܐܰܒ݂ܘܗ̇, ܐܰܒ݂ܘܢ, etc.

2. In Feminines; *a*) the suffix in the sing. is attached to the form of the emphat. state with a union vowel preceding; e.g. ܐܰܪܡܠܬܶܗ from ܐܰܪܡܠܐ *widow*, emphat. state ܐܰܪܡܠܬܳܐ. The suffixes of the 1 sing. and of the 2 and 3 plur. are attached to the construct state without the union vowel, to avoid the concurrence of three vacant consonants; e. g. ܢܶܟ݂ܪ̈ܬܝ from ܢܶܟ݂ܪ̈ܐ, constr. state ܢܶܟ݂ܪ̈ܬ.

Rem.—From ܡܳܪܬܳܐ (emphat. state) *mistress*, is found ܡܳܪܬܗܽܘܢ. In ܒܰܪܬܳܐ *daughter*, constr. state, ܒܰܪܬ with the suff. of the 1 sing., ܰ moves forward from the first to the second consonant; e. g. ܒܪܰܬܝ. It should be remarked that the letter marked with Linea occultans is to be pronounced, if the above suffix occur; e. g. ܡܕܺܝܢ݈ܬܳܐ with suff. ܡܕܺܝܢܳܬܟ݂ܽܘܢ, ܒܪ݈ܬܳܐ with suff. ܒܪ݈ܬܝ. Amira asserts (p. 190) that the laterSyrians have the form ܡܕܺܝܢ݈ܬܗܽܘܢ, etc.

b) In the plural, feminines take singular suffixes; e. g. ܡܰܠܟ݁ܘܳܬܝ, ܡܰܠܟ݁ܘܳܬܳܟ݂, etc.

Rem.—In respect to the cardinal numbers (§ 50. 2), it should be remarked that they take both the sing. and plur. suffixes, forming with the first, possessive pronouns, and with the last, demonstrative pronouns; e.g. ܥܶܣܪ̈ܬܶܗ *his ten*, ܬܪ̈ܰܝܗܽܘܢ *those two*, ܬܰܪ̈ܬܰܝܗܶܝܢ *those two*, ܬܠܳܬ݂ܰܝܗܽܘܢ *those three*.

§ 47. *Declension of Nouns in General.*

Nouns are varied in respect to inflection (§§44.46) according to their form, either with or without any vowel changes. Thus they are divided into two principal classes, viz.; those with immutable and with mutable vowels. The latter class, on account of its diversities, may be arranged under several paradigms, and together with the former class, takes the place of the declensions of the western languages (comp. § 48).

---

§ 48. *Exhibition of Nouns according to Declension.*

A. Masculines.

Decl. I.—This includes all monosyllabic nouns as well as those having more syllables than one, with immutable vowels (ܝܺ, ܳ, ܽܘ, ܳܘ) e. g. ܪܺܝܫ *head,* ܡܳܪ *master,* ܡܚܽܘܫ *lean,* ܓܰܘ *midst,* ܦܽܘܠܳܓ *partition,* ܝܺܠܺܝܕ *native.* To the latter class belong likewise those nouns whose penult. syllable is either a close one; e. g. ܝܽܘܪܩܳܢ *herbage,* (gentile nouns with ܳܝ; e. g. ܢܳܨܪܳܝ *Nazarite*), or such as would have a close penult syllable, if the Syrians employed duplication of letters (= *Dagh. forte*); e. g. ܓܰܢܳܒ *thief.*

Rem.—Here also belong nouns derived from ܥܥ Verbs with ܰ, which in the plural, double the final radical letter, and mark the first of the two doubled letters with Lin. occult.; e. g. ܥܰܡ *nation,* plur. ܥܰܡܡܺܝܢ. But monosyllabic nouns having ܘ and ܝ, and in the emphat. state, which change ܺ and ܽ into ܰ, belong to segholate forms (Decl. IV); e.g. ܝܽܘܡ *day,* emphat. state ܝܰܘܡܳܐ; ܥܺܝܢ *eye,* emphat. state ܥܰܝܢܳܐ; as do those also in which under the same circumstances ܘ is transposed; e. g. ܩܽܘܕܫ *holiness,* emphat. state ܩܽܘܕܫܳܐ. In ܥܠܰܝܡ *young man,* ܓܕܺܝܳܐ *kid,* and ܦܰܪܕܰܝܣ *paradise,* ܺ falls away in the inflection and ܝ with ܰ preceding, forms *ai;* e. g. emphat. state ܥܠܰܝܡܳܐ, etc.

Decl. II. This includes nouns, with ܰ and ܶ, which have two consonants; e.g. ܫܡ *name,* or two syllables, of which the penult. is either a mixed one as in ܡܩܛܠ (part. pass. Aph.), ܡܥܫܢ *mighty;* or whose middle radical must be doubled; e.g. ܟܟܪ *a talent;* ܨܦܪ *sparrow;* or has an immutable vowel; e.g. ܥܠܡ *eternity;* ܣܗܕ *witness;* ܓܝܓܠ *wheel.* In these nouns, the vowel of the final syllable falls away, excepting in the sing. before the suff. of the 1 sing. and before the 2 and 3 plur.; e. g. emphat. state ܥܠܡܐ with suff. ܥܠܡܗ, ܥܠܡܝ, and ܥܠܡܟܘܢ.

Rem.—Here belongs also ܐܝܕ *hand,* emphat. state ܐܝܕܐ; plur. ܐܝܕܝܢ, etc. Forms also like ܡܕܒܚ *altar,* and ܡܕܒܚܐ belong here, which take a new syllable with ܶ over the first radical letter in consequence of an accumulation of consonants; e. g. ܡܕܒܚܐ (see § 15. 4). The following are examples: ܡܕܢܚ *morning,* ܡܦܬܚ *opening,* etc. From ܡܒܘܥ *fountain,* appears the emphat. state ܡܒܘܥܐ, plur. ܡܒܘܥܐ.

Decl. III. To this belong those nouns, which, throughout their inflection, lose ܶ (before gutt. ܰ) of the final syllable; but take ܰ as a helping vowel over the antepenultimate radical consonant, viz.; in participles Ethpe.; e. g. ܡܬܩܛܠ *dead,* emphat. state ܡܬܩܛܠܐ.

Decl. IV. Here are to be enumerated all nouns which correspond with Hebrew segholate forms (see Gesen. Lehrgeb. p. 568 sq). Such for the most part in Syriac, are monosyllabic nouns which begin with a vacant consonant, and have for their characteristic vowel ܰ or ܶ, which appears first in the emphat. state over the first radical. In this form the noun remains unchanged throughout its formations. They may as in Hebrew, be divided into derivatives of verbs with and without gutturals, and derivatives of ܥ"ܘ and ܥ"ܥ Verbs.

A) To the first class belong forms like ܡܠܶܟ *king*, emphat. state ܡܰܠܟܳܐ; ܣܦܰܪ *book*, emphat. state ܣܶܦܪܳܐ; ܝܠܶܕ *child*, emphat. state ܝܰܠܕܳܐ; with suff. ܡܰܠܟܶܗ, ܣܶܦܪܗܽܘܢ, ܝܰܠܕܝ. To the form with Hholem in Hebrew corresponds ܩܽܘܕܫ *holiness*, emphat. state ܩܽܘܕܫܳܐ; ܒܽܘܪܟ *knee*, emphat. state ܒܽܘܪܟܳܐ (comp. § 15. 2. B. b). The same applies :

B) In forms with gutturals; e.g. ܥܒܶܕ *slave*, emphat. state ܥܰܒܕܳܐ; ܒܥܶܠ *master*, emphat. state ܒܰܥܠܳܐ. Here belong also emphat.forms like ܐܰܪܥܳܐ *earth*, ܐܰܪܙܳܐ *cedar*, ܐܽܘܟܠܳܐ *food*, ܐܽܘܪܚܳܐ *way*.

C) Finally, derivatives of Verbs ܥ"ܝ and ܥ"ܘ lose ܶ or ܳ belonging to the middle quiescent radicals ܝ or ܘ. In connection with ܰ, ܝ and ܘ form the dipthongs *ai* and *au* ; e.g. ܥܶܝܢ *eye*, emphat. state ܥܰܝܢܳܐ; ܚܳܘܒ *guilt*, emphat.state ܚܰܘܒܳܐ (ܒܶܝܬ constr. state, *house*, emphat. ܒܰܝܬܳܐ).

Rem.—The following forms take ܶ, viz.: ܒܣܰܪ *flesh*, ܣܛܰܪ *side*, ܡܠܰܟ *counsel*, and the emphat. forms ܐܶܒܠܳܐ *mourning*, ܝܰܡܳܐ *sea*, ܐܶܕܪܳܐ *threshing floor*, ܐܶܠܦܳܐ *ship*, ܐܶܡܪܳܐ *lamb*; from ܐܒܶܠ, etc. Some words which would in Hebrew, take Pattah, in Syriac, take ܶ; e.g. ܪܶܓܠ *foot*, emphat.state ܪܶܓܠܳܐ, etc. ܐ is considered as a guttural when at the end of ܛܰܡܳܐ *impure*, emphat. state ܛܰܡܳܐܳܐ, plur. absol. ܛܰܡܳܐܺܝܢ, constr. ܛܰܡܳܐܰܝ̈, emphat. ܛܰܡܳܐ̈ܶܐ; and in the emphat. form ܬܶܕܐܳܐ, plur. ܬܶܕܐܺܝܢ (also ܬܰܕܐܺܝܢ) from the absolute form ܬܕܳܐ *grass*.

Decl. V. Here belong derivatives (mostly participles and infinitives) of Verbs ܠ"ܐ (comp. § 40.) ending in ܶܐ, ܝ and ܺܝ. The distinguishing characteristic is, that ܐ is changed into ܝ, and is movable as well as both the other endings in the emphat. state sing. and before the suffixes with the union vowel; e.g. ܪܳܥܶܐ emphat. state ܪܳܥܝܳܐ, with suff. ܪܳܥܝܶܗ. But before the suff. of the 1 sing. and 2 and 3 plur. ܐ quiesces in

—; e. g. ܓܠܝܗܘܢ. The same is true in the plur. which ends with ـܝ̈ (§ 44. Rem. 1) with the falling away of ܐ; e.g. ܓ̈ܠܝܟܝ. The suffix is attached to the emphatic state ending with ـܝܐ as well as to the constr. state ending with ـܝ. In respect to the changes of the vowels, it should be remarked that the form with ـܐ takes ـ in the emphatic state, if it be a monosyllable and begin with a vacant consonant; e. g. ܓܠܝܐ from ܓܠܐ *revealed.* In words of two or more syllables the preceding vowel remains unchanged; e. g. ܡܟܣܝܐ from ܡܟܣܐ, ܡܓܠܝܐ from ܡܓܠܐ. Monosyllabic nouns with ـܝ mute likewise retain their vowels; e.g. ܚܡܪܐ from ܚܡܪ *wine.* Finally nouns ending with ـܝ (part. pass. of Pa. and Aph. see § 32. 1), lose ـ in the emphat. state sing.; e. g. ܡܫܒܩܐ from ܡܫܒܩ *abandoned;* but ـ appears again in the emphat. state plur.; e. g. ܡܫܒܩ̈ܐ.

Rem.—From monosyllabic nouns ending with ـܐ we find forms with —; e. g. ܟܣܝܐ (Matt. vi. 4) from ܟܣܐ. Also from ܛܠܐ we have the plur. emphat. ܛ̈ܠܝܐ as though from ܛܠܝ. Here belongs also ܦ̈ܬܝܐ from the obsolete form ܦܬܐ, constr. state plur. ܦ̈ܬܝ. The part Pe. act. differs from the noun of the same form by being inflected as usual, while the noun, in the plur. takes the form of feminines of decl. IV., and ܐ is changed into ܘ movable with ـ preceding; e.g. ܪܥܐ *pasturing,* plur. ܪ̈ܥܝܢ, constr. ܪ̈ܥܝ, emphat. ܪ̈ܥܝܐ; ܪܥܐ *herdsman,* on the contrary, becomes in the plur. ܪ̈ܥܘܢ, ܪ̈ܥܘܬ, ܪ̈ܥܘܬܐ. From ܡܪܐ *master,* both forms of the plur. occur; the latter form in ܟܘܪܣܝܐ *throne.* The noun ܢܒܝܐ *prophet,* in the plur., contracts ـܝ and ܐ into ـܝ, ܢܒ̈ܝܐ; while the adjective ܫܦܝ takes yet another ܐ, emphat. ܫܦܝܐܐ, plur. ܫܦܝܐܝܢ, ܫܦܝܐܝ, ܫ̈ܦܝܐܐ.

B. Feminines.

Decl. I. This includes all the Feminines ending with ܬܐ, which have an immutable vowel in the penult syllable. In this case the penult syllable has either a vowel with a letter quiescing in it; e. g. ܒܬܘܠܐ *virgin*, or the noun is a derivative of Verbs ܥܥ, in which case in the plural, the first of the duplicate radicals reappears, and takes Linea occultans; e.g. ܥܠܐ (also ܥܠܠܐ) *pretense* from ܥܠ; ܟܠܐ *bride*, plur. ܟܠܠܢ. The suff. of the 1. sing. is appended to the constr.state without the union vowel; e. g. ܒܬܘܠܬܝ. The suff. in other persons is joined with the form of the emphat. state; e. g. ܒܬܘܠܬܟܘܢ, etc. (comp. § 46. 2).

Rem.—From ܟܘܬܝܢܐ *waistcoat*, appears the plur. ܟܘܬܝܢܝܢ as if from ܟܘܬܝܢܝܬܐ or ܟܘܬܝܢܝܬ. Some forms with final ܢܐ take Linea occult. in the emphat. state under ܢ; e.g. ܡܕܝܢܐ *city*, emphat. state ܡܕܝܢܬܐ; or ܢ falls entirely away as in ܐܚܪܢܐ *another*, emphatic state ܐܚܪܬܐ.

Decl. II. Here belong all nouns fem. whose final syllable begins with two consonants. They have the peculiarity, that between these two consonants, in the emphat. sing., ܰ or ܶ is inserted. This vowel is determined by the vowel belonging to corresponding masculine terminations; e. g. ܐܪܡܠܐ *widow*, (from ܐܪܡܠܐ masc.), emphat. state ܐܪܡܠܬܐ; ܡܠܟܐ (from ܡܠܟܐ masc.), emphat. state ܡܠܟܬܐ; before gutturals ܰ is always the vowel inserted between the two consonants in the emphat.; e.g. ܦܪܚܐ *fowl*, emphat. state ܦܪܚܬܐ. In the reception of suffixes this declension agrees with decl. I; e. g. ܐܪܡܠܬܝ, ܐܪܡܠܬܗ, ܡܠܟܬܝ and ܡܠܟܬܗ.

Rem.—Some insert ܘ; e. g. ܡܦܠܐ *fall*, emphat. ܡܦܘܠܬܐ. So too ܬܕܡܪܐ *wonder*, ܬܚܒܒܐ *love*.

Decl. III. This includes those nouns fem. whose vowel of the first syllable is moved forward, in the emphat. state to the second vacant consonant; e. g. ܚܒܪܐ *female companion*, emphat. ܚܒܪܬܐ; ܬܘܪܐ *cow*, emphat. ܬܘܪܬܐ. Nouns of this class, taking a suff. in the sing., are treated like nouns in decl. I. and II.

Rem. — Some nouns have several emphatic forms. Thus ܙܕܩܐ *alms*, has three emphatic forms; e. g. ܙܕܩܬܐ, ܙܕܩܬܐ, ܙܕܩܬܐ. In the same manner also are inflected ܩܘܪܒܐ *offering*, ܗܘܬܐ *terror*, ܢܩܒܐ *woman*, ܕܚܠܐ *fear*, etc. The following contractions in the emphat. state should be mentioned: ܚܕܬܐ for ܚܕܬܬܐ *new*, ܓܦܬܐ for ܓܦܢܬܐ from ܓܦܢܐ *vine*, ܠܒܢܬܐ for ܠܒܢܬܬܐ from ܠܒܢܐ *brick*.

Decl. IV. This includes fem. derivatives of Verbs ܠܐ̈ ending in ܝܐ and ܘܐ. It should be remarked in reference to them that the immutable vowel of the penult syllable is retained, and ܝ and ܘ, in the emphat. state sing., quiesce in ܺ and ܽ; e. g. ܚܘܣܝܬܐ from ܚܘܣܝܐ *reproach*, ܚܝܘܬܐ from ܚܝܘܐ *animal*. If the masc. be monosyllabic the vowel of the first syllable falls away; e. g. ܛܠܝܬܐ from ܛܠܝܐ *girl*, (ܛܠܐ masc.). But in the constr. state, and in all the plurals, ܝ and ܘ are movable; e. g. ܚܘܣܝܬ, ܚܝܘܬ, ܛܠܝܬ, plur., ܚܘܣܝܢ, etc.

Rem.—Here belongs also the participle act. of Pa. and Aph.; but the fem. participle pass. in the same conjugations, ending, in the masc., with ܰܝ, takes ܰ instead of ܺ in the emphat. state. With this vowel ܝ forms the dipthong *ai*; e. g. ܡܓܠܝܐ, emphat. ܡܓܠܝܬܐ from ܡܓܠܝ.

Decl. V. To this belong mostly monosyllabic derivatives of Verbs ܠܐ̈ ending with ܘ and ܝ (some end in ܬܐ), which begin with two consonants; e. g. ܡܚܘ *calamity*, ܒܪܝ *creature*. Also dissyllabic nouns belong here with immutable vowels in the penult syllable; e.g. ܙܟܘܬܐ *victory*, ܬܘܕܝܬܐ *thanks*, whose ܘ and ܝ quiesce, throughout in the sing. But in the plur. where ܘ and ܝ are movable, some nouns (derivatives of Pa.) take ܰ after the second radical letter; e. g. ܒܥܘܬܐ *entreaty*, plur. ܒܥܘܢ, ܒܥܘܬܐ, ܒܥܘܬܐ. Nouns ending with ܬܐ belong here, which in the plur. take ܘ with the falling away of ܬ; e. g. ܡܘܗܒܬܐ *offering*, plur. ܡܘܗܒܢ, ܡܘܗܒܬܐ, ܡܘܗܒܬܐ. Other nouns (derivatives of Pe.) take ܳ after the first radical letter; e.g. ܕܡܘܬܐ *resemblance*, plur. ܕܡܘܢ, ܕܡܘܬܐ, ܕܡܘܬܐ; or with gutturals following, they take ܰ; e. g. ܡܚܘܬܐ *blow*, plur. ܡܚܘܢ, etc.

Rem.—The same peculiarity of taking a new vowel is found also in ܫܘܠܛܢܐ *authority*, plur. ܫܘܠܛܢܝܢ, etc.; ܥܢܐ *sheep*, plur. ܥܢܘܢ and ܡܐܐ *a hundred*, plur. ܡܐܘܬܐ as if from ܥܢܘܐ and ܡܐܘܐ. So also in some nouns which are not derivatives of ܠܝ; e. g. ܦܠܓܘܬܐ *partition*, plur. ܦܠܓܘܢ; ܣܗܕܘܬܐ *testimony*, plur. ܣܗܕܘܬܐ, and even ܡܠܟܘܬܐ, ܡܠܟܘܢ, besides ܡܠܟܘܢ, and some others.

---

§ 49. *Anomalous Nouns.*

Some nouns of very frequent occurrence are inflected in a manner varying more or less from the above mentioned paradigms (§§ 47, 48). This arises either from an attempt to unite different ground-forms, or from the simple ground form conforming less closely to the general laws of inflection.

These nouns are the following:

MASCULINES.

Plural.			Singular.			
emphat.	constr.	absol.	emphat.	constr.	absol.	
ܐܒܗ̈ܐ / ܐܒܗܬܐ	ܐܒܗ̈ܝ / ܐܒܗܬ	ܐܒܗ̈ܝܢ / ܐܒܗܢ	ܐܒܐ	ܐܒ	ܐܒ	*Father.*
ܒ̈ܢܝܐ	ܒ̈ܢܝ	ܒ̈ܢܝܢ	ܒܪܐ	ܒܪ	ܒܪ	*Son.*
ܒ̈ܬܐ	ܒ̈ܬܝ	ܒ̈ܬܝܢ	ܒܝܬܐ	ܒܝܬ	ܒܝܬ	*House.*
ܫܡܗ̈ܐ / ܫܡܗܬܐ	ܫܡܗ̈ܝ / ܫܡܗܬ	ܫܡܗ̈ܝܢ / ܫܡܗܢ	ܫܡܐ	ܫܡ	ܫܡ	*Name.*
ܐܬܪ̈ܘܬܐ	ܐܬܪ̈ܘܬ	ܐܬܪ̈ܘܢ	ܐܬܪܐ	ܐܬܪ	ܐܬܪ	*Place.*

FEMININES.

emphat.	constr.	absol.	emphat.	constr.	absol.	
ܐܡܗܬܐ	ܐܡܗܬ	ܐܡܗܢ	ܐܡܐ	ܐܡ	ܐܡ	*Mother.*
ܒ̈ܢܬܐ	ܒ̈ܢܬ	ܒ̈ܢܢ	ܒܪܬܐ	ܒܪܬ	—	*Daughter.*
ܐܚ̈ܘܬܐ	ܐܚ̈ܘܬ	ܐܚ̈ܘܢ	ܚܬܐ	—	—	*Sister.*
ܐܡܗܬܐ	ܐܡܗܬ	ܐܡܗܢ	ܐܡܬܐ	ܐܡܬ	ܐܡܐ	*Maiden.*
ܐܡ̈ܐ	ܐܡ̈ܝ	ܐܡ̈ܝܢ	ܐܡܬܐ	ܐܡܬ	ܐܡܐ	*Ell.*
ܐܡܘܬܐ	ܐܡܘܬ	ܐܡܘܢ	ܐܘܡܬܐ	ܐܘܡܬ	ܐܘܡܐ	*People.*
ܫ̈ܢܐ	ܫ̈ܢܝ	ܫ̈ܢܝܢ	ܫܢܬܐ	ܫܢܬ	ܫܢܐ	*Year.*
ܣܦܘܬܐ	ܣܦܘܬ	ܣܦܘܢ	ܣܦܬܐ	—	—	*Lip.*
ܕܘܟ̈ܝܬܐ	ܕܘܟ̈ܝܬ	ܕܘܟ̈ܝܢ	ܕܘܟܬܐ	ܕܘܟܬ	ܕܘܟܐ	*Place.*

Paradigms of Nouns

A. Masculine Nouns.

Singular.	Decl. II.	Decl. IV.	Decl. V.	
Stat. absol.	ܣܳܗܶܕ	ܡܶܠܶܟ	ܛܠܳܐ	ܡܶܫܬܶܐ
	Witness.	*King.*	*Boy.*	*Drink.*
Suff.Sing. 1 c.	ܣܳܗܕܝ	ܡܰܠܟܝ	ܛܰܠܝܝ	ܡܶܫܬܝܝ
2 m.	ܣܳܗܕܳܟ	ܡܰܠܟܳܟ	ܛܰܠܝܳܟ	ܡܶܫܬܝܳܟ
2 f.	ܣܳܗܕܶܟܝ	ܡܰܠܟܶܟܝ	ܛܰܠܝܶܟܝ	ܡܶܫܬܝܶܟܝ
3 m.	ܣܳܗܕܶܗ	ܡܰܠܟܶܗ	ܛܰܠܝܶܗ	ܡܶܫܬܝܶܗ
3 f.	ܣܳܗܕܳܗ̇	ܡܰܠܟܳܗ̇	ܛܰܠܝܳܗ̇	ܡܶܫܬܝܳܗ̇
Suff.plur. 1 c.	ܣܳܗܕܰܢ	ܡܰܠܟܰܢ	ܛܰܠܝܰܢ	ܡܶܫܬܝܰܢ
2 m.	ܣܳܗܕܟܽܘܢ	ܡܰܠܟܟܽܘܢ	ܛܰܠܝܟܽܘܢ	ܡܶܫܬܝܟܽܘܢ
2 f.	ܣܳܗܕܟܶܝܢ	ܡܰܠܟܟܶܝܢ	ܛܰܠܝܟܶܝܢ	ܡܶܫܬܝܟܶܝܢ
3 m.	ܣܳܗܕܗܽܘܢ	ܡܰܠܟܗܽܘܢ	ܛܰܠܝܗܽܘܢ	ܡܶܫܬܝܗܽܘܢ
3 f.	ܣܳܗܕܗܶܝܢ	ܡܰܠܟܗܶܝܢ	ܛܰܠܝܗܶܝܢ	ܡܶܫܬܝܗܶܝܢ

(To the suff. 1 sing. of the forms ܛܠܳܐ and ܡܶܫܬܶܐ add ܛܰܠܝܝ and ܡܶܫܬܝܝ, compare ܡܶܫܬܝ § 46. 1. *a*).

Plural.	ܣܳܗܕܶܐ	ܡܰܠܟܶܐ	ܛܠܳܝܶܐ	
Suff.sing. 1 c.	ܣܳܗܕܰܝ	ܡܰܠܟܰܝ	ܛܠܳܝܰܝ	ܛܠܳܝܢܰܝ
2 m.	ܣܳܗܕܰܝܟ	ܡܰܠܟܰܝܟ	ܛܠܳܝܰܝܟ	ܛܠܳܝܢܰܝܟ
2 f.	ܣܳܗܕܰܝܟܝ	ܡܰܠܟܰܝܟܝ	ܛܠܳܝܰܝܟܝ	ܛܠܳܝܢܰܝܟܝ
3 m.	ܣܳܗܕܰܘܗܝ	ܡܰܠܟܰܘܗܝ	ܛܠܳܝܰܘܗܝ	ܛܠܳܝܢܰܘܗܝ
3 f.	ܣܳܗܕܶܝܗ̇	ܡܰܠܟܶܝܗ̇	ܛܠܳܝܶܝܗ̇	ܛܠܳܝܢܶܝܗ̇
Suff.plur. 1 c.	ܣܳܗܕܰܝܢ	ܡܰܠܟܰܝܢ	ܛܠܳܝܰܝܢ	ܛܠܳܝܢܰܝܢ
2 m.	ܣܳܗܕܰܝܟܽܘܢ	ܡܰܠܟܰܝܟܽܘܢ	ܛܠܳܝܰܝܟܽܘܢ	ܛܠܳܝܢܰܝܟܽܘܢ
2 f.	ܣܳܗܕܰܝܟܶܝܢ	ܡܰܠܟܰܝܟܶܝܢ	ܛܠܳܝܰܝܟܶܝܢ	ܛܠܳܝܢܰܝܟܶܝܢ
3 m.	ܣܳܗܕܰܝܗܽܘܢ	ܡܰܠܟܰܝܗܽܘܢ	ܛܠܳܝܰܝܗܽܘܢ	ܛܠܳܝܢܰܝܗܽܘܢ
3 f.	ܣܳܗܕܰܝܗܶܝܢ	ܡܰܠܟܰܝܗܶܝܢ	ܛܠܳܝܰܝܗܶܝܢ	ܛܠܳܝܢܰܝܗܶܝܢ

with Suffixes.

B. Feminine Nouns.

Comp. § 49.	Table.	Decl. 1.	Decl. IV.	Decl V.
ܒܪ	ܐܒ	ܒܬܘܠܬܐ	ܛܠܝܬܐ	ܒܥܘ
Son.	*Father.*	*Virgin.*	*Maiden.*	*Petition.*
ܒܪܝ	ܐܒܝ	ܒܬܘܠܬܝ	ܛܠܝܬܝ	ܒܥܘܬܝ
ܒܪܟ	ܐܒܘܟ	ܒܬܘܠܬܟ	ܛܠܝܬܟ	ܒܥܘܬܟ
ܒܪܟܝ	ܐܒܘܟܝ	ܒܬܘܠܬܟܝ	ܛܠܝܬܟܝ	ܒܥܘܬܟܝ
ܒܪܗ	ܐܒܘܗܝ	ܒܬܘܠܬܗ	ܛܠܝܬܗ	ܒܥܘܬܗ
ܒܪܗ	ܐܒܘܗ	ܒܬܘܠܬܗ	ܛܠܝܬܗ	ܒܥܘܬܗ
ܒܪܢ	ܐܒܘܢ	ܒܬܘܠܬܢ	ܛܠܝܬܢ	ܒܥܘܬܢ
ܒܪܟܘܢ	ܐܒܘܟܘܢ	ܒܬܘܠܬܟܘܢ	ܛܠܝܬܟܘܢ	ܒܥܘܬܟܘܢ
ܒܪܟܝܢ	ܐܒܘܟܝܢ	ܒܬܘܠܬܟܝܢ	ܛܠܝܬܟܝܢ	ܒܥܘܬܟܝܢ
ܒܪܗܘܢ	ܐܒܘܗܘܢ	ܒܬܘܠܬܗܘܢ	ܛܠܝܬܗܘܢ	ܒܥܘܬܗܘܢ
ܒܪܗܝܢ	ܐܒܘܗܝܢ	ܒܬܘܠܬܗܝܢ	ܛܠܝܬܗܝܢ	ܒܥܘܬܗܝܢ

Comp. § 49. Table.	Decl. 1.	Decl. IV.	Decl V.
ܡ̈ܝܐ	ܒܬܘ̈ܠܬܐ	ܛܠܝ̈ܬܐ	ܒܥ̈ܘܬܐ
Flood, Waters.			
ܡ̈ܝܝ	ܒܬܘ̈ܠܬܝ	ܛܠܝ̈ܬܝ	ܒܥ̈ܘܬܝ
ܡ̈ܝܟ	ܒܬܘ̈ܠܬܟ	ܛܠܝ̈ܬܟ	ܒܥ̈ܘܬܟ
*	ܒܬܘ̈ܠܬܟܝ	ܛܠܝ̈ܬܟܝ	ܒܥ̈ܘܬܟܝ
ܡ̈ܝܘܗܝ	ܒܬܘ̈ܠܬܗ	ܛܠܝ̈ܬܗ	ܒܥ̈ܘܬܗ
ܡ̈ܝܗ	ܒܬܘ̈ܠܬܗ	ܛܠܝ̈ܬܗ	ܒܥ̈ܘܬܗ
ܡ̈ܝܢ	ܒܬܘ̈ܠܬܢ	ܛܠܝ̈ܬܢ	ܒܥ̈ܘܬܢ
ܡ̈ܝܟܘܢ	ܒܬܘ̈ܠܬܟܘܢ	ܛܠܝ̈ܬܟܘܢ	ܒܥ̈ܘܬܟܘܢ
	ܒܬܘ̈ܠܬܟܝܢ	ܛܠܝ̈ܬܟܝܢ	ܒܥ̈ܘܬܟܝܢ
*	ܒܬܘ̈ܠܬܗܘܢ	ܛܠܝ̈ܬܗܘܢ	ܒܥ̈ܘܬܗܘܢ
ܡ̈ܝܗܘܢ, ܡ̈ܝܗܘܢ *	ܒܬܘ̈ܠܬܗܝܢ	ܛܠܝ̈ܬܗܝܢ	ܒܥ̈ܘܬܗܝܢ

§ 50. *Adjectives and Numerals.*

1. Adjectives being derivatives of verbs (see § 40. and tables) and having the same form as nouns, are inflected according to the same laws (see §§ 44, 45, 48). In respect to denominative adjectives, see § 41. 2.

Rem.—The Syriac has no special forms for the comparative and superlative. For the manner in which these are expressed, see Syntax § 77.

2. Numerals are either *cardinal* or *ordinal*. In the former we should notice the peculiarity, that masculines from 3 to 10, as in Hebrew, have feminine endings; but feminines, on the contrary, have masculine endings. From 20 to 100 there is only one form for both genders.

The numbers from 1 to 10 are the following:

CARDINALS.

Fem.	Masc.		Fem.	Masc.	
ܚܕܐ	ܚܕ	1.	ܫܬ	ܫܬܐ	6.
ܬܪܬܝܢ	ܬܪܝܢ	2.	ܫܒܥ	ܫܒܥܐ	7.
ܬܠܬ	ܬܠܬܐ	3.	ܬܡܢܐ	ܬܡܢܝܐ	8.
ܐܪܒܥ	ܐܪܒܥܐ	4.	ܬܫܥ	ܬܫܥܐ	9.
ܚܡܫ	ܚܡܫܐ	5.	ܥܣܪ	ܥܣܪܐ	10.

Rem.—Upon the union of these numerical words with suffixes, see § 46. 2. b. Rem.

The tens from 30 to 90 are expressed by the plural of the cardinals from 3 to 9; e. g. ܬܠܬܝܢ 30, ܐܪܒܥܝܢ 40, ܚܡܫܝܢ 50, ܫܬܝܢ 60, ܫܒܥܝܢ 70, ܬܡܢܝܢ 80, ܬܫܥܝܢ 90. The plural of 10 (ܥܣܪܝܢ) represents 20. All plurals are of the common gender. ܡܐܐ signifies 100, ܡܐܬܝܢ 200, ܬܠܬܡܐܐ or ܬܠܬ ܡܐܘܬܐ 300, etc., with the preceding unit in the feminine. ܐܠܦ signifies 1000 (instead of ܐܠܦ or ܐܠܦ, emphat. ܐܠܦܐ, plur. ܐܠܦܝܢ, ܐܠܦܐ); ܬܪܝܢ ܐܠܦܝܢ signifies

2000, ܬܠܬܐ ܐܠܦܝ̈ܢ 3000. etc. (with the preceding unit in the masculine).

The intermediate numbers from 11 to 19 are formed by the union of units with 10 in one word, in the following manner:

Fem.	Masc.		Fem.	Masc.	
ܚܕܥܣܪܐ	ܚܕܥܣܪ	11.	ܫܬܥܣܪܐ	ܫܬܥܣܪ ܫܬܬܥܣܪ	16.
ܬܪܬܥܣܪܐ	ܬܪܥܣܪ	12.	ܫܒܥܣܪܐ	ܫܒܥܣܪ	17.
ܬܠܬܥܣܪܐ	ܬܠܬܥܣܪ	13.	ܬܡܢܥܣܪܐ	ܬܡܢܥܣܪ ܬܡܢܬܥܣܪ	18.
ܐܪܒܥܣܪܐ	ܐܪܒܬܥܣܪ	14.	ܬܫܥܣܪܐ	ܬܫܥܣܪ	19.
ܚܡܫܥܣܪܐ	ܚܡܫܥܣܪ ܚܡܫܬܥܣܪ	15.			

The intermediate numbers from 21 to 29, 31 to 39, etc., are formed by the numeral representing the number of tens, followed by the numeral under ten preceded by ܘ; e. g. ܬܠܬܝܢ ܘܬܠܬܐ masc. 33, ܫܬܝܢ ܘܚܡܫ fem. 65. Sometimes the units precede; e. g. ܐܪܒܥܐ ܘܥܣܪܝܢ 24, etc. So if the number of numerical words combined be large, the greater numerals are always placed before the smaller; e. g. ܐܠܦ ܘܬܡܢܡܐܐ ܥܣܪܝ̈ܢ ܘܫܒܥܐ 1827.

3. The ordinal numbers, from 3 to 10, are formed from the cardinal numbers by adding the terminations ܝܐ masc., ܝܬܐ fem., and inserting ܝ before the ultimate radical. For *the first*, a particular word is used, and for *the second*, a form differing somewhat from the form of the cardinal for 2.

ORDINALS.

Fem.	Masc.		Fem.	Masc.	
ܩܕܡܝܬܐ	ܩܕܡܝܐ	*the first.*	ܫܬܝܬܝܬܐ	ܫܬܝܬܝܐ	*the sixth.*
ܬܪܝܢܝܬܐ	ܬܪܝܢܐ	*the second.*	ܫܒܝܥܝܬܐ	ܫܒܝܥܝܐ	*the seventh.*
ܬܠܝܬܝܬܐ	ܬܠܝܬܝܐ	*the third.*	ܬܡܝܢܝܬܐ	ܬܡܝܢܝܐ	*the eighth.*
ܪܒܝܥܝܬܐ	ܪܒܝܥܝܐ	*the fourth.*	ܬܫܝܥܝܬܐ	ܬܫܝܥܝܐ	*the ninth.*
ܚܡܝܫܝܬܐ	ܚܡܝܫܝܐ	*the fifth.*	ܥܣܝܪܝܬܐ	ܥܣܝܪܝܐ	*the tenth.*

The tens of ordinals from 20 are expressed, as in Hebrew, either by cardinal numbers or by the addition thereto of the terminations ـܝܐ masc., ـܝܬܐ fem.; e. g. ܥܣܪܝܢܝܐ, ܬܠܬܝܢܝܐ, ܐܪܒܥܝܢܝܐ, etc. The units are put after; e. g. ܬܠܬܝܐ ܥܣܪܝܢܝܐ.

The intermediate numbers from 11 to 19, etc., are formed by uniting the ordinal number 10 with a unit of the cardinals, into one word, the unit preceding; e. g. ܚܕܥܣܪܝܬܐ fem., ܚܕܥܣܪܝܐ masc. *the eleventh*, ܬܪܬܥܣܪܝܬܐ fem., ܬܪܥܣܪܝܐ masc. *the twelfth*, etc. Sometimes the ordinal 10 is united with a cardinal number and the word is preceded by ܕ; e.g. ܕܚܕܥܣܪ, ܕܬܪܬܥܣܪ, etc.

Rem.—The Syrians, like the Hebrews, express the idea of *a part*, by a feminine form and the insertion of ܘ after the first radical letter; e.g. ܬܘܠܬܬܐ, ܪܘܒܥܐ, ܚܘܡܫܐ *third part*, etc. Upon the other relations of numbers comp. Syntax § 78.

CHAPTER FOURTH.

PARTICLES.

To Particles belong adverbs, prepositions, conjunctions and interjections. In respect to their origin they may be considered as primitive, derivative, or transferred from other parts of speech. The last are by far the most numerous.

---

§ 51. *Adverbs.*

1. The following may be considered as primitive adverbs: ܐܝܟ *so*, ܠܐ, ܠܘ *not*, ܬܡܢ *there*, ܗܪܟܐ *here*.

2. Those derived from nouns and adjectives with the characteristic endings ـܝܬ, ـܘܬ and ـܐܝܬ, are the following;

ܐܚܪܝܐܝܬ *at last,* ܩܕܡܝܐܝܬ *at first,* ܬܢܝܢܘܬ *again,* ܐܠܗܐܝܬ *godly,* ܦܣܝܩܐܝܬ *in short,* ܥܒܪܐܝܬ *Hebraically,* ܝܘܡܢܐ *today.*

3. As transferred from other parts of speech are to be considered those :

a) from substantives; α) with a preposition; e. g. ܒܚܪܬܐ *finally,* ܒܫܪܪܐ *truly,* ܒܙܒܢܐ *once,* ܠܓܘ *inwardly,* ܡܫܠܝܐܠܝܢ *immediately,* ܡܢ ܪܝܫ *anew ;* β) without a preposition; e. g. ܣܟ *(want) not,* ܣܦܩܐܝܬ *enough,* ܟܠܗ, ܟܠ *wholly, entirely,* also in the plural ܙܒܢ̈ܐ *sometimes ;* *b*) from adjectives, numerals and pronouns; e. g. ܛܒ, ܝܬܝܪ *very,* ܠܚܘܕ, ܒܠܚܘܕ *only,* ܐܟܚܕ, ܐܟܚܕܐ *at once,* ܡܚܕܐ *immediately,* ܟܡܐ *how much?* ܠܡܢܐ, ܡܛܠ *why?* *c*) from verbal forms, as the infinitive, ܬܘܒ *again ;* or participles ܠܡܣܬܟܢ, ܡܢ ܡܣܬܟܢ *almost.*

Rem.—Some adverbs are transferred from the Greek; e. g. ܡܠܠܘܢ μαλλον, ܡܠܝܣܛܐ μαλιστα, ܐܝܩܐ εἰκη. The Syriac language is especially rich in compound adverbs. Such are the following: ܐܝܟܐ *where?* ܥܕܡܐ ܠܐܝܟܐ *wherefore?* ܠܐ ܥܕܟܝܠ *not yet,* ܥܕܡܐ ܠܐܡܬܝ *how long?* ܗܫܐ *now,* ܥܕܡܐ ܠܗܫܐ *until now,* etc. Among compound adverbs may also be placed the circumlocutory ܠܝܬ *not to be* (see § 38). The simple interrogation is either not expressed at all, or by the addition of ܟܝ : the negative interrogation, is expressed by ܠܐ, and ܠܐ ܗܘ. The syllable ܐܝ prefixed to pronouns and adverbs expresses an interrogation; e.g. ܡܢ ܐܝܟܐ *whence?* ܐܝܢܐ *who?*

---

§ 52. *Prepositions.*

1. To the original Prepositions belong the prefixes ܒ, ܕ (gen.), ܠ (dat. and acc.) which are always joined with a noun or pronoun, and are vacant when the noun or pronoun begins with a regular consonant; e. g. ܒܣܦܪ, ܠܡܠܟܐ. Prefix prepositions take the vowel, which is usually ◌ܰ, when

the following consonant is vacant; e. g. ܒܡܫܚܐ, ܠܡܠ̈ܟܐ, or when the vowel falls back from the quiescents ܐ or ܗ; e. g. ܒܡܐܢܐ from ܡܐܢܐ for ܡܐܢܐ; ܠܝܼܗܘܕܝܐ for ܠܝܗܘܼܕܝܐ. Before words which begin with ܐ, ܝ or ܝܗ, the vowels, in which these letters quiesce, fall back upon the preceding prefix; e. g. ܒܐܪܥܐ, ܒܐܢܫܐ, ܠܐܝܕܐ, ܠܝܠܝܕܐ, ܒܝܗܘܕ from ܐܪܥܐ, etc.

Rem.—Before ܫܬܐ 6, and ܫܬܝܢ, these prepositions take ‒, probably because they were also written ܐܫܬܐ and ܐܫܬܝܢ. In ܩܘܒܠ and ܩܘܕܡ the preposition ܠ quiesces in ܘ, * which falls back (comp. § 15. 2. B. c. and the tables following); e.g. ܠܘܩܒܠ, ܠܘܩܕܡ, except when suffixes are appended with a union vowel, in which case the ‒ of the second syllable falls away and the original form reappears; e.g. ܠܘܩܒܠܗ, etc. Among the original prepositions may also be reckoned the monosyllables ܥܡ *with*, ܠܘܬ *by*, ܠܘܬ *to*.

2. Most of the other prepositions are considered as transferred from other parts of speech; *a*) substantives in the constr.state; e. g. ܩܕܡ *before*, ܚܠܦ *instead*, ܡܛܠ *for*, ܒܝܢ and ܒܝܬ *between*, ܚܕܪ and ܚܕܪܝ *about*, ܬܚܬ and ܬܚܝܬ *under*, ܡܢ (from ܡܢܬ *part*) *from*, ܒܬܪ *after*; *b*) substantives with prefixes; e.g. ܒܣܬܪ *according to*, ܠܘܩܒܠ *against*, ܠܘܩܕܡ *before*; *c*) compounds; e. g. ܥܕܡܐ ܠ *until to*, ܠܥܠ *over*, ܡܢ ܒܠܥܕ *without*, ܡܢ ܚܕܪ *around, about*, ܡܢ ܠܘܩܒܠ *against*.

3. Several of the prepositions seem to have been originally plural nouns, on which account they are united with plural suffixes. Here belong ܥܠ *over*, ܨܐܕ, ܨܝܕ *after, against*, ܡܛܠ *for*, ܩܕܡ *before*, ܬܚܬ *under* (comp. § 16. 2. C. and the following paradigms).

---

*Instead of saying that ܠ quiesces in ܘ the author should have said that ܠ takes the vowel ‒ with ܘ quiescing in it, as ܠ is not a quiescent (see § 13).—Tr.

Prepositions with Suffixes.

(§ 16. II. C. and § 52).

	A. With Suff. of the Sing.				B. Of the Plur. Masc.	Fem.
	ܒ	ܠܘܳܬ	ܒܳܬܰܪ	ܠܽܘܩܒܰܠ	ܥܰܠ	ܡܶܛܽܠ
	in.	*to.*	*after.*	*against.*	*over.*	*on account of.*
Sing.						
1 c.	ܒܝ	ܠܘܳܬܝ	ܒܳܬܪܝ	ܠܽܘܩܒܠܝ	ܥܠܝ	ܡܶܛܽܠܳܬܝ
2 m.	ܒܳܟ	ܠܘܳܬܳܟ	ܒܳܬܪܳܟ	ܠܽܘܩܒܠܳܟ	ܥܠܰܝܟ	ܡܶܛܽܠܳܬܳܟ
2 f.	ܒܶܟܝ	ܠܘܳܬܶܟܝ	ܒܳܬܪܶܟܝ	ܠܽܘܩܒܠܶܟܝ	ܥܠܰܝܟܝ	ܡܶܛܽܠܳܬܶܟܝ
3 m.	ܒܶܗ	ܠܘܳܬܶܗ	ܒܳܬܪܶܗ	ܠܽܘܩܒܠܶܗ	ܥܠܰܘܗܝ	ܡܶܛܽܠܳܬܶܗ
3 f.	ܒܳܗ	ܠܘܳܬܳܗ	ܒܳܬܪܳܗ	ܠܽܘܩܒܠܳܗ	ܥܠܶܝܗ	ܡܶܛܽܠܳܬܳܗ
Plur.						
1 c.	ܒܰܢ	ܠܘܳܬܰܢ	ܒܳܬܪܰܢ	ܠܽܘܩܒܠܰܢ	ܥܠܰܝܢ	ܡܶܛܽܠܳܬܰܢ
2 m.	ܒܟܽܘܢ	ܠܘܳܬܟܽܘܢ	ܒܳܬܪܟܽܘܢ	ܠܽܘܩܒܠܟܽܘܢ	ܥܠܰܝܟܽܘܢ	ܡܶܛܽܠܳܬܟܽܘܢ
2 f.	ܒܟܶܝܢ	ܠܘܳܬܟܶܝܢ	ܒܳܬܪܟܶܝܢ	ܠܽܘܩܒܠܟܶܝܢ	ܥܠܰܝܟܶܝܢ	ܡܶܛܽܠܳܬܟܶܝܢ
3 m.	ܒܗܽܘܢ	ܠܘܳܬܗܽܘܢ	ܒܳܬܪܗܽܘܢ	ܠܽܘܩܒܠܗܽܘܢ	ܥܠܰܝܗܽܘܢ	ܡܶܛܽܠܳܬܗܽܘܢ
3 f.	ܒܗܶܝܢ	ܠܘܳܬܗܶܝܢ	ܒܳܬܪܗܶܝܢ	ܠܽܘܩܒܠܗܶܝܢ	ܥܠܰܝܗܶܝܢ	ܡܶܛܽܠܳܬܗܶܝܢ

Rem.—The following take no suffixes: ܒܓܰܘ *in*, ܠܒܰܪ *without*, ܠܓܰܘ *within*, ܠܥܶܠ *over*, ܠܬܰܚܬ *under*, ܥܕܰܡܳܐ ܠ *until to*, and ܣܛܰܪ ܡܶܢ *except*.

§ 53. *Conjunctions and Interjections.*

1. The original Conjunctions are the copulative ܘ, ܕ *that, because* (ܠ before infinit.), ܐܢ *if,* ܟܕ *as, since,* ܐܘ *or,* ܟܝܠ *hence,* ܠܡ (for this preposition in questions see § 51. 3. Rem.) *namely,* ܕܠܡ *lest.*

Rem.—ܘ and ܕ, like ܒ and ܠ, are prefixed (see §52. 1).

2. Compound Conjunctions are; *a*) with ܐܢ; e. g. ܐܠܘ *if,* ܐܠܐ ܐܢ and ܐܠܘܠܐ *unless,* ܐܦܢ *although,* ܐܢܗܘ ܕܝܢ and ܐܢܕܝܢ *if but,* ܐܢ ܗܘ — ܐܢ ܗܘ *be it—be it;* *b*) with ܕ; e.g. ܕܠܐ *lest,* especially after prepositions; e. g. ܐܝܟ ܕ *as,* ܡܛܠ ܕ, ܥܠ ܕ and ܡܛܘܠ ܕ *because,* ܦܢ ܕ *lest,* ܥܕܡܐ ܕ *until;* *c*) with other conjunctions; e. g. ܗܟܝܠ *hence,* ܡܟܝܠ *now,* ܟܝ ܗܘ *therefore,* ܟܕ ܗܘ *although.* From the Greek are borrowed ܐܠܐ ἀλλα, ܓܝܪ γαρ, ܕܝܢ δε, ܡܢ μεν.

3. Interjections as primitives are mostly onomatopoetic; e. g. ܐܘ, ܐܘܝ *O!* ܘܝ *wo!* ܗܐ *behold!* ܗܘܝ *hey! ha!* They are sometimes borrowed from other parts of speech; e.g. ܐܠܘܦ, ܠܘܝ *if yet!* ܒܒܥܘ *I pray you!*

PART THIRD.

SYNTAX.

CHAPTER FIRST.

THE PRONOUN.

§ 54. *Use of the Separable Personal Pronouns and Suffixes.*

A. Separable Personal Pronouns.

1. These pronouns at the beginning of a sentence, denote a certain emphasis, and stand in various relations to the verb which follows in the same person. This relation is not only; *a*) that of the nominative absolute; e. g. Rom. xiv. 10. ܐܢܬ ܕܝܢ ܩܐ ܡܘܢܐ ܕܐܢ ܐܢܬ ܠܐܚܘܢܘܟ *but thou, why judgest thou thy brother!* Eph. iv. 20., Acts xix. 15., II Tim. iv. 5; but it may be also represented; *b*) by the oblique cases; e.g. *α*) by the genitive; e.g. Matt. iii. 11. ܗܘ ܕܠܐ ܗܘܐ ܐܢܐ ܠܡܫܪܝܬܐ ܡܣܐܢܘܗܝ *whose shoes I am not worthy to unloose*, John xix. 11., Ephes. vi. 20; *β*) by the dative; e. g. Kirsh. ii. 2. ܘܐܢܫܐ ܠܐ ܩܐܬܐ ܠܟܠܝ ܐܢܫ *but no one comes to me*, Luke xxiii. 41; *γ*) by the accusative; e.g. Kirsh. iv. 7.–9. ܗܘ ܡܕܝ ܕܐܢܬܘܢ ܒܥܝܬܘܢ ܐܢܬܘܢ ܒܠܠܝܐ ܕܒܝܘܡܐ ܕܡܫܟܚܬܐ ܐܢܐ ܒܥܝܢ ܡܫܟܚܢܗ ܘܠܐ ܡܫܟܚܢܗ *what you seek to find in the night, I seek to find in the day time, and find it not.*

Rem.—They are also emphatic after the verb; e.g. Luke iii. 14. ܡܳܢܳܐ ܢܶܥܒܶܕ ܐܳܦ ܚܢܰܢ *what then shall we do?* Upon ܐܶܢܽܘܢ and ܐܶܢܶܝܢ as accusatives, comp. § 16. Rem. 1. and the preceding table.

2. United with substantives, adjectives or adverbs they mark the Present; *a*) of the substantive verb ܗܘܳܐ (see §38); e.g. ܫܰܪܺܝܪܳܐ ܗ̱ܝ *she is true*; Matt. xxiv. 26. ܒܡܰܕܒܪܳܐ ܗ̱ܘ *he is in the desert*; verse 23. ܗܳܪܟܳܐ ܗ̱ܘ *he is here*; *b*) of the finite verb with its participle; e. g. ܐܳܡܰܪ ܐ̱ܢܳܐ *I say*, ܡܶܬܺܝܠܶܕ ܐ̱ܢ݇ܬ *thou art born* (comp. § 64).

Rem.—(Upon ܐ̱ and ܗ̱ see § 12. 1. B).—The contraction of the pronoun with the participle or adjective into one word is found in the 1 pers. plur.; e. g. ܩܳܪܶܝܢܰܢ *we read*, ܩܰܕܺܝܫܺܝܢܰܢ *we are holy*. It is also found sometimes in other persons; e. g. Eph. iii. 13. ܡܦܺܝܣܢܳܐ *I beseech*; Gal.v.3. ܚܰܝܳܒܽܘ *he is guilty*; iii.11 (comp. §20.and§37.E).

3. Farther in these cases; *a*) the pronoun of the same person may be doubled, so that the former will denote the subject and the latter the substantive verb; e. g. John i. 20. ܐ̱ܢܳܐ ܐ̱ܢܳܐ *I am*; xiv. 20. ܐܰܢ̱ܬܽܘܢ ܒܺܝ ܐܰܢ̱ܬܽܘܢ *ye are in me*; Matt. xxvi. 73; or the part. present of the finite verb is placed between; e.g. Matt. iii. 11. ܐ̱ܢܳܐ ܡܰܥܡܶܕ ܐ̱ܢܳܐ *I baptize*; xxvii. 4; John xiii. 13; Barh. 68, 16; 105, 14; 148, 15.

b) In the simple pronoun may be contained both the subject and substantive verb; e. g. Gen. xxix. 4. ܐܰܝܡܶܟܳܐ ܐܰܢ̱ܬܽܘܢ — ܡܶܢ ܚܰܪܳܢ ܚܢܰܢ *whence are ye?—we are from Haran*; Assem. I. 33; 12. 13.

c) The pronoun ܗܽܘ, as substantive verb, may follow the 1 and 2 person as subject; e. g. Acts xxii. 8. ܐ̱ܢܳܐ ܗ̱ܘ ܝܶܫܽܘܥ *I am Jesus*; Luke xxii. 67. ܐܶܢ ܐܰܢ̱ܬ ܗ̱ܘ ܡܫܺܝܚܳܐ *if thou art the Messiah*; verse 70; xxiv. 18; Ephr. I. 214. E; Barh. 173, 18–20. Also ܐܶܢܽܘܢ and ܐܶܢܶܝܢ, follow the 1 and 2 pers. as subject; e. g. Matt. v. 13. ܐܢ̱ܬܘܢ ܐܢܘܢ ܡܠܚܗ ܕܐܪܥܐ *ye are the salt of the earth;* I. Cor. iii. 17; Barh. 133. 1.

Rem.—Instead of the pronouns, the Philoxenian version of the N.T. uses ܐܝܬ with suff.; e. g. ܐܢܐ ܐܝܬܘܗܝ *I am*; ܐܝܬܝܟܘܢ ܐܢ̱ܬܘܢ *ye are.*

B. Suffixes

1. The pronominal suffixes of the verb denote the accusative; rarely, and for the most part in translations from the Hebrew, the dative; e. g. ܝܗܒܬܢܝ for ܝܗܒܬ ܠܝ *thou hast given to me.*

Rem.—This imitation of the Heb. is neglected in passages of the O. T.; e. g. Zach. vii. 5. comp. with Ephr. II. 296. B. and Isa. xxiv. 4, comp. with II. 65. C.

2. In the relation of genitive, the suffixes are attached to the *nomen rectum* or to the genitive proper; e.g. Ez. xvi. 18. ܡܐܢܐ ܕܨܒܬܟܝ *thy embroidered garments,* literally *of thine embroidery* or *ornament*; vii. 20; xi. 15; xxvii. 16, 27; Matt. vi. 11. ܠܚܡܐ ܕܣܘܢܩܢܢ *our necessary bread,* literally *of our need.*

Rem.—The suffix is seldom found with the *nomen regens;* e.g. Ez. xvi. 27. ܡܢ ܐܘܪܚܬܟܝ ܕܙܢܝܘܬܐ *of thy lewd ways,* usually in connection with ܝܡܝܢܐ *the right,* and ܣܡܠܐ *the left;* e.g. Acts. iii. 7. ܒܐܝܕܗ ܕܝܡܝܢܐ *on his right hand*; Matt.v.29; Rev.i.17. Sometimes a double suffix occurs; e.g. Ephr. I. 204. B. and C. ܠܒܪܝ ܒܘܟܪܝ *thy first born.*

3. The noun taking a suffix stands before an adjective connected with it; e. g. Ps. lxxxvii. 1. ܒܛܘܪܗ ܩܕܝܫܐ *in his holy mountain*; Ez. vi. 9; Ephr. I. 284. A. ܐܘܨܪܗ ܛܒܐ *his good treasure.*

4. The suffix to the noun is often understood objectively; e. g. Exod. xx. 20. ܕܚܠܬܗ *fear before him*; I Cor. xi. 25. ܠܥܘܗܕܢܝ *in remembrance of me*; John xv. 10. ܚܘܒܗ *love to him*; Barh. 218, 14.

Rem. 1.—Possessives are also expressed by ܕܝܠ with suff. (§ 16. B); e. g. Barh. 49. 7. ܪܒ ܚܝܠܐ ܕܝܠܗ *his commander*; 146, 10.

This manner of expression is used particularly when a stronger emphasis is required than is indicated by the mere suffix; e. g. Matt. vi. 13. ܕܝܠܟ ܗܝ ܡܠܟܘܬܐ *thine is the kingdom ;* Barh. 146, 1. ܥܕܬܐ ܪܒܬܐ ܕܝܠܢ ܕܒܚܪܢ *our great church in Haran.* If the suff. to the noun be also repeated, it indicates (emphatically) the Greek possessives ἐμὸς σὸς, &c.; e. g. John iv. 34. ܡܐܟܘܠܬܝ ܕܝܠܝ ἐμὸν βρῶμα ; vii. 6 ; xv. 9 ; Rom. 3.7. The same repetition of the suffix occurs also in prepositions; e. g. II Cor. v. 19. ܒܢ ܕܝܠܢ ἐν ἡμῖν ; I John ii. 2, and in certain forms of expression; e.g. Matt. xxvii. 4. ܠܢ ܡܐ ܠܢ τί πρὸς ἡμᾶς ; John xxi. 22.

Rem. 2.—We should mention the use of the suff. in ܡܪܝ, ܡܪܢ, for the pronoun of the second, and in ܥܒܕܝܟ, ܐܡܬܟ, ܥܒܕܟ, for the pronoun of the first person, when the discourse is addressed to superiors; e. g. Genesis xliv. 16. ܡܢܐ ܢܐܡܪ ܠܡܪܝ *what shall we say to thee* (*my lord*)*?* ܣܟܠܘܬܐ ܠܥܒܕܝܟ *our* (*thy servants'*) *iniquity ;* verse 32. So kings in speaking of themselves use ܡܠܟܐ; e. g. Esth. viii. 8. ܟܬܘܒܘ ܒܫܡܐ ܕܡܠܟܐ *write in* (*my*) *the king's name ;* and in reference to God, ܐܠܗܐ is used; e. g. Gen. v. 1. Also ܡܪܝ stands connected with the second and third persons; e. g. Mark xii. 37. ܩܪܐ ܠܗ ܡܪܝ *he calls him his* (*my*) *Lord*, and differs from ܡܪܢ, in that the former is the common form of salutation, while the latter marks the *pluralis majestatis*, and is used of Christ in the version of the New Testament; e. g. Acts i. 1; Rom. xiv. 8.

Rem. 3.—It is rather to be considered as an imitation of a Hebrew idiom, when the suffix relates to a noun which does not occur till later in the discourse (comp. Gesenius Lehrgeb. p. 739); or when the noun itself is repeated instead of the pronoun; e.g. Gen. xvi. 16.

§ 55. *Pleonastic Use of Pronouns.*

A. Separable Personal Pronouns.

Here belongs the pronoun of the third person ܗܘ (ܗ̄ܘ) (comp. § 12. 1. B) united with nearly all persons of the sing. and plur., by which an emphasis is denoted, which is disregarded in the later language. It is found still in such passages as John viii. 26. ܗܠܝܢ ܗܘ ܡܡܠܠ ܐܢܐ ܒܥܠܡܐ *that* (*exactly*) *I speak before the world;* verse 28; xv. 16; Rom. iii. 31; Heb. ix. 17. It is to be considered merely as pleonastic in Luke vii. 19. ܐܘ ܠܐܚܪܢܐ ܗܘ ܡܣܟܝܢܢ *or shall we wait for another?* Rom. xiv. 8; Heb. xiii. 22; I Tim. i.4; v. 9; Barh. 133, 3; Assem. I. 221, A.5, especially where it occurs with a feminine noun; e. g. Rom. iii. 28. ܒܗܝܡܢܘܬܐ ܗܘ ܡܙܕܕܩ ܒܪܢܫܐ *by faith is a man justified.* ܗܘ is sometimes connected with a plural; e. g. Ephr. I. 214, D. ܡܛܠ ܢܫܘܗܝ ܗܘ ܘܒܢܘܗܝ *on account of his wives and children.*

Rem.—Sometimes also the fem. ܗܝ (still more emphatic), is found; e. g. Rev. xxi. 2. ܘܠܡܕܝܢܬܐ ܗܝ ܩܕܝܫܬܐ — ܚܙܝܬ *and I saw* (*it*) *the holy city;* xxii. 19, and the plur. ܗܢܘܢ Assem. I. 77, A. 20, 21. ܗܘ and ܗܘ are sometimes united together without emphasis; e.g. John v.9. ܘܗܘ ܗܘ ܝܘܡܐ *and this day;* Barh. 148, 3. Also in the plur.; e.g. Matt. iii. 1. ܒܗܘܢ ܕܝܢ ܒܝܘܡܬܐ ܗܢܘܢ *but in these days.* The pleonastic use of ܗܘ is confirmed from the fact that the Philoxenian version omits it altogether.

B. Suffixes.

1. The suffix is often used pleonastically with the verb, when the object with ܠ as though by way of explanation follows; e. g. Matt. i. 21. ܗܘ ܓܝܪ ܢܚܝܘܗܝ ܠܥܡܗ *for he shall bless* (*it*) *his people;* verse 24; ii. 6, 11; Mark xiv. 47. Without ܠ in Matt. xxv. 25. ܛܡܪܬܗ ܟܟܪܟ *I buried* (*it thy talent;* xxvii. 5; I Tim. vi. 14.

Rem. 1.—The suffix also occurs pleonastically with ܠ after verbs of *motion, going, coming,* &c.; e.g. Gen. xxvii.43. ܙܠ ܠܟ *go;* Luke viii.37. ܘܐܙܠ ܠܗ *therewith he departed;* Matt.x.6; John xi.31; iv.3. ܘܐܬܐ ܠܗ ܬܘܒ *and he came again;* Assem. 1.44, A.17. ܢܦܩ ܠܗ *he went out;* 186, A.30. ܫܢܐ ܗܘܐ ܠܗ ܠܟܦܪܐ ܐܚܪܢܐ *he had gone to the Aramæans;* Ephr. I. 226, B. ܩܳܡ ܠܶܗ ܡܽܘܫܶܐ *Moses stood up;* Matt. iii. 2. ܩܪܶܒܰܬ ܠܳܗ̇ ܡܰܠܟܽܘܬܳܐ ܕܫܡܰܝܳܐ *the kingdom of heaven is near;* the same is true frequently, after ܫܢܳܐ (= *to depart from this life*); e. g. John xi. 14. ܠܳܥܳܙܰܪ ܫܢܺܝ ܠܶܗ *Lazarus is dead;* Mark ix. 26; Assem.I. 367, 9; Ephr.1.204,A; sometimes with verbs which have not the signification of motion; e. g. ܗܰܝܡܶܢ *to believe;* John xi. 31; ܥܒܰܕ *to make,* Barh. 217, 10; ܫܛܳܐ *to be foolish,* Rom. i. 22; and even after ܗܘܳܐ John i. 15.

Rem. 2.—On the contrary, the suffix in active verbs, sometimes, falls away when it can either be easily supplied from the context, or the same object has already preceded; e. g. Barh. 424. 9. ܐܰܦܶܩ ܟܽܠ ܕܺܝܢܳܪ̈ܶܐ ܘܰܪܡܳܐ - ܩܽܘܡܳܐ ܩܕܳܡܰܘܗ̱ܝ *he brought out all of the silver coin and heaped (it) up before him;* particularly the neuter; e. g. Gen. xxiv. 49. ܚܰܘܳܐܘܢܝ *inform me thereof.* In many verbs following each other the suffix which is to be repeated falls away; e.g. Matt. xiv. 19; I Cor. xi. 23, 24. Where two follow each other the suffix is usually added to the latter verb; e.g. Barh. 419,5. ܡܝܰܩܪܺܝܢܰܢ ܘܰܡܫܰܒܚܺܝܢܰܢ ܠܶܗ *we esteem and honor it.*

2. The suffix is also pleonastic in the *nomen regens,* which precedes the genitive with ܕ; e. g. John iii. 18. ܒܫܡܶܗ ܕܺܝܚܺܝܕܳܝܳܐ *in the name of the only begotten;* xii.3. ܠܪ̈ܶܓܠܰܘܗ̱ܝ ܕܝܶܫܽܘܥ *the feet of Jesus;* verse 31; Acts v. 2; Ephr. I. 87, B.

Rem.—Here belongs also the repetition of the suff. before ܕܺܝܠ (§ 54. B. 4. Rem. 1) and after ܟܽܠ = *all,* without ܕ following it; e.g. Matt. xiii. 2. ܟܽܠܶܗ ܟܶܢܫܳܐ *the whole multitude;* ii. 3, 4; Kirsh. 114, 10. ܟܽܠܗܶܝܢ ܡܕ̈ܺܝܢܳܬܳܐ *all cities.* Sometimes ܟܽܠ with suffix occurs after the noun; e.g. Barh. 71, 6. ܥܰܡܳܐ ܕܶܝܢ ܟܽܠܶܗ *but the whole people;* Matt. vi. 33. ܗܳܠܶܝܢ ܟܽܠܗܶܝܢ *all these things.* Without the suffix ܟܽܠ signifies *each, every;* e. g. Matt. iv. 4. ܟܽܠ ܡܶܠܬܳܐ *every word;* Acts xviii. 4.

3. Finally, a pleonastic suffix is attached to prepositions thus; *a*) ܕ is placed before the accompanying noun and is

considered either as a sign of the genitive (§ 52. 2) or as a relative; e. g. I Tim. i. 8. ܐܝܟܘܬܗ ܕܢܡܘܣܐ *according to (it) the law;* John i. 42. ܠܘܬܗ ܕܝܫܘܥ *to (him) Jesus;* xviii. 15; ܥܡܗ Rev. v. 11; ܠܘܬܗ Luke xxiii. 7; ܡܛܠܗ Rom. viii. 3. ܡܛܠܬܗ ܕܚܛܝܬܐ *for (it) sin;* ܡܢܝ Acts iii. 6; ܠܗܠܝܢ Rom. xiii.6; Barh. 74,18. ܠܘܩܒܠܗ ܕܛܪܘܢܐ *against (him) the tyrant;* ܠܘܬܗ 76, 11; ܡܨܥܬܗ Luke v. 19; *b*) or the preceding preposition with the suffix is repeated before the noun; e. g. Luke ii.8. ܒܗ ܒܐܬܪܐ *in (it) the field;* Barh.192,7; Assem.I. 27, 1, 29; Ephr.I.87,B; ܠܗ John ii. 2. ܠܗ ܠܡܫܬܘܬܐ *to (it to) the feast;* ܡܢܗ Acts viii. 35; ܠܗܠܝܢ Acts ix. 21, etc.

General Remark on Personal Pronouns.

In Syriac, we also find in personal pronouns *enallage; a*) of *number* in ܐܝܬ; e.g. Barh. 166, 6. ܐܝܬܝܗܘܢ ܗܘܘ ܒܗܘܢ ܥܣܪܝܢ ܢܫܐ ܘܥܣܪܐ ܛܠܝܐ *there were among them twenty women and ten children;* in words whose plural only is used; e.g. Luke xxiii. 45. ܘܐܬܦܪܝܬ ܐܦܝ ܬܪܥܐ ܕܗܝܟܠܐ ܡܢ ܡܨܥܬܗ *the vail of the temple was rent (in its midst) in twain.* The same is true in the dual; e. g. Hebrews xi. 26. ܣܝܡܬܗ ܕܡܨܪܝܢ *the treasures (of it) Egypt;* Barh. 108, 2; *b*) of *gender;* e. g. Michael. Chr. 20, 9, 10. ܠܟܠܗܘܢ ܐܬܪܘܬܐ — ܒܗܝܢ *all places —in these; c*) of *gender* and *number* together, if by collectives sing. fem. are signified names of countries and cities, men or inhabitants; e.g. Barh. 565, 18, 19. ܐܫܟܚܘ ܐܢܫܘܬܐ ܣܓܝܐܬܐ — ܘܐܦ ܠܗܘܢ ܕܒܪܘ ܫܒܝܬܐ *they found a great many men, — and these also they led into captivity;* ܛܝܒܘܬܐ 580, 1, 2; ܡܕܝܢܬܐ 591, 5, 6; ܐܦܪܝܩܝ 150, 11, 12.

§ 56. *Use of the Relative Pronoun* (§ 17. 2).

1. The Relative ܕ gives to adverbs of interrogation, place, time, etc., a relative signification; e. g. ܐܝܟܐ *where?* ܐܝܟܐ ܕ *there, where,* John i. 28. ܐܝܟܐ ܕܡܥܡܕ ܗܘܐ ܝܘܚܢܢ *there, where John baptized;* verse 40; Barh.82,2; ܠܐܝܟܐ *whither?* ܠܐܝܟܐ ܕ *thither, where;* e. g. John xiii. 36. ܠܐܝܟܐ ܕܐܙܠ ܐܢܐ *whither I go;* Barh. 198, 13; Assem.I. 27; 2.3.v. E; ܐܝܟܢܐ *how?* ܐܝܟܢܐ ܕ *just as:* e. g. John iii. 14; v. 26; xiii. 33; ܐܡܬܝ *when?* ܐܡܬܝ ܕ *when, as;* e. g. v. 25. ܐܡܬܝ ܕܢܫܡܥܘܢ *when they shall hear;* ܟܡܐ *how much?* ܟܡܐ ܕ *so much;* e. g. John vi. 11. ܟܡܐ ܕܨܒܘ *as much as they would.* ܕ gives the same meaning sometimes to nouns; e.g. ܐܬܪ *place;* ܐܬܪ ܕ *where;* e.g. John iii. 8.

2. The oblique cases are formed by some mark of the case followed by a suffix; *a*) the genitive is indicated by the suffix added to the *nomen regens;* e. g. John ix. 11. ܕܫܡܗ ܝܫܘܥ *whose name is Jesus;* Assem.I. 165, A. 14; *b*) the dative, according to the following example; Rom. i. 9. ܕܠܗ ܡܫܡܫ ܐܢܐ *whom I serve;* verse 31; *c*) the accusative, thus; e. g. John i. 26. ܕܐܢܬܘܢ ܠܐ ܝܕܥܝܢ ܐܢܬܘܢ ܠܗ *whom ye know not.* The accusative is also expressed by the suffix attached to the verb; e. g. iii.34. ܕܐܠܗܐ ܫܕܪܗ *whom God hath sent; d*) the ablative by ܒ; e.g. John i.48; by ܡܢ Rom.i.6. In a similar manner the relative is united with the preposition; e.g. ܥܡ, John iii.2. ܕܐܠܗܐ ܥܡܗ *with whom is God,* etc.

REM.—In connection with the suffix of the 1 and 2 person, added to the verb, it (the relative) forms, with reference to a preceding subject of the same person, the oblique cases *who, I, whom, me,* like the Lat. *qui;* e. g. Gen. xlv. 4. ܐܢܐ ܐܢܐ ܝܘܣܦ ܕܙܒܢܬܘܢܝ *I am Joseph whom (me) ye have sold;* Num. xxii. 30; Isa. xli. 8 (Ephr. II.88. E) ܐܝܣܪܝܠ ܐܢܬ ܕܓܒܝܬܟ *thou art Israel whom (thee) I have made strong.* The same occurs with prepositions; e. g. Num. xxii. 30. *thy she ass* ܕܪܟܒܬ ܐܝܬ ܒܟܝ *upon whom (me) thou hast ridden.* The relative alone sometimes marks the accusative, particularly the neuter; e. g. Gen. i. 31. ܟܠ ܕܥܒܕ *all that he made.* The relative is sometimes used before the mark of the case; e.g. Barh. 43, 12. ܕܠܙܒܢܗ *to which time;* 137, 5. ܕܠܛܝܝܐ ܗܘܐ *which belonged to the Arabians.*

3. The Syrians express the relative with a demonstrative preceding *he*, or *this, who, that, which*, etc., as follows; *a*) by ܗܘ ܕ, ܗܘ ܕ, ܗܢܐ ܕ masc., ܗܝ ܕ, ܗܕܐ ܕ fem., and in the plur. ܗܢܘܢ ܕ masc., ܗܢܝܢ ܕ fem.; e. g. John vii. 16. ܐܠܐ ܕܗܘ ܕܫܕܪܢܝ *but his, who has sent me;* Rom.iv. 5; vii. 6; Phil. ii.6. ܗܕܐ ܕܐܝܬܘܗܝ *that, which was;* John i.24. ܗܢܘܢ ܕܐܫܬܕܪܘ *those who were sent;* Barh. 17, 2; 170,5; *b*) by ܡܢ ܕ masc. and fem., and ܡܕܡ ܕ neut.; e. g. Matt. xiii. 12. ܠܡܢ ܕܐܝܬ ܠܗ ܢܬܝܗܒ *to him who hath, shall be given;* John iv. 34; v.30; vii.17, 18; Matt.xiii.17. ܡܕܡ ܕܚܙܝܢ ܐܢܬܘܢ *that which ye see;* Rom. i. 28; viii. 25; *c*) by ܐܝܢܐ ܕ masc., ܐܝܕܐ ܕ fem. and plur. ܐܝܠܝܢ ܕ com.; e. g. Rom. ii.29. ܐܝܢܐ ܕܒܟܣܝܐ ܗܘ *he who is inwardly;* John ix. 8; Rom. ii. 2, 3; iv. 7; v. 14; Barh. 85, 3; *d*) frequently by the participle; e.g. Rom.vii.1. ܝܕܥܝ ܢܡܘܣܐ *those who know the law.*

Rem.—If a particular emphasis is to be indicated the demonstrative is doubled; e. g. John ix. 8. ܗܢܘ ܗܘ ܕܝܬܒ ܗܘܐ *this very one is he who sat.* Sometimes, like the Greek attraction, the demonstrative is wanting; e. g. John iv. 14. ܡܝܐ ܕܐܢܐ ܐܬܠ ܠܗ τοῦ ὕδατος οὗ ἐγώ δώσω αὐτῷ; or the relative is wanting; e. g. Heb. v.2. ܘܐܝܢܐ ܡܫܟܚ *and he (or this) who can;* less frequently are both wanting, according to Hebrew usage; e. g. Job xxiv. 19. Finally the relative occurs pleonastically before participles; e.g. Amos vi. 1. ܘܝ ܠܕܡܫܝܛܝܢ ܠܨܗܝܘܢ *woe to those who depise Zion;* Ephr.II.274.D.

§ 57. *Use of Demonstrative and Interrogative Pronouns.*

The *demonstrative* is neither used for the *relative*, nor does it give, as in Hebrew, a special emphasis to particles and numerals (comp. Gesen. Lehrgeb. p. 750 sq.). It is used only in its proper signification.

Rem.—It is emphatic in connection with ܗܘܿ and ܗܝܼ (§ 17. 1. Rem.); e. g. Matt. v. 47. Sometimes ܗܳܢܳܐ may be translated by *hicce;* e. g. John xix. 19.

2. The *interrogative* pronoun (§ 17. 3) is united with nouns of both genders and numbers; e. g. Matt. xii. 48. ܡܰܢ ܗ̱ܝ ܐܶܡܝ ܘܡܰܢ ܐܢܽܘܢ ܐܰܚܰܝ̈ *who is my mother and who are my brethren?* The *oblique cases* are either so expressed that, in the genitive, the noun in the constr. state precedes; e. g. Gen. xxiv. 23. ܒܪܰܬ ܡܰܢ ܐܰܢ̱ܬܝ *whose daughter art thou?* or so that ܡܰܢ follows with ܕ preceding; e. g. I Sam. xii. 3. ܡܶܢ ܐܺܝܕܳܐ ܕܡܰܢ *from whose hand?* or ܕܡܰܢܘ stands before the noun; e. g. Matt. xxii. 20. ܕܡܰܢܘ ܨܰܠܡܳܐ ܗܳܢܳܐ ܘܟܬܳܒܳܐ *whose image and writing is this?* The other cases are formed by the special case-signs preceding, or by prepositions; e.g. Assem. 1. 34, 6. ܠܡܰܢ ܐܶܬܶܠ *to whom shall I give?* Matt. xii. 27. ܒܡܳܢܳܐ *whereby?*

Rem.—Sometimes ܐܰܝܢܳܐ occurs instead of the relative in the indirect question, without ܕ following it; e. g. Matt. xxiv. 42. ܒܰܐܝܕܳܐ ܫܳܥܬܳܐ ܐܳܬܶܐ ܡܳܪܟܽܘܢ *at what hour your lord will come?* and ܡܰܢܘ includes ܗ̱ܘܳܐ; e. g. John xviii. 38. ܡܰܢܘ ܫܪܳܪܳܐ *what is truth?* vii. 20.

---

§ 58. *Pronouns for which the Syrians have no special forms.*

A. Reflexive Pronouns.

The Syrians express the *reflexive pronoun* (§ 17. 4) as follows; *a*) by the passive (comp. § 21. 2. § 22. 2. § 24. 2); *b*) often, particularly in the third person, by the personal pronoun ; e. g. Barh. 54, 15. ܗܽܘ ܠܶܗ ܩܛܰܠ *he killed himself ;* 77, 5. ܐܰܩܺܝܡܘ ܠܗܽܘܢ ܡܰܠܟܳܐ *they chose themselves a king ;* 83, 16 ; by prepositions ; e.g. Barh. 164,12. ܘܐܶܬܕܰܒܰܪܘ ܒܰܠܚܽܘܕܰܝܗܽܘܢ *and they lead by themselves ;* c) by ܢܰܦܫܳܐ and ܩܢܽܘܡܳܐ. The former is used in reference to persons ; e.g. Matt. xxiii. 12. ܡܰܢ ܕܶܝܢ ܕܢܰܪܺܝܡ ܢܰܦܫܶܗ *he who exalteth himself ;* Barh. 56, 2 ; 84, 15 ; 144, 12 ; less frequently, in reference to things ; e. g. Luke xi. 17. ܟܽܠ ܡܰܠܟܽܘ ܕܬܶܬܦܠܰܓ ܥܰܠ ܢܰܦܫܳܗ *every kingdom which is divided against itself.* ܩܢܽܘܡܳܐ is used in reference to both persons and things ; e.g. II Cor. xii. 15. ܩܢܽܘܡܝ ܐܶܬܶܠ *I give myself ;* Luke xi. 17. ܒܰܝܬܳܐ ܕܥܰܠ ܩܢܽܘܡܶܗ ܡܶܬܦܠܰܓ *a house which is divided against itself.*

Rem. — Less frequently occur in a reflexive signification, ܠܶܒܳܐ *heart ;* e.g. Luke ii .51 ; ܪܺܫܳܐ *head ;* ܪܽܘܚܳܐ *spirit ;* e.g. Dan. iv. 5, 9 ; ܚܰܝܶܐ *life ;* Ps. vii. 6. The pronouns ܢܰܦܫܳܐ and ܩܢܽܘܡܳܐ by way of periphrasis for other pronouns ; e. g. Rom. x. 3. ܙܰܕܺܝܩܽܘܬܳܐ ܕܢܰܦܫܗܽܘܢ *their own righteousness ;* 1 Cor.vi.19 ; Phil.ii.4,5 ; Rom. ix. 3. ܐܶܢܳܐ ܩܢܽܘܡܝ *I myself ;* Heb. i. 3 ; ix. 28.

B. Other Pronouns.

The other pronouns are thus expressed :

1. *This, that,* see § 56. 3.

2. *Each, every,* are expressed ; a) as substantives, by ܓܰܒܪܳܐ Gen. xl. 5 ; ܐ݈ܢܳܫ I Cor. iii. 8 ; vii. 2, 3 ; Gal. vi. 4 ; the latter is doubled in Acts ii. 38, 45 ; I Cor. vii. 17 ; xi. 21 ; II Cor. v. 10 ; I Thess. iv. 4. Sometimes they are expressed by ܟܽܠ ܢܰܦܫ Rom. xiii. 1 ; ܟܽܠ ܚܰܕ ܚܰܕ Eph. v. 33 ; ܟܽܠ ܐ݈ܢܳܫ ܡܶܢ Luke xiv. 33 ; ܟܽܠܒܰܪܢܳܫ or ܟܽܠ ܒܰܪܢܳܫ Rom. xii. 18 ; b) as adjectives ; α) by ܟܽܠ Matt. vii. 17 ; 1 John iv. 3 ; ܟܽܠܚܰܕ ܡܶܢ Assem. I. 11, A. 19 ; β) by a repetition of the noun defined by *each, every ;* e. g. II Kings

xvii. 29. ܥܰܡ ܥܰܡ *every nation;* Matt. xx. 10; *γ*) by the plural; e.g. Amos iv. 4. ܠܨܰܦܪ̈ܐ *every morning;* sometimes by the singular which is to be considered as a distributive; e. g. Jer. xxxvii. 21. ܒܝܰܘܡܳܐ *each day.* The neuter is expressed by ܟܽܠ ܡܶܕܶܡ John iv. 25.

3. *Whosoever,* (*quicunque*), is expressed by ܟܽܠ ܐ̱ܢܳܫ or ܟܽܠܢܳܫ John i. 7; 1 Cor. iii. 13; ܟܽܠ ܕ Matt. xiii. 19; ܟܽܠ ܐܰܝܢܳܐ ܕ I John iii. 3; ܡܰܢ ܕ Mark vii. 16; Barh. 195, 3; 198,12. The neuter by ܟܽܠܡܳܐ ܕ Acts iii.22; iv. 23; ܡܶܕܶܡ ܕ Matt. x. 27.

4. *Somebody, anybody* (*aliquis*), in interrogative and conditional clauses, are expressed; *a*) by ܐ̱ܢܳܫ and ܒܰܪܢܳܫܳܐ John iv. 33. ܠܡܳܐ ܐ̱ܢܳܫ ܐܰܝܬܺܝ ܠܶܗ ܡܶܕܶܡ ܠܡܶܐܟܰܠ *hath any one brought him aught to eat?* vii. 48; I Tim. vi.3. ܐܶܢ ܐܺܝܬ ܐ̱ܢܳܫ ܕܡܰܠܶܦ *if any one teach;* Rev. xxii. 18; *b*) by ܡܰܢ ܕ Mark vii. 16. ܡܰܢ ܕܐܺܝܬ ܠܶܗ *hath any one?* *c*) sometimes by ܡܰܢ Rom. iii. 3. ܐܶܢ ܡܶܢܗܽܘܢ εἰ τινες; Mark xii. 5; or more in accordance with the Hebrew idiom, by ܢܰܦܫܳܐ Lev. iv. 2; v. 1, 2, 4; vii. 27. The neuter is expressed; *a*) by ܡܶܕܶܡ Acts v. 36; ܕܡܶܕܶܡ ܗ̱ܘܳܐ ܗܽܘ *that he was something* (*great*)*;* John vii.4; I John ii. 15; *b*) sometimes by ܡܶܢ Lev.v.9. ܡܶܢ ܕܡܳܐ *some* (*of the*) *blood;* or ܡܶܠܬܳܐ (= דָּבָר) Gen. xviii.14.

5. *Nobody, no one;* *a*) as substantives, are expressed by ܠܳܐ ܐ̱ܢܳܫ Matt.ix.16; John i.18; James i.13; ܐ̱ܢܳܫ ܠܳܐ Acts xviii. 10; I Cor.ii.11; ܠܳܐ ܒܰܪܢܳܫ Num.xxxi.49; ܠܳܐ ܒܰܪ ܐ̱ܢܳܫ Jer. li.43; ܠܰܝܬ ܐ̱ܢܳܫ John vii.4; sometimes by ܠܰܝܬ ܕܐ̱ܢܳܫ John xv.13; ܠܰܝܬ ܕ or simply by ܠܰܝܬ with an adjective or participle following; e.g. Matt.xix.17. ܠܰܝܬ ܛܳܒ *no one is good.* The neuter, by ܠܳܐ ܡܶܕܶܡ or ܡܶܕܶܡ ܠܳܐ Phil. ii. 3; I Tim. vi. 7; ܠܰܝܬ fol-

lowed by ܡܕܡ Matt. x. 26; with ܡܕܡ preceding, II Cor. vi. 10; without ܡܕܡ James iv. 2; *b*) as adjectives, by ܠܐ after the noun, with the verb, I Cor. ii.9. ܥܝܢܐ ܠܐ ܚܙܬ *no eye hath seen it;* before the noun, Rom. viii. 39. ܠܐ ܒܪܝܬܐ *no creature;* by ܠܝܬ with the noun following, Luke iv. 24. ܠܝܬ ܢܒܝܐ *no prophet;* Heb.iv.13; with the noun preceding, Eph. v. 5; with the words standing between, John xv. 22. ܠܝܬ ܗܘܬ ܠܗܘܢ ܚܛܝܬܐ *they would have had no sin.*

6. *Some, any,* are expressed; *a*) by ܐܝܬ ܕ Matt. xvi. 14. ܐܝܬ ܕܐܡܪܝܢ *some say;* John ix. 9; with words interposed, vii. 12. ܐܝܬ ܗܘܘ ܓܝܪ ܕܐܡܪܝܢ *for some said;* ܐܝܬ ܐܢܫܐ ܕ I Cor. viii. 7; xv. 34; II Thes. iii. 11; *b*) by ܐܢܫ ܐܢܫ Phil. i. 15; I Tim. iv. 1; ܐܢܫܐ ܡܢ John ix. 16; *c*) eliptically, by ܡܢ, Matt. xxiii. 34. ܡܢܗܘܢ ܬܩܛܠܘܢ ܐܢܘܢ *some shall ye kill;* Mark xii. 5; Acts xvii. 32; Rom. iii. 3; *d*) sometimes by the plural of the noun; e. g. Dan. viii. 27. ܝܘܡܬܐ *some days;* ܝܘܡ̈ܐ, Gen. xxix. 20. The neuter is expressed by ܐܝܬ ܕ, Matt. xiii. 4. ܐܝܬ ܕܢܦܠ *some fell;* also in verse 8.

7. *Some, others,* are expressed; *a*) by ܐܢܫܝܢ — ܐܚܪ̈ܢܐ, Acts xxviii. 24; or by ܐܢܫ ܐܢܫ — ܐܢܫ ܐܢܫ Phil. i. 15; *b*) by ܐܝܬ ܕ — ܐܚܪ̈ܢܐ Matt. xvi. 14; John vii. 12; or with ܐܝܬ ܕ repeated, Assem. I. 10. Rem. 1, 2; *c*) by ܡܢܗܘܢ — ܡܢܗܘܢ Acts xvii. 32; Barh. 105, 10; with the sign of the case prefixed, 114,14. ܠܡܢܗܘܢ ܩܛܠܘ ܘܠܡܢܗܘܢ ܥܘܪ ܣܡܝܢܗܘܢ *some they killed, others he blinded;* finally by ܡܢ — ܐܚܪ̈ܢܐ, Barh. 93, 18.

Rem.—When *some* signifies the *greater part,* it is expressed by

ܐ̈ܢܫܐ ܗܟܢ — ܐ̈ܚܪܢܐ, John vii. 40. *Some this—others that*, by ܐ̈ܚܪܢܐ ܐ̈ܚܪܢܝܬܐ Acts xix. 32.

8. *The one, the other*, (*alter*) are expressed; *a*) of persons, by ܚܒܪ masc. ܚܒܪܬܐ fem., repeated; or by ܚܕܐ — ܚܒܪ Isa. iii. 5; ܐܢܫ — ܚܒܪ Gen. xiii. 11; also of inanimate objects, Matt. xii. 13. ܦܫܛ ܐܝܕܗ ܘܬܩܢܬ ܐܝܟ ܚܒܪܬܗ *he stretched forth his hand and it became sound as the other;* I Cor. xiv.7; Col. iii. 13. ܐܢ ܐܝܬ ܠܐܢܫ ܥܠ ܚܒܪܗ ܪܘܥܡܐ *if one hath an accusation against another;* Phil. ii. 3, 4; *b*) by ܚܕ or ܗܢܐ repeated, Rom. xii. 10; ܚܕ ܠܚܕ *one to the other* (=*each other*, comp. Remark); Matt. xxiv. 10; John xiii. 35; also by ܚܕ - ܐܚܪܢܐ Matt. vi. 24. ܐܚܪܝܢ — ܐܚܪܝܢ John iv. 37; *c*) by the repetition of the same noun, Acts xxi. 34. ܐ̈ܢܫܐ - ܡܕܡ ܡܕܡ *one this, another that;* or by ܚܕ̈ܕܐ Gal. vi. 2. ܛܥܘܢܘ ܝܘܩܪܐ ܕܚܕ̈ܕܐ *let one bear another's burden.*

Rem.—*One another* is represented by ܚܕ ܚܕ, with a preposition interposed between, John xiii. 14; xxii. 34, 36; sometimes by the simple preposition with suffix, Rom. i. 24. ܒܗܘܢ *among one another;* or in like manner by ܚܕ̈ܕܐ John xvi. 19; Barh. 41, 18.

9. *The same, himself, herself, itself*, are expressed; *a*) by a personal pronoun doubled, with ܒܗ placed between; e. g. Heb. x. 11. ܗܘ ܒܗ ܗܘ ܕܒܚܐ *the same sacrifice;* Phil. iii. 1. ܗܢܝܢ ܒܗܝܢ ܗܢܝܢ *the same;* also without ܒܗ; e.g. Assem. I. 44, 13. ܒܗܘ ܒܗܘ ܙܒܢܐ *at the same time;* *b*) by a compounding of the demonstrative pronoun (§ 17. 1. Rem.; § 57. 1. Rem.); *c*) by the pleonastic suffix before the noun; e.g. Mark i. 42. ܒܗ ܒܫܥܬܐ *at the same hour;* Heb. ii. 14; ix. 24. ܠܗ ܠܫܡܝܐ *into heaven itself;* Matt. xxvi. 44; Heb. ix. 21.

ܡܶܢܶܗ ܡܶܢ ܕܡܳܐ *with the same blood ;* with ܕܺܝܠ and the noun following ; e.g. Assem. I.415,3. ܕܺܝܠܶܗ ܕܫܰܢ݈ܬܳܐ *the same year ;* 416, 1 ; *d*) sometimes by ܢܰܦܫܳܐ and ܩܢܽܘܡܳܐ with suffix (§ 58. A), Matt. iv. 6 ; John v. 26, 43.

Rem.—More definite are ܗܽܘܝܽܘ ܗܽܘ , equivalent to *just the same, exactly the same* ;John i. 15 ; vii. 25 ; Barh. 26, 2.

10. *A certain (one) ; a*) by ܚܰܕ masc. ܚܕܳܐ fem. ; John iv. 46. ܡܰܠܟܳܐ ܚܰܕ *a certain king ;* v. 2. ܕܽܘܟܬܳܐ ܚܕܳܐ *a certain place ;* Barh.116,10 ; 117,3 ; with ܡܶܢ following; e.g. Assem. I. 33; 22, 27 ; Barh. 93, 6 ; *b*) by ܡܶܕܶܡ relating to things ; e.g. Barh. 170, 3. ܟܰܕ ܥܰܠ ܠܒܰܝܬܳܐ ܡܶܕܶܡ *when he had entered into a house ;* 178, 2 ; 194, 3.

Rem.—In proper nouns it is sometimes expressed, by circumlocution, by ܐ̱ܢܳܫ ܕܫܡܶܗ ;e. g. Assem. 350, 18 ; 351, 2.

11. *As great—as (tantus quantus)* is expressed by ܐܰܝܟ ; e.g. Barh. 190, 16. ܠܳܐ ܚܙܰܘ — ܐܰܝܟ ܐܽܘܠܨܳܢܳܐ ܕܝܰܘܡܳܐ ܗܰܘ *they saw no need so great as on this day. Of which nature—of such,* or *so as (talis--qualis)*, are expressed by ܐܰܝܟܰܢܳܐ ܕ — ܗܳܟܰܢܳܐ ; e.g. Assem. I.39 ; 17,18. ܐܰܝܟܰܢܳܐ ܕܚܙܰܝܬ ܐܺܝܬ ܠܨܰܠܡܽܘܬܳܐ - ܗܳܟܰܢܳܐ ܐܺܝܬܰܘܗ̱ܝ *as the statue which thou hast seen, so is he.* This latter idea alone is also expressed by ܐܰܝܟ and a pronoun following ; e.g. John iv. 23; ܕܐܰܝܟ ܗܳܠܶܝܢ *such ;* Barh. 55, 13 ; 70, 18.

CHAPTER SECOND.

THE VERB.

---

§ 59. *General View.*

The use of the *Preterit* and of the *Future*, as in the Hebrew, is so comprehensive, that by them almost all the other relations of time are designated, in accordance with definite rules (comp. § 65). This, however, is usually in such a manner that the preterite designates those tenses which stand in connection with past time, while the *future* has the same influence upon *future* time.

---

§ 60. *Use of the Preterit.*

1. In the *Past* it designates ;

a) the absolutely *past* tense ; e.g. Matt. ii. 2. ܚܙܝܢ ܟܘܟܒܗ *we have seen his star ;* ܐܬܝܢ ܠܡܣܓܕ ܠܗ *we are come to worship him ;* John iii. 16 ; Assem. I. 361, 26, 27 ;

b) the *Narrative* tense (*Aorist*) ; *α*) mostly *before the subject ;* e.g. Mark xi. 11. ܥܠ ܝܫܘܥ ܠܐܘܪܫܠܡ *Jesus came to Jerusalem ;* John ii. 22. ܐܬܕܟܪܘ ܬܠܡܝܕܘܗܝ *his disciples remembered ;* *β*) after particles (when something *actual* is denoted), e. g. ܡܢ, Barh. 68,12. ܡܢ ܠܐ ܩܒܠܘ *since they did not receive;* line 4. ܥܕܡܐ ܕ *until that ;* Matt. i. 25. ܥܕܡܐ ܕܝܠܕܬ *until she brought forth ;* Barh. 24, 6 ; ܥܕܡܐ ܕܡܝܬ *until he died ;* 213, 18 ; 217, 3 ; Assem. I. 31,17 ; Ephr. I. 196, F ;

c) the *Pluperfect*; *a*) in relative clauses which define the principal action, and in point of time, precede it; e.g. Matt. i. 24. ܥܒܕ ܐܝܟܢܐ ܕܦܩܕ ܠܗ ܡܠܐܟܗ ܕܡܪܝܐ *he did as the angel of the Lord had commanded;* Mark xi. 6; *b*) after particles; e.g. ܡܐ ܕ *when, after;* Matt. ii. 1. ܡܐ ܕܐܬܝܠܕ ܝܫܘܥ *when Jesus was born;* verse 9; John ii. 22; vi. 23, 24; Barh. 90, 9; Assem. 84, B. 6. ܒܬܪ ܕ *after that;* Barh. 39,7. ܒܬܪ ܕܩܛܠܗ ܠܕܪܝܘܫ *after that he had slain Darius;* 164,8. ܡܢ ܒܬܪ ܕ, ibid; Assem. I. 213, A. 25; ܡܚܕܐ ܕ *so soon as;* Barh. 79, 12.

Rem.—More frequently, however, for the pluperfect, stands the periphrastic form of the preterite with ܗܘܐ (§ 65).

2. It denotes the *Present Tense;*

a) in verbs of *quality* and *condition;* e. g. Matt. xvi. 2, 3. ܣܡܩ ܫܡܝܐ *the sky is red;* John iv. 35. ܐܪ̈ܥܬܐ ܕܚܘܪܝ *the fields which are white;* Isa. i. 3; Ephr. II. 117, A; *b*) in general designations of time, denoting simply what is *usual* and *customary;* e. g. Ps. xiv. 2. ܡܪܝܐ ܐܕܝܩ *the Lord looks down;* xxv. 2; *c*) when it denotes a state or condition; e.g. Gen. iv. 6. ܠܡܢܐ ܐܬܚܡܬ ܠܟ *why art thou angry?*

3. It marks the *Future Tense;*

a) in prophecies, asseverations, and the like, (for the most part, however, only in translations from the Hebrew), which are viewed as already fulfilled and accomplished; e.g. Isa. ix. 2. ܚܙܘ ܢܘܗܪܐ ܪܒܐ *they shall see a great light;* Gen. xvii. 20; sometimes after verbs in which is involved the idea of a future action; e. g. Barh. 80, 1. ܐܡܪ ܕܢܬܠ *he promised that he would give;* *b*) the *completed future* (*futurum exactum*) after ܡܐ ܕ; e.g. Mark xii.25. ܡܐ ܕܩܡܘ ܡܢ ܡܝ̈ܬܐ *when they shall rise from the dead;* John iv. 25.

4. In exhortations, and in clauses which contain conditions or conclusions, the preterite also expresses the relation of the subjunctive; *a*) of the *present tense*, (ܗܘܐ with a participle or adjective); e. g. I Thess. v. 6. ܢܗܘܐ ܥܝܪܝܢ *let us be watchful;* verse 8; Eph. ii. 11; Tit. ii. 9, 10; *b*) of

the *imperfect:* e. g. John ix. 41. ܐܠܘ ܣܡܝܐ ܗܘܝܬܘܢ، ܠܝܬ ܗܘܬ ܠܟܘܢ، ܚܛܝܬܐ *if ye were blind, then would ye have had no sin;* xv. 19; c) of the *pluperfect;* e. g. John xi. 21. ܐܠܘ ܬܢܢ ܗܘܝܬ ܠܐ ܡܐܬ ܗܘܐ ܐܚܝ *hadst thou been here my brother had not died;* Barh. 93, 10; Ephr. I. 225, E.

Rem.—In the first case (under *a*, above) ܗܘܐ is sometimes wanting; e. g. Matt. ix. 17. ܕܠܐ ܡܨܛܪܝܢ ܙܩܐ *the bottles do not thereby burst;* xxv. 24; Mark i. 44; ii. 21,22; Luke v. 36; the imperfect subjunctive is more frequently expressed by the future (§ 61); and sometimes the preterite with ܠܘܝ *oh, that,* denotes the *optative* (§ 65); e.g. Rev. iii. 15. ܠܘܝ ܩܪܝܪܐ ܗܘܝܬ *oh, that thou wert cold;* Ephr. III. 284. ܠܘܝ ܠܐ ܗܘܝܬ ܡܢ ܒܢܝ̈ܗ *would that I were not of her children.* This idea seems also involved in the cases under *c.*

5. Finally, the preterit also stands for the *Imperative* and the *Infinitive;*

a) the preterit ܗܘܐ occurs as an *Imperative* in connection with an adjective or participle; e. g. Mark v. 34. ܗܘܝ ܚܠܝܡܐ ἴσθι ὑγιής; II Tim. iv. 5; Rom. xii. 9, 10. ܗܘܝܬܘܢ، ܪܚܡܝܢ ܠܐܚܝ̈ܟܘܢ *love your brethren;* I Pet. ii. 13; iv. 9; after preceding imperatives; e. g. Luke x. 37. ܙܠ ܐܦ ܐܢܬ ܗܟܢܐ ܗܘܝܬ ܥܒܕ πορεύου, καὶ σὺ ποίει ὁμοίως; I Pet. iii. 15;

b) the preterit stands as an *Infinitive* after verbs signifying *to come, to go, to send,* etc., without the copula; e. g. Barh. 415,2. ܐܬܐ ܪܡܐ ܟܠܐ ܥܟܘ *he came to besiege Acco;* 402, 8; with the copula, Barh. 403, 16, 17. ܫܕܪܘ ـ ܘܒܥܘ *they sent to entreat;* especially after ܫܪܝ; e. g. Barh. 68, 1. ܫܪܝ ܦܬܚ — ܘܩܪܒ *he began to open — and to offer up.*

Rem.—But this union frequently denotes merely the aorist; e. g. *Assem. I.* 288, 2. ܩܡܘ ܐܙܠܘ *they arose to go* i. e. *they went.*

---

§ 61. *Use of the Future.*

1. The Future stands;

a) for the *Absolute Future;* e. g. Matt. xxiv. 35. ܫܡܝܐ ܘܐܪܥܐ ܢܥܒܪܘܢ ܘܡܠܝ ܠܐ ܢܥܒܪܢ *Heaven and earth shall pass away, but my word shall not pass away;* i. 21, 23; Luke xviii. 8; John xiv. 13;

b) for the *Complete Future* in conditional clauses, (with the future in the conclusion of the sentence); John v. 43. ܐܢ ܐܚܪܢܐ ܢܐܬܐ ܒܫܡ ܢܦܫܗ ܠܗܘ ܬܩܒܠܘܢ *if another shall have come in his own name, him will ye receive;* viii. 28. xv. 7, 10.

2. Furthermore, it denotes, the following relations of time;

a) the *Present* although more rarely than in Hebrew; e.g. John iv. 13. ܟܠ ܕܢܫܬܐ ܡܢ ܗܠܝܢ ܡܝܐ ܬܘܒ ܢܨܗܐ πᾶς ὁ πίνων ἐκ τοῦ ὕδατος τούτου, διψήσει πάλιν; with ܐܢ verse 48, after ܩܕܡ ܕ Luke xxii. 61. ܩܕܡ ܕܢܩܪܐ ܬܪܢܓܠܐ *before the cock crows;* *b*) the *Imperfect;* *α*) after such verbs as ܫܪܝ ܕ; Assem. I. 27, 20. ܫܪܝ ܕܢܐܡܪ ܠܗ *he spake to him* (*began to speak*); *β*) after particles ܥܕܡܐ ܕ *until;* ܩܕܡ ܕ *before;* e. g. Luke ii. 21. ܩܕܡ ܕܬܬܒܛܢ ܒܟܪܣܐ *before he was conceived in his mothers womb;* Barh. xi. 15; *c*) more rarely the Perfect; e. g. Jud. v. 8. ܢܓܒܐ ܐܠܗܐ *God hath chosen;* Isa. xliii. 17, 19; *d*) the *Pluperfect;* after ܥܕܠܐ, ܩܕܡ ܕ *before;* e. g. Jer. i. 5.

3. It serves to express the following Moods;

A) the *Subjunctive;* *a*) of the *Present;* *α*) in general;

John vii. 37. ܢܐܬܐ ܠܘܬܝ ܘܢܫܬܐ *let him come to me and drink;* Barh. 79, 1. ܡܟܝܠ ܢܡܘܬ *now let him die;* β) after ܕ, ܕܠܐ with a preceding present or imperative; e. g. John v. 10. ܠܐ ܫܠܝܛ ܠܟ ܕܬܫܩܘܠ ܥܪܣܟ *it is not lawful that thou should'st carry thy bed;* vi. 12. ܟܢܫܘ — ܕܠܐ ܢܐܒܕ ܡܕܡ *gather—that nothing be lost;* Matt.xxvi.41; Assem.I.377,10, 11,13; *b*) of the *Imperfect;* *a*) in conditional clauses; John ix. 22. ܐܢ ܐܢܫ ܢܘܕܐ ܒܗ *if any man should confess concerning him;* β) after a preceding imperfect; e. g. John ii. 25. ܠܐ ܣܢܝܩ ܗܘܐ ܕܐܢܫ ܢܣܗܕ *it was not needful that any one should testify;* after a preterite; v.27. ܐܫܠܛܗ ܕܢܗܘܐ ܥܒܕ ܕܝܢܐ *he gave him authority that he should execute judgment;* i. 31; Barh. 80, 3; Assem. I. 359, 5; after the pluperfect; e. g. John iv. 8. ܐܙܠܘ ܗܘܘ — ܕܢܙܒܢܘܢ *they were gone that they might buy;* γ) sometimes with ܗܘܐ appended; e.g. Ephr. I. 223, C. ܐܝܟܢܐ ܢܥܒܕܝܘܗܝ ܗܘܐ *how he would do;* Assem. I. 297, B. 3. v. E; *c*) of the *Perfect* sometimes, in conditional clauses, after ܐܢ and ܐܠܐ ܐܢ (*in case that*); e.g. John vii. 51; Ephr. I. 237, B. and E; *d*) of the *Pluperfect*, more rarely, and only with ܗܘܐ appended; e. g. Ephr. I. 40, B. ܡܢܐ ܡܣܪܚܢܘܬܐ ܗܘܬ ܗܘܐ ܒܗܕܐ ܕܫ̈ܒܠܐ ܛܒܐ ܝܠܕܐ ܗܘܐ *what harm would have arisen because it had brought forth good ears?*

Rem.—*May*, *might*, *can*, *should*, *must*, and the like, are also expressed by the future; e. g. Ephr. I. 203, F. ܕܢܐܙܠ ܘܢܚܙܐ *that he might go and see;* John iv. 40. ܒܥܘ ܡܢܗ ܕܢܗܘܐ ܠܘܬܗܘܢ *they entreated him that he would remain with them;* verse 47; v. 14; Rom. vi. 1. ܡܢܐ ܢܐܡܪ ܢܩܘܐ *what shall we say, shall we continue?* Gen. ii. 16, 30, 31; Luke xviii. 7; John vi. 28; Heb.

i. 6; Barh. 63, 19. ܟܠ ܕܠܐ ܢܩܪܒ ܢܡܘܬ *every one who offered not should die*; 68, 18; Mark ix. 49. ܟܠ ܕܒܚܬܐ ܒܡܠܚܐ ܬܬܡܠܚ *every sacrifice should be salted with salt*; Prov. xx. 9; ܡܢ ܢܐܡܪ *who can say?* By way of circumlocution, *may* and *should* are expressed by ܫܠܝܛ ܕ; e. g. I Cor. xi. 7; *must*—by ܘܠܐ ܕ with a future following; e. g. John iv. 24; I Tim. iii. 2.

B) The *Imperative*; *a*) in Prohibitions; e.g. Matt. i. 20. ܠܐ ܬܕܚܠ *fear not;* John iii. 7; vi. 20; I Cor. xv. 33, 34. ܠܐ ܬܚܛܘܢ *sin not;* *b*) after a preceding imperative; e. g. John i. 40. ܬܘ ܘܬܚܙܘܢ ἔρχεσθε καὶ ἴδετε, verse 47; viii. 11.

Rem.—The third person of the imperative, which is wanting, is always expressed by the future; e. g. Gen. i. 3. ܢܗܘܐ ܢܘܗܪܐ *let there be light.*

C) The future marks the *Infinitive* after verbs which involve the intention of some action; e. g. Barh. 34, 4, 5. ܒܥܐ ܕܢܩܛܘܠ *he sought to kill;* 90,7,8. ܐܬܚܫܒ ܕܢܩܛܠܝܘܗܝ *he thought to kill him;* Matt. ii. 22. ܕܚܠ ܕܢܐܙܠ *he feared to go;* Assem. 1. 33, 25. ܫܪܝ ܕܢܨܘܡ ܘܢܨܠܐ *he began to fast and to pray;* John iii. 3. ܠܐ ܡܫܟܚ ܕܢܚܙܐ *he cannot see;* verses 4, 5; xv. 4 (without ܕ following, Matt. viii. 28). In like manner occur ܐܬܐ Matt. v.17; ܨܒܐ xvi. 3; ܦܩܕ Luke viii. 55; Acts i. 4; and many others.

Rem.—The infinitive with ܠ also follows these verbs. Compare § 63. B.

4. Finally, the future is also expressed by ܥܬܝܕ *ready, about to be* (= μέλλειν) and a following infinitive; e.g.Matt. xi. 14. ܕܥܬܝܕ ܠܡܐܬܐ *he who is to come;* John iii. 14. ܗܟܢܐ ܥܬܝܕ ܠܡܬܬܪܡܘ ܒܪܗ ܕ ܐܢܫܐ *even so the Son of Man is to be lifted up;* vi. 6; vii. 35; in the plural; Luke xxi.

9. ܥܬܝܕ̈ܢ ܐܢܝܢ ܗܠܝܢ ܠܡܗܘܐ *this will come to pass;* verse 36. The implied idea of the imperfect is expressed by ܗܘܐ appended; e. g. John vii. 39. ܪܘܚܐ ܕܥܬܝܕܝܢ ܗܘܘ ܠܡܩܒܠܘܗ̇ *the spirit which they were to receive.*

Rem.—Also occurs ܥܬܝܕ ܕ with a following future; e. g. Assem. I. 481, 22. ܕܥܬܝܕ ܟܗܢܐ ܕܢܫܪܐ *the priest shall begin*; 37, 17; Ephr. I. 197, D; in the plural; John vi. 15. The idea of *willing, purposing,* is also expressed by ܨܒܐ; *a*) with ܕ and a future following; especially Matt. xvi. 24. ܡܢ ܕܨܒܐ ܕܢܐܬܐ ܒܬܪܝ whoso will follow after me; v. 40; Barh. 68,6; or without ܕ; e. g. Luke xviii. 13. ܠܐ ܨܒܐ ܗܘܐ — ܢܪܝܡ *he would not—lift up;* b) with an infinitive following; John i.44. ܨܒܐ ܠܡܦܩ *he would go forth.*

---

§ 62. *Use of the Imperative.*

1. The Imperative expresses either a *command;* e.g. John v. 8. ܩܘܡ ܫܩܘܠ ܥܪܣܟ ܘܗܠܟ *arise, take up thy bed and walk;* or *encouragement* and *permission;* e. g. Mark i. 38. ܗܠܟܘ ܠܩܘܪ̈ܝܐ *go into the city;* John xi. 15.

Rem.—In the same signification the Syriac appends the imperative of ܐܬܐ (vid. § 28. 1.Rem.; 2. Rem.) to the future of the finite verb, especially of ܬܐ and ܬܝ in the singular, when *two,* are intended; e. g. Gen. xxxi. 44. ܬܐ ܢܩܝܡ ܩܝܡܐ *let us make a covenant;* xix. 32; and ܬܘ in the plural, when *several* are meant; e.g. John xi. 7. ܬܘ ܢܐܙܠ *let us go.*

2. The imperative standing after the future, sometimes acquires a future signification; e. g. Gen. xlv. 18. ܐܬܠ ܠܟܘܢ — ܘܐܟܘܠܘ *I will give to you—and ye shall eat;*

or the latter of two imperatives, following each other without a copula, denotes the infinitive; e. g. John iv. 16. ܙܠ ܩܪܝ *go to call ;* verse 29. ܬܘ ܚܙܘ *come to see ;* Ephr. I. 201, E; or with the copula they stand in the relation of *cause* and *effect ;* e. g. Gen. xlii. 18. ܗܕܐ ܥܒܕܘ ܘܚܝܘ *do this and live*, i. e., *if ye would live.*

Rem.—In this latter case the future also follows the imperative; e. g. Isa. viii.10. ܡܠܠܘ ܡܠܬܐ ܘܠܐ ܬܬܩܝܡ *speak a word, it shall not be fulfilled.*

3. Of two successive imperatives, when one is negative, it is expressed by the future (§ 61. 3. B); e. g. John viii. 11. ܙܠ ܘܡܢ ܗܫܐ ܬܘܒ ܠܐ ܬܚܛܐ *go and henceforth sin no more ;* Rom. xi. 20; Eph. iv. 26.

Rem.—Concerning the third person of the imperative, compare § 61. 3. B. Rem. On the use of ܗܘܐ to designate this person. see § 60. 5. *a.*

---

§ 63. *Use of the Infinitive.*

The Syriac, which has not, like the Hebrew, a double form for the infinitive absolute and construct, denotes the latter by ܠ prefixed (compare § 19. B. 3).

A. Infinitive Absolute.

The infinitive without ܠ is mostly used adverbially, and in connection with its finite verb, which it precedes, denotes; *a*) a *strenthening* of the action; e. g. Hebr.vi. 14. ܡܒܪܟܘ ܐܒܪܟܟ ܘܡܣܓܐܘ ܐܣܓܝܟ *I will bless thee exceedingly and multiply thee greatly* ; I Sam. xx. 6; xxiii. 22; John ix. 9. ܡܕܡܐ ܕܡܐ ܠܗ *he is very like him* ; Acts v.

28; Philem. verse 9; *b*) *certainty, confirmation;* e.g. Barh. 15, 13. ܡܕܥ ܬܕܥ *thou shall know with certainty.* Negatively with ܠܐ before the finite verb it is equivalent to, *by no means;* e.g. John xx. 5. ܡܥܠ ܠܐ ܥܠ *he by no means went in;* Rom. ix. 6.; *c*) it sometimes denotes *continuance;* e.g. Isa. xxx.19. ܡܒܟܐ ܠܐ ܬܒܟܘܢ *ye shall not always weep;* Exod. xxxiv. 7.

Rem.—By the infinitive absolute are also expressed, rather however after the idiom of the Hebrew, other minute points of the language; e. g. *much, much more;* Jer. xxii. 10. ܡܒܟܐ ܒܟܘ *weep much; somewhat, indeed* (Germ. *etwa*), Gen. xxxvii. 8. ܡܡܠܟܘ ܡܡܠܟ ܐܢܬ ܥܠܝܢ *wilt thou indeed rule over us? then, truly;* xliii.7. ܡܕܥ ܝܕܥܝܢ ܗܘܝܢ *could we then know? perhaps, indeed;* Acts vii. 34. ܡܚܙܐ ܚܙܝܬ *I have indeed seen.* More frequently it is merely pleonastic; e. g. Luke i. 22; John xiii. 29; Acts vii. 45; and it is appended to the imperative; e. g. Isa. vi. 9. ܫܡܥܘ ܡܫܡܥ *hear ye.* The negative sometimes stands before it; e.g. Gen. iii. 4. ܠܐ ܡܡܬ ܬܡܘܬܘܢ *ye surely shall not die.* The case *a*, in translations of passages from the Old Testament, is also expressed by the noun formed from the finite verb; e. g. Gen. ii.17. ܡܘܬܐ ܬܡܘܬ מוֹת תָּמוּת *thou shalt surely die* (compare Ephr. I. 24, A), which is closely connected with the ordinary Syriac mode of expression; as ܚܕܝ ܚܕܘܬܐ ܪܒܬܐ ܛܒ *rejoice exceedingly;* see § 67. 1. c.

B. Infinitive with ܠ or the Construct form.

The Infinitive with ܠ stands;

a) after verbs which denote a *purpose, wish, determination, capacity, command,* etc.; e. g. Luke xi. 54. ܒܥܝܢ ܠܡܨܕܘ ܡܕܡ *they sought to catch something;* Matt. xxi. 46;

John v. 16; vii. 1. ܠܐ ܨܒܐ ܗܘܐ ܠܡܗܠܟܘ *he would not go;* Matt. xiv. 5; Barh. 14, 18; 83, 6; Matt. vi. 24. ܠܐ ܐܢܫ ܡܫܟܚ ܠܡܦܠܚ *no man can serve;* Mark ii. 7; John iii. 2; x. 21; Barh. 192,20. ܐܦܠܐ ܠܬܡܢ ܐܫܟܚ ܠܡܩܘܝܘ *here also could he not remain;* Luke xv. 15. ܫܕܪܗ ܠܡܪܥܐ *he sent him to feed;* John iv. 33. ܐܝܬܝ — ܠܡܐܟܠ *he brought—to eat;* Ephr. I. 230, D. ܢܣܒܘܢ — ܠܡܘܩܕܘ *they shall take — to kindle;* John xi. 31. ܕܠܩܒܪܐ ܐܙܠܐ ܠܡܒܟܐ *that she goeth unto the grave to weep;* Barh. 12, 20; *b*) after verbs signifying *to begin, to cease, to be accustomed;* e. g. Matt. iv. 17. ܫܪܝ ܠܡܟܪܙܘ *he began to preach;* xvi. 21; Barh. I, 1, 2; 5, 2; Assem. I. 513, B. 20; Acts v. 42. ܠܐ ܫܠܝܢ ܗܘܘ ܠܡܠܦܘ *they ceased not to teach;* Eph. i. 16; Barh. 5. 10. ܡܕܪܒܝܢ ܠܡܫܚܠܦܘ *they were accustomed to changes.*

Rem. 1.—The infinitive with ܠ (which can sometimes, viz. in passages translated from the Hebrew, be rendered by *while,* or *when;* e.g. Gen. ii. 3. ܕܒܪܐ ܐܠܗܐ ܠܡܥܒܕ *which God created, when he made it*); forms, after ܥܬܝܕ (§ 61. 4) and after ܗܘܐ, a circumlocution for the future; e.g. Gen. xv.12. ܗܘܐ ܫܡܫܐ ܠܡܥܪܒ *the sun shall go down.* But of the Hebrew idiom, by which the infinitive, joined with a preposition or conjunction, is explained by the finite verb, there occurs in Syriac, only the construction with ܡܢ ܕ before ܠ; e.g. Assem. I. 42,8. ܘܠܐ ܫܠܐ ܗܘܐ ܡܢ ܕܠܡܠܦܘ *and he ceased not to teach;* negatively, in Hebr. iv. 1. ܕܩܘܡ ܡܢ ܕܠܡܥܠ *who should refrain from entering,* i. e., *who should not enter;* or comparatively, without ܕ; Gen. iv. 13. ܪܒܐ ܗܝ ܡܣܟܠܘܬܝ ܡܢ ܠܡܫܒܩܘ *my crime is greater, than can be forgiven me.*

Rem. 2.—In the poets we sometimes meet with a transition

from the infinitive to the finite verb; e. g. Ephr. III. 129, F. ܦܩܚ ܗܘ ܠܟ ܒܙܒܢ ܨܗܝܐ ܡܝ̈ܐ ܠܡܫܬܐ ܘܠܐ ܢܟܘܠ ܚܠܦ ܡܫܬܝܐ ܡܒܘ̈ܥܐ ܢܟܘܠ *far better is it, in time of thirst to drink water, than, instead of drinking to measure fountains* (literally, *and we will not measure*); and likewise conversely; which seems to be done for the sake of the metre (compare Hahn et Sieff. Chr. p. 7, Anm.). The Syriac also expresses the infinitive by the future, with or without ܕ prefixed (§ 61. 3. C) or by the participle (§ 64. 3. B).

---

§ 64. *Use of the Participle.*

1. Participles may be considered either as Adjectives or as Substantives:

A) As *Adjectives*, they assume the number and gender of their subject; and take their object in the case or with the preposition of the verb from which they are formed; thus; *a*) the *Active Participle;* e. g. John ii. 14. ܗܢܘܢ ܕܡܙܒܢܝܢ ܬܘܪ̈ܐ ܘܥܪ̈ܒܐ ܘܝܘ̈ܢܐ *those who sold oxen, sheep, and doves;* verse 16; viii. 44; Barh. 52, 4, 5; 74, 20. ܡܠܟܐ ܕܕܚܠ ܠܐܠܗܐ *a king who fears God;* Assem. I. 270, A. Rem. 9; Acts vi. 3. ܡܠܝܢ ܪܘܚܐ ܕܩܘܕܫܐ *full of the Holy Ghost;* Rom. i. 29; John iii.15. ܟܠܢܫ ܕܡܗܝܡܢ ܒܗ *every one who believes on him;* *b*) the *Passive Participle*, with the case or the preposition of its active; e. g. Ez. ix. 2. ܠܒܝܫ ܒܘܨܐ *clothed in Byssus;* Barh. 32, 14; 108, 6; 170, 19. ܦܫܝܓ ܐܝܕܐ *maimed in the hand;* Lev. ii. 4. ܪ̈ܩܝܩܢ ܡܫܝܚܢ ܒܡܫܚܐ *cakes anointed with oil;* I Sam. ii.18. ܒܪܝܟ ܠܡܪܝܐ *blessed of the Lord.*

B) As *Substantives*, participles stand, in a genitive relation, in the construct state, before the noun; thus *a*) the

Active Participle; e.g. Gen. xxiii. 10. ܥܳܐܠܰܝ̈ ܬܰܪܥܳܐ *those who went in at the gate*; Rom. vii. 1. ܝܳܕ̈ܥܰܝ ܢܳܡܽܘܣܳܐ *those who know the law* (literally, *the knowers of the law*); Barh. 195, 11. ܫܳܠ̈ܦܰܝ ܣܰܝ̈ܦܳܐ *who had drawn the sword*; 214, 1; even before prepositions; II Tim. iii. 2. ܟܳܦܪ̈ܰܝ ܒܛܰܝܒܽܘܬܳܐ *who deny* (i. e. *refuse to acknowledge*) favors; I Tim. i.10. ܥܳܒܪ̈ܰܝ ܥܠ ܡܰܘܡܳܬܳܐ *breaker of their oath*; *b*) the *Passive Participle*; Gen. xxiv. 31. ܒܪܺܝܟܶܗ ܕܡܳܪܝܳܐ *blessed of God*; xxvi. 29.

2. Participles mark the following relations of time:

A) The *present*, in connection with the separable pronoun denoting the subject (§ 54. 2); e. g. John iv. 9. ܨܳܠܶܐ ܐܢ̱ܬ *thou prayest* (*art praying*); xv. 15; Assem. I. 34, 9. ܠܳܐ ܦܩܺܝܕ ܐ̱ܢܳܐ ܡܶܢ ܡܳܪܰܢ *I have no command from our Lord.*

Rem.—In the third person which is usually already rendered definite by a preceding noun or pronoun, the separable pronoun is omitted; e. g. Luke xv. 5. ܘܫܳܩܶܠ ܠܶܗ *and he beareth it* (*the sheep*); verse 6. ܘܐܳܬܶܐ ܠܒܰܝܬܶܗ ܘܩܳܪܶܐ ܠܪ̈ܳܚܡܰܘܗ̱ܝ *and cometh into his house and calleth his friends*; John iii. 18, 20; iv. 36; vii. 17; viii. 47; iv. 23. ܐܶܠܳܐ ܐܳܬܝܳܐ ܫܳܥܬܳܐ *but the time cometh.*

B) The *past*; *a*) the *Imperfect*; *α*) in connection with ܗ̱ܘܳܐ (§ 65); *β*) without ܗ̱ܘܳܐ after a preceding imperfect; e. g. John. iii. 22. ܡܬܰܘܶܐ ܗ̱ܘܳܐ ܥܰܡܗܽܘܢ ܘܡܰܥܡܶܕ *he tarried with them and baptized*; iv. 27, 31; vi. 2; *γ*) after the preterite in a relative parenthetical clause; e. g. John vi. 5. ܘܚܙܳܐ ܟܶܢܫܳܐ ܣܰܓܺܝܐܳܐ ܕܐܳܬܶܐ ܠܘܳܬܶܗ *and he saw a great company who came to him*; verse 11; Assem. I. 75, A.36; joined with ܘ copulative; e. g. Barh. 4, 3. ܗܳܠܟܽܘ ܠܟܽܘܬܳܐ

ܕܚܪܡܘܢ، ܘܝܬܒܝܢ *they went up on Mount Hermon and abode;* b) the *Perfect*; John vii. 52. ܒܨܝ ܘܚܙܝ ܕܢܒܝܐ ܡܢ ܓܠܝܠܐ ܠܐ ܩܐܡ *search and see, that out of Galilee hath arisen no prophet.*

Rem.—It is to be regarded as a mere imitation, and not as a constant idiom of the language, when the Hebrew infinitive הָלוֹךְ or the participle הֹלֵךְ, (by which, coming before the finite verb, is indicated the continuance or gradual progress of an action), is expressed in Syriac by the participle of ܐܙܠ; e. g. Gen. viii. 5. ܘܡܝܐ ܐܙܠܝܢ ܗܘܘ ܘܡܬܒܨܪܝܢ (וְהַמַּיִם הָיוּ הָלוֹךְ וְחָסוֹר) *and the waters decreased more and more;* I Sam. ii. 26. ܘܛܠܝܐ ܐܙܠ ܘܪܒܐ ܘܛܒ (וְהַנַּעַר הֹלֵךְ וְגָדֵל וָטוֹב) *and the boy grew from day to day.*

C) The *Future; a*) the *Absolute Future; α*) in general propositions; e. g. John xi. 23. ܩܐܡ ܐܚܘܟ *thy brother shall rise again; β*) after a present; John xi. 24. ܝܕܥ ܐܢܐ ܕܩܐܡ *I know that he shall rise again;* iv. 25; *γ*) after a preterite, Barh. 80, 20; 81, 1. ܐܡܪ ܠܗ ܕܒܬܠܬܐ ܝܘܡܝܢ ܡܫܠܡ ܐܢܐ ܠܗ ܠܡܕܝܢܬܐ *he said to him that in three days he would surrender the city;* John iv. 25; *δ*) after a future; John xiv. 23. ܐܒܝ ܢܪܚܡܝܘܗܝ ܘܠܘܬܗ ܐܬܝܢܢ *my Father will love him, and we will come to him;* Assem. I. 362, 5, 8. ܐܢ ܢܬܠܗܒ ܠܝ ܕ — ܟܪܝܣܛܝܢܐ ܗܘܐ ܐܢܐ *if it shall be granted me that — then will I become a christian; ε*) after an imperative; Mark xi. 24. ܗܝܡܢܘ ܕܢܣܒܝܢ ܐܢܬܘܢ *believe that ye shall receive; ζ*) after ܗܐ, John xvi. 32. ܗܐ ܐܬܝܐ ܫܥܬܐ *behold the hour shall come;* Gen. vi. 17; xlviii. 4; Exod. ix. 18; *η*) in direct and indirect questions;

e. g. John vii. 41. ܕܠܡܐ ܡܢ ܓܠܝܠܐ ܐܬܐ ܡܫܝܚܐ *shall the Messiah come out of Galilee?* verse 31; viii. 22; xiii. 27. ܡܕܡ ܕܥܒܕ ܐܢܬ *what thou wilt do;* b) the *futurum exactum;* a) after particles; e. g. John vii. 27. ܐܡܬܝ ܕܐܬܐ *when he shall have come;* verse 31. Barh. 133, 2. ܡܐ ܕܫܡܝܥܐ ܐܢܬ *as soon as thou shalt have heard;* β) in conditional clauses; e.g. Ephr. I. 218, F. ܐܠܐ ܕܝܗܒ ܐܢܐ ܠܗ ܡܝܐ *unless I shall have given him water.*

3. In like manner, participles indicate various *Moods;*

A) The *Subjunctive;* viz. a) of the *Imperfect* (with ܗܘܐ, compare § 65) after ܐܢ; e. g. Barh. 38, 10. ܐܢ ܬܒܝܪܐ ܡܬܬܒܪ܆ ܐܪܥܐ — ܠܐ ܡܬܬܒܪܐ܆ *even though the vessel broke, the ground — would not break;* Assem. I. 379, 2. ܐܢ ܟܦܪ܆ ܒܡܫܝܚܐ ܚܝܐ ܘܐܠܐ ܡܐܬ *if he denied Christ then should he live, if not, he should die;* after ܐܠܐ ܕ, Barh. 56, 12. ܐܠܐ ܕܠܐ ܕܒܚܝܢ ܠܡܕܒܚܘܗ *besides that they would not sacrifice;* in relative clauses depending upon a future (= imperfect subjunctive); e. g. Assem. I. 362, 19. ܦܩܕ ܕܢܬܝܗܒ ܠܗܘܢ ܐܦܝܣܩܘܦܐ ܡܢ ܕܫܐܠܝܢ *he ordered that he should be given them as Bishop, whom they should ask;* b) of the *Pluperfect,* with ܗܘܐ in conditional clauses (compare § 60. 4. c); e. g. Gal. iv. 15. ܐܠܘ ܡܫܟܚܐ ܗܘܬ ܥܝܢܝܟܘܢ ܢܩܪܬܘܢ ܗܘܝܬܘܢ ܘܝܗܒܬܘܢ ܠܝ *had it been possible ye would have plucked out your own eyes, and given them to me;* Heb. x. 2; xi. 15; I John ii. 19.

B) The *Infinitive,* after verbs signifying *to begin, to cease, to permit, to command, to be able,* etc.; e. g. Matt. xii. 1. ܫܪܝܘ ܡܠܩܛܝܢ *they began to pluck;* Mark i. 45; Luke v. 21;

xv. 14; I John ii. 8. ܢܘܗܪܐ ܫܪܝܘ ܚܙܝܢ *they began to see the light;* Assem. I. 37,15. ܫܪܝ ܩܪܐ *he began to call;* 50, 5; Barh. 96, 7; 108, 19; 160, 7; 180, 5; 83, 12; ܫܠܐ ܡܢ ܒܢܐ ܥܕ̈ܬܐ *he ceased to build churches;* Matt. xiii. 30. ܫܒܘܩܘ ܪܒܝܢ *suffer to grow;* Luke xviii. 16; John xi. 44; xviii. 8; Luke x. 40. ܐܡܪ ܠܗ̇ ܡܥܕܪܐ ܠܝ *bid her help me;* Mark ii. 2. ܠܐ ܐܚܕ ܐܢܫ ܐܢܘܢ *it could not hold them;* vii. 15; John v. 19; viii. 43; Acts x. 47; Mark vi. 37. ܢܬܠ ܠܗܘܢ ܠܡܐܟܠ *we will give them to eat.*

Rem.—Sometimes ܕ also stands before such a participle; e. g. Matt. xxiv. 30. ܢܚܙܘܢ ܠܒܪܗ ܕܐܢܫܐ ܕܐܬܐ *they shall see the Son of man coming;* John v. 19; Acts xxi. 32. ܫܠܘ ܡܢ ܕܡܚܝܢ ܗܘܘ ܠܦܘܠܘܣ ἐπαύσαντο τύπτοντες τὸν Παῦλον.

4. The *Absolute Participle* is distinguished by a) ܟܕ preceding it; e.g. Matt. xiv. 25. ܐܬܐ ܠܘܬܗܘܢ ܝܫܘܥ ܟܕ ܡܗܠܟ ܥܠ ܡܝܐ *Jesus came to them walking upon the sea;* xv. 32; John ix. 7. ܘܐܬܐ ܟܕ ܚܙܐ *he came seeing;* Barh. 62, 6. ܟܕ ܡܫܓܫ ܒܩܪܒܐ ܡܝܬ *disquieted by war he died;* 73, 4. ܠܐ ܟܕ ܩܐܡ ܐܠܐ ܟܕ ܪܟܝܢ ܐܪܥܐ *not standing, but bowed to the earth;* b) by ܕ preceding; e. g. Mark ii. 14. ܕܝܬܒ ܒܝܬ ܡܟܣܐ *sitting at the receipt of custom;* xi. 2, 4; Matt. xiv. 26; xxvi. 64.

Rem.—If to such a participle, a noun be appended, this construction sometimes expresses the Latin ablative absolute; e. g. Matt. xv. 20. ܟܕ ܠܐ ܡܫܝܓܢ ܐܝ̈ܕܝܗܘܢ *with unwashed hands;* Mark vii. 2, 5; John xi. 44. ܟܕ ܐܣܝܪܢ ܐܝ̈ܕܘܗܝ ܘܪ̈ܓܠܘܗܝ *bound hand and foot.* In the translation of the New Testament, the participle is sometimes to be understood as in the person of the finite verb following it; e. g. Matt. ii. 8. ܙܠܘ ܒܥܘ πορευθέντες ἐξετάσατε, verses 9, 10, 11, 13.

5. The passive participles frequently have an active signification; *a*) those from transitive verbs; e. g. Matt. viii. 18. ܕܚܕܝܪܝܢ ܠܗ *those surrounding him;* Luke vii. 14. ܕܫܩܝܠܝܢ ܗܘܘ ܠܗ *those bearing him;* John v. 4. ܡܙܝܥ ܗܘܐ ܠܡܝܐ *troubling the water;* Acts xxi. 16; Assem. I. 30, 4. ܟܕ ܫܩܝܠܐ ܠܛܠܝܐ *bearing the child;* 34,9; 37,8; 377, 2. ܠܒܝܟܐ ܗܘܬ ܠܗ ܒܐܝܕܗ *she drew him by the hand;* *b*) those from intransitive verbs; e. g. Matt. v. 4. ܛܘܒܝܗܘܢ ܠܐܒܝܠܐ *blessed are those who mourn;* Mark vii. 30; John xi. 19. ܐܬܝܢ ܗܘܘ *they were come;* xii. 15. ܪܟܝܒ ܥܠ ܥܝܠܐ *riding upon a foal;* Barh. 170, 2; 223, 1. ܟܕ ܣܡܝܟ ܥܠ ܥܪܣܐ *sitting upon a bed.*

Rem. — Participles sometimes have the signification of the Latin participle in *-ndus;* e. g. Barh. 128, 2. ܕܚܝܠ *timendus.* Here also belong (compare No. 5) such constructions as ܫܒܝܩ ܠܝ ܟܠ *I have forsaken all;* ܟܦܝܪ ܠܝ ܒܟ *I deny thee;* ܐܝܟ ܕܨܒܝܐ ܠܝ *as I will.*

6. Finally participles are also used impersonally thus; *a*) the *Masculine;* Rom. xvi. 2. ܐܝܟ ܕܦܐܐ ܠܩܕܝܫܐ *as it becometh saints;* Heb. viii. 3; Philem. 8; Assem. I. 33,20. ܒܪܝ ܦܐܐ ܠܟ *my son, it behoveth thee;* 455, A. 24, 41. ܠܐ ܦܐܐ ܠܥܒܕܐ ܕܡܪܝܐ *it behoveth not a servant of the Lord;* John iii. 30. ܠܗܘ ܗܘ ܘܠܐ ܗܘܐ ܠܡܪܒܐ *he must increase;* ix. 4. ܠܝ ܘܠܐ *I must;* Acts xxv. 27; xxvi. 1; Rom. xiv. 4; Mark iv. 38. ܠܐ ܒܛܝܠ ܠܟ ܕܐܒܕܝܢܢ οὐ μέλει σοι, ὅτι ἀπολλύμεθα; *b*) the *Feminine;* especially to denote the neuter; e. g. Gal. vi. 9. ܠܐ ܬܗܘܐ ܡܐܢܐ ܠܢ *let it not be burdensome to us;* Barh. 45, 13. ܗܕܐ ܕܡܝܐ *this is probable;*

Assem. I.179,B.22. ܐܠܝܨܐ ܗܘܬ *it was necessary;* 482, 24. ܦܐܝܐ ܘܙܕܩܐ *it is honorable and right;* 519, A. 4.

Rem.—Here belongs also Rom. xiv. 4. ܡܛܝܐ ܠܐܝܕܘܗܝ *it comes into his hands;* i. e. *he can;* and in the feminine, Acts v. 39. ܠܐ ܡܛܝܐ ܠܐܝܕܝܟܘܢ *ye cannot.*

---

§ 65. *View of the manner of designating all the Tenses and Moods; of the Imperfect, Pluperfect, and Optative in particular.*

1. The *Indicative;*

A) of the *Present* is expressed; *a*) by the preterit (§60. 2); *b*) sometimes by the future (§61. 2. a); *c*) usually by the participle (§ 54. 2. b, and § 64. 2. A);

B) of the *Imperfect*; *a*) usually by the participle joined with ܗܘܐ (§ 18.4. Rem., and § 38; also without the substantive verb, § 64. 2.B. β); e.g. Matt. ii.9. ܐܙܠ ܗܘܐ *he went;* verse 20. ܗܢܘܢ ܕܒܥܝܢ ܗܘܘ ܢܦܫܗ ܕܛܠܝܐ *who sought the child's life;* iii. 5. ܢܦܩܐ ܗܘܬ ܟܠܗ ܝܗܘܕ *all Judea went out;* John xvii. 12. ܢܛܪ ܗܘܝܬ *I kept;* *b*) by the preterite (§ 60. 1. b), and rarely; *c*) by the future (§ 61. 2. b);

C) of the *Perfect,* besides cases noted in (§ 60. 1); *a*) rarely by the future (§ 61. 2. c); *b*) by the participle (§ 64. 2. B. b);

D) of the *Pluperfect;* *a*) usually by ܗܘܐ in the same person and number added to the preterit; e. g. Luke v. 9

ܬܶܡܗܳܐ ܐܰܚܕܳܗ̇ ܗ̱ܘܳܐ *terror had seizĕd him;* John iv. 8. ܥܰܠܘ ܗ̱ܘܰܘ *they had gone into;* v. 13. ܐܶܬ݂ܛܰܫܺܝ ܗ̱ܘܳܐ *he had hidden himself;* x. 22. ܗ̱ܘܳܐ ܗ̱ܘܳܐ *he had been;* *b*) by the preterit (§ 60. 1. c); *c*) rarely by the future (§ 61. 2. d);

E) of the ***Future*** besides cases noted in § 61. 1., sometimes; *a*) by the Preterit (§ 60. 3. a); *b*) by the imperative (§ 62. 2); *c*) by the participle (§ 64. 2. C);

F) of the ***Futurum exactum;*** *a*) by the preterit (§ 60. 3. b), more frequently; *b*) by the future (§ 61. 1. b), sometimes; *c*) by the participle (§ 64. 2. C. b).

II. The ***Subjunctive;***

A) of the ***Present*** is given; *a*) by the preterit of ܗ̱ܘܳܐ (§ 60. 4. a), very often; *b*) by the future (§ 61. 3. A. a);

B) of the ***Imperfect;*** *a*) usually like the indicative of the same tense, by the participle with ܗ̱ܘܳܐ in conditional clauses; e. g. John viii. 19. ܐܶܠܘܽ ܠܺܝ ܝܳܕ݂ܥܺܝܢ ܗ̱ܘܰܝܬܽܘܢ ܐܳܦ ܠܐܳܒ݂ܝ ܝܳܕ݂ܥܺܝܢ ܗ̱ܘܰܝܬܽܘܢ *if ye knew me, ye would also know my father;* verses 39, 42; xviii. 30, 36; xxi. 25; *b*) by the future (§ 61. 3. A. b), sometimes; *c*) by the participle alone (§ 64. 3. A. a);

C) of the ***Perfect;*** sometimes by the future (§ 61. 3. A. c);

D) of the ***Pluperfect;*** *a*) by the preterit (§ 60. 4. c); *b*) by the future (§ 61. 3. A. d), more frequently; *c*) by the participle with ܗ̱ܘܳܐ (§ 64. 3. A. b).

III. The ***Optative*** is expressed; *a*) by the interrogative pronoun with a preterit or future following; e. g. Judges ix. 29. ܡܰܢ ܢܶܬܶܠ ܐܡܠܟܘܗ ܠܥܡܐ ܗܢܐ ܒܐܝܕܝ *oh that I had (who will give over to me) this people in my power!* Ps. iv. 7; lv.7; *b*) by the particles ܠܘܝ and ܐܬܘܣ *oh that*, with a preterit following (§ 60. 4.Rem.); the *Future;* e.g. Gen. xvii.18. ܐܬܘܣ ܢܐܚܐ *oh that he might live*; or the participle with ܗܘܐ; e. g. II Cor. xi.1. ܐܬܘܣ ܡܣܝܒܪܝܢ ܗܘܝܬܘܢ ܠܝ *may ye yet bear with me!*

Rem—The optative is sometimes also expressed by ܐܘ or ܠܘܝ; e.g. Ps.lxxxi.13. ܠܘܝ ܥܡܝ ܫܡܥܢܝ *would that my people would hearken to me*; by verbs that denote a wish with a following ܕ; e.g. Exod. xvi. 3. ܨܒܝܢ ܗܘܝܢ ܕܡܝܬܢ *would that we were dead!* When the substantive verb denotes a wish, it is omitted; e. g. Luke. ii.14. ܫܘܒܚܐ ܠܐܠܗܐ *glory to God.* Sometimes instead of the Hebrew מִי יִתֵּן occurs the almost correspondent ܡܢ ܝܗܒ ܕ; e. g. Job xxiii. 3; but it is literally translated in Cant. viii. 1. ܡܢ ܢܬܠܟ ܐܚܐ ܠܝ *oh that thou wert my brother.*

IV. The *Imperative*, besides the cases under § 62, is expressed; *a*) by the preterit of ܗܘܐ (§ 60. 5. a); *b*) by the future, especially negatively (§ 61. 3. B).

V. The *Infinitive*, finally, besides the cases under § 63, is expressed; *a*) by the preterit (§ 60. 5. b); *b*) by the future (§ 61. 3. C), and more frequently; *c*) by the participle (§ 64. 3. B).

---

§ 66. *The Persons of the Verb.*

1. The third singular masc. and fem. of the active and passive conjugations is sometimes used impersonally thus;

a) the *masculine;* *α*) of the preterit; e. g. Heb. x. 34. ܟܪܐ ܠܟܘܢ *it pained you;* Luke x.34. ܐܬܒܛܠ ܠܗ ܒܝܘܨܦܗ *he cared for him;* *β*) of the future, Deut. vi. 24. ܢܛܐܒ ܠܢ *it would be good for us;* Jer. vii.6. ܢܒܐܫ ܠܟܘܢ *it would harm you;* *b*) the *feminine;* *α*) of the preterit, Ps. xcv.10. ܩܢܛܬ ܠܝ ܡܢ ܕܪܐ ܗܘ *it shames me, (I am ashamed) of this generation;* Ps. xxxi.9. ܥܩܬ ܠܝ *it grieves me;* Luke xviii. 23. ܟܪܬ ܠܗ *it pained him;* *β*) of the future, Gal. vi. 9. ܠܐ ܬܐܡܠ ܠܢ *it will not be grievous to us;* Ps. lxix. 20. ܠܡܢ ܕܬܟܪܐ ܠܗ *whom it grieved.*

2. In like manner in Syriac, the *neuter* is usually expressed; *a*) by the third person singular feminine of the verb, thus; *α*) in impersonal phrases, as Luke vi. 13. ܢܓܗܬ *it was light;* John vi. 17. ܚܫܟܬ *it was dark;* passively, Barh. 84,14. ܐܫܬܡܥܬ *the report was spread abroad;* Assem. I. 298. A.11. ܐܬܓܠܝܬ ܠܗ *it was revealed to him;* 481, 7; *β*) in connection with the demonstrative pronoun or with adjectives as subjects; e. g. John i. 28. ܗܠܝܢ ܒܒܝܬ ܥܢܝܐ ܗܘܝ *this came to pass at Bethany;* i. 3. ܐܦܠܐ ܚܕܐ ܗܘܬ *there was not any thing;* Ephr. I. 240, F. ܫܦܪܬ ܗܕܐ ܒܥܝܢܝ ܡܘܫܐ *it seemed good to Moses;* passively, Assem. I. 380, 4. ܘܙܕܩܐ ܐܬܚܙܝܬ ܠܢ *it seemed just to us.* Yet we also find for the neuter; *b*) the third person singular masculine; e.g. Isa. xxiii. 12. ܠܐ ܢܢܘܚ ܠܟܝ *there will be no rest for thee;* Barh. 133, 8. ܐܬܐܡܪ ܠܗ *it was said to him;* Assem. I. 362, 5. ܐܢ ܢܫܬܒܩ ܠܝ *it shall be permitted to me.*

3. When the subject of the verb is general or indefinite, it is expressed, in Syriac, in various ways, as in the English, thus; *a*) by the third person singular; e. g.

Gen. xi. 9. ܩܳܪܶܐ *he calls;* (i. e. *one calls, it is called*); to which is also appended by way of explanation, after the Hebrew idiom, the participle or participial noun of the same verb; e. g. Isa. xvi. 10. ܕܳܝܶܫ ܕܳܝܽܘܫܳܐ *the wine treaders shall tread* (no more wine; i. e. *no one shall tread*); or ܐ̱ܢܳܫܳܐ and ܓܰܒܪܳܐ; e.g. I Sam. ix. 9. ܐܳܡܰܪ ܗ̱ܘܳܐ ܓܰܒܪܳܐ *he* (i. e. *any one*) *said;* John iii. 4. ܐܰܝܟܰܢܳܐ ܡܶܫܟܰܚ ܕܢܶܬܺܝܠܶܕ ܓܰܒܪܳܐ ܟܰܕ ܣܳܒ݂ܳܐ *how can one be born when he is old?* or passively Matt. xxvi. 13. ܢܶܬܡܰܠܰܠ *it shall be told;* Acts xvi. 13. ܠܰܡ ܡܶܬܚܰܙܝܳܐ ܗ̱ܘܳܐ ܬܰܡܳܢ ܕܨܠܽܘܬ݂ܳܐ *there prayer was wont to be made;* Barh. 58, 13, 15; *b*) by the third person plural; e.g. Isa. lxiv. 3. ܠܳܐ ܫܡܰܥܘ *they* (i. e., *men* in general) *have not heard;* xlvii. 1; Dan. i. 12; Heb. xi. 3. ܗܳܠܶܝܢ ܕܡܶܬ݂ܚܰܙܝܳܢ ܗ̱ܘܰܝ̈ *what they see* (i. e. *what any one sees, what is seen*); also with an explanatory participle or adjective; e.g. Isa. xxiv. 16. ܟܽܘܠܳܐ ܐܶܬ݂ܟܰܠܘ *they failed;* *c*) by the second singular; e. g. Luke ii. 4. ܟܰܕ ܬܰܩܪܶܒ *when thou bringest;* I Tim. ii. 1. ܕܬܶܗ̱ܘܶܐ ܡܩܰܪܶܒ *that thou offerest* (i. e. *that there be offered*); sometimes the verb is in the second plural, Matt. vi. 24; *d*) sometimes by the first plural; e.g. Mark vii. 27. ܕܢܶܣܰܒ — ܘܢܶܪܡܶܐ (or by the infinitive with ܠ, Matt. xv. 26. ܠܡܶܣܰܒ — ܘܠܡܶܪܡܳܝܽܘ xxii. 17), *that we* (i. e. *any one*) *should take*—and cast; *e*) more frequently by the participle alone; e.g. Matt. vii. 16. ܠܡܳܐ ܠܳܩܛܺܝܢ *do men gather?* v. 15; ix. 17; x. 29; I Cor. iv. 12; Barh. 6. 2. ܐܳܡܪܺܝܢ *they say;* 58, 9.

Rem.—Here belongs also ܡܶܬ݂ܐܡܰܪܳܐ *they say, it is said;* and impersonal phrases with an infinitive following; e. g. Matt. xii. 12. ܫܰܠܺܝܛ ܠܡܶܥܒܰܕ *one may do;* Acts v. 29. ܘܳܠܶܐ ܠܡܶܫܬܰܡܳܥܽܘ *we* (*any one*) *must obey.*

4. When the Deity or those in high stations (e.g. Kings), speak of themselves, the first person plural denotes the *pluralis excellentiæ;* e. g. Gen. i. 26. ܢܶܥܒܶܕ ܐ̱ܢܳܫܳܐ *let us* (i. e. *I will*) *make man*; xi. 7; Barh. 90, 9. ܗܳܐ ܟܬܰܒܢܰܢ *behold we* (i.e. *I, Justinian*), *have written;* 11. ܟܬܽܘܒܘ ܠܰܢ *write to us* (*me*).

Rem.—Sometimes though for the most part only in passages translated from the Old and New Testaments, the construction changes from one person to the other, viz.; *a*) from the third to the second, or *vice versa;* Micah vii. 18. ܠܰܝܬ ܐܰܠܳܗܳܐ ܐܰܟܘܳܬܳܟ ܕܫܳܒܶܩ ܚܰܘܒܶ̈ܐ ܘܡܰܥܒܰܪ ܣܰܟܠܘܳܬܳܐ ܕܫܰܪܟܳܐ ܕܝܳܪܬܽܘܬܶܗ ܘܠܳܐ ܐܰܚܕܬ ܐܰܝܟ *there is no God as thou, who forgiveth sins, and remitteth the transgressions of the remnant of his heritage, and retainest not* (compare Ephr. II. 284, A. B); Mal. ii. 15; Gal. iv. 21. ܐܶܡܰܪܘ ܠܺܝ ܐܰܝܠܶܝܢ ܕܨܳܒܶܝܢ ܕܢܶܗܘܽܘܢ ܬܚܶܝܬ ܢܳܡܽܘܣܳܐ λέγετέ μοι, οἱ ὑπὸ νόμον θέλοντες εἶναι; Rom. ii. 1; Matt. xxiii. 37; *b*) from the first to the third person; e. g. Isa. xlii. 24, 25. ܡܶܛܽܠ ܕܚܛܰܝܢ ܠܶܗ — ܐܶܫܕ ܥܠܰܝܗܽܘܢ *because we have sinned against him, — hath he poured out upon them* (*us*).— Here also belong the instances where writers include themselves, in the first person plural, in what they declare of their ancestors; e. g. Psalm lxvi. 6. ܬܰܡܳܢ ܢܶܚܕܶܐ ܒܶܗ *then did we rejoice in him.* When several verbs having different subjects follow each other in the same person, it appears to be rather according to the Syriac idiom, not to indicate more particularly the difference of the subject; e.g. II Sam. xi. 13.

---

§ 67. *Construction of the Verb with various Cases and Prepositions.*

I. Verbs with the Accusative.

1. With an *Accusative* are construed;

a) *Transitive Verbs;* e. g. Matt. ii. 6. ܕܗܽܘ ܢܶܪܥܶܝܗܽܘܢ

ܠܥܡܝ *who shall feed my people* ; iv. 16 ; even intransitives, having at the same time a transitive signification ; e.g. Barh. 214, 2. ܪܟܒ ܗܘܐ ܚܡܪܐ *he rode upon an ass* ; 215, 11.

Rem.—Here also belong such verbs as in other languages govern other cases ; e. g. ܦܩܕ *to command* ; Matt. xxviii. 20. ܗܝܡܢ *to believe* ; John xii. 38 ; Romans x. 16, (with ܒ John ii. 23) ; ܥܢܐ *to answer* ; Ephr. III. 285 ; ܣܒܪ *to announce* ; Acts xvi. 10. etc.

b) Here belong the following classes of verbs ; *α*) those signifying to *put on* or *put off* clothing, *to adorn, to gird, to cover with anything* ; ܠܒܫ I Cor. xv. 53 ; Eph. vi. 11 ; Barh. 223, 12. ܕܢܠܒܫ ܠܒܘܫܝܢ *that he put on our garments* ; ܫܠܚ Col. iii. 9 ; ܐܣܪ I Sam. ii. 4 ; Acts xii. 8 ; even passive verbs ; e.g. ܐܬܚܙܩ Acts xii. 8 ; ܐܬܥܛܦ Ps. civ. 2 ; and *β*) those denoting a *want* or *excess* ; e. g. Acts vi. 8. ܡܠܐ ܗܘܐ ܗܝܡܢܘܬܐ ܘܚܝܠܐ *he was full of faith and power* ; xiii. 10 ; Rom. i. 29 ; Mark viii. 36. ܐܢ ܢܦܫܗ ܢܚܣܪ *if he suffer harm as to his soul.* Furthermore here belong ; *γ*) verbs of *remembering* and *forgetting*, ܥܗܕ John xv. 20 ; Luke i. 72 ; ܐܬܕܟܪ John ii. 17, 22 ; ܛܥܐ Heb. vi. 10 ; and finally ; *δ*) verbs of *coming* and *going* to a place ; e. g. Matt. xv. 21. ܘܐܬܐ ܠܬܚܘܡܐ ܕܨܘܪ *he came into the region of Tyre* ; Mark v. 38 ; Luke ii. 51 ; John iv. 5 ; ܐܙܠ Luke iv. 42 ; John vi. 1 ; ܗܦܟ Luke ii. 39 ; iv. 14 ; ܡܛܐ Acts ix. 3 ; ܢܚܬ John ii. 12 ; ܢܦܩ i. 44 ; ܣܠܩ v. 1 ; ܥܠ xviii. 33 ;

c) several neuters also take an accusative, viz ;

a) in connection with a noun, as their object, formed from the same verb ; e. g. Judg. xiv. 12. ܐܚܕ ܐܘܚܕܬܐ *to propose a riddle;* Ez. xvii. 2; Acts ii. 17. — ܚܙܐ ܚܙ̈ܘܢܐ ܚܠܡ ܚܠܡ̈ܐ *to have visions — dreams;* Matt. xiii. 24; Ephr. I. 251, C; 253, A; especially β) when the noun is more accurately defined by an adjective; e. g. Matt. ii. 10. ܚܕܝܘ ܚܕܘܬܐ ܪܒܬܐ *they rejoiced exceedingly;* John iii. 29; Assem. I. 362, 18; Gen. xxvii. 34. ܐܝܠܠ ܐܝܠܠܬܐ ܪܒܬܐ *he lamented sorely;* Zach. i. 14.

Rem.— ܗܘܐ, in the sense of *to befall, to happen to* any one, also governs the accusative of the object; e. g. Luke xiii. 2. ܕܗܕܐ ܗܘܐ ܠܗܘܢ, *because this has befallen them;* Acts vii. 40. ܡܢܐ ܗܘܐ ܠܗ *what has happened to him;* Acts xxviii. 5, 6.

2 The following govern a double accusative;

a) verbs in *Pa.*, *Aph.*, and *Sha.*, *Pe.* of which takes an accusative, viz.; α) verbs of *putting on* or *off* clothing, *adorning, covering* with anything; e. g. ܐܠܒܫ, ܠܒܫ, Mark xv. 17, 20; Ephr. I. 239, A. ܘܐܠܒܫ ܐܢܘܢ ܟܘܬܝܢ̈ܝܬܐ *he clothed them with garments;* II. 178, D; John xix. 2. ܘܐܠܒܫܘܗܝ ܠܒܫܐ ܕܐܪܓܘܢܐ *they put upon him a purple robe;* Ez. xvi. 10; β) verbs of *filling up, satisfying;* e. g. Ephr. I. 527, A. ܐܪܡܠܬܐ ܡܠܝܐ ܡܐܢ̈ܐ ܡܫܚܐ *the widow filled the vessels with oil;* Luke i. 53. ܟܦܢ̈ܐ ܡܠܐ ܛܒ̈ܬܐ *the hungry he fills with good things;* γ) those which denote *teaching,* or *showing;* e. g. John xiv. 26. ܢܠܦܟܘܢ ܟܠܡܕܡ *he will teach you all things;* I Tim. iv. 6; John xiv. 8. ܚܘܝܢ ܐܒܐ *show us the Father;* verses 10, 32;

b) verbs in *Peal* with a double accusative signification. Here belong; *a*) verbs of *clothing, covering* (also with ܒ of the thing); e. g. Ephr. 1. 239, A. ܐܟܣܝ ܐܢܘܢ ܬܟܣܝ̈ܬܐ *he girded them with girdles;* ܡܫܚ *to anoint*, Ps.xlv.7; ܙܪܥ *to sow;* Lev. xix. 19; β) verbs of *filling up* (also with ܒ and ܡܢ); e.g. John ii. 7. ܡܠܘ ܐܢܘܢ ܡܢܐ ܠܐܓܢܐ *fill (them) the water pots with water;* verse 9; Barh. 212, 2; Assem. I. 332, A. 12; γ) verbs of *commanding, ordering*, (also with ܡܢ and ܠ of the person and thing); e.g. Gen. vi.22. ܟܠܡܐ ܕܦܩܕܗ *all that he had commanded him;* Mark viii.11. ܫܐܠܝܢ ܗܘܘ ܠܗ ܐܬܐ *they demanded of him a sign;* δ) verbs of *showing* or *doing* any thing *to* any body, or *making* a person or thing *to be* thus and so; e. g. Gen. xvii. 5. ܐܒܐ ܣܡܬܟ *I have made thee a Father;* John viii.53. ܡܢܘ ܥܒܕ ܐܢܬ ܢܦܫܟ *what makest thou thyself?* Heb. i. 2; Assem. I. 346, A. 4. v. E. Also with an accusative of the material of which anything is formed; e. g. I Kings viii. 32. ܒܢܐ ܐܢܘܢ ܠܟܐܦܐ ܡܕܒܚܐ *he built of (them) the stones an altar;* ε) verbs of *naming*, ܩܪܐ Isa. lx. 18; I John iii. 1.

II. Verbs with Prepositions.

1. Verbs are construed with ܒ which in English are joined with *in*, *on*, *upon*, *about*, *concerning*, etc. Here belong especially; *a*) verbs which denote some state or emotion of the mind; e.g. Luke i.14. ܢܚܕܘܢ ܒܡܘܠܕܗ *they shall rejoice at his birth;* Barh.90,20; ܨܒܐ ܒ *to have pleasure in something;* Matt. iii. 17; Heb. x. 38; ܐܬܕܡܪ ܒ *to wonder at;* Matt. xxii. 33; Luke ii. 47; ܣܒܪ ܒ *to hope in;* Matt. xii. 21; John v.45; ܗܝܡܢ ܒ *to believe on;* Mark i. 15; John ii. 11; ܚܪ ܒ *to look at;* John i. 36, 43; Barh. 190, 13; Assem. I. 89, A. 17; ܒܗܬ ܒ *to be ashamed of;* Rom. i.

16; ܟܐܪ ܒ *to rebuke;* I Tim. v. 1; ܟܐܐ *ibid.* or *threaten;* Matt. viii. 26; Luke iv. 41; Barh. 53, 10; ܒܙܚ ܒ *to mock at;* Matt. xx.19; xxvii. 31; ܓܚܟ ܒ *to laugh at;* Acts ii. 13; *b*) verbs that denote *acknowledging, denying, swearing by, calling upon;* e. g. Matt. x. 32, 33. ܟܠܢܫ ܕܢܘܕܐ ܒܝ *whosoever shall confess me;* Mark i. 5; Acts xxiii. 8; Rom. x. 9, 10; Matt. x. 33. ܡܢ ܕܢܟܦܘܪ ܒܝ *whosoever shall deny me;* xxvi. 34; I Tim. v. viii; Assem. I. 341,A. 23; 372, 8, 9; Matt. xxvi. 63. ܡܘܡܐ ܐܢܐ ܠܟ ܒܐܠܗܐ ܚܝܐ *I adjure thee by the living God;* Mark v. 7; I Thess. v.27; ܩܪܐ ܒ *to call upon;* Gen. iv. 26. Here also belong; *c*) some verbs which denote a *doing* something *for* or *against* some one; e. g. ܚܫܒ ܒ, ܐܪܫܥ and ܢܩܫ *to prove against some one;* Acts xxiv. 27; xxv. 9; Rom. ix. 17; I Tim. i. 16; ܣܗܕ ܒ (also with ܥܠ) *to testify against;* Deut. xxxi. 28. Of verbs of *motion,* here belong; *d*) ܦܓܥ ܒ *to encounter;* Luke viii. 27; xxii. 10; and ܐܬܐ ܒ *to come with* (i. e. *bring*) something; Psalms lxvi. 13.

Rem.—Here also belongs ܫܬܐ ܒ *to drink from;* Gen. xliv. 5. ܟܣܐ ܕܫܬܐ ܒܗ ܡܪܝ *the cup from which my Lord drinks.* Some times ܒ denotes a *part* of the object; e.g. II Sam. xxiii. 10. ܚܪܒ ܒܦܠܫܬܝܐ *he made an overthrow among the Philistines;* and here are to be placed ܦܠܚ ܒ and ܥܡܠ *to labor at* something; I Kings ix. 23.

2. The following verbs are construed with ܠ as a sign of the dative; *a*) those of *giving, permitting, commending;* e. g. John xiv.27. ܫܠܡܐ ܕܝܠܝ ܝܗܒ ܐܢܐ ܠܟܘܢ *my peace give I to you;* Matt. viii.21,31. ܐܦܣ ܠܝ - ܠܢ *permit me — us;* Mark v. 13; Luke viii. 32; Acts xx. 32. ܡܓܥܠ

ܐܢܐ ܠܟܘܢ ܠܐܠܗܐ *I commend you to God;* I Peter iv. 19; *b*) those of *pleasing* and *displeasing;* e. g. John viii. 29. ܡܕܡ ܕܫܦܪ ܠܗ *that which pleases him;* Rom. xv. 2, 3; Heb. xiii. 16; or *c*) those that denote *likeness, similarity;* e.g. Luke xiii. 18. ܠܡܢܐ ܕܡܝܐ ܡܠܟܘܬܐ ܕܐܠܗܐ *to what is the Kingdom of God like?* verses 9, 20; Heb. ii. 17; Barh. 137, 12. ܕܡܐ ܐܢܬ ܠܗ *thou art like him.*

Rem.—Here also belong impersonal phrases, such as ܘܠܐ ܠ *it is fitting for,* and ܐܝܬ ܠ equivalent to *to have;* e. g. Matt. iii. 9; Luke xvi. 28,29; John x. 16. (with the accusative of the object in relation to ἔχειν, II John 9. ܗܢܐ ܘܠܐܒܐ ܘܠܒܪܐ ܐܝܬ ܠܗ οὗτος καὶ τὸν πατέρα καὶ τὸν υἱὸν ἔχει), and ܠܝܬ ܠ equivalent to *not to have;* Matt. xiii. 21; John xiv.30. In the same signification occurs also ܗܘܐ ܠ; e.g. Barh. 66, 4. ܬܠܬܐ ܗܘܘ ܠܗ ܒܢܝܐ *he had three sons.*

3. With ܡܢ are connected; *a*) verbs which denote *to fear, flee, guarding oneself, refraining, ceasing, releasing;* e.g. Luke xxiii. 40. ܐܦܠܐ ܡܢ ܐܠܗܐ ܕܚܠ ܐܢܬ *fearest thou not God?* John ix. 22; Barh. 94,9; Rom. ii.3. ܕܐܢܬ ܬܥܪܘܩ ܡܢ ܕܝܢܗ ܕܐܠܗܐ *that thou shalt escape the judgment of God;* I Cor. vi. 18; x. 14; Barh. 170, 4; Matt. x. 17. ܐܙܕܗܪܘ ܡܢ ܒܢܝܢܫܐ *beware of men;* xvi. 6, 12; Luke xii. 15; xx. 46; John xvii. 15. ܕܬܛܪ ܐܢܘܢ ܡܢ ܒܝܫܐ *that thou shouldst keep them from evil;* I Peter ii. 11. ܐܬܪܚܩܘ ܡܢ ܪܓܝܓܬܗ ܕܒܣܪܐ *abstain from lusts of the flesh;* Acts xv. 29; I Pet. iv.1. ܦܣܩ ܠܗ ܡܢ ܚܛܗܐ *he ceaseth from sin;* Barh.102,9; Assem. I. 42, 8; II Thess. iii. 3. ܢܢܛܪܟܘܢ ܡܢ ܒܝܫܐ *he*

will keep you from evil; *b*) those of *filling up, lacking*, and *failing;* Luke xv. 16. ܠܡܡܠܐ ܟܪܣܗ ܡܢ ܚܪܘܒܐ *to fill his belly with husks*; Barh. 69,1; I Tim. vi.10. ܡܢ ܗܝܡܢܘܬܐ ܛܥܘ *they came short of the faith;* II Tim. ii. 18; *c*) those of *asking, beseeching;* John iv. 31. ܒܥܝܢ ܗܘܘ ܡܢܗ *they besought him;* verse 40; I Peter ii. 11.

REM.—ܡܢ also expresses the Latin *præ;* e. g. ܡܡܬ ܡܢ *to die before;* or *per*, with ܥܠ and ܣܠܩ, John x. 1, 2.

4. With ܥܠ are construed verbs, which, in English, may be followed by *about, concerning*, viz.; *a*) some which express an *affection of the mind;* e.g. Matt.xv.22. ܐܬܪܚܡ ܥܠܝ *be merciful to me;* xvii. 15; Rom. ix. 15; xi. 32; Matt.vi. 28. ܥܠ ܠܒܘܫܐ ܡܢܐ ܝܨܦܝܢ ܐܢܬܘܢ *why take ye thought for raiment;* Luke xii. 26. ܝܨܦ ܥܠ *to be anxious;* Matt.v.22. ܐܬܒܣܡ ܥܠ *to rejoice over;* Rev. xviii.20. ܒܟܐ ܥܠ *to weep over*; Luke xxiii.27,28. ܐܬܡܠܟ ܥܠ *to take counsel concerning*; Matt. xxvi. 4; *b*) those which denote *power* or *authority over* something; e. g. Luke xix. 14. ܕܢܡܠܟ ܥܠܝܢ ܗܢܐ *that this person should rule over us*; Rom. vi. 14; vii. 1; Barh. 40, 6; Matt. xxiii. 35. ܢܐܬܐ ܥܠܝܟܘܢ *shall come upon you*; Luke xxi. 34; John xviii. 4; Luke i. 12. ܕܚܠܬܐ ܢܦܠܬ ܥܠܘܗܝ *fear fell upon him*; *c*) those which denote a *doing for* or *against*, or an *occupation with* something; e. g. Acts vii. 58. ܐܝܠܝܢ ܕܐܣܗܕܘ ܥܠܘܗܝ *those who testified against him;* Matt. xxvi. 62; John i. 8. ܕܢܣܗܕ ܥܠ ܢܘܗܪܐ *that he might bear witness of the light;* iii. 26; v. 31. ܐܟܣ ܥܠ *to accuse;* John viii. 46; ܟܬܒ ܥܠ *to write of, concerning*, John i. 46; v. 46; Acts xxi. 25. ܐܡܪ ܥܠ and

ܡܠܠ ܥܠ *to speak of, about;* John i. 22, 30; xiii. 22; vii. 13; *d*) verbs of *covering, protecting,* or *burdening;* e. g. Matt. xvii. 5. ܥܢܢܐ ܢܗܝܪܐ ܐܛܠܠ ܥܠܝܗܘܢ *a bright cloud covered them;* Luke i. 35. ܚܝܠܗ ܕܡܪܝܡܐ ܢܓܢ ܥܠܝܟܝ *the power of the Most High shall cover thee;* ܚܦܐ ܥܠ and ܛܥܢ have the same signification; Jer. xviii. 23; II Sam. xiii. 25. ܕܠܐ ܢܐܩܪ ܥܠܝܟ *so that we shall not burden thee.* And finally; *e*) several verbs that denote a *charge, command* or *petition;* e. g. ܦܩܕ ܥܠ *to charge one;* II Chron. xxxvi. 23; ܦܣܩ ܥܠ *to prescribe for one;* II Kings xxii. 13. ܨܠܐ ܥܠ *to pray for;* John xvii. 9. ܫܐܠ ܥܠ *to ask after;* Assem. I. 50, 6.

Rem.—Here also belong phrases compounded with nouns derived from these verbs; e. g. I Peter v. 7. ܘܨܦܬܟܘܢ ܪܡܘ ܥܠ ܡܪܝܐ *cast your cares upon the Lord;* Barh. 77, 5. ܥܠ ܡܠܟܐ ܨܦܘ ܨܦܝܠܘܬܐ *they took care for the King;* Isa. i. 14. ܗܘܘ ܥܠܝ ܠܛܥܘܢܝܐ *they are a burden to me;* Job vii. 20.

5. With ܒܝܬ, ܒܝܢܝ and ܒܝܢܬ *between,* are construed verbs which denote *dividing, separating, distinguishing;* e.g. Gen. i.4. ܦܪܫ ܒܝܬ ܢܘܗܪܐ ܠܚܫܘܟܐ *he separated between light and darkness;* Ruth i. 17. ܦܪܫ ܒܝܬ and ܚܙܐ *to see, to perceive a difference between;* II Sam. xix. 35; Mal. iii. 18.

6. With ܒܬܪ *after,* are joined verbs which signify *to go* (equivalent to *to follow*); e. g. Matt. iv. 25. ܐܙܠܘ ܒܬܪܗ *they followed him;* xii. 15; Mark x. 32; Matt. iv. 19. ܬܘ ܒܬܪܝ *follow after me;* xix. 2; John viii. 12; ܪܗܛ ܒܬܪ I Tim. vi. 11; II Tim. ii. 22.

Rem.—More in accordance with the Hebrew idiom we find ܩܕܳܡ with verbs signifying *to put away, destroy*: e. g. I Kings xiv. 10; xxi. 21.

General Remarks.

To *seem*, to *appear*, are expressed, as in Hebrew, by ܒܥܰܝܢܰܝ in the relation of genitive or with the suffix belonging to the person; e. g. Gen. xix. 14. ܗܘܳܐ ܒܥܰܝܢܰܝ ܚܰܬ݂ܢܰܘܗ̱ܝ *he seemed to his sons-in-law;* II Sam. x. 3. ܒܥܰܝܢܰܝܟ݂ (he) *seems to thee.* When rendered more definite by the adjectives *good* or *bad*, they are expressed either by ܫܰܦܺܝܪ ܠ and ܒܺܝܫ, or ܐܶܬ݂ܛܰܐܒ without ܒܥܰܝܢܰܝ; e. g. Acts vi. 5; Rom. xv. 2. 3; Gen. xxi. 11; Matt. xxi. 15; or in connection with ܒܥܰܝܢܰܝ; e. g. Ephr. I. 240,F. ܫܰܦܺܝܪ ܗܘܳܐ ܟܒ ܒܥܰܝܢܰܝ ܡܳܪܝܳܐ *would this seem good to God?* In the translation of the New Testament, δοκεῖ is usually expressed by ܡܶܣܬܰܒܪܳܐ ܠ; e. g. Matt. xvii. 25; xviii. 12; xxi. 28; xxii.17: Luke x. 36.

To *suffer*, *permit*, are expressed either by ܦܩܰܕ *to command*, or ܥܒܰܕ *to cause* (without the copula following); e.g. Barh. 72, 12; or they are expressed in such a manner that the thing to be done is implied in the imperative itself; Barh. 27, 2; 114, 14.

III. Passives and their Construction.

1. The active cause in passives is usually expressed by ܠ; e.g. Matt. vi. 16. ܕܢܶܬ݂ܚܙܽܘܢ ܠܒܢܰܝܢܳܫܳܐ *that they may be seen by men;* Luke viii. 29. ܚܛܺܝܦ ܗܘܳܐ ܠܗ *he was caught by*

him; Assem. 1. 39,14, and 16. ܐܫܬܡܥ ܠܗ ܩܠܐ *there was a voice heard by him;* Barh. 152, 11.

Rem.—Yet we also frequently find ܡܢ, Matt. iii. 14. ܕܡܢܟ ܐܬܥܡܕ *that I should be baptized of thee;* v. 13; xx. 23.

2. Passives whose actives govern a double accusative, sometimes retain one of them; e. g. Luke i. 41. ܐܬܡܠܝܬ ܪܘܚܐ ܕܩܘܕܫܐ *she was filled with the Holy Ghost;* ii. 40; Barh. 32, 14. ܓܒܪܐ ܕܠܒܝܫ ܒܘܨܐ *a man who was clad in Byssus;* 90, 14; 108, 6; 223, 15; Assem. I. 86, A. 27, 28.

3. When passives, especially in verbs relating to the mind, have an active signification, they are joined with the accusative; e.g. I Thess. i. 2. ܡܬܕܟܪܝܢܢ ܠܟܘܢ ܒܨܠܘܬܢ *we remember you in our prayers;* ܐܬܚܫܒ *to think,* Rom. ii. 3; xv. 5; ܐܫܬܘܕܥ *to recognize,* Acts xix. 15; ܐܫܬܡܥ *to obey,* Eph. vi. 1; Col. iii. 22; ܐܬܪܓܪܓ *to wish,* I Tim. vi. 10.

Rem.—Here also belong such passives as ܐܬܓܘܪܪ *to chew the cud,* Lev. xi. 3,5; and hence also may be explained why participles passive of the *Pe.* (§ 64. 5) take the accusative of the object.

4. Passives have also frequently a reflective signification (§ 21, 2; § 22. 2; § 24.2; § 58. A. a); e. g. John viii. 6. ܝܫܘܥ ܠܬܚܬ ܐܬܓܗܢ *Jesus bowed himself down;* verse 8; Mark i. 7; I Tim. v. 14. ܐܝܠܝܢ ܕܛܠܝܢ ܬܬܢܤܒܢ *those who are young shall marry;* iv. 13; ܐܬܚܝܠ *to wax strong,* Acts xix. 16; xxiii. 11; ܐܬܛܫܝ *to hide,* John viii. 59; ܐܬܦܢܝ *to turn around,* Matt. ix. 22., etc.

Rem.—Many neuters take a passive signification; e. g. ܛܠܐ *to err*, Luke xxi. 8. ܠܐ ܬܛܥܘܢ μὴ πλανηθῆτε ; ܝܩܕ *to burn*, Matt.xiii.40. ܝܩܕܝܢ ܒܢܘܪܐ καὶ πυρὶ καίεται ; ܢܦܠ *to fall*, iii.10. ܢܦܠ ܒܢܘܪܐ εἰς πῦρ βάλλεται ; ܢܦܩ *to go out*, viii. 12. ܢܦܩܘܢ ἐκβληθήσονται etc.

Upon the use of verbs for adverbs, see § 82. 1.

Appendix to § 67.

Mode of expressing Greek Composites.

To the subject of the construction of verbs with cases and prepositions, belongs also the manner of rendering Greek Composites, which in the Syriac translation of the New Testament, are expressed as follows :

1. By simple verbs, in the signification of which ; *a*) the idea of the Greek preposition is included ; e. g. Matt. xx. 18. ܣܠܩܝܢ ܚܢܢ ἀναβαίνομεν ; viii. 1. ܟܕ ܢܚܬ καταβάντι ; iii. 2. ܬܘܒܘ μετανοεῖτε ; xvi. 5. ܛܥܘ ἐπελάθοντο ; or by verbs which ; *b*) without respect to the Greek preposition, answer to the simple Greek verb ; e. g. Matt. xi. 5. ܚܙܝܢ ἀναβλέπουσι ; Acts xxiii. 33. ܥܠܘ ἀναδόντες ; Rom. 14. 9. ܚܝܐ ἀνέζησεν ; Luke xv. 24, 32 ; x.31,32. ܥܒܪ ἀντιπαρῆλθεν ; Acts xxvi. 5. ܝܕܥܝܢ προγινώσκοντες ; Rom. xv. 4. ܐܬܟܬܒ προεγράφη.

2. By verbs ; *a*) with a preposition answering to the Greek ; e.g. ܠܘܩܒܠ = ἀντὶ ; Luke xiii.17. ܕܩܝܡܝܢ ܗܘܘ ܠܘܩܒܠܗ οἱ ἀντικείμενοι αὐτῷ ; Acts vi.10 ; Rom.xiii.2. ܥܠ = ἐπί and κατά; Luke x. 34. ܐܬܒܛܠ ܠܗ ܥܠܘܗܝ καὶ ἐπεμελήθη αὐτοῦ ; Matt. xxvi.62. ܡܣܗܕܝܢ ܥܠܝܟ καταμαρτυροῦσίν σου ; ܥܡ = σὺν ; Rom.

vi.8. ܢܚܐ ܥܡܗ συζήσομεν αὐτῷ, Heb. iv. 15 ; II Tim. i. 8. ܩܕܡ = πρὸ ; Acts vii. 40. ܕܢܐܙܠܘܢ ܩܕܡܝܢ οἵ προπορεύσονται ἡμῶν ; Matt. ii. 9 ; or *b*) by an adverb of similar signification ; e. g. ܡܢ ܕܪܝܫ = ἀνά, I Peter i.3; ܐܘܠܕܢ ܡܢ ܕܪܝܫ ἀναγεννήσας ἡμᾶς, Heb. vi. 6. ܡܢ ܩܕܝܡ = πρὸ, II Cor. xiii. 2 ; ܡܢ ܩܕܝܡ ܐܡܪܬ προείρηκα, Rom. i. 2 ; Col. i. 5.

3. By another verb representing the preposition, which usually stands first, without any connective particle, in the same tense, number, and gender with the finite verb ; e. g. ܩܕܡ (*to come before*) = πρὸ, Mark xiii. 23. ܩܕܡܬ ܐܡܪܬ προείρηκα, Acts vii. 52; Rom. iii. 9 ; xi. 35. This verb sometimes follows ; e. g. John xx. 4. ܪܗܛ ܩܕܡܗ προέδραμεν.

4. If the composite is formed from a noun or adjective and a verb, it is usually resolved into its components ; e. g. Mark iv. 20. ܡܝܬܝܢ ܦܐܪܐ καρποφοροῦσιν ; iii. 4. ܠܡܥܒܕ ܕܛܒ ܐܘ ܕܒܝܫ ἀγαθοποιῆσαι ἢ κακοποιῆσαι ; Matt. xix. 18. ܠܐ ܬܣܗܕ ܣܗܕܘܬܐ ܕܫܘܩܪܐ οὐ ψευδομαρτυρήσεις.

Rem.—It seems to be merely pleonastic, where in John iv. 4. διέρχεσθαι is translated by ܕܢܐܬܐ ܢܥܒܪ.

---

§ 68. *The Substantive Verb, and some other Peculiarities chiefly relating to the Construction of the Verb.*

A. Use of ܗܘܐ, ܐܝܬ and ܠܝܬ (§ 38).

Instead of ܗܘܐ *to be* (with which, according to § 65. B. and D, the imperfect and pluperfect are formed), the Syriac also uses ܐܝܬ, and in negative phrases ܠܝܬ with suffixes, and with them also in connection with the former (ܗܘܐ), forms the imperfect; e.g. John ix.24. ܐܝܬܘܗܝ ܗܘܐ he was; verse 14. ܐܝܬܝܗܘܢ ܗܘܘ *they were*, etc.

Rem. — ܗܘܐ sometimes stands pleonastically with the preterit, without giving it the signification of the pluperfect; e.g. Mark i.45. ܫܪܝ ܗܘܐ *he began*; Luke i. 8; John iii. 25. It is sometimes omitted as present or imperfect, according to § 54. 2; or when it would be a mere copula between the subject and object; e. g. Matt. xxvii. 29 (§ 65. III. Rem.); Luke i.27. It seems to mark emphasis after ܠܐ (in the Philoxenian version ܠܘ *nowise*); e.g. John vi. 32. ܠܐ ܗܘܐ ܡܘܫܐ ܝܗܒ ܠܟܘܢ *Moses has not given you;* verses 38, 58; xiii. 11, 18; Heb. ii.5,16; or in interrogations with ܠܐ = *nonne*); e. g. Matt. xiii. 55. ܠܐ ܗܘܐ ܗܢܐ *is this not?* xx. 13; Mark vi. 3; Luke xi. 40; xvii. 17. Concerning ܗܘܐ, ܐܝܬ and ܠܝܬ with ܠ = *to have—not to have*, compare § 67. II. 2. Rem.

B. Indirect Discourse.

The indirect discourse is usually expressed directly, commencing with ܕ (= כִּי — ὅτι), e. g. John iv. 17. ܫܦܝܪ ܐܡܪܬܝ ܕܠܝܬ ܠܝ ܒܥܠܐ *thou hast rightly said, I have no husband;* verse 53; ii. 17; vi. 31; Barh. 51, 11. ܟܕ ܐܡܪ ܕܫܡܥܬ *as he said; I (he) have heard;* 135,10; 69,7. ܗܘ ܕܝܢ ܝܡܐ ܕܡܠܟܐ ܠܥܡܡܐ ܠܐ ܗܘܐ ܐܢܐ *he swore, he would (I will) be no King of the heathen;* 223, 11, 12.

Rem.—Sometimes ܕ is wanting at the beginning of the direct discourse (especially before ܐܘ); e.g. Barh. 131, 11, 12; 374, 13; 443, 8; more frequently ܐܡܪ; e. g. Barh. 106,3; 183,9; 219,5;

243, 10; 486, 5; 543, 19; 596, 11. Compare Assem. I. 479, A. 24, with 480, 1. The indirect discourse also occurs; e. g. Barh. 79, 19. ܐܡܪܘ ܠܗ ܕܠܐ ܣܦܩܐ ܠܗܘܢ، ܡܕܐܬܐ *they said to him, the tribute is not sufficient for thee;* 94, 1—3; 97, 1. Sometimes the direct discourse passes over into the indirect; e. g. 276, 8—10 and vice versa; 166, 19, 20; 513, 5, 6.

C. Ellipsis—Zeugma—Paronomasia, and Puns.

1. When a verb has previously been used in the protasis, it is usually omitted in the apodosis, where it would properly be repeated; e. g. Matt. i. 22. ܗܕܐ ܕܝܢ ܟܠܗ ܕܗܘܬ ܕܢܬܡܠܐ *but what has happened (has happened) that it might be fulfilled;* xxi. 4; John xx. 31; Rom. v. 20; I Cor. ix. 25. ܗܠܝܢ ܕܪܗܛܝܢ ܕܢܣܒܘܢ *those who run (run) that they may obtain;* II Cor. v. 13; Heb. vii. 19; viii. 3; I Peter iv. 11; I John iii. 6. Sometimes the verb is to be supplied from the context; Matt. 27,25. ܕܡܗ ܥܠܝܢ *his blood (come) upon us;* Acts xxiv. 6. ܐܝܟ ܕܒܢܡܘܣܢ *as it (is written) in our law.*

Rem.—The ellipsis must be considered as a peculiarity of the Syriac language, where the Philoxenian translation, omitting the ܕ in the apodosis, adheres strictly to the Greek words; e. g. Matt i. 22. ܗܕܐ ܕܝܢ ܟܠܗ ܗܘܬ τοῦτο δὲ ὅλον γέγονεν; John xx. 31. Concerning the omission of ܐܡܪ see B. Rem. above; and concerning the elliptical use of ܗܘܐ see A. Rem.

2. Sometimes a verb, by its signification, can belong to only one of two connected nouns (*Zeugma*), so that to the other noun another verb must be mentally supplied;

e. g. Job iv. 10. ܢܗܡܬܐ ܕܐܪܝܐ ـ ܘܫܢܐ ܐܬܬܒܪ *the roaring of the lion (is stilled) and the teeth are broken;* x. 12.

3. Paronomasia and puns occur but rarely in Syriac. The former is a mere imitation of the Hebrew original in Ps. xl. 3. ܢܚܙܘܢ ܣܓܝܐܐ ܘܢܕܚܠܘܢ (יִרְאוּ רַבִּים וְיִירָאוּ) *that many see it and rejoice.* Puns occur mostly in names where the language does not require any such alteration to be assumed; e.g. Gen. xlix. 8. ܝܗܘܕܐ ܠܟ ܢܘܕܘܢ *Judah (thy brethren) shall praise thee.* verses 16, 19.

CHAPTER THIRD.

The Noun.

---

§ 69. *Use of the Noun in General.*

1. Abstract nouns not unfrequently in Syriac take the place of adjectives and then they stand in the relation of genitive to the noun, with ܕ; e. g. Matt. iii. 11. ܒܪܘܚܐ ܕܩܘܕܫܐ *with the Holy Ghost;* John xv. 1. ܓܦܬܐ ܕܫܪܪܐ *the true vine;* I Cor. xv. 44. Especially does this union, as in Hebrew, occur with adjectives which denote the material or substance of which a thing is composed; e. g. John ii. 6. ܐܓܢܐ ܕܟܐܦܐ *stone water-pots;* Heb. ix. 4. ܩܣܛܐ ܕܕܗܒܐ

a golden box; II Cor. x. 4; II Tim. ii. 20; Barh. 11, 7, 8; 20, 10; 88, 2; 172, 8; 228, 7. ܥܰܡܽܘܕܳܐ ܕܢܽܘܪܳܐ *a fiery pillar.*

Rem.—Adjectives of material, however, do occur; e.g. Barh. 59,4. ܐܣܦܰܝܪܳܐ ܢܚܳܫܬܳܢܳܐ *a brazen celestial sphere;* and in the same construction adjectives of quality with ܕ prefixed, used for substantives; e.g. Michael. Chr. 85. ܫܰܒܬܳܐ ܕܚܶܘܳܪܶ̈ܐ *week of the white (clothes).* Abstract nouns with ܕ in connection with a pronoun, supply the place of the predicate; e. g. Rom. vii. 14. ܐܶܢܳܐ ܕܶܝܢ ܕܒܶܣܪܳܐ ܐ̱ܢܳܐ *but I am carnal;* or with a preposition prefixed they supply the place of an adjective to which a noun is to be supplied; e. g. Heb. ii. 17. ܒܰܐܠܳܗܳܐ *in divine (things);* Luke viii. 49. ܐ̱ܢܳܫ ܡܶܢ ܕܒܶܝܬ *one of the household;* even with suffixes, ܕܫܺܐܕܰܘ̈ܗܝ δαιμονιζόμενος. Some abstract nouns, in the relation of genitive with ܕ following, precede as *nomen regens;* e. g. Barh. 170, 20. ܣܽܘܓܳܐܐ ܕܟܬܳܒܶ̈ܐ *many writings;* 172, 4; 178, 5; 195,16. ܫܰܪܟܳܐ ܕܚܶܣܢܶ̈ܐ *in the remaining fortresses;* 198,13. Here also belongs ܟܽܠ according to § 55. B. 2. Rem.

2. Especially are adjectives or concrete substantives denoting *possession, custom, similarity,* etc., expressed by way of circumlocution, by means of the nouns ܒܰܪ *son;* ܒܰܪܬ *daughter;* ܒܥܶܠ and ܡܳܪܳܐ *lord, master;* ܪܰܒ and ܪܺܝܫ *prince, ruler;* and ܒܰܝܬ *house.* In respect to the use of these nouns it is to be observed;

a) ܒܰܪ designates; *a) Gentile names, inhabitants,* etc. e. g. Tit. i. 12. ܒܢܰܝ̈ ܩܪܺܝܛܳܐ *Cretans;* Barh. 167,1; Acts xxi. 12; ܒܢܰܝ̈ ܐܰܬܪܳܐ οἱ ἐντόπιοι; Barh. 80, 17. ܒܢܰܝ̈ ܡܕܺܝܢ݁ܬܳܐ *citizens;* 91, 2; *β*) the idea of *race, species, kindred;* e.g. Rom. xi.14. ܒܰܪ ܓܶܢܣܳܐ *a kinsman;* Deut. xxiii.2; I Cor. vii.22. ܒܰܪ ܚܺܐܪܳܐ

a freeman; John xviii. 35. ܒܢ̈ܝ ܚܢ̈ܦܐ *heathen;* Michael. Chr. 5. ܒܪ ܗܪܣܝܣ *a heretic;* Assem. II.248. ܒܪ ܦܠܛܝܢ *a courtier;* Rev. ii. 14, 20. (Here also belongs ܒܪܢܫܐ); γ) *participation, likeness,* (= σὺν ὅμος); e. g. Eph. iii. 6. ܒܢ̈ܝ ܝܪܬܘܬܐ συγκληρόνομοι; I Thess. ii. 14; Acts xviii. 3; xix. 24. ܒܪ ܐܘܡܢܘܬܐ ὁμότεχνος; Dan. i. 10. ܒܢ̈ܝ ܫܢܐ *contemporaries;* Phil. iv. 3; Gal. i. 14; δ) *locality, situation,* and other circumstances; e.g. Isa. xxvi. 1. ܒܪ ܫܘܪܐ *a moat;* Psalms cxxxii. 2. ܒܪ ܨܘܪܐ *a neck chain.* And finally; ε) the adverbial phrase ܒܪ ܫܥܬܗ *forthwith, immediately;* Matt. xiii. 5, 20; John v. 9; xiii. 30; Acts x. 33; xxi. 32.

b) ܒܪܬ plur. ܒܢܬ forms; *a*) rarely *abstracts;* e.g. ܒܪܬ ܓܙܪܐ *circumcision;* more frequently *concretes* in the feminine; e. g. I Macc. xi. 7. ܒܪܬ ܚܐܪܐ *one born free;* or it denotes; β) the *product* of anything; e. g. ܒܪܬ ܛܘܛܡ̈ܬܐ *grapes;* ܒܪܬ ܢܡܟܬܐ *gum on sea-weed;* and tropically ܒܪܬ ܩܠܐ *voice;* Rom. x. 16, 18; Gal. iv. 20; and in the plural, Acts xii. 22; γ) *implements, clothing,* ܒܪܬ ܟܦܢܬܐ *napkin;* ܒܪܬ ܢܝܪܐ *ring;* δ) *descendants, nations,* etc.; e. g. Luke xiii. 16. ܒܪܬ ܐܒܪܗܡ *the Hebrews;* Matt. xxi. 5. ܒܪܬ ܨܗܝܘܢ *Jerusalem,* or its *inhabitants.*

c) ܒܥܠ denotes; α) mostly *concretes;* e. g. Rom. xi. 34. ܒܥܠ ܡܠܟܐ *counselor;* Matt. v. 25; xiii. 28, 39; II Chron. xiv. 5. ܒܥܠ ܫܒܒܘܬܐ *neighbor;* β) sometimes nations; e. g. ܒܥܠ ܡܟܡܟܘܬܐ *an Ethiopian.* In like manner;

d) ܡܪܐ Luke vii. 41. ܡܪܐ ܚܘܒܐ *debtor;* Ephr. II. 360, C;

e) ܪܒ forms; α) principally *concretes* of masculine offices

e. g. II Sam. xviii. 1. ܪܒ ܐܠܦܐ *a chiliarch;* Luke xvi. 1. ܪܒ ܒܝܬܐ οἰκονόμος; Heb. iv. 14. ܪܒ ܟܘܡܪ̈ܐ ἀρχιερεύς; I Pet. v. 4; Luke xix. 2; β) *abstracts;* e. g. Luke xvi. 2. ܪܒ ܒܝܬܘܬܐ οἰκονομία. In like manner;

f) ܪܫ; α) *concretes* of masculine offices; e. g. Luke viii. 41. ܪܫ ܟܢܘܫܬܐ ἀρχισυνάγωγος; John ii. 8, 9; Acts ii. 29; I Thess. iv. 16; β) more rarely *abstracts;* e. g. Matt. xxiii. 6. ܪܫ ܡܣܡܟܐ πρωτοκαθεδρία. Sometimes it denotes; γ) the *extremity* of a thing; e. g. ܪܫ ܐܣܛܘܡܟܐ *orifice of the stomach;* ܪܫ ܦܘܡܐ *aperture of the mouth.* Finally;

g) ܒܝܬ denotes; α) the *place* or *receptacle*, in which a thing is found or kept; e. g. Acts. xii. 17. ܒܝܬ ܐܣܝܪ̈ܐ *prison;* Matt. xiv. 2. ܒܝܬ ܩܒܘܪܐ *grave;* Acts xvii. 19. ܒܝܬ ܕܝܢܐ *judgment hall;* Luke xix. 29. ܒܝܬ ܙܝܬܐ *olive garden;* Heb. ix. 4. ܒܝܬ ܒܣܡܐ *censer* (literally, *house of incense*); II Tim. iv. 13; β) *countries, cities,* etc.; e.g. Assem. I. 169,B.7. ܒܝܬ ܪ̈ܗܘܡܝܐ *the Roman dominions;* Michael. Chr. 10. ܒܝܬ ܦܪ̈ܣܝܐ *Persia.*

Rem.—Here, however, do not belong ܒܝܬ ܢܗܪ̈ܝܢ *Mesopotamia,* and ܒܝܬ ܥܝܢܐ *forehead,* where ܒܝܬ signifies *between.* More rarely we find similar compositions with ܐܒ *father,* and ܐܡ *mother.* Of the latter only occur ܐܡܐ ܕܪܫܐ *the crown of the head,* and ܐܡܐ ܕܡ̈ܝܐ *hydraulics.* The Syriac also, though more rarely than the Hebrew, uses the names of countries and cities for nations and inhabitants; e. g. Barh. 150, 12. ܐܦܪ̈ܝܩܝ *Africans;* 248, 6. ܬܓܪܝܬ *Tagritians.*

---

§ 70. *Gender of Nouns.*

1. Nouns which in the plural take the termination of

another gender (§ 44. Rem. 2 and 3), retain the gender of the singular, and in this case respect is rarely had to the termination. Here belong; *a*) *masculines* with a feminine termination in the plural; e. g. Matt. xii. 43. ܐܬܪ̈ܘܬܐ ܕܡ̈ܝܐ ܠܝܬ ܒܗܘܢ *place in which there is no water;* I Cor. x. 9. ܘܐܘܒܕܘ ܐܢܘܢ ܚܘ̈ܘܬܐ *the serpents destroyed them;* ܡܠܐܟ̈ܘܬܐ (from ܡܠܐܟܐ) Luke ii. 13; ܝܘܡ̈ܬܐ (from ܝܘܡܐ) Matt. xxviii. 20; ܟܐܒ̈ܘܬܐ (from ܟܐܒܐ) Luke xxi. 34; ܢܗܪ̈ܘܬܐ (from ܢܗܪܐ) Matt. vii. 25, 26., etc.; *b*) *feminines* with a masculine termination; e. g. John xi. 35. ܐܬܝ̈ ܗܘܘ ܕܡ̈ܥܘܗܝ ܕܝܫܘܥ *tears came into the eyes of Jesus;* ܫܒ̈ܠܐ (from ܫܒܠܬܐ) Matt. xiii. 30; ܡ̈ܠܐ (from ܡܠܬܐ) xxiv.35; ܡܢ̈ܝܢ (from ܡܢܝܬܐ) x. 30; ܦܢ̈ܝܢ (from ܦܝܬܐ) Acts xxiv. 17; ܦܟ̈ܝܢ (from ܦܟܬܐ) xix. 34., etc.

2. When the abstract stands for the concrete, or when the noun takes another than its proper signification, the gender in both cases, is regulated by the sense. Concerning the former of these cases, compare § 80. B; to the latter belongs ܡܠܬܐ λόγος = *Christ;* e. g. John i. 1—4. ܐܝܬܘܗܝ ܗܘܐ ܡܠܬܐ *it was the word;* verse 14; or ܚܝܘܬ ܫܢܐ (literally, *beast of tooth*) = αντίχριστος, Rev. xiii. 1; xvi. 2,13; xvii. 7, 8. ܪܒܘ *a myriad* (*of men*); Acts xxi. 20; Barh. 55, 9, 10; 334, 6; 395, 19. ܢܦܫܐ, in the plural, = *inhabitants;* Barh. 159, 10; 236, 8; 548, 20., etc.

3. In Syriac the neuter of nouns, as of verbs, is designated by the feminine (§ 66. 2); e. g. Rom. vii. 18. ܛܒܬܐ ἀγαθὸν, ܒܝܫܬܐ κακὸν; in the plural, Assem. I. 218.

B. 11. ܐܣܠܝܘ ܠܥܬܝܩܬܐ ܘܚܕ̈ܬܐ *they despised the old and the new.*

---

§ 71. *Number.*

1. Some nouns, particularly those which denote cohesive materials (liquids, metals and the like), form a plural only when they may be conceived of as consisting of several parts; e.g. ܣܥܪܬܐ *barley*, plur. ܣܥܪ̈ܐ *barley-corns ;* in like manner ܚܛ̈ܐ from ܚܛܬܐ *wheat* ; Matt. iii. 12; John vi. 13; I Cor. xv. 37; and ܩܝ̈ܣܐ *timber ;* I Cor. iii. 12.

2. Some nouns singular have a plural signification (*collectives* § 44. Rem. 7), and then they take *Ribui* § 6. 2. As such they are joined either with the plural; e. g. John iv. 30. ܘܢܦܩܘ ܐ̱ܢܫ̈ܐ *there came out people ;* or with the singular; e. g. John x. 3. ܥܢ̈ܐ ܫܡܥܐ ܩܠܗ *the sheep hear his voice ;* verses 4—8.

Rem.—1. As collective plural forms, the following sometimes occur, ܩܡܨ̈ܐ *locust ;* Michael. Chr. 63, 11 ; 79, 6. ܡܢܘ̈ܬܐ (properly *part*) *remainder, members ;* 102, 5, 8.

Rem.—2. As *pluralis excellentiæ*, the Syriac has, merely by imitation of the Hebrew ܐܕܢܝ or ܐܕܘܢܝ = אֲדֹנָי, Michael. Chr. 30. ܒܐܕܘܢܝ ܝܡܝܬ ܐ̱ܢܐ *I swore by the Lord.*

---

§ 72. *Apposition and Duplication of Nouns.*

1. A noun in apposition, usually includes a more accurate definition or explanation of the previous noun, as for

example in the names of cities, ܡܕܝܢܬܐ, ܩܪܝܬܐ, ܡܕܝܢܬܐ, Assem. I. 349, 3. ܐܢܛܝܘܟܝܐ ܡܕܝܢܬܐ ܪܒܬܐ *Antioch, a great city.* The noun in apposition takes the number and case of its subject; e. g. Matt x. 3. ܡܬܝ ܡܟܣܐ *Matthew the Publican;* Barh. 32, 7. ܨܠܡܐ ܕܒܥܠ ܐܠܗܐ ܕܒܒܠܝܐ *the image of Baal (of a) god of the Babylonians;* 11, 8; 12, 2. ܡܢ ܡܠܟܝܙܕܩ ܟܢܥܢܝܐ *from Melchisedeck (from the) Canaanite.*

Rem.—Sometimes the noun in apposition stands before the principal noun; e. g. Barh. 39, 11. ܢܣܒ ܐܢܬܬܐ ܠܪܘܟܣܢ *he took for wife Roxane;* so too with nouns of *weight, measure, and time,* in the genitive; e. g. Rev. vi. 6. ܬܠܬܐ ܩܘܢܝܩܣ ܕܣܥܪ̈ܐ *three measures (of) barley.*

2. The duplication of the noun denotes; *a*) a *great number* or *quantity;* e. g. Ephr. III. 154. ܐܝܬ ܒܗ ܒܝܡܐ ܢܘܢܝܢ ܢܘܢܝܢ *there are many fish in the sea;* *b*) the distributive sense expressed in English by *each, by;* e. g. Matt. xx. 9, 10. ܕܝܢܪ ܕܝܢܪ *a penny each;* Barh. 85, 6. ܟܢܫܝܢ ܟܢܫܝܢ *by heaps;* 424, 10; 165, 19. Especially in respect to numbers; e. g. Mark vi. 7. ܬܪܝܢ ܬܪܝܢ *two each;* verse 40. ܡܐܐ ܡܐܐ *a hundred each;* II Cor. xi. 24; *c*) it forms a circumlocution for *all, every* (§ 58. B. 2); e. g. Matt. xxiv. 7. ܒܕܘܟܐ ܕܘܟܐ κατὰ τόπους; Tit. i. 5. ܒܡܕܝܢܐ ܡܕܝܢܐ κατὰ πόλιν; *d*) a *diversity, variety;* e. g. Mark ii. 17. ܟܘܪܗܢ ܟܘܪܗܢ *various diseases;* John v. 4; Acts x. 46. ܒܠܫܢ ܠܫܢ *with different tongues;* xxi. 34; xxv. 19; Assem. I. 13, A. 6. v. E. ܡܐܡܪ̈ܐ ܕܟܠ ܡܕܡ ܡܕܡ *discourses having various contents;* 191, A. 7. v. E; 280.

B. 13. v. E; *e*) a *strengthening* of the sense (§ 77. B. b); e.g. John vi. 7. ܩܠܝܠ ܩܠܝܠ *very little*; II Thess. iii.6.

---

§ 73. *The Emphatic State.*

1. The Emphatic State expresses the noun with the article with less definiteness, from the fact, that in many nouns this form also denotes the absolute state (§ 45. 1), which is no longer in use; e. g. Matt. x. 9. Sometimes also it supplies the place of the indefinite article; e. g. John iv. 7. ܐܬܬ ܐܢܬܬܐ ܡܢ ܫܡܪܝܢ *there came a woman of Samaria;* ix. 1; Acts vii. 37; xi. 24; even with ܚܕ *masc.* ܚܕܐ *fem.* appended; e. g. Luke xix. 12. ܓܒܪܐ ܚܕ *a man.*

Rem.—From this should perhaps be distinguished the cases in which ܚܕ is used numerically; e. g. Eph. iv. 6.

2. Hence to avoid any ambiguity ܗܘ is also sometimes joined with the emphatic state in order to designate it as such. It stands either before the noun; e. g. Matt. ix. 33. ܡܠܠ ܗܘ ܚܪܫܐ *the dumb spake;* John xviii. 16; or follows it; e. g. John v. 9. ܐܬܚܠܡ ܓܒܪܐ ܗܘ *the man became whole.*

Rem.—In the first case the absolute state usually occurs, when ܕ follows ܗܘ; e. g. Luke xxii. 27. ܗܘ ܕܡܫܡܫ *the servant.*

3. Hence also the emphatic state with ܕ following is used in the relation of genitive; e. g. Rev. xviii. 2.

ܡܥܡܪܬܐ ܕܫܐܕܐ ܘܢܛܘܪܬܐ ܕܟܠ ܪܘܚܐ ܛܢܦܬܐ *a habitation of devils and a hold of all unclean spirits.*

---

§ 74. *The Construct State and the Genitive.*

1. In the Syriac also the *Construct state* serves to denote the relation of genitive, more frequently, however, in the plural of the masculine and the singular of the feminine, where it can at once be recognized by its special form; e.g. Matt. xi. 12. ܡܢ ܝܘܡܝ ܝܘܚܢܢ *since the days of John;* xiii. 48. ܣܦܘܬܝ ܝܡܐ *the shores of the sea;* Acts xxiv. 16; Assem. I. 2, B. 1. ܗܝ ܫܢܬ ܬܠܬܝܢ ܘܚܕܐ *that is the thirty-first year;* 37, 3, 4. ܒܡܨܥܬ ܩܠܝܪܘܣ *in the midst of the clerus;* 40, 4. ܒܨܝܪܘܬ ܗܝܡܢܘܬܗܘܢ *their deficient faith,* literally, *the deficiency of their faith.*

Rem.— Yet the masculine singular of the noun occurs also before the genitive in the construct state; e. g. Matt. x. 41. ܒܫܡ ܢܒܝܐ *in the name of the Prophet;* xiii. 2. ܥܠ ܣܦܪ ܝܡܐ *on the shore of the sea;* verse 50. In addition to the nouns which supply the place of adjectives (§ 69. 2) it also occurs in ܓܘ *midst,* and ܝܕ *hand,* etc.; e. g. Matt. xiii. 1; Gal. iii. 19; Barh. 255. 11. ܒܓܘ ܗܝܟܠܐ *in the interior of the palace.* Here belongs moreover the use of the construct state in adjectives and participles (§ 64. 1. B), followed by the noun with a preposition or particle belonging to both, by which is denoted either the genitive relation; e. g. Luke i. 28. ܒܪܝܟܬ ܒܢܫܐ *blessed of (among) women;* II Tim. iii. 3. ܡܫܥܒܕܝ ܠܪܓܝܓܬܐ *slaves of passion;* I Tim. i. 10. ܥܒܪܝ ܥܠ ܡܘܡܬܐ *violator of an oath;* or a more accurate definition of the adjective or participle; e. g. Luke i. 7, 18. ܡܥܠܝܢ ܒܝܘܡܬܗܘܢ *far advanced in their years;* Rev. xiv. 4. ܙܒܝܢܝܢ ܡܢ ܐܪܥܐ *redeemed from the earth*; Acts. xxiii. 23.

2. Far more usual is; *a*) the connection of the emphatic state as *nomen regens*, with a following ܕ before the genitive; e. g. Matt. x. 5. ܠܐܘܪܚܐ ܕܥܡܡܐ *into the way of the Gentiles;* verse 15. ܒܝܘܡܐ ܕܕܝܢܐ *at the day of Judgment;* verse 42; xii. 42. ܡܠܟܬܐ ܕܬܝܡܢܐ *the queen of the south;* xiii. 11, 45; xxiii. 35; xxiv. 3; John viii. 47. ܡ̈ܠܐ ܕܐܠܗܐ *the word of God;* or *b*) with a pleonastic suffix referring to the genitive following, (§ 55. B. 2); e. g. Matt. xii. 8. ܡܪܗ ܕܫܒܬܐ *Lord of the Sabbath;* xi.2. ܥܒܕܘܗܝ ܕܡܫܝܚܐ *the work of the Messiah*; xii. 40. ܒܠܒܗ ܕܐܪܥܐ *in the heart of the earth.*

Rem.—Rarely, and chiefly in foreign words, ܕ stands after the construct state before the genitive; e. g. Matt. xiii. 22. ܛܘܥܝܝ ܕܥܘܬܪܐ *the deceitfulness of riches;* John x. 23. ܐܣܛܘܐ ܕܫܠܝܡܘܢ *the porch of Solomon.* But it is commonly used when one or more words are interposed between the *nomen regens* and the genitive; e.g. Barh. 421.13,20. ܐܬܪܐ ܗܘ ܕܐܘܪܫܠܡ *the region, that is of Jerusalem;* or when several genitives follow each other; e. g. Assem. I. 83, B. 21. ܕܝܪܐ ܕܒܝܬ ܝܠܕܬ ܐܠܗܐ ܕܣܘܪ̈ܝܝܐ ܕܡܕܒܪܐ ܕܐܣܩܝܛܝܣ *the convent of the Mother of God, of the Syrians in the Scythian desert;* Barh. 81, 2. The *nomen regens* is sometimes wanting, and the genitive is then to be distinguished by ܕ; e. g. Rom. xiv. 8. ܕܡܪܢ ܚܢܢ *the Lords are we;* Matt. xxii. 21. Sometimes ܕ is wanting when the noun forms an apposition with a preceding genitive; e. g. Matt. xii. 39. ܐܬܗ ܕܝܘܢܢ ܢܒܝܐ *the sign of Jonah the prophet.* ܕ stands before proper nouns, especially the names of countries and cities, when they thereby acquire a more de definite designation; e. g. Matt. ii. 1, 6. ܒܝܬ ܠܚܡ ܕܝܗܘܕܐ *Bethlehem in Judea.* In some instances, especially in the superscriptions of some Psalms; e. g. Ps. iv, v, vi, ܠ (ܠ *auctoris*) supplies the place of ܕ; very rarely elsewhere; e. g. Barh. 17, 4. ܦܘܪܩܢܐ ܠܡܪܝܐ *the deliverance of the* (i.e. *by the*) *Lord;* Assem. I. 346, A. 25, 26. So too with ܡܢ, when origin or descent is indicated; e.g. Barh. 372, 16. ܢܣܒ ܚܡܫܝܢ ܡܕܝܢܢ ܡܢ ܦܪܢܓܝܐ *he took fifty cities of the Franks;* or when there is indicated a choice or selection from several; e.g. 271, 1. ܚܕ ܡܢ ܥܒܕܘܗܝ *one of his slaves;* 270, 18. ܣܓܝܐܐ ܡܢ ܛܘܪܟܝܐ *many of the Turks.*

3. The genitive is sometimes to be understood objectively; e.g. Mark xi. 22. ܗܝܡܢܘܬܐ ܕܐܠܗܐ *faith of* (i. e. *in*) *God;* John ii. 17. ܛܢܢܗ ܕܒܝܬܟ *the zeal of* (i. e. *for*) *thine house;* vii. 13; Hebr. xi. 26. ܚܣܕܗ ܕܡܫܝܚܐ *the reproach of Christ* (i.e. *that attached to him*).

Rem.—Other turns of expression imitating the Hebrew are Isa. xvii. 2. ܩܘܪܝܐ ܕܥܪܘܥܝܪ *cities of* (*about*) *Aroer;* Exod.xxii.11. ܡܘܡܬܗ ܕܡܪܝܐ *an oath of* (*by*) *the Lord;* Ez. xxxv. 5. ܥܘܠܐ ܕܡܦܘܠܗܘܢ *iniquity of* (*at*) *their downfall;* Isa.liv.9., etc. Not unfrequently is this genitive of the object connected with the preposition of the verb, from which the *nomen regens* is derived; e. g. Barh. 53, 18. ܗܝܡܢܘܬܐ ܕܡܪܢ *the faith in our Lord;* Assem. I. 347,20.

4. Sometimes, especially when geographical references are made, the genitive occurs (as in English) where apposition would be more strictly correct; e. g. Acts vii. 40. ܡܢ ܐܪܥܐ ܕܡܨܪܝܢ *from the land of Egypt;* xx. 6; Rom. xi. 8; Barh. 114, 13. ܠܟܠܗ ܛܘܪܐ ܕܠܒܢܢ *the whole mountain of Lebanon.*

5. Standing after adjectives, the genitive is often used merely to define them more accurately; e.g. Luke xxiv. 25. ܐܘ ܚܣܝܪܝ ܪܥܝܢܐ ܘܝܩܝܪܝ ܠܒܐ *O fools and slow of heart*; Acts vii. 51. ܐܘ ܩܫܝ ܩܕܠܐ *O ye stiff necked*; Cant. ii. 5. ܟܪܝܗܬ ܕܚܘܒܐ *sick for love.*

Rem.—Sometimes a noun in the genitive takes the place of an adjective; e. g. John. xviii. 10. ܐܕܢܗ ܕܝܡܝܢܐ *his right ear;* xxi. 6 (§ 54. B. 2. Rem.); and *vice versa* the *nomen regens;* e. g. Luke iv. 25. ܣܓܝܐܢ ܐܪܡܠܬܐ πολλαὶ χῆραι; John ii. 12. In the first case the Philoxenian translation uses, instead of ܕ, the explanatory ܗܘ and ܗܢܘ, equivalent to *that is, namely;* e. g. ܐܕܢܗ; ܗܢܘ ܝܡܝܢܝܬܐ and ܕ is to be understood as a relative, when it follows prepositions with suffixes; e. g. Assem. I. 30, 17. ܥܡܗܘܢ ܕܐܦܝܣܩܘܦܐ *with (them) the bishops.* Compare § 55. B. 3.

---

§ 75. *Designation and Use of the other Cases.*

1. The dative and accusative have ܠ for their common sign, which may be omitted before the accusative; e. g. Matt. xvii. 4. ܢܥܒܕ ܬܠܬ ܡܛܠܝܢ *let us make three tabernacles;* Barh. 60, 9. ܪܕܘܦܝܐ ܪܒܐ ܐܩܝܡ *he raised a great persecution.* No difficulty is thereby occasioned even when the two cases stand together; e. g. Acts xiii. 21. ܝܗܒ ܠܗܘܢ ܠܫܐܘܠ *he gave them Saul;* xx. 32.

Rem. With verbs having a double accusative (§ 67. I. 2) ܠ falls away in both cases. The same is also to be recognized in the preceding pleonastic suffix to the verb (§ 55. B. I). Usually

ܝܳܬ (= אֶת־) stands before the noun in the emphatic state; e. g. Barh. 14, 9; or before proper names, 11, 20. ܒܢܳܗ̇ ܠܢܺܝܢܘܶܐ *he built Nineveh.* For this, in Gen. i. 1—3, the Peshito has ܝܳܬ = אֶת (compare Ephr. I. 116, D), which moreover occurs in Eccl. ii. 3; iii. 17; iv. 1; viii. 9, 17; Cant. iii. 5; viii. 4.

2. The accusative is also used adverbially, and then denotes; *a*) direction towards a place (§ 67. I. b); e. g. John vii. 14, 35; viii. 14; xviii. 3; Barh. 58, 18, 19; *b*) in indicating time it denotes; α) the question, *How long?* e.g. Barh. 7, 5, 6. ܗܘܳܐ ܡܶܛܪܳܐ ܐܰܪܒܥܺܝܢ ܝܰܘܡܺܝܢ *the rain continued forty days;* 3, 15, 16. ܐܶܬܐܰܒܠܘ ܥܠܰܘܗܝ ܡܳܐܐ ܫܢܺܝܢ *they mourned for him a hundred years;* 24, 7, 8; 85, 19, 20; 195, 6, 7; Assem. I. 18, A. 1; β) *When?* Luke i. 59. ܗܘܳܐ ܠܝܰܘܡܳܐ ܬܡܺܝܢܳܝܳܐ *it came to pass on the eighth day;* Ps. i. 2. ܐܺܝܡܳܡܳܐ ܘܠܺܠܝܳܐ *by day and night;* *c*) in reference to measure and weight; *How long? How high?* etc.; e. g. Barh. 38, 19. ܐܘܪܟܶܗ ܗܘܳܐ ܬܠܳܬ ܐܰܡܺܝܢ *it was three cubits long;* 20, 6; 179, 13. ܬܠܓܳܐ ܩܳܡ — ܐܰܪܒܰܥ ܨܶܒܥܺܝܢ *the snow lay four fingers deep;* *d*) *concerning, in relation to, as to;* e. g. Barh. 37, 16. ܦܰܐܝ ܒܕܡܘܬܳܐ ܗܘܳܐ *he was beautiful as to form;* 17. ܙܥܘܪ ܥܰܝܢ̈ܶܐ ܘܦܘܡܳܐ *he had small eyes and a small mouth;* 38, 4; Assem. I. 74, A. 30; 77, A. 22; 86, A. 25.

Rem.—In indicating time, *How old?* is commonly expressed by ܒܰܪ or ܒܰܪܬ with the addition of the years; e. g. John viii. 57. ܒܰܪ ܚܰܡܫܺܝܢ ܫܢܺܝܢ *fifty years old;* Barh. 3, 20.

3. Derivative nouns also take the accusative instead of the genitive of their verbs, viz.; *a*) participial forms; Heb.

xii. 2. ܫܘܡܠܝܐ ܠܗܝܡܢܘܬܢ *the finisher of our faith;* James iv.6; *b*) infinitive forms; e.g. Kirsch.Chr.136,1. ܡܟܒܫܢܘܬܐ ܠܩܘܣܛܢܛܝܢܘܦܘܠܝܣ *the conquest of Constantinople.*

4. The vocative is distinguishable in part by its connection; e.g. Matt. xxvi. 39, 42. ܐܒܝ ܐܢ ܡܫܟܚܐ *my Father if it be possible;* Rom. viii. 15; partly by ܐܘ, prefixed; e. g. Rom. ii. 1. ܐܘ ܒܪܢܫܐ *O man;* verse 3; I Tim. vi. 11; James v. 1.

Rem.—The Philoxenian translation imitates in Greek nouns the vocative termination belonging to that language; e. g. Luke i. 3, and Acts i. 1. ܐܘ ܬܐܘܦܝܠܐ ὦ Θεόφιλε; I Tim. vi.20.

5. Finally the ablative is distinguishable by the prepositions, ܒ, ܡܢ, ܠܘܬ, etc.. prefixed.

Rem.—Time, *When?* is frequently expressed in a similar manner; e. g. Gen. viii. 11. ܒܥܕܢ ܪܡܫܐ *at eventide;* Prov. vii. 9; Assem. I. 37, A. 11.

---

§ 76. *The Case Absolute.*

By the case absolute is meant a noun, which, at the beginning of a sentence, by itself and without connection with what follows, forms a clause, and is usually to be explained by supplying, *as to, concerning*, and the like. Here belong especially;

1. the *Nominative absolute*, which; *a*) either forms the subject of the following clause; e. g. Gen. xxii. 24. ܘܦܠܓܫܬܗ ـ ܝܠܕܬ ܐܦ ܗܝ *and his concubine — she also bore;*

or *b*) is to be rendered by an oblique case, which a suffix to the noun in the clause following shows to be; *α*) a *genitive*; e.g. Ephr. I. 242, E. ܐܢܫܐ ܟܕ ܢܗܘܐ ܒܡܫܟܐ ܕܓܘܫܡܗ ܡܘܡܐ *if there be found on the skin of the body of a man a blemish;* I. 110, D; Matt. iii. 4; or the suffix to the preposition indicates it as; *β*) a *dative;* e. g. I Cor. vii. 7. ܟܠܢܫ ܡܘܗܒܬܐ ܝܗܝܒܐ ܠܗ ܡܢ ܐܠܗܐ *to each one is given a gift from God;* Acts xv. 21; *γ*) an *accusative;* e. g. Ephr.I. 223, F. ܡܘܫܐ — ܠܐ ܝܕܥܝܢ ܚܢܢ ܡܢܐ ܗܘܐ ܒܗ *we know not what has befallen Moses;* (§ 67. 1. c. Rem.) Ps. lxxiv. 17; *δ*) an *ablative* (with a following ܒ and ܡܢ); e.g. Heb. x. 1. ܢܡܘܣܐ ܛܠܠܝܬܐ ܐܝܬ ܗܘܐ ܒܗ ܕܛܒܬܐ ܕܥܬܝܕܢ *in the law is the shadow of the good things to come;* Ephr. I. 237, A. ܟܠ ܚܡܝܪ ܘܟܠ ܕܒܫܐ ܠܐ ܬܩܪܒܘܢ ܡܢܗ ܩܘܪܒܢܐ ܠܡܪܝܐ *of anything leavened and of honey, bring ye no gift to the Lord.*

2. The *accusative absolute;* e. g. Gen. xlvii. 21. ܘܠܥܡܐ ܥܒܪ ܐܢܘܢ ܡܢ ܣܦܪܐ ܠܣܦܪܐ *the people led he* (literally *led he it*) *from one city to the other.*

3. *Cases with prepositions;* e. g. Gen. ii. 17. ܡܢ ܐܝܠܢܐ ܕܝܕܥܬܐ ܕܛܒܬܐ ܘܕܒܝܫܬܐ ܠܐ ܬܐܟܘܠ ܡܢܗ *of the tree of the knowledge of good and evil* (*of it*) *shalt thou not eat.*

Rem.—Sometimes, instead of the suffix, the preceding noun absolute is repeated; e. g. Esth. vi. 7—9. ܠܓܒܪܐ — ܘܢܠܒܫܘܢܗ ܠܓܒܪܐ *as for the man — thus let him be clothed;* likewise with the pronoun; e. g. Jer. xxvii. 8.

§ 77. *Comparison of Adjectives.*

A. The Comparative.

The comparative is usually expressed by the simple adjective, with ܡܶܢ = *præ* following and before the object compared; e. g. John viii. 53. ܠܡܳܐ ܐܢܬ ܪܰܒ ܐܢܬ ܡܶܢ ܐܰܒܽܘܢ ܐܰܒܪܳܗܳܡ *art thou, then, greater than our father Abraham*; vii. 31; xiii. 16; xiv. 12; xix. 11; Assem. I. 378, 19. ܐܶܡܝ ܝܰܩܺܝܪܳܐ ܠܝ ܡܶܢ ܡܰܠܟܬܳܐ *my mother is dearer to me than the queen*; 372, 3. v. E; Barh. 82, 20. ܘܡܶܢ ܟܽܠܗܽܘܢ ܒܢܰܝ̈ܢܳܫܳܐ ܐܰܪܺܝܟܳܐ ܗ̱ܘܳܬ ܐܰܡܬܳܐ *she was a cubit taller than any man.*

Rem.—Besides ܡܶܢ, sometimes also ܛܳܒ *very*, or ܝܰܬܺܝܪ *more*, equivalent to *by far*, is added to the adjective in order to strengthen the meaning; e. g. Acts xx. 35. ܛܽܘܒܰܘܗܝ ܠܰܐܝܢܳܐ ܕܝܳܗܶܒ ܝܰܬܺܝܪ ܡܶܢ ܐܰܝܢܳܐ ܕܢܳܣܶܒ *happier by far is he who gives than he who receives*; Heb. iii. 3; iv. 12. The simple adjective is used as a comparative in stating the age of two persons; e. g. Ez. xvi. 61. ܕܢܰܣܒܰܬܝ ܠܰܐܚ̈ܘܳܬܶܟܝ ܠܰܩܫ̈ܺܝܫܳܬܳܐ ܘܰܠܙܥܽܘܪ̈ܝܳܬܳܐ *since I have received thy sisters, the elder and the younger*; Barh. 27, 6, 7. Rarely after the Hebrew idiom, are we obliged to supply the comparative adjective from the context; e. g. Job xi. 17; more frequent is ܡܶܢ = *too*; e. g. Deut. xiv. 24. ܣܰܓܺܝܐܳܐ ܗ̱ܝ ܡܶܢܳܟ ܐܽܘܪܚܳܐ *the way is too great for thee*; or before an infinitive with ܕ = *than that*; e. g. Gen. iv. 13. ܪܰܒܳܐ ܗ̱ܝ ܡܶܢ ܠܡܶܫܬܒܳܩܽܘ *greater than that it can be forgiven.* This construction with ܡܶܢ occurs also with verbs of quality; e. g. Lam. iv. 7. ܕܰܟܘ ܡܶܢ ܬܰܠܓܳܐ ܘܰܚܘܰܪܘ ܡܶܢ ܚܰܠܒܳܐ *they are purer than snow and whiter than milk.* The adverbial *more* or *less*, in respect to numbers, is expressed by ܝܰܬܺܝܪ ܡܶܢ and ܒܨܺܝܪ; Barh. 156, 2; Assem. I. 414, 3.

B The Superlative.

The Superlative is expressed; *a*) by the *positive*, with the noun following in the genitive plural; e.g. I Cor. xv.9. ܙܥܘܪܗܘܢ ܕܫܠܝ̈ܚܐ *the least of the Apostles;* or with ܒ instead of the genitive; e. g. Matt.ii.6. ܙܥܘܪܐ ܒܡܠܟ̈ܐ ܕܝܗܘܕܐ *the least among the (princes) towns in Judah;* or simply by the emphatic state; e.g. Matt. v.19. ܙܥܘܪܐ *the least;* Barh. 85, 7. ܪܗܘܡܝ ܡܕܝܢܬܐ ܪܒܬܐ ܕܐܝܛܠܝܐ *Rome, the greatest city of Italy;* Assem. I. 323, A. 20; 335, A. 14. v. E; in the plural, ICor.vi.2. ܙܥܘܪ̈ܐ ἐλάχιστα; II Pet.i.4. ܪܘܪ̈ܒܐ μέγιστα; or when a preference is given to one individual over a whole species, by ܡܢ ܟܠ and a following plural; e. g. Ephr.I. 204, C. ܪܒܐ ܡܢ ܟܠ ܡܚܘ̈ܬܗ *the greatest of all evils;* *b*) by doubling the adjective or noun, so that the latter stands in the relation of genitive in the plural; e.g. Gen.ix.25. ܥܒܕ ܥܒ̈ܕܝܢ *the meanest slave;* Exod.xxvi.33. ܩܘܕܫ ܩܘܕܫ̈ܐ *the holy of holies,* i. e. *the holiest place;* Num. iii. 32; Barh. 530, 3, 4. ܡܠܟ ܡܠܟ̈ܐ *the king of kings,* i.e. *the mightiest king;* *c*) by ܛܒ and ܝܬܝܪ before the adjective; e. g. Rev. xviii. 12. ܩܝܣܐ ܝܬܝܪ ܡܝܩܪܐ *the most precious wood;* Barh. 87, 3.

Rem.—To denote the superlative, use is also made of the words ܪܝܫ and ܡܝܬܪܐ; e.g. Barh. 170, 13. ܪܝܫ ܐܣܘ̈ܬܐ *the most excellent physician;* Assem. 1. 335, B. 4, 5. ܡܝܬܪܐ ܕܪ̈ܚܡܢܐ *the most merciful;* more like the Hebrew, by ܐܠܗܐ; e. g. Ps. xxxvi. 6. ܛܘܪ̈ܐ ܐܠܗܐ *the mountains of God,* i.e. *the greatest mountains.* In verbs, a strengthening is denoted by ܛܒ *much;* e. g. Barh. 56, 11. ܛܒ ܐܬܕܠܚ *he was much disquieted;* or, by ܪܒ *many* (§ 67.1. c. *β*); e.g. Barh. 6, 5; 135, 1. To be noted also are such forms as ܕܝܕܝܥܐ ܚܟܡܬܗ, literally, *whose wisdom (is known) for the wisest.*

§ 78. *Construction of Numerals* (§ 50).

A. Cardinal Numbers.

The cardinals from three upwards, are connected with nouns in the following manner; *a*) the *object numbered* precedes the emphatic state plural; e.g. Luke i.56. ܝܪ̈ܚܐ ܬܠܬܐ *three months;* Barh. 133, 16. ܫܢ̈ܝܐ ܥܣܪܝܢ ܘܬܪܬܝܢ *twenty-two years;* 4, 5. ܫܢ̈ܝܐ ܡܐܬܝܢ ܘܚܡܫ *two hundred and five years;* or *b*) it follows in the absolute state; e. g. Matt. x. 29. ܬܪܝܢ ܨܦܪ̈ܝܢ *two Sparrows;* xiv. 20. ܬܪܬܥܣܪ ܩܘܦܝܢܝܢ *twelve baskets;* John v. 5; Acts xx. 3; Barh. 135, 10.

Rem.—Exceptions to this rule, however, occur, the object numbered standing after the number in the emphatic state; e. g. Barh. 160, 17. ܬܡܢܝܐ ܐܠܦܝܢ ܥܒܕ̈ܐ *eight thousand slaves;* 121, 8; 164, 4; or the cardinal, though rarely, stands as *nomen regens* in the construct state; e. g. Matt. iv. 25. ܥܣܪܬ ܡܕ̈ܝܢܬܐ *ten cities,* (literally, *the ten of the cities*). Some nouns, such as ܫܢܬܐ, ܝܘܡܐ also follow the numeral in the singular; e. g. Assem. I. 213, A. 21, 22. ܟܕ ܥܒܪܘ ܚܡܫܝܢ ܘܚܕ ܝܘܡܐ *when fifty-one days had passed;* Barh.10,16. Concerning the designation of age by ܒܪ and ܒܪܬ comp. § 75.2. Rem.; Assem.I. 31,21; 377, 1; Ephr.I.195,D; Barh. 50,13; 179,4; with the omission of ܫܢܝܢ; Barh. 5, 12. ܒܪ ܡܐܐ ܘܫܬܝܢ ܘܚܡܫ *one hundred and sixty-five years old.* For the combination of numerals without any numbered object, compare § 50; in respect to which it is to be noticed that, contrary to the He brew usage the smaller numbers follow the larger; e. g. Num. iv. 43; 1 Kings v. 11. Concerning suffixes to cardinal numbers, see § 46. 2. b. Rem.

B. Ordinal Numbers.

1. Ordinals are connected like adjectives with their nouns in the same number and case; e. g. Matt. xiv. 25. ܡܛܪܬܐ

ܒܡܛܪܬܐ ܕܠܠܝܐ *in the fourth watch of the night ;* Rev. iv. 7 ; vi. 9. ܠܚܬܡܐ ܚܡܝܫܝܐ *the fifth seal ;* verse 12 ; xvii. 11.

2. The cardinal numbers also supply the place of ordinals as follows ; *a*) the units, especially in designating time ; *a*) with the noun standing before the numeral in the emphatic state plural; e. g. John xix. 14. ܐܝܟ ܫ̈ܥܐ ܫܬ *about the sixth hour ;* β) with the noun after the numeral, in the absolute state ; e. g. John iv. 6. ܐܝܬܝܗ̇ ܗܘܬ ܫܬ ܫ̈ܥܝܢ *it was the sixth hour ;* verse 52 ; Acts iii. 1 ; x. 9, 30 ; but more especially ; *b*) in numbers above ten with the noun preceding in the construct state ; e.g. Luke iii. 1. ܒܫܢܬ ܚܡܫܥܣܪܐ *in the fifteenth year ;* Assem. I. 2, A. 1. 2, v.E. ܒܫܢܬ ܡܐܐ ܘܫܒܥܣܪܐ *in the one hundred and seventeenth year ;* p. 3, A. 17. B. 19 ; 388, 3 ; 389, 1, 3, 5; 407, 10 ; or with ܕ following in the emphatic state ; e.g. Barh. 4, 16. ܒܫܢܬܐ ܕܥܠܡܐ ܕܐܠܦܐ *in the year of the world one thousand ;* or *c*) the ܕ prefixed raises the cardinals to ordinals ; e. g. Matt. xxii. 26. ܕܬܪܝܢ *the second;* ܕܬܠܬܐ *the third ;* verse 39 ; Luke xii. 38. ܕܬܪܝܢ ܐܘ ܕܬܠܬܐ *the second or the third ;* especially in designating the years of the reign of a sovereign; e. g. Barh. 10, 14; 11, 1; 86, 11.

Rem.—Sometimes also, in accordance with Hebrew usage, the object numbered is repeated after the numeral in the absolute state plural; e.g. Gen. vii.11. ܒܫܢܬ ܫܬ ܡܐܐ ܫܢܝܢ *in the six hundredth year;* and the years of the reign are given with ܕܡܠܟ with a suffix ; e. g. Barh. 19, 9. ܒܫܢܬ ܥܣܪ ܕܡܠܟܗ *in the tenth year of his reign ;* 60, 8. In giving the days of the month, either ܒ without ܝܘܡܐ is repeated after the numeral, before the name of the month ; e. g. Assem. I. 2, B. 12. v. E. ܒܬܠܬܥܣܪ ܒܢܝܣܢ *on the 13th of Nisan(April);* 272,B.31 ; 399,19,20 ; 407,8,9 ; or, reversely, after the name of the month, before the numeral following it ; e. g. 397, 13. ܒܚܙܝܪܢ ܒܬܫܥܐ ܒܗ *on the 9th of June ;* or with ܒܝܘܡܐ

before the numeral and the name of the month which follows with ܒ repeated; e. g. 398, 7. ܒܝܘܡ ܥܣܪܝܢ ܘܫܒܥܐ ܒܝܪܚ ܟܢܘܢ *on the 27th of December*; 274, 30; or reversely, so that ܒܝܘܡ stands after the name of the month, before the numeral; e. g. 399, 14. ܒܝܪܚ ܐܒ ܒܝܘܡ ܬܪܝܢ ܘܥܣܪܝܢ ܒܗ *on the 22nd of August.* This takes place even in designating the days of the week; e.g. Matt. xxviii. 1. ܚܕ ܒܫܒܐ *the first day of the week*; John xx. 19; Assem. I. 2, B. 12. v. E.

C. Other Relations of Numbers.

1. *Distributives* are formed; *a*) by doubling the cardinal numbers (§ 72. 2. b); e. g. Mark vi. 40; Barh. 19, 14; *b*) sometimes by circumlocution by means of ܟܠ; e. g. Barh. 41, 16. ܠܟܠ ܬܪܝܢ ܚܕ *two each*; 17.

2. *Numerical adverbs*; *a*) in answer to the question, *How many times?* (Multiplicatives); *α*) by ܚܕ and ܒ before a cardinal number following, which more clearly defines it; e.g. Gen. iv. 15. ܚܕ ܒܫܒܥܐ *seven-fold*; Luke viii. 8; without ܒ, Jer. xvii. 18. ܚܕ ܬܪܝܢ *twofold*; *β*) by the simple numeral with ܒ, Luke xix. 8. ܒܐܪܒܥܐ (i.e. ܐܪܒܥܐ) *fourfold*; *b*) in answer to the question *How often?* *α*) with the signification of a cardinal, by means of ܙܒܢ *time*, plural ܙܒܢܝܢ *times*, as in English; e. g. II Cor. xi. 24, 25. ܚܕܐ ܙܒܢ *once*; ܚܡܫ ܙܒܢܝܢ *five times*; Matt. xviii. 22; Luke xvii. 4; John xiii. 38; by ܙܒܢܬܐ plural ܙܒܢ̈ܬܐ, Asssem. 1. 484, 27, 30; sometimes by ܟܪ *time*, plural ܟܪ̈ܝܢ, Barh: 10, 19; more rarely by ܐܘܪܚܐ *way*, or merely by the feminine of the ordinal number; e. g. Gen. iv. 24; *β*) in an ordinal signification, in such a manner that either ܙܒܢܐ of the cardinal precedes with ܕ, and is repeated after it in the plural; e.g. ܙܒܢܐ ܕܬܠܬܐ

ܬܠܝܬܝܬ (also elliptically ܙܒܢܐ ܕܬܠܬ or ܬܠܝܬܝܬ ܕܬܠܬ) *for the third time;* or by adverbs of the ordinals in ܐܝܬ, e. g. Jude, verse 12. ܬܢܝܢܘܬ *for the second time.*

3. Fractions are represented ; *a*) by special forms derived from the cardinal numbers; e. g. Rev. viii. 7. ܬܘܠܬܐ *one-third;* vi. 8. ܪܘܒܥܐ *one fourth;* Heb. vii.2 ; *b*) by circumlocution ; e.g. Rev. xi.13. ܚܕ ܡܢ ܥܣܪܐ *one-tenth ;* Ephr. I.204, D; Ez. v. 2. ܚܕܐ ܡܢ ܬܠܬ ܡܢܘܢ.

---

§ 79. *Connection of the Noun with Adjectives.*

The adjective is related to the noun either as epithet or predicate.

I. As epithet it follows the noun in the same gender and number ; e. g. Matt. xvii. 1. ܛܘܪܐ ܪܡܐ *an high mountain ;* xvi. 4. ܫܪܒܬܐ ܒܝܫܬܐ ܘܓܝܪܬܐ *a wicked and adulterous generation ;* xi. 8. ܢܚܬܐ ܪܟܝܟܐ *soft raiment ;* John xi. 47. ܐܬܘܬܐ ܤܓܝܐܬܐ *many miracles.* The same is true in respect to pronouns and participles; e.g. Matt. xv. 8. ܥܡܐ ܗܢܐ *this people ;* verse 12 ; xix. 1 ; Rev. iii. 8. ܬܪܥܐ ܦܬܝܚܐ *an open door.* Collectives in the singular are followed by the adjective in the plural ; e. g. Assem. I. 78, A. 4. ܥܡܐ ܢܛܪܝ ܢܡܘܣܐ *the people who hold to the law ;* so also with nouns in the plural having a singular signification ; e. g. John vii. 38. ܡܝܐ ܚܝܐ *living water ;* Heb. x. 24 ; or in the singular *ad sensum ;* e. g. Num. iv. 5. ܐܦܝ ܬܪܥܐ ܕܦܪܝܣܝܢ *the vail which was spread out.*

REM.—The pronoun frequently comes first ; e. g. John xi. 47. ܗܢܐ ܓܒܪܐ *this man ;* Matt. xviii. 1 : xvii. 18. Adjectives are also used emphatically, especially in titles; e.g. Assem.1.25,A.14. ܛܘܒܢܐ ܡܪܝ ܐܦܪܝܡ *the pious Ephraem;* 117,B.23. ܩܕܝܫܐ ܡܪܝ ܝܘܚܢܢ *the holy John;* 286, A. 1. If an adjective is appended to the demonstrative pronoun for the sake of more particular designation, the pronoun usually stands between the noun and the adjective; e. g. Ephr. 1. 124,E. ܢܘܗܪܐ ܗܘ ܩܕܡܝܐ ܐܬܦܪܣ *this light first spread abroad*; 127, D; or before both, 132, F. ܗܘ ܡܠܦܢܐ ܪܒܐ *this great teacher.*—ܟܠ occurs (as a noun) exclusively before the noun; e.g. Matt. xv. 13. ܟܠܗ̇ ܢܨܒܬܐ ܐܝܕܐ *this whole planting,* (with suffix, compare §55.B. 2.Rem.). A word, generally a particle, sometimes stands between the noun and the adjective; e. g. Acts xvii. 20. ܡ̈ܠܐ ܓܝܪ ܢܘܟ̈ܪܝܬܐ *strange words indeed.* But very rarely the adjective follows in a gender different from that required by the noun; e. g. Barh. 454, 18. ܕܝܪܐ ܩܕܝܫܐ (fem. ܩܕܝܫܬܐ) *the holy cloister.* Or with nouns of the common gender, the gender of several adjectives following one after the other, is interchanged; e. g. Michael. Chr. 61. 1, 2.

2. As predicate (with the substantive verb expressed or to be supplied) the adjective precedes the noun, which follows in the absolute state, or with a suffix; e. g. Mark xv. 23. ܚܡܪܐ ܕܡܚܠܛ ܒܗ ܡܘܪܐ *wine with which myrrh was mingled;* verse 26. ܟܬܝܒܐ ܗܘܬ ܥܠܬܐ *as reason was written;* Matt.xv. 28. ܪܒܐ ܗܝ ܗܝܡܢܘܬܟܝ *great is thy faith.* In like manner the pronoun; e. g. Mark xv. 26. ܗܢܘ ܡܠܟܐ ܕܝܗܘܕܝܐ *that is the King of the Jews;* Luke ii. 12. ܗܢܐ ܢܗܘܐ ܠܟܘܢ ܐܬܐ *that shall be for you the sign.*

Rem.—Sometimes the adjective, as predicate, follows the noun, viz.: when several words follow which define more closely the signification of the adjective; e. g. Gen. xix. 20. ܡܕܝܢܬܐ ܗܕܐ ܩܪܝܒܐ ܗܝ ܠܡܥܪܩ ܠܬܡܢ *this city is nigh to flee unto;* or an adverbial idea is embraced in the preposition; e. g. Gen xxix. 7. ܥܕܟܝܠ ܝܘܡܐ ܪܒ *it is yet high day,* i. e. *high in the day.* Sometimes the adjective singular, as predicate, stands before the plural noun; e.g. Barh. 542, 14, 15. ܠܗ̇ ܟܬܝܒ ܗܘܐ ܡ̈ܠܐ *to that same were the words written;* or it follows a plural, being itself in the singular; e.g. Assem. I. 21,5, 6. ܩܝ̈ܢܬܐ ܘܡܕܪ̈ܫܐ ܡܬܥܒܕ ܠܗ *songs and hymns were composed by him.* But especially the adjective in the plural follows collectives; e. g. Rev. xix. 1. ܟܢܫܐ ܣܓܝܐܐ ܕܐܡܪܝܢ *a great multitude, who said;* Barh. 88, 4. The predicate is also expressed by a noun; e. g. I Cor. xii. 27. ܦܓܪܗ ܐܢܬܘܢ ܕܡܫܝܚܐ *ye are the body of Christ;* Eph. v. 30.

3. When several nouns of different genders are connected, the adjective as epithet and predicate, usually conforms to the masculine; e.g. Luke i. 5, 6. ܙܟܪܝܐ ܘܐܢܬܬܗ ܐܠܝܫܒܥ — ܬܪܝܗܘܢ ܙܕܝܩܝܢ ܗܘܘ ܩܕܡ ܐܠܗܐ *Zacharias and his wife Elizabeth both feared God;* verses 6,7; Barh. 106,9.

Rem.—Concerning the neuter the same rules prevail as in § 66. 2, and § 70. 3; e.g. Assem. I. 36, 6. ܗܘ ܕܟܬܝܒܐ *that which has been written;* 372, 19; Ephr. I. 241,B; Barh.24, 18. ܥܒܕ ܕܒܝܫ *he did that which was evil.*

---

§ 80. *Connection of the Noun with the Verb.*

The Verb conforms in number and gender to the subject; but to this there are many exceptions, which may be referred to the following cases. Compare *Agrell Comment. de varietate generis et numeri in LL. OO. Lundæ*, 1815, 4.

A. In regard to Number.

Here it should be remarked:

1. That collectives or those nouns which are regarded as such, are connected with plural verbs. Here belong, ܚܝܠܐ; e.g. Barh. 94, 10. ܚܝܠܐ ܕܪ̈ܗܘܡܝܐ ܟܪܟܘܗ̇ ܐܦܣܘܣ *the Roman army*

proceeded towards Persia; 96, 9; ܟܽܠ; e. g. Acts xxvi. 13. ܟܽܠ ܕܰܥܡܝ ܗ̱ܘܰܘ *all who were with me*; Michael. Chr. 15,5; and its compounds, ܟܽܠܢܳܫ; e.g. Assem. I. 39,3—5. ܟܽܠܢܳܫ ܐܰܟܬܶܒܘ *all—wrote*; ܟܽܠܡܶܢ; e.g. Michael. Chr. 14,15. ܟܽܠܡܶܢ ܕܶܐܡܰܪܘ *all who said*; ܟܽܠ ܐ̱ܢܳܫ; e.g. Barh. 277,6. ܕܟܽܠܐ̱ܢܳܫ ܬܡܰܗܘ *that every one wondered*; also ܟܶܢܫܳܐ; e.g. Luke xxiii. 1. ܘܩܳܡܘ ܟܽܠܗ ܟܶܢܫܗܽܘܢ *the whole multitude arose*; ܚܰܝ̈ܠܳܐ; e.g. Barh. 422,10. ܐܶܬܰܘ ܚܰܝ̈ܠܳܐ *a great multitude came*; Assem. I. 386,15,16; ܥܰܡܳܐ; e.g. John v. 3. ܒܗܳܠܶܝܢ ܪܡܶܝܢ ܗ̱ܘܰܘ ܥܰܡܳܐ ܤܰܓܝܐܳܐ ܕܟܰܪܝܗ̈ܶܐ *in these (pools) lay a great multitude of invalids*; Assem. I. 483, 19; Barh. 95, 6,7; 227,8; 312,7; ܫܰܪܟܳܐ; e.g. Barh. 211,8. ܫܰܪܟܳܐ ܥܪܰܩܘ ܠܡܰܥܰܪ̈ܬܳܐ *the others fled*; 342, 19. According to the same construction are names of places put for their inhabitants; e.g. ܕܰܝܪܳܐ *cloister*; Assem. I. 411, Note B. 4—6. ܕܰܝܪܳܐ ـ ܟܰܕ ܚܙܰܐܘܗ̱ܝ *when the monks saw him*.

REM.—The same nouns also are found with the verb singular; e.g. ܚܰܝܠܳܐ, Barh. 551, 13; ܟܽܠ, 288,12, and its compounds, ܟܽܠܢܳܫ; e.g. 309,14; ܟܽܠܡܶܢ; e.g. 314,2; ܟܽܠ ܐ̱ܢܳܫ or ܟܽܠܐ̱ܢܳܫ; e.g. 373,1; also ܟܶܢܫܳܐ; e.g. Acts xiv. 4; ܥܰܡܳܐ; e.g. Acts v. 26; Barh. 301,9,10. In like manner, abstract feminines occur for concretes; e. g. ܐ̱ܢܳܫܽܘܬܳܐ, Barh. 490, 18. ܟܽܠܗ ܐ̱ܢܳܫܽܘܬܳܐ ܥܪܰܩ *all men fled*; ܫܒܺܝܬܳܐ for *prisoner*; Assem. I. 490, A. 31; ܡܕܺܝܢ݁ܬܳܐ for *inhabitants*; e.g. Acts xiii. 44; ܥܺܕܬܳܐ for *congregation*; e.g. I Cor. xiv. 23. Still more remarkable is the construction of these nouns in one and the same period with a singular and plural verb; e.g. ܚܰܝܠܳܐ, Barh. 212,1. ܟܰܕ ܙܟܳܝܗ̱ܝ ܚܰܝܠܳܐ ـ ܘܰܐܫܒܝܽܘܗ̱ܝ *an army conquered him and took him captive*; ܟܽܠ ܐ̱ܢܳܫ e.g. 388,3, 4; ܥܰܡܳܐ; e.g. Acts xxi. 36; Barh. 371, 8.

2. Nouns with a plural form having a singular signification (§ 44. Rem. 6), are either; *a*) in respect to form

connected with the plural verb; e. g. ܐܦܐ, II Cor. iii. 18. ܒܐܦܐ ܓܠܝܬܐ *with uncovered face;* Barh. 201, 1; ܚܝܐ; e.g. John iii.15. ܢܗܘܘܢ ܠܗ ܚܝܐ ܕܠܥܠܡ *he shall have eternal life;* v.26; Barh.219,12; ܡܝܐ; e.g. John v.7. ܡܐ ܕܐܬܬܙܝܥܘ ܡܝܐ *when the water was troubled;* Barh. 194, 3; 268, 7, 8, 12; and ܫܡܝܐ; e.g. Mark i 10. ܕܐܬܦܠܓܘ ܫܡܝܐ οὐρανοὶ σχιζόμενοι; James v. 18. ܫܡܝܐ ܝܗܒܘ ܡܛܪܐ ὁ οὐρανὸς ὑετὸν ἔδωκεν; or *b*) more rarely, in respect to signification, they are connected with the singular verb; e. g. Luke xxiii. 45. ܐܨܛܪܝ ܐܦܝ ܬܪܥܐ *the vail was rent;* John i. 4. ܒܗ ܚܝܐ ܗܘܐ *in him was life;* Num. xxxiii. 14. ܠܐ ܗܘܐ ܬܡܢ ܡܝܐ *there was no water there;* Luke iii. 21. ܐܬܦܬܚ ܫܡܝܐ *the heaven was opened;* as feminine, II Petr. iii. 5. ܫܡܝܐ ܐܝܬܝܗܘܢ ܗܘܬ ܡܢ ܩܕܝܡ οὐρανοὶ ἦσαν ἔκπαλαι; Barh. 228, 10.

3. With the noun plural also is connected the verb singular; *a*) when the verb preceding is used impersonally; *α*) ܐܝܬ and ܠܝܬ; e. g. John vi. 9. ܐܝܬ ܠܗ ܚܡܫ ܓܪܝܨܢ ܕܣܥܪܐ ܘܬܪܝܢ ܢܘܢܝܢ *he has five barley-loaves and two fishes;* xxi. 25; I Cor. xv. 40; Barh. 144, 8; with ܗܘܐ, John v. 2. ܐܝܬ ܗܘܐ ܒܗ ܚܡܫܐ ܐܣܛܘܢ *there were in the same five porches;* Assem. I. 352, 13; *β*) other verbs relating to persons; e. g. Luke ii. 13. ܐܬܚܙܝ ܚܝܠܘܬܐ ܣܓܝܐܐ ܕܫܡܝܐ *there appeared many of the heavenly host;* Barh. 124, 11. ܥܒܕ ܛܝܝܐ ܫܝܢܐ *the Arabians made peace;* 133, 12. ܡܝܬ ܐܪܒܥܐ ܐܠܦܝܢ - *there died four thousand;* 177, 14; 339, 9; or *b*) when the verb follows though more rarely; *α*) ܐܝܬ and ܠܝܬ; e.g. Barh. 148, 10. ܚܡܫܐ ܫܘܪܐ ܐܝܬ ܗܘܐ ܠܟܝܣܘܡ *Chisum had five walls;* *β*) other verbs relating to persons; e. g.

Barh. 112, 10. ܣܓܝܐܐ ܐܬܩܛܠ *many were slain*; 125, 14,15. ܛܝܝܐ ܐܡܠܟܘ *the Arabians chose for king*; 190, 9. ܡܢ ܕ ܡܥܡܪܢܝܐ - ܡܢ ܕܕܚܠ *since the inhabitants feared*; 298, 17; 513, 3; 532, 19.

Rem.—Some have attempted to explain this singular of the verb as the third plural pret. defectively written (§ 6; comp. Agrell a. a. O.p. 12,13); still it is remarkable that one and the same author, as Barhebræus, should employ interchangeably both ways of writing. On the contrary this construction is found in Hebrew and more frequently in the Arabic; and to both of these languages, such a defective form of the 3 pret. plur. is unknown. When a plural is to be considered as distributive (*one of them*, or *each one of them*), the Syriac uses not only the singular but the plural also, and marks this construction more accurately by ܟܠܚܕ, ܚܕ ܡܢܗܘܢ or ܟܠ ܡܢܗܘܢ; e.g. Barh. 434, 12. ܗܢܘܢ ܐܙܠ ܟܠܚܕ ܠܐܬܪܗ *each one of them went into his country*; 101, 14, 15. ܟܕ ܥܢܐ ܟܠܚܕ ܡܢ ܡܢܗܘܢ *each one of them had answered.*

4. The dual, which is used in four words only, (§ 44), is connected with the plural verb; e. g. Matt. xxiv. 40. ܬܪܝܢ ܢܗܘܘܢ *two shall be*; xviii. 19; xix. 5; Barh. 165, 19. ܘܝܠܕܝ ܬܪܝܗܘܢ *and they both brought forth.*

Rem.—Sometimes, also, according to the sense, the verb in the singular is found with ܡܨܪܝܢ; e.g. Barh.396,12. ܕܢܬܩܪܐ ܡܨܪܝܢ ܡܢ ܐܡܗ *that it should be called Egypt*; 433, 20. Similar is Barh. 121, 11. ܢܦܩ ܬܪܝܢ ܡܫܪܝܢ *there departed two armies.*

B. In respect to Gender.

1. Nouns masculine, singular and plural, sometimes take the verb, whether it precede or follow, in the feminine when they are masculine in respect to the termination, but not as to signification (compare § 43. Rem. 2, and § 70. 1. b).

Rem.—It must be considered as a solecism or a designation of the neuter when the verb feminine is found with a noun masculine; e.g. Barh.527,16. ܟܕ ܗܘܬ ܪܡܫܐ *when it was evening;* compared with Matt. viii. 16; xiv. 15; or Barh. 152, 14. ܗܘܬ ܡܨܘܬܢܐ *there arose a quarrel;* compared with Matt. xxvi. 5; Acts xxiii. 10.

2. Feminines take a verb in the masculine; *a*) when they are feminine merely in respect to termination (compare § 70. 1. a); *b*) when abstracts stand for concretes (compare § 70. 2); e. g. ܐܢܫܘܬܐ, ܒܢܝܢܫܐ *for mankind;* Barh.236,8. ܐܝܟ ܚܡܫܝܢ ܐܠܦܝܢ ܐܢܫܘܬܐ ܡܝܬܘ *there died about fifty thousand men;* 548, 20; 585, 14. ܡܫܪܝܬܐ *army;* 581, 12. ܐܬܟܢܫܘ ܗܠܝܢ ܡܫܪܝܬܐ *these armies were assembled;* or ܦܠܚܘܬܐ *military* for *soldiers;* 607, 20.

Rem.—These nouns are also found with the verb feminine; e. g. Barh. 341, 10, 11. ܡܝܬܬ ܐܝܟ ܬܪܬܥܣܪ ܐܠܦܝܢ ܒܢܝܢܫܐ *there died about twelve thousand men;* 348, 15, 16. But the preceding verb masculine is to be considered as impersonal in such cases as Barh. 612, 14. ܐܬܝܗܒ ܥܠܬܐ *there was occasion given;* compared with 579, 14. ܥܠܬܐ ܪܒܬܐ ܗܘܬ *there was much occasion;* or 606, 19, 20. ܗܘܐ ܠܗ ܕܚܠܬܐ *he had fear;* compared with 136, 6. ܢܦܠܬ ܕܚܠܬܐ ܥܠ ܡܠܟܐ *fear fell upon the king.*

3. Sometimes the noun is connected, in the same sentence, with the masculine and feminine of the verb; not only, *a*) nouns of the common gender; e.g. Mark v. 13. ܢܦܩܘ ܪܘܚܐ ܗܠܝܢ ܛܢܦܬܐ ܘܥܠܘ *these unclean spirits went out and entered;* but *b*) such also as have a determinate gender; e. g. Barh. 268, 10. ܬܪܬܝܗܘܢ ܢܦܠ ܘܐܬܚܢܩܘ *they both (mother and daughter) fell and were suffocated;* 260, 11, 12.

C. *In respect to both Gender and Number.*

1. Collectives feminine often take, in accordance with the meaning, the plural masc. of the verb; e. g. Barh. 561, 6, 7. ܐܢܫܘܬܐ — ܥܪܝܩܝܢ ܗܘܘ *the inhabitants had fled;* Gen. xli. 57. ܟܠܗ ܐܪܥܐ ܐܬܘ *the whole people (country) came;* Matt. viii. 32. ܟܠܗ ܒܩܪܐ ܗܘ — ܢܦܠܘ *this whole herd — perished;* Assem. I. 53, 17. ܐܬܟܢܫܘ ܟܠܗ ܡܕܝܢܬܐ ܘܒܟܘ *all the inhabitants (the whole city) assembled and wept.* So too the names of cities; e. g. Assem. I. 51, Note B. 1. ܐܘܪܗܝ ܢܦܩܘ ܠܡܬܩܛܠܘ *the inhabitants of Edessa went out to be slain;* Barh. 248, 6, 7. ܛܝܝܘܬܐ for *Mohammedans;* Barh. 580, 1, 2.

2. With nouns plural feminine, sometimes occur verbs singular masculine, as well before as after the noun; e. g. Isa. iii. 16. ܐܬܬܪܝܡ ܒܢܬܗ ܕܨܗܝܘܢ *the daughters of Zion are haughty;* Barh. 215, 7. ܐܬܒܙܙ ܟܠܗܘܢ ܩܢܝܢܘܗܝ *all of his goods had been plundered;* Ephr. II. 145, A. ܟܬܝܒ ܗܘܐ ܥܠܝܗܘܢ ܟܬܒܬܐ *there were writings composed concerning them;* Jer. xiv.5. ܐܝܠܬܐ — ܝܠܕ ܘܫܒܩ *the hinds calved and forsook;* Barh. 368, 11, 12; 10, 9. ܬܠܬ ܥܝܢܝܢ ܐܝܬܘܗܝ *there were three eyes.*

Rem.—Seldom are cases found, where the verb singular feminine stands with the noun plural masculine; e. g. Job xxxix.13, 14. ܫܒܩܬ ܒܝܥܐ ܢܥܡܝܬܐ *the ostrich leaveth her eggs.*

D. *Construction of sentences when there is more than one subject, or where the subject is compound.*

1. When the subject of a sentence is compounded of a nominative and genitive, the verb conforms; *a*) usually to the

nominative; e. g. Barh. 228, 7. ܐܶܬ݂ܚܙܺܝܬ݂ ܕܡܽܘܬ݂ܳܐ ܕܥܰܡܽܘܕܳܐ *there was seen the form of a pillar;* 613, 14. ܩܳܠܳܐ ܕܡܶܣܟܢ̈ܶܐ ܐܶܫܬܡܰܥ *the cry of the poor was heard;* 348, 20; *b*) the verb conforms to the genitive, when the latter contains the principal idea; e. g. Job xxxii. 7. ܣܽܘܓܳܐܐ ܕܫܢ̈ܝܳܐ ܡܰܠܦܳܢ *the multitude of years shall teach;* Barh 96,8,9. ܣܽܘܓܳܐܗ̇ ܕܡܕܺܝܢ̱ܬܳܐ ܢܦܰܠ *a great part of the city was destroyed;* 141, 10; 241, 10, 11; 188, 7, 8. ܐܽܘܟܠܳܣ ܩܛܝ̈ܠܳܐ — ܡܶܬ݂ܩܰܒܪܺܝܢ ܗ̄ܘܰܘ *a multitude of the dead were buried.*

Rem.—In the last connection ܟܽܠ, almost always is found; e. g. Matt. viii. 34; Acts xxi. 30; I Cor. xiv. 23; to which the verb rarely relates, as Barh.611,3. ܢܶܬ݂ܡܰܠܝ̈ܳܢ ܟܽܠܗܶܝܢ ܒܳܥܘܳܬ݂ܶܗ *all of his petitions should be granted.*

2. When it has several subjects connected by *and*, the verb stands as follows; A) when they are of the same gender; *a*) in the plural; thus *α*) before the subjects; e. g. John xxi. 2. ܐܺܝܬ݂ܰܝܗܽܘܢ ܗ̄ܘܰܘ ܐܰܟ݂ܚܕ݂ܳܐ ܫܶܡܥܽܘܢ ܟܺܐܦ݂ܳܐ ܘܬܳܐܘܡܳܐ ܘܢܰܬ݂ܢܳܐܝܶܠ *there were together Simon Peter, Thomas and Nathaniel;* Barh. 19, 7. ܐܶܬ݂ܩܰܛܠܘ ܫܳܐܘܽܠ ܘܝܽܘܢܳܬ݂ܳܢ *Saul and Jonathan were slain;* 78, 8; 193, 17; Assem. I. 30, A. 1, 2. ܟܰܕ ܟܢܺܝܫܺܝܢ ܩܠܺܝܪܳܘܣ ܘܟܽܠܗ ܥܰܡܳܐ *when the clergy and the whole congregation were assembled;* Ephr. 1. 223, A; *β*) after the subjects; Exod. xvii. 10. ܡܽܘܫܶܐ ܘܰܐܗܪܽܘܢ ܘܚܽܘܪ ܣܠܶܩܘ *Moses, Aaron and Hur, went up.* But the verb is also frequently found; *b*) in the singular; *α*) before the subjects; e.g. Matt. xxviii. 1. ܐܶܬ݂ܶܬ݂ ܡܰܪܝܰܡ ܡܰܓܕܠܳܝܬܳܐ ܘܡܰܪܝܰܡ ܐ̱ܚܪܺܬܳܐ *then came Mary Magdalene and the other Mary;* Barh. 106, 4, 5; 121, 19; 159, 9; 160, 13. ܗܘܳܐ ܟܰܦ݂ܢܳܐ ܘܡܰܘܬܳܢܳܐ *there arose famine and pestilence;* 193, 19; Assem. I. 272, A. 35, 36; Ephr. I. 216,B;

230,D ; β) after the subjects ; e.g. John ii.2. ܐܦ ܗܘ ܝܫܘܥ ܘܬܠܡܝܕܘܗܝ ܐܬܩܪܝܘ *Jesus and his disciples were invited ;* Barh.111,10 ; Assem. I. 234, A. 5. v. E ; B) when the subjects are of different genders, the verb conforms ; *a*) to the gender of that standing nearest to it ; e. g. Barh. 106, 9. ܟܕ ܟܢܫܝܢ ܗܘܘ ܓܒܪ̈ܐ ܘܢܫ̈ܐ ܘܛܠܝ̈ܐ *when men, women and youth had assembled together ;* 192, 10. ܐܬܚܙܝܘ ܛܘܪ̈ܐ ܘܓܙܪ̈ܬܐ *mountains and islands appeared ;* 195, 4 ; or *b*) the masculine is preferred, especially if the verb follow the subjects ; e.g. Barh. 74, 12, 13. ܬܐܘܕܘܣܝܘܣ ܘܚܬܗ ܡܬܪ̈ܒܝܢ ܗܘܘ *Theodosius and his sister were educated ;* 77, 7 ; 78, 2 ; Ephr.I. 253, A ; C) finally, when there are several subjects, if the construction commence with the singular of the verb, in the continuation of the sentence, the plural of the verb is used ; e.g. Barh. 137, 14. ܩܡ ܓܒܠܐ ܘܫܘܬ̈ܦܘܗܝ ܘܥܪܩܘ *Gabala and his confederates arose and fled ;* 155, 16. ܢܦܩ ܠܘܬܗ ܕܝܢܐ ܘܩܫܝܫ̈ܐ ܘܩܪܒܘ *the judge and the elders went out and brought.*

Rem.—The verb in the plural also follows, when several subjects are united by ܥܡ *with ;* e.g. Barh. 197,5,6. ܟܕ ܢܝܩܦܘܪܘܣ ܥܡ ܡܫܪܝܬܐ ܕܪ̈ܗܘܡܝܐ ܗܦܟܘ *when Nicephorus with the Roman army returned ;* 72, 2 ; 85, 9. When there are two different subjects, of which one is a pronoun of the first person, the verb follows in the first person plural ; e. g. Luke ii. 48. ܐܢܐ ܘܐܒܘܟ ܒܟܪܝܘܬܐ ܣܓܝܐܐ ܒܥܝܢ ܗܘܝܢ ܠܟ *I and thy father (we) have sought thee with much sorrow ;* Assem. I. 173, B. 23—25. Yet sometimes when the subjects are in the first and third persons, the verb is in the first person singular ; e.g. Assem. 1, 347, 28, 29. ܐܢܐ ܘܡܫܝܚܐ ܚܕ ܟܝܢܐ ܐܝܬܝ *I and the Messiah are (am) one nature.*

§ 81. *Peculiarities relating to Nouns.*

A. *Ellipsis.*

1. If the subject of a sentence would be repeated in the predicate, before a genitive for the purpose of defining it more accurately, that subject is omitted, and only the genitive is used; e. g. Matt. iii. 4. ܐܝܬܘܗܝ ܗܘܐ ܠܒܘܫܗ ܕܣܥܪܐ ܕܓܡ̈ܠܐ *his clothing was (a clothing of) camel's hair;* John v. 36. ܣܗܕܘܬܐ ܕܪܒܐ ܡܢ ܕܝܘܚܢܢ *a witness which is greater than that of John;* x. 21; xi. 4; Heb. iii. 3; v. 14. ܕܓܡܝܪ̈ܐ ܡܐܟܘܠܬܐ ܥܫܝܢܬܐ *to those who are of full age belongs strong meat;* Col. iii. 22.

Rem.—This Ellipsis also occurs in designations of time and place, with ܫܢܬܐ; e. g. Assem. I. 394, 6, 7. ܩܕܡ ܫܢܬܐ ܕܗܘܬ ܒܗ ܣܘܢܗܘܕܘܣ ܕܢܝܩܝܐ *a year before the Nicene council,* for ܫܢܬܐ, ܩܕܡ ܫܢܬܐ; l. 11. ܒܬܪܗ ܕܫܢܬܐ *the year thereafter,* for ܫܢܬܐ, ܒܬܪܗ ܕܫܢܬܐ; Mark xiv. 9. ܟܠ ܐܝܟܐ ܕܬܬܟܪܙ ܣܒܪܬܝ ܗܕܐ (viz: ܐܬܪ) *where-ever this my gospel shall be preached.*

2. Sometimes the accusative is wanting with the active verb, when the object can be easily supplied from the signification of the verb; e. g. ܕܒܪ *to plough,* literally *to drive* (ܦܕܢܐ *the yoke—plough*), I Sam. viii. 12. (in full, Luke xvii. 7); ܝܠܕ *to bring forth,* Aph. ܐܘܠܕ *to beget* (ܒܢ̈ܝܐ), Gen. xvi. 1; xxx. 1; ܢܣܒ *to marry,* literally *to take* (ܐܢܬܬܐ); Ezra. ix. 2, 12 (in full, Barh. 39, 11); ܐܪܡܝ *to cast lots,* literally *to cast* (ܦܣܐ *a lot*); I Sam. xiv. 42 (in full, Ps. xxii. 19); also nouns with prepositions; ܣܡ *to consider,* literally *to lay* (ܒܠܒܐ *in the Heart*); Job xxxiv. 23 (in full, Acts v.

4); ܪܕܐ *to ship*, literally *to go*, (ܒܝܡܐ *upon the sea*); Mark vi. 48; Luke viii. 23.

Rem.—Here also seem to belong impersonal phrases (§ 66. 1, 2) like ܟܪܝܐ ܠܝ, ܥܩܬܐ ܠܝ to which may be supplied ܢܦܫܐ or ܪܘܚܐ; and ܛܐܒ ܠܝ to which may be supplied ܠܒܐ. To ܢܗܪܬ *it is clear*, and ܚܫܟܬ *it is dark*, it is forced and unnecessary to supply ܐܐܪ or ܫܘܡܠܐ.

B. Zeugma and Hendiadys.

Zeugma occurs with the noun as well as with the verb (§ 68. C. 2); e.g. Gen. ii. 1. ܫܡܝܐ ܘܐܪܥܐ ܘܟܠܗ ܚܝܠܗܘܢ *the heavens and the earth and all their host*; or *Hendiadys*; e.g. Gen. iii. 16. ܟܐܒܝܟܝ ܘܒܛܢܟܝ *thy sorrow and thy conception*, i. e. *the sorrow of thy conception*; Job iv. 16. Cases of Paronomasia are merely imitations of the Hebrew; e.g. Isa. xxviii. 10, 13; and passages of accidental assonance; e.g. Barh. 102, 18. ܠܐ ܒܦܝܣܐ ܐܠܐ ܒܣܝܦܐ *not by persuasion but by the sword.*

APPENDIX.

The Rendering of Composite Greek nouns.

The Syrians render the Greek composite noun as well as the verb (compare Appendix to § 67) into their language, in the following manner; 1) by simple Syriac words of like signification; e. g. I Tim. iv. 13. ἀνάγνωσις ܩܪܝܢܐ; παράκλησις ܒܘܝܐܐ; i. 9. ἀσεβεῖς ܪܫܝܥܐ; ἀνόσιοι ܛܢܦܐ; Matt. xviii. 28. σύνδουλος ܟܢܬܐ; or 2) by writing two words for one; *a*) in the relation of genitive; e.g. Acts ii. 23. πρόγνωσις ܡܩܕܡܘܬ ܝܕܥܬܐ; II Tim. iii. 2. ἀχάριστοι ܟܦܘܪܝ ܛܝܒܘܬܐ; or *b*) by two nouns, of which the latter stands in apposition; e.g. John xi.16. συμμαθηταὶ αὐτοῦ ܠܬܠܡܝ̈ܕܐ ܚܒܪ̈ܘܗܝ; c) by a participle and noun which correspond with the verb; e. g. Acts iv. 13. αγράμματοι ܠܐ ܝܕܥܝܢ ܣܦܪܐ: or by participles and adjectives and the noun with ܠܐ prefixed; e. g. II Pet. iii. 16. δυσνόητος ܥܣܩܝܢ ܠܡܣܬܟܠܐ; or *d*) by the pronoun and verb; e. g. I Cor. vii. 8. ἄγαμοι ܐܝܠܝܢ ܕܠܝܬ ܠܗܘܢ ܢܫ̈ܐ. If the composites are formed from adjectives and nouns; 3) they are frequently resolved into their component parts, and rendered in the same manner as in cases mentioned above; *a*) in the relation of genitive; e. g. Mark xvi. 14. σκληροκαρδία ܩܫܝܘܬ ܠܒܐ; Col. ii. 14. χειρόγραφον ܫܛܪ ܚܘ̈ܒܝܢ; Matt. xxiv. 24. ψευδοπροφῆται ܢܒܝ̈ܐ ܕܕܓܠܘܬܐ; *b*) by the noun and adjective; e. g. Phil. ii. 3. κενοδοξία ܫܘܒܗܪܐ ܣܪܝܩܐ; II Cor. xi. 13. ψευδαπόστολοι ܫܠܝ̈ܚܐ ܕܓܠ̈ܐ; 4) sometimes we can trace definite laws of rendering; *a*) nouns, adjectives, and adverbs compounded with πᾶς, take ܟܠ; e. g. Luke xi. 22. πανοπλία ܟܠܗ ܙܝܢܗ; xxiii. 18. παμπληθεί ܟܠܗ ܟܢܫܐ; Sap. xviii. 15. παντοδύναμος ܕܟܠ ܡܫܟܚܢܐ; *b*) when they are compounded with α privative, the latter is represented by ܠܐ and ܕܠܐ; e. g. I Cor. xv. 53. ἀθανασία ܠܐ ܡܝܘܬܘܬܐ; Eph. i. 4. ἄμωμος ܕܠܐ ܡܘܡ; Matt. iii. 12. ἄσβεστος ܕܠܐ ܕܥܟܐ. Finally, in composites formed with σὺν, this is often rendered by ܥܡ; e. g. Philem. verse 23. συναιχμάλωτός μου ܫܒܝܐ ܕܥܡܝ; Rom. xvi. 9. ὁ συνεργὸς ἡμῶν ܡܥܕܪܢܐ ܕܥܡܢ.

CHAPTER FOURTH.

PARTICLES.

§ 82. *Construction and union of Adverbs.*

1. Besides the formation of adverbs described in § 51, is to be noticed as a special peculiarity the expressing of them by certain verbs, which, either stand in the same tense, number, and gender, with the finite verb, with or without the copula, or the infinitive of the verb follows with ܠ. In this connection stand ; *a)* ܗܦܟ *to return*, and ܐܘܣܦ *to continue*, for *once more, farther, again* ; e. g. Gen. viii. 10. ܗܦܟ ܘܫܕܪܗ̇ *again he sent her out* ; Ps. lxxi. 20. ܬܗܦܟ ܬܣܩܢܝ *thou shalt bring me again* ; Job vii.7. ܠܐ ܬܗܦܘܟ ܠܡܚܙܐ *they shall no more see* ; Luke xx. 11, 12. ܐܘܣܦ ܘܫܕܪ *he sent again* ; Assem. I. 203, A. 7, 8 ; Gen. iv. 2. ܐܘܣܦܬ ܠܡܐܠܕ *she bare again* ; Barh. 152, 3 ; also by adding pleonastically ܬܘܒ *again* ; Gen. viii. 21. ܠܐ ܐܘܣܦ ܬܘܒ ܠܡܠܛܗ̇ ܠܐܪܥܐ *I will no more curse the earth* ; *b)* ܐܣܓܝ *to make much*, for *very* ; e. g. Barh. 92, 14. ܐܣܓܝ

ܝܰܬܺܝܪ *he esteemed very much ;* II Cor. viii.15 ; II Kings xxi. 6. ܐܰܣܓܺܝ ܠܡܶܥܒܰܕ ܕܒܺܝܫ *he did much evil ; c)* ܫܰܠܶܡ *to end,* for *wholly, completely;* e.g. Gen. xxiv. 15. ܠܳܐ ܫܰܠܶܡ ܠܡܰܡܠܳܠܽܘ *he had not yet done speaking ; d)* ܩܰܕܶܡ *to precede* (always without the copula) for *before ;* e. g. ܩܰܕܡܶܬ ܐܶܡܪܶܬ *I have said before ;* Acts ii. 31 ; vii. 52 ; Rom. iii. 9, 25; viii. 28,30; xi. 35 ; xii. 11 ; I Cor. ii. 7; Gal. iii. 8.

Rem.—More according to the Hebrew, seems to be the expression in Hos. vi. 4 ; ܛܰܠܳܠܳܐ ܕܡܰܩܕܶܡ ܘܳܐܙܶܠ (טַל מַשְׁכִּים הֹלֵךְ) *the dew, which early is scattered ;* Gen. xxxvii. 7 ; or II Kings ii. 10. ܐܰܣܓܺܝܬ ܫܶܐܠܬ (הִקְשִׁיתָ לִשְׁאוֹל) *thou askest too great a thing;* compare Ephr. I. 519, D. E ; הִפְלִיא in II Chron. xxvi. 15, is expressed by ܐܰܣܓܺܝ ; compare Jer. iv. 5, and onward. If the finite verb already precede, it may be omitted in adverbial usage ; e. g. I Sam. xx. 41. ܒܟܰܘ ـ ܕܳܘܺܝܕ ܕܶܝܢ ܐܰܣܓܺܝ *they mourned — but David the most.*

2. Adverbs like adjectives, are connected with nouns and stand ; *a)* before them ; e. g. Luke iv. 25. ܣܰܓܺܝ ܐܰܪ̈ܡܠܳܬܳܐ *many widows ;* John ii. 12. ܩܰܠܺܝܠ ܝܰܘ̈ܡܳܬܳܐ *few days ;* Barh. 78, 1 ; 105, 3 ; 106, 8 ; Assem. I. 30, 15, 21 ; 270, A. 6. v. E; with words standing between; 284, A. 10. v. E. ; *b)* more seldom after the noun ; e. g. I Cor. v. 6. ܚܰܡܺܝܪܳܐ ܩܰܠܺܝܠ *a little leaven ;* II Chron. ii. 9. ܩܰܝ̈ܣܳܐ ܣܰܓܺܝ *much wood ;* Barh. 80, 16. ܢܽܘܪܳܐ ܣܳܡ ܠܬܰܚܬ *the fire placed under.*

Rem.—Sometimes nouns represent the adverb by a following genitive ; e. g. Ephr. I. 219, A. ܐܺܝܬܰܝܗܽܘܢ ܠܗܽܘܢ ܐܰܡܺܝܢܽܘܬܳܐ ܕܥܢܳܢܳܐ ܘܥܰܡܽܘܕܳܐ *they had continually the cloud and the pillar.* Particularly should be noticed ; ܩܪܝܒ ܒܩܠܝܠ *almost* ; or ܩܠܝܠ ܡܢ ܩܠܝܠ ܐܘ ܡܢ, ܡܢܬ *partly*, etc.

3. The repetition of the adverb indicates ; *a*) a strengthening or increase of the meaning ; e. g. Gen. vii. 19. ܛܒ ܛܒ *quite ready* ; Matt. iv. 24. ܒܝܫ ܒܝܫ *very bad* ; John vi. 7 ; Barh. 65, 14. ܩܠܝܠ ܒܩܠܝܠ and 84, 17. ܦܣܩ ܦܣܩ *by degrees* ; *b*) sometimes a diversity is expressed by adverbs of place ; e. g. I Kings xx. 40. ܠܗܪܟܐ ܘܠܗܪܟܐ *here and there.*

---

§ 83. *Use of the Interrogation, Affirmation, and Negation.*

A. Upon the construction of the interrogation, it should be remarked ;

1. That the simple direct question is distinguished ; *a*) either by being preceded by an interrogatory pronoun or particle ; e.g. Luke xxii. 27. ܡܢܘ ܪܒ *who is the greatest ?* John ix. 26. ܡܢܐ ܥܒܕ ܠܟ *what has he done to thee ?* verse 10. ܐܝܟܢܐ ܐܬܦܬܚ ܥܝܢܝܟ *how were thine eyes opened ?* verse 19 ; vii. 35 ; Assem. I. 33, 15 ; 179, B. 25. ܡܢ ܐܝܟܐ ܝܕܥܝܢ ܗܘܘ ܗܠܝܢ *whence know they this ?* or *b*) by the position of the words employed, the prominent word in forming the question being generally placed first ; e. g. Matt. xxvii. 11. ܐܢܬ ܗܘ ܡܠܟܐ ܕܝܗܘܕܝܐ *art thou the king of the Jews ?* Assem. I. 33, 17. ܐܝܬ ܠܟ ܨܒܝܢܐ *is it thy wish ?*

2. A question with ܠܐ usually contains an affirmation ; e.g. John iv. 35. ܠܐ ܐܢܬܘܢ ܐܡܪܝܢ ܕܒܬܪ ܐܪܒܥܐ ܝܪܚܝܢ ܐܬܐ ܚܨܕܐ *say ye not, that after four months cometh the harvest ?*

xviii.26; but with ܠܡܐ it embraces a negation; e.g.John v. 45. ܠܡܐ ܡܣܒܪܝܢ ܐܢܬܘܢ ܕܐܢܐ ܡܩܛܪܓ ܐܢܐ ܠܟܘܢ *believe ye that I shall accuse you?* x. 21; xviii.35; or a doubt; e.g. Matt. xxvi. 22. ܠܡܐ ܐܢܐ ܡܪܝ *Lord is it I?* John ix. 27; xviii.25; so also with ܟܒ; e. g. Ephr. I. 240, F, ܡܫܦܪ ܗܘܐ ܟܒ ܩܕܡܘܗܝ ܡܪܝܐ *would this please God?* Luke xviii. 8; xxiv. 18; John vii. 35.

Rem.—The direct question is also found with ܐܪܐ (ἆρα), Barh. 131, 12; with ܡܟܢܐ for ܠܡܐ 119, 10.

3. The indirect question is indicated by ܐܢ = *whether*; e.g. Matt. xxvi. 63. ܐܢ ܐܢܬ ܗܘ ܡܫܝܚܐ ܒܪܗ ܕܐܠܗܐ *whether thou art the Christ the son of God.* The disjunctive (*whether—or* (*utrum—an*) is marked by ܐܘ in the second part; e. g. Matt. xi. 3. ܐܢܬ ܗܘ ܗܘ ܕܐܬܐ ܐܘ ܠܐܚܪܝܢ ܗܘ ܡܣܟܝܢܢ *art thou he who should come or shall we look for another?* John ix. 2; Assem. I. 87, B. 12, 13; 377, 20, 21.

Rem.—The affirmation or negation of a question is usually expressed by a repetition of the leading verb with the personal pronoun; e.g. Assem. I. 375, 7. ܫܡܥܬܘܢ ܐܚܝ ܡܕܡ ܕܐܡܪܬ — ܘܐܡܪܘ ܫܡܥܢ ܟܠܡܕܡ ܕܐܡܪܬ *have you heard, my brethren, what I have said? and they answered, yes, all;* 10. ܫܪܝܪ ܐܘ ܠܐ — ܘܥܢܘ ܕܫܪܝܪ *is it true or not? and they answered it is true,* i. e. *yes;* sometimes by another verb; e.g. Matt.xxvii.11. ܐܢܬ ܐܡܪܬ *thou hast said it,* i. e. *yes;* in the negative with the same repetition; e. g. Assem. I. 378, 7, 11. Sometimes only ܠܐ = *not*, appears; e. g. Assem. I. 33,19. ܘܐܡܪ ܠܐ ܐܒܝ *and he said, No, my father.*

B. The negative particles ܠܐ and ܠܘ (and *nonne?*) are distinguished from ܠܝܬ by this latter forming the negation to ܐܝܬ, and with nouns, adjectives, and participles (§ 58. B. 5) or with suffixes (§ 38. 2), it includes the substantive verb.

Rem.— ܠܐ is repeated in the latter of two negative clauses; e. g. I Cor. xi. 11, 16 (but the negative sense is lost when the particle is to be taken affirmatively; as in Matt. v. 25; Luke xxi. 34). To adjectives and participles it gives a negative or privative signification (= *un, in, -less*); e. g. Eph. i. 4. ܠܐ ܡܘܡܐ *spotless;* Rom. i. 23. ܠܐ ܡܬܚܒܠܢܐ *imperishable.* Before nouns it signifies *nothing less than;* e.g. Deut. xxxii.21. ܠܐ ܥܡܝ *nothing less than my (God's) people.* Before the future (equivalent to an imperative) it is prohibitory; compare § 61. 3. B, and § 62. 3. Doubled (ܘܠܐ — ܘܠܐ or ܘܠܐ — ܠܐ), it signifies *neither — nor;* John viii. 19; ix. 3.

---

§ 84. *Prepositions.*

1. When prepositions come together, in many instances; *a*) the signification of one of them is only apparently lost. Thus for example, ܡܢ; *α*) before prepositions, denotes the direction from a place whose position is more closely defined by those which follow; e. g. Assem. I. 46, 21. ܡܢ ܠܬܚܝܬ ܟܐܦܐ ܢܦܩ *out from under a rock,* 1. 37,19; *β*) after prepositions it denotes a removal from the place more closely defined by those which precede; e. g. Assem. I. 54, 7. ܩܒܪܘܗܝ ܠܬܚܝܬ ܡܢ ܥܕܬܐ *they buried him under the Church;* Barh. 200, 16. ܠܩܕܡ ܡܢ ܡܕܝܢܬܐ *before the city;* 72, 19, 20; 66, 13. ܠܥܠ ܡܢ ܫܘܪܐ *from below,* (i. e. *above*) *the walls;* figuratively, 31, 17. ܠܥܠ ܡܢ ܟܠܗܘܢ ܝܘܬܪܢܐ *above all excellence;* one of the prepositions is; *b*) merely pleonastic; e. g. Eccl. x. 14. ܡܢ ܒܬܪܗ *after him;* Assem. I. 36, 22.

ܡܶܢ ܠܘܳܬܳܟܝ *from thee;* 37, 1; Dan. v. 24. ܡܶܢ ܩܕܳܡܰܘܗܝ *before him;* Barh. 65, 9. ܠܘܳܬ ܠܡܰܠܟܳܐ *to the King.*

2. Several of the prepositions have a peculiar consecution; e.g. *betwixt—and between,* ܒܶܝܢܰܝ — ܘܰܠ; e.g. Matt. xx. 17. ܒܶܝܢܰܘܗܝ ܠܒܶܝܢܰܝܗܘܢ *between him and them;* frequently without the copula, xix. 10; ܒܶܝܬ — ܠ; e. g. Barh. 60, 13. ܒܶܝܬ ܚܪܳܢ ܠܐܘܪܗܝ *between Haran and Edessa;* 75, 17, 18; 83, 15; 146, 13; rarely ܠ — ܠ; e. g. Barh. 60, 8; *from—to,* ܡܶܢ — ܕܰܡܳܐ ܠ; e.g. Matt. i. 17. ܡܶܢ ܐܰܒܪܳܗܳܡ ܕܰܡܳܐ ܠܕܰܘܺܝܕ *from Abraham to David;* in more general designations also without ܕܰܡܳܐ; e. g. Barh. 99, 17; 105, 7.

3. Besides the cases mentioned in § 55. B. 3. b) prepositions are repeated with several nouns which follow after one another, and depend upon one and the same preposition; e. g. Barh. 82, 10; 104, 11, 13; but the preposition is quite as frequently omitted after the first noun; e. g. Barh. 6, 1; 40, 12; 66, 6.

Rem.—As special idioms, are to be regarded the following; *a*) ܒ sometimes stands for ܠ (ἐν = εἰς); e. g. Luke ii. 3. ܐܳܙܶܠ ܗܘܳܐ ܟܽܠܢܳܫ — ܒܡܕܺܝܢܬܶܗ *each went to his own city;* iii. 3; Barh. 66, 16, 17; or serves to designate the value or price of a thing, equivalent to *for;* Barh. 64, 6. ܒܡܳܐܬܰܝܢ ܘܰܚܡܶܫܺܝܢ ܡܳܥܶܝܢ *for two hundred and fifty oboli;* 149, 8, 9; 191, 1, 2; 193, 19; *b*) ܠ denotes direction towards a place (§ 67. 1. b. δ); with numerals, with ܕܰܡܳܐ preceding = *about to; c*) ܠܘܳܬ and ܓܰܒ show, sometimes a possession in a physical and intellectual sense (= *penes*); e.g. Job xv. 9. ܕܠܳܐ ܗܘܳܐ ܠܘܳܬܰܢ *which stands not in our power;* 23. 14; *d*) ܡܶܢ forms adverbs (§ 51. 3. a); expresses the pronouns *anybody — some* (§ 58. B. 4, 6, 7), and sometimes indicates the direction to a place; e. g. Assem. I. 485, 28. ܡܶܢ ܡܰܕܢܚܳܐ *towards morning* ; I. 29 ; *e*) ܟܠܐ often occurs before a duty or obligation (§ 67. II. 4. b) ; Ezra x. 4. It may also in respect to signification, be considered as a preposition ; *f*) ܕܠܐ *without* ; e. g. Barh. 227,5. ܕܠܐ ܐܝܕܝܐ ܘܕܠܐ ܪܓܠܐ *without hands and without feet.*

---

§ 85. *Conjunctions.*

The Syriac language, in common with the other semitic dialects, is very deficient in conjunctions ; but affluence of periodic diction in all languages arises from this class of words. Hence in syriac, upon the one hand, the periods are wanting in variety and continuance ; and on the other hand the connective particles which do exist have many significations. In general the following may be observed :

I. Those conjunctions (e. g. *when*, *then*) are frequently omitted, which, in the protasis indicate the relation to the apodosis, and the two members are united by *and ;* e. g. Gen. xix. 23. ܫܡܫܐ ܢܦܩ ܘܠܘܛ ܥܠ *when the Sun had arisen, Lot came ;* xliv. 4.

REM.—Moreover the following fall away ; *a*) ܘ (*asyndeton*) after verbs of motion ; e. g. Matt. ix. 7. ܩܡ ܐܙܠ *he arose and went ;* Barh. 25, 1; 197, 19 ; especially in earnest discourse ; e. g. I Sam. xv. 6 ; *b*) ܐܘ *or ;* e.g. II Kings ix. 32. ܬܪܝܢ ܬܠܬܐ ܡܗܝܡܢܐ *two or three eunuchs ;* *c*) ܕ more in accordance with Hebrew usage ; e. g. Isa. l. 2. ܠܡܢܐ ܐܬܝܬ ܘܠܝܬ ܐܢܫ *wherefore was, I came, (when I came), no one there.* On the other hand ܘ is often repeated (*polysyndeton*) ; e. g. Barh. 51, 20. ܘܡܝܬ ܘܐܬܩܒܪ ܘܩܡ ܘܣܠܩ ܠܫܡܝܐ *he died, was buried, arose, and went to heaven ;* 82, 17 ; 38, 5, 6.

2. As correlatives, conjunctions are used doubled in a

sentence; *a*) the same word; e. g. ܘ — ܘ and ܐܦ — ܐܦ *as well—as, both—and;* e. g. Assem. I. 291, A. 10, 11, v. E; ܐܘ — ܐܘ *either—or;* Barh. 112, 4; 223, 4, 5; ܐܢ — ܐܢ *whether—or;* e.g. 217,13; or *b*)different words; e.g. ܐܝܟ — ܗܟܢܐ *like—as;* Assem. I. 75, B. 11, 13, v. E; 374, 23, 24; with ܐܝܟܢܐ ܕ preceding; Ephr. I. 214, E; ܐܦܢ — ܐܠܐ *although—yet;* e. g. Barh. 91, 12, 13.

3. The conjunctions ܕ = *that, thereby,* or ܕܠܐ = *that not,* are usually connected with the future (§ 61.3.A); e. g. Assem. I. 515, B.32; Barh. 213, 6; but in as far as they have the signification of *since, because,* (*quod*), they are connected with the preterite; e.g. Matt. ix. 8. ܫܒܚܘ ܠܐܠܗܐ ܕܝܗܒ *they praised God, because he had given;* 12, 41; 13, 11; Barh. 24, 9.

4. Concerning the use of particular conjunctions, the following may be noted;

a) ܐܘ is sometimes used in comparisons (= ܡܢ); e. g. Matt. xi. 22; xix. 24; and likewise *b*) ܐܝܟ in comparing one thing with another of the same species; e. g. Isa. i. 7; Job xxiv. 14; Assem. I. 75, A. 1. v. E; 168, B. 29; with numerals it signifies *really, about;* Barh. 104,13; *c*) ܐܠܘ *if,* (= לוּ ἐάν) denotes, in doubtful cases, the relation of the subjunctive; ܐܢ = אם εἰ in cases of certainty, denotes the indicative, and also occurs in indirect questions (§ 83.3); it is negative in those passages containing asseverations under oath, yet only in those which are translated, and which, according to the Hebrew idiom, are without any negation; with a negative ܠܐ ܐܢ, ܐܢ ܠܐ or ܐܢ ܠܐ, it is affirmative (compare אם and לא אם, Gesenius Lehrg. p. 844); e. g. Cant. 2. 7.

ܐܢ ܬܥܝܪܘܢ ܘܐܢ ܬܥܝܪܘܢ *wake not, rouse not ; d)* ܕ (for the further use of which see § 56 ; § 69.1 ; 73. 3 ; § 74. 2.; § 78.B. 2) ; *α*) from particles which it follows, forms conjunctions ; e. g. ܐܝܟ ܕ *just as*, Assem. I. 34, 17 ; *so that*, Matt. ii. 13 ; ܐܝܟܢܐ ܕ *just as*, John viii. 28 ; Ephr. I. 214, E ; ܐܡܬܝ ܕ (of time) *as, when*, Assem.I. 485, 15 ; ܡܛܠ ܕ *since, because*, Barh. 112, 7, 8 ; 160, 12 ; ܒܬܪ ܕ, 39,7, and ܡܢ ܒܬܪ ܕ, Assem. I. 213, A. 25, *afterwards ;* ܒܫܥܬܗ ܕ *as soon as*, I.218, 27 ; ܡܐ ܕ (of time) *when*, I.485,20 ; ܡܛܘܠ ܕ, Barh.160, 16, and ܚܠܦ ܕ, 158,12, *since,because ;* ܥܕܡܐ ܕ *until, that*,(including the *terminus ad quem*), Ephr. II. 125, B ; 242, A ; ܥܕܡܐ ܠܗܝ ܕ *so much that*, Barh.193,2 ; ܩܕܡ ܕ *before*,150,13 ; *β*) in the signification of *that*, ܕ is sometimes omitted before the future ; e.g. John xxi. 3. ܐܙܠ ܐܢܐ ܐܨܘܕ ܢܘܢܐ *I go thatI may catch fish ;* after ܥܕ, John v. 7. ܥܕ ܐܢܐ ܐܬܐ ܐܢܐ *until that I come ;* or it is pleonastic after ܐܢ ; e. g. Matt. x. 13. ܐܢ ܗܘ ܕܫܘܐ ܒܝܬܐ *when the house is worthy ;* Mark viii. 3 ; Luke vi. 7 ; John viii. 36 ; after ܐܦܢ, Matt. ix. 21 ; ܠܘܠܐ Mark 13, 20 ; *e*) the copula ܘ also denotes *α*) *that*, especially after verbs of ***sending, entreating, commanding***, etc ; e. g. Assem. I. 77, 23, 24 ; Barh. 11, 18 ; 97, 8; 105, 1 ; 152, 5; 221, 2; it forms *β*) the apodosis ; e.g. Barh. 39, 7. 8 ; and is *γ*) equivalent to *but* ; e. g. Barh. 11, 16; 16, 9 ; *δ*) it sometimes supplies the place of the comparative ܐܝܟ ; e. g. Job v. 7. Also the Hebrew אוּלָם is translated by the frequently occurring ܒܪܡ ***yet, nevertheless.***

§ 86. *Interjections.*

1. The Interjection which denotes an imprecation or cry of distress, is usually connected with ܠ following; e. g. Eccl. x. 16. ܘܝ ܠܟܝ *woe to thee!* ii. 16. ܘܝ ܠܟܘܢ *woe to you!* Matt. xviii. 7; xxiii. 13–16; xxiv. 19; Ephr. II. 135, E. ܘܝ ܠܡܠܟܐ ܕܝܗܘܕܐ *woe to the king of Judah!* 274, D. ܘܝ ܠܕܡܬܚܫܒܝܢ ܢܟܠܐ *woe to those who meditate deceit!* 351, C. ܘܝܐ ܠܚܘܒܝܢ; or with ܐ appended; e.g. ܘܝܐ ܠܝ *woe to me!* Ez. xxx. 2. ܐܘܗ ܠܝܘܡܐ *woe for the day!* sometimes with ܥܠ; e. g. Jer. l. 27. ܘܝ ܥܠܝܗܘܢ *woe to you!* or ܡܢ, Amira p. 449. ܐܘܗ ܡܢ ܫܪܒܬܐ ܗܕܐ *woe to this generation.* Without an intervening preposition, they are the usual expressions of grief and mourning, and the noun is then to be taken in the accusative; e. g. Judges xi. 35. ܐܘܗ ܒܪܬܝ *alas, my daughter!* Rev.xviii.10,16,19.

Rem.—Sometimes ܐܘ occurs as an ordinary exclamation, with ܠ as a sign of the accusative; e. g. Barh. 333, 3, 4. As a particle of exclamation sometimes also occurs ܐܝܢ, properly, *verily, truly;* compare Amira p. 436.

2. Concerning the construction of particular interjections, the following may be observed:

a) ܗܐ *lo! behold*, is frequently pleonastic; e.g. Ephr. III. 149, B. ܦܓܪܐ ܡܝܘܬܐ ܠܘܬ ܗܘ ܡܬܬܠܝܐ ܗܐ ܐܟܙܢܐ ܢܦܫܐ *the mortal body is thus dependent upon the soul;* or at the beginning of a period it serves to give animation to the discourse; e. g. Ephr.III.247,C. ܗܐ ܦܪܝܫ ܗܘܐ ܐܚܘܢ *lo! our brother (member) is separated;* in designations of time, like the Greek ἤδη, it signifies *now, already;* e. g. Matt. iii. 10. ܗܐ ܢܪܓܐ ܣܝܡ ܥܠ ܥܩܪܐ ܕܐܝܠܢܐ *the axe is already laid at the roots of the tree;* Num. xxii. 28. ܗܐ ܬܠܬ ܙܒܢܝܢ *already the third time;* Assem. I. 369, 30; with ܡܢ ܕ following, *since that;* e.g. Acts

x. 30. ܗܘܐ ܡܢ ܕܨܡܬ ܐܢܐ *since that I have fasted;* Col. i. 4; preceded by ܠܐ (ܠܐ ܗܘܐ, from which comes ܠܘ) οὐχί, *nonne?* e.g. Matt. v. 46. ܠܐ ܗܘܐ ܐܦ ܡܟܣܐ ܗܢܘܢ ܗܕܐ ܥܒܕܝܢ *do not even the publicans the same?* verse 47; xiii. 27;

b) ܚܣ *far be it*, with ܠ of the person and ܕ before the future of the finite verb; e.g. Matt. xvi. 22. ܚܣ ܠܟ ܡܪܝ ܕܬܗܘܐ ܠܟ ܗܕܐ *far be it from thee, my lord, that this should happen to thee;* Assem 1. 341, A. 30. ܚܣ ܠܢ ܕܢܟܦܘܪ ܒܐܠܗܐ *far be it from us that we should deny God;* 375, 13. Sometimes the participle follows; e.g. Assem. I. 51, 12, 13. ܚܣܝ ܚܣ ܠܢ ܕܟܦܪܝܢܢ *far be it from us that we should deny;* the verb follows in the future, with ܐܢ preceding (=אִם compare § 85. 4. c); e. g. I Sam. xxiv. 7; or in the infinitive with ܠ; e. g. Gen. xliv. 7;

c) ܛܘܒܝ *hail!* (= אַשְׁרֵי) with suffix plural, and the noun following with ܠ, to which the preceding suffix relates; e.g. Matt. v. 3. ܛܘܒܝܗܘܢ ܠܡܣܟܢܐ ܒܪܘܚ *hail to the poor in spirit;* verses 4–11; with a word interposed; e.g. Assem. I. 95, A. 3, 6, v. E. ܛܘܒܝܟ ܐܦ ܠܟ ܫܡܥܘܢ ܟܐܦܐ *hail also to thee, Simon Peter;* frequently absolute without ܠ; B. 3. v. E. ܛܘܒܝܟܝ ܐܘ ܫܟܝܡ *hail to thee O Sichem;* 96, A. 17, 19. —The Hebrew נָא is, in the Peshito, expressed by ܬܐ; e. g. I Kings xxii. 12.

APPENDIX.

Peculiarities in the Position of Words.

In the position of words, which, as in the Hebrew, is very easy and natural, besides the peculiarities referred to in the preceding chapters, the following deviations from the usual collocations occur; *a*) the verbs ܗܘܐ and ܐܡܪ are interposed between words, which, according to their grammatical connection, cannot be separated; e. g. Exod. vii. 7. ܡܘܫܐ ܒܪ ܬܡܢܝܢ ܗܘܐ ܫܢܝ̈ܢ *Moses was eighty years old;* Luke v. 3; Exod. v. 16. ܘܠܒܢ̈ܐ ܐܡܪܝܢ ܠܢ ܥܒܕܘ *and bricks, say they to us, make ye.* The same is true; *b*) of personal pronouns, having the signification of ܗܘܐ; e.g. John viii. 33. ܙܪܥܗ ܚܢܢ ܕܐܒܪܗܡ *we are Abraham's seed;* verse 37; Heb. vii. 28. ܢܡܘܣܐ ܟܘܡܪ̈ܐ ܗܘ ܒܢ̈ܝܢܫܐ ܡܩܝܡ ܒܟܘܪܗܢܐ *it is the law which makes priests of feeble men;* *c*) more rarely the same occurs with the noun; e. g. Matt. xvi. 1. ܫܐܠܝܢ ܠܗ ܐܬܐ ܡܢ ܫܡܝܐ ܕܢܚܘܐ ܐܢܘܢ *they besought him that he would give them a sign from heaven;* *d*) more frequently it occurs with particles; e. g. Mark i. 45. ܓܠܝܐܝܬ ܕܢܥܘܠ ܠܡܕܝܢܬܐ *he should go openly into the city.* Compare ܗܘܐ and ܠܐ ܗܘܐ (§ 86. 2. a).

EXERCISES

IN

SYRIAC GRAMMAR,

AND

A CHRESTOMATHY,

PREPARED WITH REFERENCE TO

THE TRANSLATION OF

UHLEMANN'S SYRIAC GRAMMAR.

BY ENOCH HUTCHINSON.

NEW YORK:
1855.

INTRODUCTORY REMARKS.

The following Exercises are designed for beginners, who need something simple, and at the same time, something which will lead them into a *thorough knowledge of the grammar.*

A small portion of Syriac, perhaps a page, should be selected and carefully analyzed in reference to all the important phenomena of the language. Every peculiarity in respect to each word should be critically examined. Perhaps the best course would be to trace one peculiarity throughout the page, searching the grammar and other helps; then trace another, and so on, until every peculiarity shall have been examined. Thus the most important facts will be strongly impressed upon the memory.

The great difficulty, especially with beginners, is. that they often attempt to investigate too many subjects at once and thus do not obtain clear ideas of any. There is frequently a great inclination to press forward and translate rapidly. Hence, many important subjects of investigation are entirely neglected, Superficial scholarship, is the unavoidable result of such a course.

That nothing may escape observation, a few general directions are presented to aid the learner in making his analysis. In mentioning those points, which are to be examined, the exact order in which they occur in the grammar, has not been followed, but they have been so arranged, it is hoped, as best to facilitate the progress of the student; and they are intended to embrace the most important phennomena necessary to be attended to by the learner.

Before commencing the examination the pupil should be directed to the Introduction of the grammar, that he may become somewhat acquainted with the history and literature of the Syriac Language. The grammar should be studied rather as a book of reference than as one, which must be committed to memory. The student, at first, should consult it as an aid in analyzing. At the commencement of the analysis, he will feel the need of assistance, and that assistance he must find in the grammar. When he there discovers a principle of the language and perceives its application in parsing, he can easily retain it in his memory. By the time that he has carefully studied the Exercises and Chrestomathy through, he will not only have a considerable knowledge of the language; but will have most of the grammar *committed to memory*, with but very little effort, and no loss of time in learning rules and principles, whose application he does not perceive, and which consequently are apt to escape from the mind. After the pupil, in the course of his analysis, shall have become somewhat familiar with the grammar, he may recite it regularly through, and it will not be an unmeaning nor an uninteresting exercise.

The general divisions, in the Exercises, are marked by the character ¶, to distinguish them from similar divisions in the grammar marked §. Smaller divisions are inserted under Remarks and Explanations.

GENERAL DIRECTIONS FOR ANALYZING.

I. Find the *Guttural Letters* on page first of the Chrestomathy. Vid. Gram. § 1. Rem. 3, 4.

II. " " *Aspirates*, or on what letters *Kushoi* and *Rukok* are found. Vid. Gram. § 1. Rem. 4; § 5.

III. " " *Diacritical Points*, for which the vowels are designed to compensate, formerly used instead of vowels and for other purposes. Vid. § § 2, 3, 4, and Rem.

IV. " " *Long* and *Short Vowels*. Vid. § 3. Rem. 3.

V. " " *Simple* and *Mixed* syllables.

VI. " " *Pure* and *Impure*, *Mutable* and *Immutable* vowels. Vid. § 45. A; § 48. A.

VII. " " *Dipthongs*, *Quiescent* and *Otiant* letters. Vid. § 3. Rem. 4; § 13; § 14.

VIII. " " *Lineæ Marhetono*, *Mehagyono* and *Sheva*.

IX. " " *Linea Occultans*. Vid. § 8.

X. Find on what syllables the *Tone* is to be found. Vid. § 9.

XI. Examine the *Marks* of *Punctuation*. Vid. § 10.

XII. Find *Ribui*. Vid. § 6.

XIII. Read the *Syriac*.

XIV. *Translate*.

XV. Examine the *Changes* of *Consonants*—assimilated—transposed—dropped—added and exchanged. Vid. § 12.

XVI. Find the *Changes* of *Vowels*—thrown back—exchanged—transposed—dropped and added. Vid. § 15.

XVII. Find the *Suffixes* and *Prefixes*, *Sufformatives* and *Preformatives*. Vid. § 16; § 36; § 46.

XVIII. *Parse.* In respect to *Verbs*—ascertain whether they are *Simple* or *Compound*—Their *Conjugation*—*Voice*—*Regular* or *Irregular*—*Active*, *Passive* or *Neuter*—*Number*—*Person*—*Gender*—*Mood*—*Tense*—*Conjugate* and *Inflect* them to the Case, Mood, Tense, etc., where they are found—*Rule.* Vid. § 19., etc.; § 59., etc.

Nouns — *Signification* — *Suffix* or *Prefix* — *Adjective* or *Substantive*—*Derivation* and *Formation*—*Declension*—*Person*—*Number*—*Gender*—*State*—*Case*. Vid. § 43; § 70; § 44; § 71; § 45; § 73; § 74; § 46; § 47; § 48; § 50; § 77., etc.

Pronouns—What kind—Person—Number—Gender—Case—Suffix—Rule. Vid. § 16; § 17; § 54., etc.

Participles—Derivation—Active or Passive—Conjugation—Rule.

Adverbs—Primitive or Derivative—What they qualify. Vid. § 51; § 82.

Numerals—Cardinal or Ordinal—Gender—Decline—To what they belong.

Prepositions—Suffixes—What they govern. Vid § 52; § 84.

Conjunctions—What kind—Suffix or Prefix—What they connect. Vid. § 53. 1, 2; § 85.

Interjections—Primitive or Derivative. Vid. § 53. 3; § 86.

EXERCISES IN SYRIAC GRAMMAR.

EXERCISE FIRST.

VID. GRAM. § 1. REM. 3, 4.

¶ 1.

Find the Gutturals on the first page of the Chrestomathy.

1. Select all those letters which are EVER used as Gutturals; thus:

ܗ ܐ ܗ ܐ ܗ ܗ ܐ ܐ ܗ̣ ܐ ܐ ܗ̣ ܐ ܐ ܗ ܗ ܐ ܐ ܗ ܐ ܐ ܗ ܗ ܐ
ܚ ܗ̣ ܐ ܗ ܗ ܗ ܐ ܚ ܐ̣ ܐ ܗ ܥ ܐ ܗ ܗ ܐ̣ ܐ ܗ̣ ܐ ܐ ܗ ܗ ܐ ܐ̣
ܐ ܐ̣ ܐ ܗ ܗ̣ ܐ ܐ̣ ܐ̣ ܚ ܗ̣ ܐ̣ ܚ ܐ ܗ ܗ ܐ̣ ܐ ܗ ܗ̣ ܐ ܐ̣ ܚ ܐ ܗ ܐ̣
ܐ ܗ ܐ ܗ ܗ ܐ̣ ܗ ܐ̣ ܗ̣ ܐ ܗ ܥ ܗ̣ ܐ ܗ̣ ܐ ܐ ܐ̣ ܗ ܚ ܗ̣ ܐ ܗ̣ ܐ
ܗ ܐ̣ ܐ̣ ܥ ܐ ܗ ܐ̣ ܥ ܐ̣ ܥ ܐ ܐ ܗ̣ ܐ ܐ ܗ ܐ ܗ ܗ ܐ ܐ ܗ ܥ ܗ̣ ܐ̣ ܐ
ܗ̣ ܥ ܐ̣ ܐ̣ ܥ ܐ ܗ.

EXPLANATIONS.

a) The above are all guttural letters, but not all used as such in the text from which they are taken.

b) The guttural ܐ resembles the *Spiritus lenis* of the Greeks, being a scarcely audible breathing from the lungs. ܥ has always a feeble sound. The Galileans pronounced ܥ and ܚ like א of the Hebrews. An Arabian would pronounce ܥ as a sort of vowel sound like *a*. It is a kind of soft breathing (comp. Gesenius' Hebrew Grammar, by Conant, § 6). The Greeks express ܚ as well as ܥ, sometimes by *Spiritus asper*, and sometimes by γ. Usually ܚ is sounded like *hh* with a rolling of the palate. ܗ before a vowel is our *h (Spiritus asper)*; but when uttered after a vowel, it has nearly the sound of *h* in *Korah*, perhaps a little softer, as in *ah! oh!* It is difficult to ascertain exactly the sounds of these letters; still it is important that the learner should fix upon a definite pronunciation of each.

2. Find those letters which are here used as gutturals.

ܗ ܥ ܚ ܗ ܗ ܗ ܗ ܗ ܗ ܗ ܗ ܗ ܗ ܗ ܗ ܗ.

EXPLANATIONS.

a) Verse 3. word 3., ܗ is a guttural, as it would in Hebrew take a composite sheva, and it has no vowel of its own. (Some would perhaps prefer to call ܗ a regular movable consonant, and consider ܐ at the end of the word as otiant, and ܘ as quiescing in —̇).

b) Verse 3. word 4., ܥ is a guttural for the same reasons.

c) Verse 3. word 6., ܚ is a guttural for the same reasons.

d) Verse 4. word 6., ܗ is a guttural being movable. It belongs to the second syllable of the word, being preceded by a vowel (§ 15. 4. d). The other cases may be similarly explained.

Rem.—It should be remarked that there are some other guttural letters on the first page of the chrestomathy, which should be considered merely as movable consonants. It is true that all gutturals are sounded, and might be said to be movable consonants (compare Gesen. Heb. Gram., transl. by Conant, §23.2). Still we prefer to make a difference between gutturals and regular movable consonants. The latter, though guttural letters on page first, are the following :

3. Find those guttural letters which are regular movable consonants :

ܐ ܗ ܐ ܐ ܗ ܗ ܐ ܗ ܗ ܐ ܐ ܗ ܗ ܐ ܗ ܗ ܚ ܚ ܐ ܗ
ܗ ܚ ܗ ܚ ܐ ܗ ܐ ܗ ܗ ܚ ܗ ܐ ܗ ܥ ܗ ܗ ܗ ܐ ܗ
ܥ ܐ ܗ ܥ ܥ ܥ ܗ ܥ ܥ ܗ.

EXPLANATIONS.

a) Verse 1. word 2., ܐ is a regular movable consonant, and is sounded nearly like the vowel —́, and does not quiesce in its vowel. In dialects kindred to the Hebrew, ܐ melts into the vowel far more readily than the sound of the Hebrew א melts into its vowel. Still ܐ retains its power as a movable consonant. It is very common in Syriac for a guttural letter to take a long vowel, where in Hebrew, it would have a composite Sheva. This seldom occurs in Hebrew (vid. Gesenius' Heb. Gram. by Conant. § 23. 2. Rem. 2).

b) V. 1. w. 5., ܗ is movable, as it does not quiesce and is not otiant.

c) V. 1. w. 8., ܘ (not a guttural) is movable, as the preceding letter is not sounded, and the following one is quiescent.

d) V. 1. w.10., ܐ should be considered as movable though its sound so melts into the vowel, we can scarcely perceive that it has the power of a consonant.

e) V. 1. w. 11., ܐ is not movable, as it quiesces, though seldom, in ـِ (§ 13. 1. Rem).

f) V. 1. w. 11., ܗ is movable for the same reasons as others above. ـَ preceding it, belongs to the previous syllable (comp. ¶ 5. 1. f; § 15. 4. d).

g) V. 3. w. 2., ܗ is movable as it is a suffix, and = הּ of the Hebrew (§ 13. Rem.).

h) V. 9. w. 9., ܠ is movable as it has a vowel of its own, though it so flows into the sound of the vowel that it is scarcely perceptible (¶ 1. 1. b).

REM.—It should be remarked that two of the guttural letters ܐ and ܗ are sometimes used as quiescents and sometimes as otiant letters (§ 12. A. B. and Rem.; § 13; §14).

EXERCISE SECOND.

¶ 2.

Find the Aspirates or in what letters Kushoi (ܩܘܫܳܝ *a hardening, and Rukok* (ܪܘܟܳܟ) *a softening are found.*

1. Those which are *ever* aspirated (§ 1. Rem. 3).

ܒ ܓ ܓ ܓ ܓ ܓ ܬ ܓ ܓ ܓ ܒ ܓ ܬ ܒ ܒ ܕ ܒ ܕ ܦ ܕ ܬ ܕ
ܕ ܒ ܓ ܕ ܒ ܒ ܟ ܕ ܟ ܒ ܕ ܓ ܕ ܬ ܕ ܬ ܕ ܕ ܕ ܟ ܒ ܕ ܕ ܓ
ܕ ܕ ܒ ܕ ܬ ܒ ܒ ܕ ܕ.

2. Find those, which are *aspirated* on page first (§5. and Rem. by Tr.).

ܓ ܓ ܓ ܓ ܓ ܬ ܓ ܓ ܓ ܒ ܓ ܬ ܕ ܒ ܕ ܦ ܕ ܬ ܕ ܓ ܕ ܒ ܒ ܒ
ܟ ܕ ܟ ܒ ܕ ܕ ܬ ܕ ܬ ܕ ܕ ܕ ܟ ܕ ܕ ܕ ܓ ܕ ܕ ܟ ܠ ܒ ܕ ܕ.

EXPLANATIONS.

a) Verse 1. word 1., ܬ is aspirated as it closes the syllable (§5. 2. Rem. c. *a*).

b) V.1. w.2., ܬ is aspirated as it follows an open or simple syllable (§ 5. 2. Rem. c. c., and § 15. 4. d).

c) V.1. w.4., ܬ is aspirated, because a letter, which would in Hebrew, take a vocal Sheva, precedes it (§ 5. 2. Rem. c. b).

d) V. 2. w. 4., ܒ is aspirated as the preceding word ends with ܐ (§5. 2. Rem.*a*).

e) V.3. w.2., ܓ is aspirated as it follows an open syllable (§ 5. 2. Rem. c. c).

f) V.3. w.4., ܒ is aspirated because it follows a letter which would in Hebrew take a vocal Sheva, (§ 5. 2. Rem. c. b).

g) V.3. w.4., ܓ is aspirated as it is preceded by a letter which would in Hebrew take a composite Sheva and would of course be vocal (§5. 2. Rem. c. b).

h) V.3. w.5., ܦ is aspirated as it follows an open syllable (§ 5. 2. Rem. c. c).

i) V.4. w.7., ܕ is aspirated as the preceding word ends in ܐ (§5. 2. Rem. *a*).

k) V.4. w.7., ܒ is aspirated as it closes a syllable (§ 5. 2. Rem. c. *a*).

l) V.7. w.4., ܕ is aspirated as it closes a syllable (§ 5. 2. Rem. c. *a*).

m) V.10. w. 4., ܓ is aspirated as it follows an open syllable (§ 5. 2. Rem. c. c).

3. Find those which are not *aspirated*.

ܒ ܟ ܒ ܕ ܒ ܬ ܒ ܕ ܒ.

EXPLANATIONS.

a) Verse 1. word 1., ܒ is not aspirated as it begins a word (§ 5. 2. Rem. *a*).

b) V.4. w.1., ܒ is not aspirated though it is preceded by ܐ (§5. 2. Rem.*a*), because it begins a verse.

c) V.6 w.3., ܬ is not aspirated as it is preceded by a letter, which, in Hebrew, would not take a vocal Sheva, and which has no vowel (§ 5.2. Note by Tr.).

d) For the pronunciation of these aspirates see the *Alphabet*, and § 1. Rem. 3, 4.

REM.—ܒ when aspirated is sounded like *v*, and when not aspirated like *b* ; ܕ like *th* in *that*, when aspirated, but otherwise like *d* ; ܦ when aspirated is sounded like *ph* or *f*, and otherwise like *p* ; ܬ when aspirated like *th* in *thin*, in other situations like *t* ; ܓ is sounded like *g* hard whether it be aspirated or not * ; ܟ when aspirated is sounded like *hh* or *k* with a rolling of the palate ; in other situations like *k*. In general the aspirates are pronounced like the corresponding letters in Hebrew (vid. references above and Gesenius' Hebrew Grammar by Conant, § 6. 2. 3. and Note by Tr.).

EXERCISE THIRD.

¶ 3.

(§ 2 ; § 3 ; § 4 *and Rem.*).

Find the diacritical points for which the vowels are designed to compensate, formerly used instead of vowels and for other purposes :

ܘܗܘ ܗܘܐ ܕܗܘܐ ܗܘܬ· ܗܘܐ ܟܐܒ ܠܬܐ ܗܘ ܠܬܐ ܘܗܘ ܠܬܐ

ܗܘܐ ܟܐܒ ܗܘܐ ܕܐܢܐ ܗܘܐ ܗܘ ܟܐܒ ܐܢܐ ܗܘܐ.

---

* The aspiration of ܓ would be indicated by the rolling of the palate.

EXPLANATIONS.

Rem. 1.—Diacritical points sometimes mark particular tenses and persons of verbs (§ 4. Rem.).

Rem. 2.—The vowel system of the Syrians began to be introduced in the time of Mohammed. Then and even after the system was completed by introducing characters from the Greek vowels, the ancient diacritical points were used to some extent by many writers. They are now seen in the more ancient writings.

Rem. 3.—The diacritical points here presented and others, appear in ancient Syriac writings, perhaps from the fact that they have been copied from more ancient editions, and in some cases doubtless, directly from the oldest editions of the Peshito. The several editions have been copied with so much care, that even after the vowel system came into use, the diacritical points, which had been used long before, were copied as well as the more recent vowels. Thus appear sometimes two characters to represent one vowel sound. As later editions have appeared, however, those points have gradually been omitted and vowels substituted, though, some remnants of the old system are still left (§2; §3; §4).

a) Verse 1. word 4., ܠܐܳܐ. The diacritical point under ܠ, according to the principles laid down byLudov. deDieu,indicates the vowel ـ. We have then here the vowel and the ancient diacritical point for which the vowel compensates (§4.Rem.).

b) V.1. w. 5., ܘܗܘ. The point under ܗ, according to Amira, indicates ـ (§4.Rem.).

c) V.3. w. 2., ܩܐܡ. The point under ܩ indicates, according to Ludov. de Dieu, the vowel ـ (§4. Rem.).

d) V.3. w. 3., ܗܘܐ. Diacritical points are often placed under and over the radical letters of verbs,sometimes to distinguish particular persons and sometimes to indicate vowels (vid. ¶ 3. Rem. 1). In the imperative and infinitive it may be wholly omitted or inserted underneath (vid. §4.Rem.; also compare Hoffmann's Syriac Gram. § 14).

EXERCISE FOURTH.

¶ 4.

Find the Long and Short vowels (§ 3. *Rem.* 3).

I. Find the *Long* ones :

EXPLANATIONS.

a) Verse 1. word 1., are both long as they are followed by quiescent (§ 3. Rem. 3. b).

b) V.1. w.5., is long because quiesces in it.

c) V. 1. w. 11., is long as it has a quiescent (§13. 1. Rem.).

The other instances need no explanation.

2. Find the *Short* vowels :

EXPLANATIONS.

a) Verse 1. word 2., ـَ is short as it is a regular short vowel.

b) V. 1. w. 10., ـَ is short as Olaph is movable, not quiescing.

c) V. 3. w. 1., ـَ is short as it has not ܘ quiescing in it (§3. Rem.3).

Rem.—In v.1. w.2., ـَ and several other short vowels on page first, form dipthongs with ܘ and ܝ. These quiescent letters do not fully coalesce with their respective vowels; but melt into them to a greater extent than they would do in Hebrew, under similar circumstances. They can scarcely, therefore, be considered as movable consonants, as they would be in Hebrew. Still the vowels in these cases are heterogeneous and the quiescents do not sufficiently coalesce, in our estimation, to make the vowels long (vid. Gesen. Heb. Gram. by Conant, § 8. 4; Uhlemann § 1. Rem.4).

EXERCISE FIFTH.

¶ 5.

Find the Simple and Mixed Syllables (§15. 3 *and* 4).

I. Find the *Simple* Syllables:

[illegible]

[illegible]

[illegible]

[illegible]

[illegible]

ܗܳܕܶܐ ܢܦ̂ ܠܳܐ ܐ ܗܳܕܶܐ ܢܦ̂ ܗܘܳܐ ܗܘ̂ ܠܳܐ ܩܳܐ ܗܽܘܢ ܗܳܕܶܐ ܢܦ̂ ܐܢܳܐ ܗܕܽܘ
ܕܗܘܳܐ ܠܡܶܟ݂ܠ ܡܶܢ ܠܡܶܟ݂ܠ ܠܟ ܐܢܳܐ ܐܪ ܕܳܐ ܃ ܗܳܕܶܐ ܢܦ̂ ܗܘܳܐ ܠܘ̂ ܐܝܬ
ܠܳܐ ܠܡܶܟ݂ܠ ܡܶܢ ܗܘܳܐ ܩܳܐ ܠܡܶܟ݂ܠܳܐ ܡܶܢ.

EXPLANATIONS.

Rem.—A simple syllable terminates in a vowel sound, and that vowel sometimes has a vowel letter quiescing in it. A mixed syllable terminates in one or more movable consonants. Every vowel stands in a simple syllable when the following consonant takes a vowel.

a) Verse 1. word 1., ܡܰܪܝ is a simple syllable as it ends in a vowel sound, although it has a quiescent ; ܝ has a vowel of its own and is of course sounded with the following syllable (vid. ¶ 5. 1. Rem., and § 15. 4. d).

b) V.1. w.2., ܐܺܝ is simple for the same reason as last, the syllable ending with ܝ and not with ܬ (vid. §15. 4.d).

c) V.1. w.2., ܬܰܘ is a dipthong and should be considered, we think, as a simple syllable because ܘ coalesces in the vowel to such an extent that the syllable ends in a vowel sound, though the coalescence is not so perfect as in a regular case of quiescence. Some may regard ܘ as a movable consonant as it would be in Hebrew, under similar circumstances, but we incline to the former opinion (vid. ¶4. 2. Rem. ; Gesen. Heb.Gram. by Conant, § 8.4).

d) V.1. w.4., ܡܶܢ is simple (vid. reference above).

e) V.1.w.4., ܠܬܳܐ is simple, ܐ quiescing in —̇.

f) V.1. w.5., ܘܗܘ̇ is simple, the last ܘ quiescing.

g) V.1. w.10., ܐ̇ is simple as ܠ which follows Olaph has a vowel of its own.

h) V.1. w.11., ܘܐ̇ is simple, Olaph quiescing in —̇, though it seldom quiesces in that vowel (vid §13.1 Rem. ; compare ¶ 1. 3. e).

i) V. 3. w.2., ܡܳܐ is simple, ܐ quiescing in —̄ and ܝ being otiant.

k) V.3. w.5., ܐ is simple as — is a long vowel and ܒ belongs to the next syllable (§15. 4. d).

l) V.4. w.5., ܟܘܝ is a dipthong and ends in a vowel sound as ܝ melts into the vowel to such an extent that it can hardly be considered as a movable consonant as it would be in Hebrew. We choose then to place the syllable among *simple* ones ; ܢܝ in verse 4. word 7., and ܗܘܝ in verse 7. word 8, are similar instances (vid.¶4.2.Rem. ; ¶5.1.c).

m) V.4. w.6., ܢܘ is simple as ܘ quiesces in — making it a long vowel, and ܗ belongs to the next syllable (§15.4.d).

n) V.7. w.3., ܠܗ is simple as ܗ belongs to the penult syllable and follows a long vowel (§15. 4. d. ; compare ¶ 1. 2. d).

2. Find the *Mixed* Syllables :

ܟܗ ܕܗ ܡܪܝ ܗܘܬ ܡܗ ܟܠܠ ܠܘܬ ܡܝܬ ܠܘܬ ܡܝܬ
ܕܢܫ ܢܝ ܡܩܠܗ ܩܠܝ ܕܙ ܟܢ ܩܗ ܐܕ ܗܘܙ ܡܟ ܕܒ ܗܘܝ
ܕܡܟ ܕܡ ܢܪܝ ܟܠܠ ܗܕ ܕܢܫ ܗܪ ܩܠܝ ܢܡ ܩܟ ܟܠܠ ܗܕ
ܟܗ ܡܪ ܗܪ ܢܡ ܠܟܟ ܗܙ .

EXPLANATIONS.

a) Verse 1. word 1., ܡܝܬ is mixed as it ends with a consonant sound (vid. ¶ 5.1. Rem.).

b) V.1. w. 9., ܠܘܬ is mixed, ending in a consonant sound (vid. ¶ 5. 1.Rem.).

c) V.3. w.2., ܗܪ is mixed as ܗ = הָ in Hebrew and is of course movable (§ 13. Rem.).

d) V.7. w.7., ܕܟܘ is mixed as — is short when ܘ does not quiesce in it, and the following consonant has no vowel (vid. §15.4, and §3. Rem.3).

EXERCISE SIXTH.

¶ 6.

Find the Pure, Impure, Mutable and Immutable vowels (§ 45. *A*; § 48. A).

1. Find the *Pure* vowels:

EXPLANATIONS.

Rem. A pure vowel, is one with which no consonant colesces. An impure vowel is one with which a consonant coalesces.

a) Verse 1. word 2., — is pure* as the syllable ܠܘ is a dipthong (vid. § 3. Rem. 4; also Palfrey's Gram. § 2), and ܘ does not fully quiesce in —, though it so far coalesces that it can hardly be considered as a movable consonant. Still as the vowel is a heterogeneous one and ܘ does not fully coalesce in it, we scarcely feel authorized to place the vowel among the impure ones, though some may prefer to do so, (vid. ¶ 4. 2. Rem.; ¶ 5. 1. c. and l; Gesenius' Heb. Grammar by Conant, § 8.4; compare §15. 4. d; also ¶ 6.2. Rem., and ¶ 6. 1.Rem.).

b) V.1. w.9., — is pure as ܘ does not quiesce in it, being a movable consonant and ܠ preceding being pronounced with a vocal sheva.

* It is also mutable (¶ 6. 4. b).

c) V.1. w. 10., — is pure as Olaph does not quiesce in that vowel. Olaph is here a movable consonant according to the analogy of the Hebrew (vid. §1. Rem.4.; also Gesenius' Heb. Gram. by Conant, §23.2).

d) V.3. w.5., — (the first one) is pure † as ܘ being a movable consonant does not quiesce in — (vid. last references).

e) V.3. w.7., — is pure as ܘ is movable, ܗ being sounded as if it had Sheva, and forming a part of the syllable.

f) V.3. w.9., — is pure and immutable as ܗ does not quiesce in it, being a guttural (comp. ¶ I. 2. a).

g) V.4. w.5., — is pure as ܝܐ is a dipthong (vid. *a* above).

h) V.7. w.3., — is pure as ܗ is a guttural.

i) V.7. w.9., — is pure as ܗ is = הּ in Hebrew and is of course a movable consonant (vid. §13. Rem. — is also mutable according to the general rule (¶6. 2. Rem.).

2. Find the *Impure* vowels:

— — — — — — — — — — — — — — — — — —

— —

— —

— —

— — .

EXPLANATIONS.

a) Verse 1. word 1., — and — are both impure vowels as they have ܝ quiescing in them.

† — is also immutable (¶ 6. 4).

b) V.1. w.3., — is impure as ܐ quiesces in it (compare ¶ 6. 1. e).

c) V.1. w.11., — is impure as Olaph quiesces in it, though it does not often quiesce in that vowel (§ 13. 1 and Rem.). The other cases are similarly explained.

Rem.—As a general thing, those vowels, which are pure are mutable and those which are impure are immutable; but there are as in Hebrew many exceptions (vid. ¶ 6. 1. a. b. c. d. e. f. g. h. i).

3. Find the *Mutable* vowels (compare ¶ 6. 2 Rem.):

— —

— — — — — — — — — — — — — — — .

EXPLANATIONS.

a) Verse 1. word 10., — is mutable (also pure, according to the general rule (vid. ¶ 6. 1. c) as it is in a simple syllable (compare ¶ 6. 4. d).

b) V.3. w.2., — is mutable as it has no quiescent and is long.

c) V.4. w.2., — is mutable as it is in a simple syllable.

4. Find the *Immutable* vowels:

— — — — — — — — — — — — — — — — — — — —

— — — — — — — — — — — — — — — — — — — —

— —

— — — — — — — — — — — — — — — — — — — —

— — — — — — — — — — — — — — — — — — — —

EXPLANATIONS.

Rem.—Those vowels are immutable,as in Hebrew; in which either a vowel letter quiesces; or from which a vowel letter has fallen away; short vowels in mixed syllables which would inHebrew takeDaghesh forte; and vowels immutable by nature.

a) Verse 1. word 1., — — are both immutable as well as impure, having quiescents.

b) V.1. w.2., — is in a simple syllable, is pure, and cannot properly be considered as immutable though ܘ coalesces with it to some extent (vid. ¶4.2.Rem.; ¶5.1.c; ¶6.1.a).

c) V.1. w.4., — over ܡܥ is immutable by position as ܡܥܠܬܐ is derived from ܥܠܠ a ܥܥ verb, and the ܠ is in reality doubled and the first would, if expressed, take Linea occultans. This is similar to Daghesh forte in Hebrew, and makes, as in that language, the preceding vowel impure and immutable (compare §48.B.Feminines).

d) V.1. w.10., — is short but in a simple syllable (¶5. 1.*g*) and consequently not immutable.

e) V.1. w.10., — (the first one) is immutable by nature (48. A. Masculines); it is sometimes, however, like all the other vowels, mutable (vid.§ 15.1.b; § 45.2.b) as in Hebrew (vid. Stuarts' Heb. Gram. §127).

f) V.1. w.11, — is immutable as ܐ quiesces in it (¶ 6. 2. c).

g) V.3. w.1., — is immutable as it is in a short mixed syllable.

EXERCISE SEVENTH.

¶ 7.

Find the Dipthongs, Quiescents and Otiant Letters (§3.*Rem.*4; § 13; § 14).

I. Find the *Dipthongs* (§ 3. Rem. 4; Palfrey's Gram. § 2) :

[illegible]

EXPLANATIONS:

a) Verse 1. word 2., [illegible] is a dipthong as [illegible] is in the same syllable with [illegible] without fully quiescing in it, though [illegible] so melts into the vowel that the syllable may be considered as ending in a vowel sound (vid. ¶4.2.Rem.; ¶5. 1. c and 1; Gesen.Heb.Gram. by Conant, §8. 4).

b) V.3. w.4., [illegible] is a dipthong for the same reason as last.

c) V.4. w.5., [illegible] is a dipthong as [illegible] unites with [illegible] but does not fully quiesce in it (vid. references above).

Rem. It will be observed that dipthongs in Syriac as well as in Hebrew, are quiescent letters with heterogeneous vowels; but in Hebrew the quiescent letters are movable while the reverse is true in Syriac.

2. Find the *Quiescents* :

[illegible]

[illegible]

[illegible] .

EXPLANATIONS:

a) Verse 1. word 1., [illegible] is a quiescent as it unites with the sound of the preceding vowel (§13.3).

b) V.1. w.2., [illegible] is a regular quiescent letter; but does not here fully quiesce, though it forms a dipthong and so melts into the vowel that the syllable may be considered as ending with a vowel sound (vid. ¶7.1.a).

c) V.1. w.3., [illegible] is not quiescent as it is a movable consonant, [illegible] not being sounded. The following [illegible] however quiesces in the preceding vowel.

d) V·1. w.5., [illegible] (the first one) is movable as it would in Hebrew take a vocal Sheva; the second [illegible] quiesces in [illegible] .

e) V.1. w.9., [illegible] does not quiesce in [illegible] as it is movable (vid. ¶6. 1. b).

f) V.1. w.11., [illegible] quiesces in [illegible] though it is rather unusual (§13. 1.Rem.).

g) V.3. w.2., [illegible] quiesces in [illegible] .

3. Find the *Otiant* Letters:

[illegible] .

a) Verse 1. word 2., [illegible] is otiant as it is a part of the suffix and is not followed by [illegible] (vid. § 14. 2. b).

b) V.3. w.2., [illegible] is otiant because it follows a quiescent.

EXERCISE EIGHTH.

¶ 8.

Find Lineæ Marhetóno (ܡܪܗܛܢܐ), *Mehagyóno* (ܡܗܓܝܢܐ), *and Sheva, where there is no accumulation of consonants.*

1. Find instances of *Marhetóno* and *Mehagyóno*:

ܕܪ̈ .

EXPLANATIONS:

a) Verse 5. word 7., ܕܪ̈. Here is an accumulation of consonants, and to indicate that they could not all be sounded conveniently, Marhetóno (or a horizontal line) would regularly be placed over ܕ. In this case the ܕ would in Hebrew take silent Sheva. ܪ must of course be pronounced with a vocal Sheva (vid. §7).

Rem.—1. There seems to be no instance of Mehagyóno on the first page. A. T. Hoffmann in his Syriac Grammar gives ܕܡܫܠܡܐ as an instance. The ܡ is to be sounded as though a short *e* followed it (vid. § 7).

Rem.—2. It appears that Marhetóno indicates silent Sheva when there is an accumulation of vowelless consonants, but under no other circumstances, though silent Sheva, in reality, frequently occurs as in Hebrew. So Mehagyóno represents vocal Sheva only when there is a similar accumulation of vowelless consonants, though when there is no accumulation vocal Sheva often occurs.

2. Find instances of *Simple vocal Sheva*:

ܕ ܕ ܢ ܕ ܕ ܠ ܡ ܡ ܪ ܘ ܒ ܘ ܘ ܦ ܠ ܘ ܠ ܒ ܠ ܠ ܠ ܘ ܠ ܒ
ܠ ܘ ܠ ܘ ܠ ܒ ܠ ܠ ܠ .

EXPLANATIONS.

a) Verse 1. word 1., ܒ would, in Hebrew, take a vocal Sheva, and as it cannot well be pronounced without the aid of a vowel or half vowel we must use the Sheva. This cannot be considered as an instance of Mehagyóno, for there is no accumulation of consonants which are destitute of vowels (vid. § 7). According to Lud. de Dieu and Norberg, the Syrians *did use* the Sheva and pronounced consonants accordingly, as in Hebrew (vid. §5.1).

b) V. 1. w.4., ܠ should be pronounced with a vocal Sheva like ܒ under *a* (vid. references above).

Rem.—We find no characters to indicate Sheva and seldom any to indicate Marhetóno and Mehagyóno, still we are to pronounce the consonants where those characters would regularly occur, as we should if they had actually appeared.

c) V.3. w.5., ܦ is pronounced with a Sheva. The preceding syllable being simple, ܦ belongs to the final syllable.

d) V.3. w.9., ܗ makes a part of the first syllable of the word and should not be pronounced with vocal Sheva.

e) V.6. w.3., ܡ is pronounced with a vocal Sheva as it constitutes a part of the penultimate syllable, being preceded by a long vowel (§ 15.4).

f) V.9. w.9., ܠ should be pronounced with a vocal Sheva (vid. last reference).

3. Find the *silent* Shevas, where there is no accumulation of consonants destitute of vowels :

Δ Z Δ Z ܠ̈ ܗ Z ܣ ܗ ܗ, ܒ ܝ ܢ ? ܗ ; ܢ ܗ ܡ ?
ܠ̈ ܠ ܡ ܗ ܡ ? ܠ̈ ; ܡ ܝ ܢ ܠ ܡ ܗ ; ܗ . .

EXPLANATIONS.

a) Verse 1. word 1., Δ would regularly in Hebrew take a

silent Sheva (vid. Conants' Gesen. Heb.Gram. §10; also ¶8. 2. a. b and Rem.).

b) V.1. w.2., ܘ would in Hebrew take a silent Sheva, being a movable consonant at the end of a syllable; but in Syriac it so melts into its vowel, that the syllable may be considered as terminating in a vowel sound, and ܘ does not take silent Sheva (vid. ¶ 4. 2. Rem.; comp. references above).

c) V.3. w.1., ܠ takes silent Sheva as it closes a syllable.

d) V.3. w.2., ܗ is a movable consonant at the end of a syllable being equivalent to הְ in Hebrew and takes silent Sheva.

e) V.3. w.9., ܗ̣ is at the end of a mixed syllable with a short vowel, and takes silent Sheva though a guttural (vid. ¶8.4.d; ¶6.1.f; comp. Gesen. Heb. Gram. by Conant, §22. 3).

f) V.4. w.5., ܝ forms with the vowel ܼ— a dipthong. It would in Hebrew be pronounced as a movable consonant and take a silent Sheva; but in Syriac it so melts into its vowel that it can hardly be considered as a movable consonant and does not take a silent Sheva (vid. ¶4. 2. Rem.; ¶8.3.b).

g) V.9.w.5., ܥ takes a silent Sheva as it is preceded by a short vowel and ends the antepenultimate syllable.

4. Find instances of *Composite Sheva*:

ܗ̣ ܚ ܗ̣ ܗ̣ ܗ ܗ ܗ̣ ܗ ܗ ܗ̣ ܗ ܗ ܗ ܗ̣ ܗ̣ .

a) Verse 3. word.3., ܗ̣ would in Hebrew take a composite Sheva and is pronounced as though it did here (vid. Gesen. Heb. Grammar by Conant, §22. 3; ¶1.2.a).

b) Verse 3. w.6., ܚ takes composite sheva for similar reasons as in the case above.

c) V.3.w.9., ܗ does not take composite Sheva but silent Sheva simple as in Hebrew. The Gutturals take simple Sheva where other consonants would take silent Sheva (Gesen.Heb.Gram. by Conant,§22.3).

d)V.4. w.6., ܗ takes composite Sheva (vid. *a* above).

EXERCISE NINTH.

¶ 9.

Find instances of *Linea Occultans* (§8) :

ܗ̱ ܗ̱ ܗ̱ ܗ̱ ܗ̱ ܗ̱ ܗ̱ ܗ̱ ܗ̱ ܗ̱ ܗ̱ .

EXPLANATIONS.

a) Verse 1. word 2., ܗ̱ is an instance of Linea occultans, indicating that the ܗ is not sounded (vid. §8; §12.1.A. and B., also Rem.).

b) V.1. w.3., ܗ̱ is another instance of Linea occultans. The horizontal line under ܗ shows that the letter is not to be pronounced. In this case ܘ begins the syllable. The othe cases are similarly explained.

EXERCISE TENTH.

¶ 10.

Find on what Syllables the Tone rests (§ 9) :

ܒܪܫܝܬ ܐܝܬܘܗܝ ܗܘܐ ܡܠܬܐ ܘܗܘ ܡܠܬܐ ܐܝܬܘܗܝ ܗܘܐ ܠܘܬ ܐܠܗܐ ܘܐܠܗܐ ܐܝܬܘܗܝ ܗܘܐ ܗܘ ܡܠܬܐ ܗܢܐ ܐܝܬܘܗܝ ܗܘܐ ܒܪܫܝܬ ܠܘܬ ܐܠܗܐ ܟܠ ܒܐܝܕܗ ܗܘܐ ܘܒܠܥܕܘܗܝ ܐܦܠܐ ܚܕܐ ܗܘܬ ܡܕܡ ܕܗܘܐ ܒܗ ܚܝܐ ܗܘܐ ܘܚܝܐ ܐܝܬܝܗܘܢ ܢܘܗܪܗ ܕܒܢܝܢܫܐ ܘܗܘ ܢܘܗܪܐ ܒܚܫܘܟܐ ܡܢܗܪ ܘܚܫܘܟܐ ܠܐ ܐܕܪܟܗ .

EXPLANATIONS.

a) Verse 1. word 1., ܫܝܬ is the final syllable and takes the tone because it ends with a movable consonant (§9.1 and 2).

b) V.1. w.2., ܐܝ takes the tone, as ܘ in the final syllable ܬܘ is not movable (vid. ¶4. 2. Rem.; ¶8. 3. b ; §9.1 and 2). ܗ and ܝ are not sounded.

c) V.1. w.4., ܡܠ is the penultimate syllable and has the tone according to the general rule (§9.1).

d) V.3. w.2., ܕܗ is the final syllable and takes the tone because ܗ is movable.

e) V.3. w.5., ܐ is the penultimate and takes the tone. ܒ belongs to the last syllable (§15. 4. d).

f) V.4. w.5., ܘܢ takes the tone because it ends with a movable consonant.

g) V.5. w.3., ܐ is inserted above as receiving the tone according to the general rule, though it is somewhat doubtful whether, in such cases the tone was on the penultimate or ultimate syllable (§ 9. 1. Rem.). Euphony would seem to favor the former opinion; there is another instance of the same kind in v.7. w.3.

EXERCISE ELEVENTH.

¶ 11.

Find the Marks of Punctuation (§10):

. . . . ܀ . . . .

EXPLANATIONS.

a) Verse 1. word 4., . is a mark of punctuation more generally used to denote the end of a period, but sometimes used in the middle to denote a slight pause similar perhaps to our comma. It is used so here (§10.d).

b) V.1. w.15., . denotes the full close of the period.

c) V.5. w.4., ܁ indicates the end of the protasis (§10.a).

d) V.5. w.7., ܀ is supposed to indicate the longest pause of any mark of punctuation. It is sometimes written thus ⁘ (§10.c).

e) V.6. w.5., ܂ indicates the end of the apodosis(vid.§10.c).

EXERCISE TWELFTH.

¶ 12.

Find instances of *Ribui* (§6):

ܕܰܒ̈ܢܰܝܢܳܫܳܐ, ܘܚܰܝ̈ܶܐ, ܚܰܝ̈ܶܐ, ܘܰܒܠܥܳܕܰܘ̈ܗܝ,

EXPLANATIONS.

a) Verse 3. word 4., ¨ over the word is an instance of Ribui indicating that the preposition has a plural suffix (§ 6.1.Rem.; §16.C).

b) V.4. w.2., here Ribui indicates that the noun over which it is placed is in the plural number though it is rendered as if it were in the singular. This word occurs only in the plural form (§44.Rem.6). The same is true in respect to v.4. w.4.

c) V.4.w.7., Ribui indicates simply the plural form of the noun as above.

EXERCISE THIRTEENTH.

¶ 13.

Read the *Syriac*:

Verse 1., Berishith aithau vo méletho vehu mélethó aithau vo levoth aloho. valoho aithau vo hu mélethó.

V. 2., hōnō aïthau vō v^{e}rïshïth l^{e}vōth alōhō.

V. 3., kul bïdheh hh^{e}vō v^{e}vel^{e}ōdhau ōph^{e}lō hh^{e}dhō hh^{e}vōth medhém dahhvō.

V. 4., béh hhaye hh^{e}vō. v^{e}hhaye aïthayhūn nuh^{e}rō dhavnaynōshō.

V. 5., v^{e}hū nuh^{e}rō v^{e}hheshūkō manhar: v^{e}hheshūkō lō adhr^{e}keh.

V. 6., hh^{e}vō varnōshō dheshtadhar mén alōhō. sh^{e}méh yūhhanōn.

V. 7., hōnō ethō l^{e}sōh^{e}dhūthō dh^{e}nashedh al nuh^{e}rō. d^{e}kulnōsh n^{e}haymen bïdheh.

V. 8., lō hū h^{e}vō nuh^{e}rō. elō dh^{e}nashedh al nuh^{e}rō.

V. 9., aïthau vō ger nuh^{e}rō dhashrorō. dh^{e}manhar l^{e}kulnōsh dethō l^{e}ol^{e}mō.

V. 10., b^{e}ol^{e}mō h^{e}vō. v^{e}ol^{e}mō vïdheh h^{e}vō. v^{e}ol^{e}mō lō yadheh.

EXPLANATIONS.

a) Verse 1. word 1., ܒܪ is the first syllable, ܒ not making a syllable of itself. The ^{e} answers to the Sheva in Hebrew, and is pronounced like a very short *e*.

b) V. 1. w. 2., ܐܝ is perhaps best pronounced like aï, though the *a* sound is scarcely perceivable. In ܬܘ, ܘ having a heterogeneous vowel, does not fully quiesce, still it so melts into the vowel that it can hardly be considered as a movable consonant (vid ¶4.2.Rem.). ܗ is not sounded as it takes Linea occultans (§8) and the ܝ is otiant (§ 14. 2).

c) V.1. w.3., ܗ̱ܘܳܐ. ܗ̱ is not sounded on account of Linea occultans, and ܘ becomes vocal by beginning a syllable.

d) V.1. w.10., ܐܰ is pronounced ă. Olaph so unites with the *a* sound that it is scarcely perceivable in pronunciation, though being at the beginning of a syllable it is a regular movable consonant. It is at the same time a guttural letter and must have the sound of the *Spiritus lenis* of the Greeks (vid. ¶1.2.Rem.).

e) V.1. w.11., ܘܳܐ. ܳ is pronounced broad and *long* as it has a quiescent (§13.1.Rem.).

f) V.3. w.1., ܟܽܠ is pronounced thus: *kul*, *u* taking the broad and short sound. The ܽ is short here as it has no quiescent (vid. §3. Rem. 3).

g) V.3.w.2., ܒܐܝܕܶܗ bĭdhĕh. ܐ quiesces in ܺ, and ܝ is otiant. ܗ is a movable consonant though a guttural letter.

h) V.3.w.4., vᵉvelᵉothău. ܠ must be sounded with a vocal Sheva (vid. ¶8.2). ܒ being preceded by a vowel is aspirated. ܝ as well as ܗ̱ is otiant.

i) V.3. w.9., ܕܰܗܘܳܐ dahhvo. ܗ is movable and pronounced with the first syllable. ܰ has a broad and short sound.

j) V.4. w.5., ܬܰܝ thay. ܰ is short and broad as it has no quiescent though ܝ so melts into the vowel that it can hardly be considered as a movable consonant (vid. ¶ 4. 2.Rem.).

k) V.6.w.1., ܗܘܳܐ hhᵉvo. ܗ is pronounced with Sheva. ܘ is vocal and ܐ quiesces in ܳ.

EXERCISE FOURTEENTH.

¶ 14.

Translate Literally :

Verse 1. In (the) beginning was (the) Word and he (or it the) Word was with God and God was he or it (the) Word.

2. This was in (the) beginning with God.

3. Every (thing) by (the) hand of him was; and without him also not anything was which was.

4. In him life (lit. lives) was, and life was (lit. lives were) (the) light of (the) sons of man.

5. And he (or it) light, into (the) darkness, shineth (lit. causing or permitting to shine §23.2.*a.b*), and (the) darkness did not comprehend it.

6. (There) was a son of man, who was sent from God, whose name (lit. the name of him) (was) John.

7. This (man) came for a witness, who shall (should) bear witness concerning (the) light, that every man might believe through (the) hand of him.

8. He was not (lit. not he was) (the) light; but (came for a witness) who might bear witness concerning (the) light.

9. For (that light) was (the) light of truth, which shineth upon every man, who cometh into (the) world.

10. (He) was in (the) world (lit. in the world was) and (the) world was by his hand and (the) world did not know him.

EXPLANATIONS:

a) Verse 1. word 1., ܒܪܫܝܬ. In translating this word, *the* is supplied. There is no distinct character in Syriac for the definite article. It was originally expressed by the noun in the emphatic state; but this is by no means universal in laterSyriac. There are many cases, as in Hebrew, in which the definite and indefinite articles have no word nor character to represent them, and they must be supplied in translating (§45.1).

b) V.1. w.2 and 3., ܗܘܐ ܐܝܬܘܗܝ *was.* The substantive verb ܗܘܐ *to be,* in connection with the other substantive verb ܐܝܬ *to be,* (third person masculine ܐܝܬܘܗܝ) forms the imperfect tense, *was* (§38.1,2).

c) V.1. w.5., ܘܗܘ. ܗܘ is a pronoun of the masculine gender. It is pleonastic and need not be rendered (§55). As the neuter gender in Syriac is included in the masculine and feminine ܗܘ might be considered either as neuter or masculine and may mean he or it (§43).

d) V.3. w.3., ܗܘܐ is rendered *was,* and is in the imperfect without ܐܝܬܘܗܝ (vid. §65.B.*a*).

e) V.3. w.7., ܗܘܬ is rendered *was,* same as last. The same is true in respect to ܕܗܘܐ (v.3. w.9).

f) V.3. w.6., ܚܕܐ and ܡܕܡ (v.3. w.8) should be taken together. The first means *any* and the second *something* or *thing*. Taken together they should be rendered *any thing*.

g) V.4. w.2., ܚܰ̈ܝܶܐ is rendered *life*. The noun always takes the plural form though it usually takes a singular meaning and has sometimes a singular and sometimes a plural verb. Here it takes a verb singular and in v.4. w.4., a verb plural.

h) V.5. w.4., ܡܢܰܗܰܪ is a participle; but it is used instead of the present tense of the verb (§64.2.A. andRem.; also ¶ 18.5).

i) V.6. w.3., ܕܶܐܫܬ݁ܰܕܰܪ means (lit.) *is sent;* but with ܗ̄ܘܳܐ it forms the imperfect tense.

EXERCISE FIFTEENTH.

¶ 15.

Find the Changes of Consonants—Assimilated—Transposed—Dropped—Added—Exchanged (§12).

1. Find those which are changed by *assimilation :*

All of those letters which take Linea occultans, are in reality assimilated (vid. §12. and ¶9).

2. Find those which are changed by *transposition :*

ܫܬ

EXPLANATIONS.

a) Verse 6. word 3., ܕܶܐܫܬ݁ܰܕܰܪ is in the Ethpa. conjugation and ܫ and ܬ are transposed, the appropriate place for ܬ being before ܫ (§12.2).

3. Find those Consonants which have been *dropped* :

ܐܐܐܐܐܐܐܐܐܐܐܐܐܐ .

EXPLANATIONS.

a) Verse 1. word 4., ܡܠܟܬܐ is from ܡܠܟܐ, const. ܡܠܟܬ. ܐ is dropped.

b) V.3. w.2., ܩܕܡܝܗ. ܐ final is dropped to give place for the suffix.

c) V.3. w.7., ܬܗܘܐ. ܐ is dropped to form the feminine (§37 Table).

d) V.4. w.7., ܕܢܢܩܦܘܢ. ܐ is dropped before the second ܢ.

e) V.5. w.4., ܡܢܗܪ. ܐ is dropped after the preformative ܡ.

f) V.7. w.7., and v.9. w. 7., ܢܕܟܪܘܢ. ܐ is dropped before ܢ.

g) V.7. w.8., ܢܗܘܡܝܢ. ܐ is dropped before ܡ.

4. Find consonants which are *added* :

ܗܘܢ ܐ ܬܐ ܗܘܢ ܐ ܐ ܘ ܐ ܗܘܢ ܐ ܬܐ ܘ ܬܐ ܗܘܢ ܐ ܒ
ܘ ܐ ܕ ܐ ܟܘܢ ܐ ܐ ܘ ܐ ܗ ܕ ܬ ܐ ܗܘܢ ܘ ܗ ܐ ܒ ܐ ܒ
ܒ ܟܘܢ ܕ ܐ ܢ ܕ ܐ ܠ ܗ ܐ ܬ ܐ ܕ ܐ ܗ ܐ ܐ ܘ ܡ ܐ ܒ ܐ
ܒ ܐ ܘ ܐ ܒ ܐ ܠ ܕ ܠ ܡ ܕ ܐ ܕ ܐ ܗܘܢ ܐ ܐ ܢ ܕ ܐ ܗ ܐ
ܗ ܐ ܘ ܗ ܐ .

EXPLANATIONS.

a) Verse 1. word 1., ܒܫܢܬܐ. ܒ is added as a prefix.

b) V.1. w.2., ܐܝܬܘܗܝ. ܐ is prosthetic (§38.1). ܘܗܝ is a suffix.

c) V.1. w.4., ܡܠܟܬܐ. ܬ is added from the construct state and ܐ is added because the word is in the emphatic state.

d) V.1. w.10., ܠܐܠܗܐ. ܐ is added at the end to form the emphatic state (¶18.*g*).

e) V.2. w.1., ܗܢܐ. Perhaps ܐ should be considered as added here because ܗܢܐ seems to be a kind of emphatic state of ܗܢ, though we have omitted ܐ above as the word usually appears in the emphatic form.

f) V.3. w.6, ܚܕܐ. ܐ is added to form the feminine.

g) V.3. w.7., ܗܘܬ. ܬ is added to form the feminine.

h) V.4. w.2., ܫܡܝܐ. ܐ is added to form the emphatic state (¶18.*v*).

i) V.4. w.5., ܐܝܬܝܗܘܢ. ܝܗܘܢ is added in the course of inflection and ܐ at the beginning is prosthetic (§38).

k) V.4. w.6., ܢܘܗܪܐ. ܐ is added to form the emphatic state (¶18. *y*).

l) V.5. w.3., ܟܢܘܫܬܐ. ܐ is added to form the emphatic state.

m) V.5. w.4., ܡܬܚܘܪ. ܡܬ is a preformative occurring in the course of inflection.

n) V.5. w.7., ܐܕܪܟܗ. ܐ is added in the Aphel conjugation.

o) V.6. w.3., ܕܐܬܦܩܕ. ܬ and ܐ are added in the course of inflection (comp. ¶15.2.*a*).

p) V.7. w.4., ܕܢܫܡܥܘܢ. ܢ is a preformative.

q) V.7. w.8., ܢܗܘܡܟܝ. ܢܗܝ is added in the course of inflection.

r) V.8. w.6., ܕܢܡܫܗܪ. ܕ is added in the course of inflection.

s) V.9. w.9., ܠܟܠܟܡܐ. ܐ is added to form the emphatic state.

5. Find Consonants *exchanged* for each other :

There are no cases on page first. ܠ is often exchanged for ܐ before ܗ and *vice versa*. Other letters also exchange with each other (§12.4).

EXERCISE SIXTEENTH.

¶ 16.

Find the changes of vowels—thrown back—exchanged—transposed—dropped and added (§ 15).

1. Find those which are thrown back :

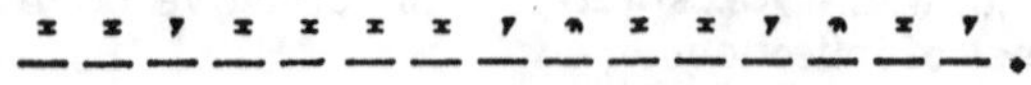

EXPLANATIONS:

a) Verse 1. word 2., ܐܬܘܗܝ. ܼ is thrown back from ܝ to ܐ (§15.2.A.b; §13,1.3).

b) V.1. w.7., ܐܬܘܗܝ — same as above.

c) V.1. w.11., ܘܐܠܗܐ. — is thrown back from ܐ to ܘ.

d) V.3. w.2., ܒܐܡܗ. — is thrown back from ܐ to ܒ on account of the suffix.

e) V.5. w.4., ܡܢܗܪ. ܐ the characteristic of Aphel is dropped and its vowel — falls back upon the preformative of the participle ܡ (§23. 1).

f) V.6. w.3., ܕܐܬܒܪܝ. — is thrown back from ܐ to ܕ.

g) V.10. w.8., ܡܫܝܚܗ. — falls back from ܝ to ܫ (§36; ¶ 18.37), as the vowel — of the original form ܡܫܝܚ is dropped and a suffix appended (¶16.2. *e*, and 4.*l*; ¶18.37).

2. Find those which are *exchanged*:

— for —, — for —, — for — .

EXPLANATIONS:

a) Verse 3. word 2., ܒܐܡܗ is derived from ܐܡ. — is dropped and — added in the course of inflection and — is thrown back from ܐ to ܒ (¶16.1.*d*) the word here being in the suffix state. Some would prefer to say that — is changed into —, (¶16.4. *c* and 5. *d*).

b) V.4. w.7., ܕܡܫܡܫܢܝ. — is changed into — in the construct plural (§45.2.*a*; ¶18.1).

c) V.5. w.4., ܡܢܗܪ. In the second syllable, — is changed into —, as the third radical of the verb from which ܡܢܗܪ is derived, is Resh (§23 1).

d) V.7. w.8., ܢܗܦܟܘܢ is derived from ܐܗܦܟ. — is changed into —, and — in the last part, into — in passing from Peal to Aphel. But it is better to say that — is dropped and ـܶ added in one case, and ـܶ dropped and ـܳ added in the other (¶16.4.h; 5.*r*).

e) V.10. w.8., ܡܫܝܚܗ is derived from ܡܫܝܚ, and ـܰ has the appearance of being changed into ـܶ on account of the suffix (§36.A.Rem.); but ـܰ is dropped and ـܶ thrown back upon ܡ (¶16.1.*g* and 4.*b*; ¶18.37).

3. Find those vowels, which are *transposed* :

ـܳ ـܳ ـܳ ـܳ ـܳ ـܳ .

EXPLANATIONS.

a) Verse 4. w.6., ܢܘܗܪܐ from ܢܗܘܪ or ܢܘܗܪ. ـܳ with ܘ is transposed in the emphatic state from the last to the first part of the word (vid.¶18.*y*).

The other cases are all similarly explained.

4. Find those vowels which are *dropped* :

ـܺ ـܶ ـܺ ـܶ ـܺ ـܶ ـܶ ـܺ ـܶ ـܰ ـܳ ـܳ ـܳ ـܶ ـܶ ـܺ ـܶ ـܶ ـܶ ـܶ
ـܶ ـܺ ـܶ ـܰ .

EXPLANATIONS.

a) Verse 1. word 2., ܐܬܠܗܘܢ has an additional syllable ܗܘܢ; but the original vowel ـܰ is not dropped as ܢ quiesces in it making it immutable (vid.§15.3; §48.A).

b) V.1 w.4., ܡܠܟܬܐ is derived from ܡܠܟܐ, construct ܡܠܟܬ. ـܺ is dropped to form the construct state and ـܶ of the construct state is dropped in the emphatic state because the additional syllable ܐ is added (vid.§15.3; compare ¶16.5.*b*).

c) V.3. w.2., ܩܐܡܬܗ is derived from ܩܐܡ. — is dropped and from the emphatic state, — is dropped to give place to the suffix (compare ¶ 16.5.*d*).

d) V.3. w.6., ܚܕܐ is the feminine form of ܚܕ. — is dropped (vid. ¶16.5. *f*).

e) V.4. w.7., ܕܒܢܝܢܫܐ. — is dropped from the plural absolute of ܒܢܝܢ in passing into the construct state (vid. §15.3, and Rem.; ¶16.5. *i*; ¶ 18.1).

f) V.5. w.7., ܐܕܟܪܗ is Aphel of ܕܟܪ with a suffix pronoun. In taking the suffix,— of the verb is dropped and — of the suffix added (vid. ¶16.5.*m*; ¶18.7).

g) V.7. w.3., ܠܣܗܕܘܬܐ is in the feminine emphatic state, from the noun ܣܗܕ, and, in the course of inflection — is dropped (vid.¶16.5.*p*; ¶18.17).

h) V.7. w.8., ܢܘܣܦܘܢ is a verb from ܐܘܣܦ, and is in the Aphel conjugation. In the course of inflection, — in the first part of the word is dropped and — in the last part, and other vowels added (vid.¶16.5. *r*; ¶18.22).

i) V.9. w.5., ܕܡܪܢܐ is compounded of ܕ and ܡܪܢܐ. The latter is a noun in the emphatic state from ܡܪ. — falls away in taking an additional syllable (§15. 3) to form the emphatic state (vid. ¶ 16. 5. *s*; ¶ 18 32).

k) V.9.w.9., ܠܡܠܟܘܬܐ is compounded of ܠ and ܡܠܟܘܬܐ, emphatic state from ܡܠܟܘ. — is dropped in forming the emphatic state (§15.3) as an additional syllable is received (¶ 16.5.*t*; ¶18.36).

l) V.10. w.8., ܫܪܟܗ is a verb with a suffix, derived from

ܫܡܗ. In taking the suffix, ─ is dropped and ─ falls back upon the first radical (§36; ¶18. 37).

5. Find those vowels which are *added* :

— — — — — — — — — — — — — — — — — — — —

— — — — — — — — — — — — — — — — — — — —

— — — — — — — — — — —

EXPLANATIONS.

a) Verse 1. word 2., ܐܬܠܘܗܝ. ─ is added in the course of inflection as a part of the sufformative of the verb.

b) V.1. w.4., ܡܠܟܘܬܐ is in the emphatic state from the construct state ܡܠܟܘܬ. ─ is dropped and ─ added (compare ¶ 16.4.*b* ; ¶18. *d*).

c) V.1. w.10., ܫܡܝܐ is in the emphatic state, but as it always appears in this state it is perhaps better not to place ─ (at the end of the word) among the vowels added.

d) V.3. w.2., ܐܒܘܗ̈ܝ is derived from ܐܒ. ─ is dropped and a new vowel, ─, added. Then from the emphatic state ܐܒܐ, ─ is dropped to give place to the suffix with which ─ is added (vid. § 46. 1. *a* ; compare ¶ 16. 4. *c* ; ¶ 18. *m*).

e) V. 3. w. 4., ܘܡܠܟ̈ܘܗܝ is from ܡܠܟ. ─ is added with the suffix.

f) V.3. w.6., ܚܝܐ is the feminine form for ܚܝ. ─ is dropped and ─ added.

g) V.3. w.9., ܕܗܘܐ. — is assumed over ܕ to aid in the pronunciation (vid.¶18.*t*).

h) V.4. w.6., ܢܘܗܪܐ is derived from ܢܗܪ or ܢܘܗܪ. — is added in the emphatic state (vid.¶18.*y*).

i) V.4. w.7., ܕܒܢܝܢܫܐ. — at the beginning of the word is assumed (vid.§15.4.*b*). The remainder of the word is compounded of ܒܢܝ and ܐܢܫܐ. The former is in the construct plural, and,in passing from the absolute to the construct plural, — is dopped and — added (vid. §15.3 and 4; ¶16. 4. *e*; ¶ 18.1).

k) V.5. w.3., ܒܚܫܘܟܐ. This is from ܚܫܘܟ though the emphatic state is the more usual form. — is added.

l) V.5. w.4., ܡܢܗܪ. This is a participle active, Aphel, from ܢܗܪ. The first — is assumed, forming a part of the preformative (vid.¶18.5).

m) V.5. w.7., ܐܕܪܟܗ is a verb in the Aphel conjugation from ܕܪܟ. — is assumed in the preformative. — is also assumed with the suffix (vid.¶16.4.*f*; ¶18.7).

n) V.6. w.2., ܓܒܪܐ is in the emphatic state and — is added (vid.¶18.9).

o) V.6. w.3., ܕܐܫܬܕܪ is compounded of ܕ and the verb ܐܫܬܕܪ, Ethpaal from ܫܕܪ. — is added as a part of the preformative. The first — is assumed in the course of inflection in Ethpaal.

p) V.7. w.3., ܠܣܗܕܘܬܐ is in the feminine emphatic state from ܣܗܕ. In the course of inflection — and — are added and — is dropped (vid.¶16.4.*g*; ¶18.17).

q) V.7. w.4., ܕܢܣܗܕ is compounded of the relative ܕ and

the verb ܢܥܗܕ, Aphel of ܥܗܕ. — is assumed in Aphel in the course of inflection (vid. §18.18).

r) V.7.w.8., ܢܗܘܡܟ is a verb in the Aphel conjugation from ܐܘܡܟ. In the course of inflection, — in the first part of the word is dropped and — added, and in the latter part of the word, — is dropped and — added (¶16.4. *h*; ¶18. 22).

s) V.9. w.5., ܕܦܪܩܐ is compounded of ܕ and ܦܪܩܐ. The latter is a noun in the emphatic state from ܦܪܩ or ܦܪܘܩ. If considered as derived from the former, — is dropped on account of the additional syllable (§15.3),and, in consequence, ܕܦ having no vowels, ܕ takes the new vowel — (§15. 4. *b*). — is also added to form the emphatic state (vid. ¶16.4. *i*; ¶18.32).

t) V.9. w.9., ܠܡܠܟܘܬܐ is compounded of ܠ and ܡܠܟܘܬܐ, emphatic state from ܡܠܟܘܬ. — is dropped in forming the emphatic state as a syllable is added (§15.3), and — is assumed (vid.¶16.4.*k*; ¶18.36).

EXERCISE SEVENTEENTH.

¶ 17.

Find the Suffixes and Prefixes, Sufformatives and Preformatives (§16; §36; §46).

1. Find the *Prefixes* :

ܒ ܘ ܘ ܒ ܒ ܘ ܕ ܒ ܘ ܕ ܘ ܒ ܘ ܕ ܠ ܕ ܕ ܒ ܕ ܕ

ܠ ܕ ܠ ܒ ܘ ܒ ܘ.

EXPLANATIONS.

a) Verse 1. word 1., ܒ is a prefix preposition.

b) V.3. w.2., ܒ is a prefix preposition with the vowel thrown back upon it.

c) V.3. w.9., ܕ. ܕ is a relative pronoun prefixed to the verb, and, two vowelless consonants occurring together, ܸ is assumed to aid in pronunciation. The other instances need no explanation

2. Find the *Suffixes* :

ܗ ܗܘܢ ܗ ܗ ܗ ܗ ܗ ܗ.

EXPLANATIONS:

a) Verse 3. word 2., ܗ is a suffix pronoun with its union vowel.

b) V.3. w.4., ܗܘܢ is a suffix pronoun added to a preposition, though the same form when attached to ܐܝܬ is a sufformative.

REM.—We use the terms sufformative and preformative to indicate those letters which are suffixed or prefixed to words as necessary appendages in order to form particular conjugations, tenses, moods, persons, numbers, genders or states, according to the course of inflection. Such are mere formative letters and properly constitute a part of the word to which they are attached, while suffixes and prefixes are appendages which have more distinct significations of themselves, and do not necessarily compose a part of the word to which they are attached.

3. Find the *Preformatives* :

ܡܳ ܢ ܢܰܗ ܢ ܐܶܬ ܐ ܡܳ .

EXPLANATIONS.

a) Verse 1. word 2., ܐ is, strictly speaking, a preformative; but the letter seems to constitute a part of the word through all of its changes and does not so properly come under this head as it does under "consonants added" (¶15.4.*b*).

b) V.5. w.4., ܡܳ is a preformative added in the course of inflection.

c) V.5. w.7., ܐ is a preformative added in the Aphel conjugation.

d) V.6. w.3., ܐܶܬ are preformative letters added in the Ethpaal conjugation.

e) V.7. w.8., ܢܰܗ is a preformative added in the Aphel future.

4. Find the *Sufformatives* :

ܐ ܗܘܢ ܬ ܐ ܘܗܝ ܬܐ ܘܗܝ ܘܗܝ ܬܐ ܬܐ ܘܗܝ
ܐ ܐ ܐ ܐ ܐ ܘܗܝ ܐ ܐ ܐ ܐ .

EXPLANATIONS:

a) Verse 1. word 2., ܘܗܝ is a sufformative as it forms, according to the inflection, the third person singular masculine preterite, though it is in reality a noun suffix attached to the original noun ܐܝܬ *being*.

b) V.1. w.4., ܬܐ is the sufformative ending of the emphatic state, or rather ܐ is the ending of the emphatic state and ܬ of the construct from which the emphatic is formed.

c) V.3. w.6., ܐ is the emphatic ending.

d) V.3. w.7., ܬ takes the place of ܐ and is a formative letter in constituting the feminine gender.

e) V.4. w.5., ܗܘܢ— is a sufformative found in the course of inflection.

f) V.4. w.7., ܐ is the ending of the emphatic state.

g) V.6. w.2., ܐ is an emphatic ending.

EXERCISE EIGHTEENTH.

¶ 18.

Parse :

a) Verse 1. word 1., ܒܪܫܝܬ is compounded of the preposition ܒ *in* and the noun ܪܫܝܬ *beginning.* ܒ is a preposition governing ܪܫܝܬ in the ablative case (§ 75.5 ; §52 ; § 84). ܪܫܝܬ is a denominative noun (§41) from the root ܪܫ *principal, chief, head* (Hebrew ראשׁ Chaldee רֵאשׁ)—formed by adding to its root the formative letters ܝܬ (§39.2). The vowel — is added and aids to form the syllable ܝܬ (§15.4; §13.3). ܪܫܝܬ is of the first declension as its vowels are immutable (§48. A) though it is somewhat irregular in its inflection (see its plural)—third person, singular number(§44).

ܪܘܚܬ, plural ܪ̈ܘܚܬܐ. The two points over ܪ in the plural compose Ribui. The point belonging to ܪ still belongs to ܪ and at the same time is part of Ribui (§6.2.Rem.)—feminine gender as it is the same as in Hebrew and is transferred from that language (§43.2.Rem.2). It ends also in ܬܐ a feminine termination in the emphatic state, ܐ being the regular emphatic termination (vid. last reference and § 45.3.*b*). In the absolute state the form is ܪܘܚܬ, emphatic ܪܘܚܬܐ (§ 45)—in the ablative case after the preposition ܒ and governed by it (§75.5).

b) V.1. w.2., ܐܝܬܘܗܝ is an auxiliary verb from ܐܝܬ *to be* (vid.Lexicon). ܐܝܬ is formed from the noun ܝܬ *being*, with a prosthetic ܐ. ܐܝܬܘܗܝ is irregular—takes the noun suffix ܘܗܝ, as it is derived from a noun, though that suffix is here to be considered as a sufformative (¶ 17.4. *a*; ¶ 17.2. Rem.)—neuter (§ 66.2 ; §19)—singular number (§38.1.Paradigm)—third person (§38. 1. Paradigm)—masculine gender (vid.last reference)—indicative mood(§65.1 ; compare (§18.4) —preterite imperfect tense,as ܗܘܐ immediately follows(§18.4. Rem.; §38.2;§68.A). Inflect to the person where it is found. First person common gender ܐܝܬܝ (*I am*), second masculine ܐܝܬܝܟ (*thou art*), second feminine ܐܝܬܝܟܝ (*thou art*), third masculine ܐܝܬܘܗܝ (*he is*) (vid.§38.1.Inflection). It agrees with its nominative ܡܠܬܐ, though of a different gender (80. B.2).

c) V.1. w.3., ܗܘܐ is a substantive verb signifying *to be* (§38.1)—a ܠܐ verb (§38. 1)—irregular (§32)—neuter (§ 19)—third person—singular number. When used with another verb it has the effect of Vau conversive in Hebrew § 38. 1)

—masculine gender and used here merely as a helping verb to the preceding, in forming the imperfect tense(§38.2).

d) V.1. w.4., ܡܠܬܐ *word* is a substantive noun, derived from ܡܠܠ *to speak*, forming in the absolute state ܡܠܐ (vid. § 39. 2. *b*. third example), construct state ܡܠܬ, emphatic ܡܠܬܐ—first declension (§45. feminines A; §48.B. feminines; ¶ 6. 4. *c*). Decline. Singular (vid.above)—plural absolute, ܡ̈ܠܝܢ, construct ܡ̈ܠܬ, emphatic ܡ̈ܠܬܐ (§ 45. 3)—third person singular—feminine—emphatic state—nominative case to ܐܝܬܘܗܝ ܗܘܐ (§80.B.2).

e) V.1. w.5., ܘܗܘ is compounded of the conjunction ܘ and the pronoun ܗܘ. ܘ is a copulative conjunction (§53. 1)—a prefix (§53. 1. Rem.). It connects the two nouns. ܗܘ may be translated by *he* or *it*, as the neuter gender in Syriac is included in the masculine and feminine (¶ 14. *c*; § 43)—a personal pronoun separate (§16)—third person singular. It is pleonastic and need not be rendered in translating (§55). For explanations of the next three words vid. *supra*.

f) V.1. w.9., ܠܘܬ *with*, a preposition governing ܐܠܗܐ (§52 ; §84).

g) V.1. w.10., ܐܠܗܐ *God*—taken from the Hebrew אֱלוֹהַּ and that probably derived from אֵל *God*. אֱלוֹהַּ is a denominative noun taking the Syriac emphatic termination ܐ is the ending of a large number of Syriac nouns, sometimes indicating the feminine and sometimes the emphatic state (§43.2; §45.3). Some nouns always appear in the emphatic or suffix state (§ 45.1.Rem.). ܐܠܗܐ has the form of the emphatic state. It is a substantive noun and may be declined like ܕܢܒ (Decl. 1. §45.masculines A)—third person singular–masculine–emphatic state—ablative case and governed by ܠܘܵܬ (§75.5).

h) V.1. w.11., ܘܲܐܠܵܗܵܐ. ܘ *and*, is a prefix conjunction continuing the sense. ܐܠܵܗܵܐ *God*, is in the nominative to ܐܝܬܘܗܝ ܗܘܐ (§80). For further explanations vid. *supra.*

i) V.1. w.14., ܗ̤ܘ is a pleonastic pronoun (vid. *supra*).

j) V.1. w.15., ܡܸܠܬ݂ܵܐ *word*, is in the nominative after ܐܝܬܘܗܝ ܗܘܐ (§80; ¶18.*b*).

k) V.2. w.1., ܗܵܢܵܐ *this, same.* It has the form of the emphatic state though it should be considered as one of the original forms of the word. The forms are ܗܵܢ and ܗܵܢܵܐ (§17)—a demonstrative pronoun—singular–masculine–nominative case to ܐܝܬܘܗܝ ܗܘܐ (§80)—used as a noun. Decline it (vid.§17).

l) V.3. w.1., ܟܠ *all, every, each,* (§58.B.2.*a*,*b*)—a pronoun used as an adjective (§58.B.2.*b*) the noun *thing* to which it belongs being implied—declined according to decl. 1. of nouns—third person–masculine–absolute state. The implied noun would be in the nominative to ܗܘܐ; or ܟܠ itself might be considered as a collective noun and in the nominative to ܗܘܐ (§80.A.1 and Rem.).

m) V.3. w.2., ܒܐܝܕܗ *by the hand of him* or *by his hand* ܒ is a prefix preposition governing ܐܝܕ. The whole word is compounded of the preposition ܒ *by*, the noun ܝܕ emphatic ܐܝܕܐ *hand,* and the suffix ܗ *of him* or *his.* ܐܝܕ is a derivative noun (§39), from ܝܕ and takes a suffix (Hebrew יָד

Chaldee יד)–2nd. declension–singular. Absolute and constr. ܐܝܕ, emphatic ܐܝܕܐ, plural absolute ܐܝܕܝܢ, construct ܐܝܕܝ, emphatic ܐܝܕܝܐ—third singular masculine (§45. masculines B)—ablative case and governed by ܒ (§75.5). ـܗ is a suffix pronoun attached to the emphatic state and ܐ falls away (§46.1. *a*)–third singular masculine (§16. Table)—genitive case (§54. B.2) and governed by ܐܝܕ (§16 ; §16.B; §74).

n) V.3.w.3., ܗܘܐ *to be* is here rendered *was*, the imperfect being sometimes thus formed (§65). It agrees with ܟܠ (¶14.*d*).

o) V.3. w.4., ܘܒܠܥܕܘܗܝ *and without him*—compounded of the conjunction ܘ, the preposition ܒܠܥܕ, and the suffix pronoun ـܘܗܝ. ܘ *and*, is a conjunction as above. ܒܠܥܕ *without* is a preposition with a suffix. It governs its suffix ـܘܗܝ. ـܘܗܝ *him*, is a noun suffix – plural (§16.Table)—third singular masculine—ablative case and governed by ܒܠܥܕ (§75.5).

p) V.3. w.5., ܐܦܠܐ *also not, neither*—compounded of ܠܐ *not*, and ܐܦ *also.* ܐܦ is a conjunction(§53.2.*a*) and continues the sense. ܠܐ *not* is an adverb and qualifies ܗܘܬ.

q) V.3. w.6., ܚܕܐ *one, any one, a certain one, certain, any*; from ܚܕ, is a pronoun (§58.10.*a* and *b*) or a numerical adjective (§50.2). Here it has the sense of an indefinite pronoun —singular feminine and belongs like an adjective to the noun ܡܕܡ (§58.10.*a*).

r) V.3.w.7., ܗܘܬ *to be* from ܗܘܐ. ܐ is changed into ܬ to form the feminine (§19.Table). Imperfect and parsed like ܗܘܐ (vid. *n. supra*)

s) V.3. w.8., ܡܶܕܶܡ *any thing*, has a similar meaning to that of ܡܳܐ above ; but has more the sense of a noun. It is sometimes used in the same manner as ܡܳܐ (§58.10.*b*). It is used here as a noun meaning *thing*, and ܡܳܐ belongs to it, as the pause between ܗܘܳܐ and ܡܶܕܶܡ is one of minor importance (¶ 11.*c*; § 10)–third singular feminine–absolute state–nominative case to ܗܘܳܬ (§80).

t) V.3. w.9., ܕܗܘܳܐ *which was*—compounded of ܗܘܳܐ and ܕ. ܕ *which* is a relative pronoun (§ 17.2)—is in the third singular—nominative to ܗܘܳܐ.

u) V.4. w.1., ܒܶܗ *in him*, compounded of ܒ *in* and ܗ *him*. ܒ is a preposition, governing the ablative (§75.5); ܗ is a suffix pronoun (§ 16.Table; § 52.Table)–third person singular—in the ablative case and governed by ܒ (§ 75.5. compare §54.B.1).

v) V.4. w.2., ܚܰܝܶܐ *life*, is a verbal noun(concrete)(§40TableA). It occurs always in the plural form(§44.Rem.6),generally with a singular signification (vid.Lexicon; §80.2)–derived from ܚܝܳܐ *to live*–appears in the emphatic form,like other plural forms mentioned(§44.Rem.6 and§45.Rem.)though this is its usual form. It is an anomalous noun having no regular declension–third person plural masculine(§45.Rem.)–nominative case to ܗܘܳܐ (§80.2.*b*).

w) V.4. w.4., ܘܚܰܝܶܐ *and life*—compounded of the conjunction ܘ *and*, and ܚܰܝܶܐ *life*. This is parsed like the same word above, only it is in the nominative to a plural verb (§80. 2. *a*).

x) V.4. w.5., ܐܝܬܝܗܘܢ *was*, literally *were* — third person plural masculine, and agrees with ܒܢܝܐ in gender and number (§80.2.*a*; vid.also *c*. and *d*. *supra*).

y) V.4. w.6., ܢܘܗܪܐ *light*, is a verbal noun from ܢܗܪ *to shine*—an infinitive form in the emphatic state like ܩܘܛܠܐ from ܩܛܠ (§ 40.Table, II. A. *a*). Infinitive absolute ܢܗܪ, ܢܗܪ or ܢܘܗܪ, emphatic state ܢܗܪܐ, ܢܗܪܐ, ܢܘܗܪܐ. The ܡ which appears in the infinitive is here dropped (compare §39.2.*b*.and §40), though the emphatic form is the one in which it usually appears–declensionIV.(§45.masculines, D)– third person singular–masculine–emphatic state, and in the nominative case after ܐܝܬܝܗܘܢ, but used as the construct before ܕ of the next word (§74.2.*a*).

1) V.4. w.7., ܕܒܢܝܢܫܐ *of the sons of men*, a composite noun (§41.1)–compounded of ܕ, ܒܢܝ and ܐܢܫܐ. ܕ *of*, is a sign of the genitive case, which follows (§74.3). ܒܢܝ *sons*, is from ܒܪ *son*, primitive—anomalous. Singular absolute ܒܪ, construct ܒܪ, emphatic ܒܪܐ, plural absolute ܒܢܝܢ, construct ܒܢܝ, emphatic ܒܢܝܐ (§49.masculines)–third person plural–masculine–construct state(in form and because the next noun is in the genitive)–genitive case, though in the construct state, as sometimes occurs in Hebrew (vid. Stuart's Hebrew Grammar, §434. *b*), governed by ܕ (§74). ܢܫܐ *man*, is from ܐܢܫܐ, the ܐ being dropped (§12.3.*a*)–derived from the Hebrew word אִישׁ *man* (Chaldee אֱנָשׁ)–a primitive noun–declension 1, but somewhat irregular (vid. Lexicon)—third person singular as it has not Ribui, though it has the same form which appears in the plural–masculine emphatic state abso-

lute and construct ܐܢܫ, emphatic ܐܢܫܐ, absolute plural ܐܢܫ̈ܝܢ or ܐܢܫ̈ܐ–genitive case and governed by the preceding noun ܒܢ̈ܝ (§74).

2) V.5. w.1., ܘܗܘ (vid. *supra e*).

3) V.5. w.2., ܢܘܗܪܐ *light*, is in the nominative absolute, with the participle ܡܢܗܪ (§76.1). For farther explanation of the word vid. *y* above.

4) V.5. w.3., ܒܚܫܘܟܐ *in (the) darkness*, is compounded of the preposition ܒ *in*, and ܚܫܘܟܐ *darkness*. ܚܫܘܟܐ is a substantive noun (the Hebrew form is חֹשֶׁךְ, a verbal noun)—declension fourth (§ 45. masculines D)—third person singular masculine–emphatic state–ablative case and governed by ܒ (§ 75.5).

5) V.5. w.4., ܡܢܗܪ *permitting to shine*–a participle from the irregular ܦ̇, active intransitive verb (§20.2) ܢܗܪ *to shine* (33) –in the Aphel conjugation (§ 19 Table; § 19.B.4; § 23.1)–an active participle (§19.B.4; §23.1). It is used here for the third person singular of the present tense (§64.2.A.Rem.) and rendered the same as though it were a verb (vid. Trans. ¶14) third person singular. Conjugate to the place where it is found. Preter. Peal ܢܗܪ, preter. Ethpeel ܐܬܢܗܪ (§ 19.Table II, and §21.1), preterite Pael ܢܗܪ (§19.Table II, and §22.1), preterite Ethpaal ܐܬܢܗܪ (§ 19. Table II, § 22. 1 and Rem.), preterite Aphel ܐܢܗܪ (§19. Table II; §23.1), future Aphel ܢܢܗܪ (§19. Table II; §19.B.2,5; §23.1), imperative Aphel ܐܢܗܪ (§ 19. Table II; § 19. B. 1; § 23.1), infinitive Aphel ܡܢܗܪܘ (§19.Table II; §19.B.3 and 9; §23.1) participle active

Aphel ܡܢܗܪ (§19.Table II; §19.B.4; §23.1). It is found in the Aphel conjugation–active participle—masculine gender, and belongs to ܢܘܗܪܐ (§ 64. 1. A), or is absolute with it.

6) V.5. w.5., ܘܚܫܘܟܐ *and the darkness.* ܘ is a conjunction as above, and ܚܫܘܟܐ is in the nominative case to ܐܕܪܟܗ. For farther explanations see 4. *supra.*

7) V.5. w.7., ܐܕܪܟܗ *comprehended it,* is an irregular active intransitive verb, composed of ܕܪܟ and ܗ. Irregular–active voice–intransitive (§19.Table1)–indicative (§65.1.B.b)–Aphel preterite. The usual form is ܐܕܪܟ. When the suffix is appended, the final vowel of the verb is dropped (§15.3) and the last consonant forms a syllable with the suffix ܗ. It is in the 3rd.person masc.; Peal ܕܪܟ, Ethpeel ܐܬܕܪܟ, Pael ܕܪܟ, Ethpaal ܐܬܕܪܟ, Aphel ܐܕܪܟ, and agrees with its nominative ܚܫܘܟܐ. The suffix ܗ is a personal pronoun—third masculine singular–accusative case (§54.B.1) and governed by ܐܕܪܟ.

8) V.6. w.1., ܗܘܐ *was,* is a Lomadh Olaph verb—Peal—active voice–3d. singular–masculine–indicative mood–present tense (32.1) and agrees with ܒܪܢܫܐ (vid. ¶18.*c*).

9) V.6. w.2., ܒܪܢܫܐ *son of man,* is a composite noun (§42. 1) compounded of ܒܪ *son* and ܐܢܫ *man* ܒܪ is a primitive noun—anomalous—singular, construct (vid. paradigm §49. masculines)—third person masculine — nominative case to ܗܘܐ. ܢܫܐ *man,* is a noun derived from ܐܢܫ *man*—primitive—declension first–third person singular masculine–emphatic state–in the genitive case and governed by ܒܪ (§74; ¶18 1).

10) V.6 w.3., ܕܐܬܫܕܪ *who was sent*, is compounded of ܕ *who*, and ܐܬܫܕܪ *was sent.* ܕ is a relative pronoun–third singular masculine, a prefix, and in the nominative case to ܐܬܫܕܪ (§17. 2; §56). ܐܬܫܕܪ is a verb in the Ethpaal conjugation—passive voice—regular—third singular masculine—indicative mood—preterit imperfect tense (§60.4), and agrees with its nominative ܕ. Peal ܫܕܪ, Ethpeel ܐܬܫܕܪ, Pael ܫܕܪ, Ethpaal ܐܬܫܕܪ. In Ethpaal and the other passive conjugations ܫ is transposed (vid.¶15.2.*a*).

11) V.6. w.4., ܡܢ *from, of,* is a preposition and governs the ablative case (§75.5).

12) V.6.w.5., ܐܠܗܐ *God,* a noun—declension first—third singular masculine—emphatic state—ablative case, and governed by ܡܢ (§75.5; ¶18.*g*).

13) V.6. w.6., ܫܡܗ *his name,* compounded of ܫܡ *name* and ܗ *his.* ܫܡ is a noun from ܫܡ—anomalous—third singular masculine. Absolute and constr. singular ܫܡ, emphatic ܫܡܐ—suffix state ܫܡܗ (vid. paradigm, § 49. masculines). ܵ of the absolute state falls away in the emphatic state, and from the emphatic is formed the suffix state by dropping ܐ and adding ܗ—(§46.1.*a*)—nominative case to ܐܝܬܘܗܝ ܗܘܐ *was* (implied). In reference to ܐܝܬܘܗܝ ܗܘܐ (vid.¶18. *b* and *c*). ܗ *his,* is a suffix pronoun, third singular masculine (§16.Table)–genitive case (§54.B. 2) and governed by ܫܡ (§16; §16.B; §74).

14) V.6. w.7., ܝܘܚܢܢ *John,* a noun proper–anomalous–third singular masculine, absolute state–nominative case after ܐܝܬܘܗܝ ܗܘܐ.

15) V. 7. w. 1., ܗܘ *same, this*—a demonstrative pronoun, singular, masc. nominative case to ܐܬܐ (vid. ¶18. *k*).

16) V. 7. w. 2., ܐܬܐ *came*—Lomath Olaph (ܠܐ)—active voice–Peal conjugation–pret. imperfect–3d pers. singular, masc. indicative mood and agrees with ܗܘ (§27 Tab.; §32).

17) V. 7. w. 3., ܠܣܗܕܘܬܐ *for a witness*—compounded of ܠ *for*, and ܣܗܕܘܬܐ *witness*. ܣܗܕܘܬܐ is a noun derived from the verb ܣܗܕ *to witness*. The form ܣܗܕ appears as a noun of the 2d declension. Absolute and construct ܣܗܕ, emph. ܣܗܕܐ (§45. masculines B). The feminine absolute has the same form as the emphatic masc. viz. ܣܗܕܐ. In many nouns ܬ is inserted before the final ܐ in the feminine ; ܘ with ܬ is also sometimes inserted (§45. 3 and Rem. 3) as in this word. It has the form here of the emph. feminine. That indeed seems to be the usual form in which the word appears—3d pers. singular, dative case and governed by ܠ (§75. 1).

18) V. 7. w. 4., ܕܢܣܗܕ *who shall (should) bear witness*—compounded of ܕ *who*, and ܢܣܗܕ *shall (should) bear witness*, or *cause to bear witness* (§23. 2. *a*) ܢܣܗܕ is a verb from ܣܗܕ *to beget, to bear witness*–Aph. conjugation–active voice–regular (§26)–intransitive. 3d sing. Peal ܣܗܕ, Ethpe. ܐܬܣܗܕ, Pa. ܣܗܕ, Ethpa. ܐܬܣܗܕ, Aph. pret. ܐܣܗܕ, Aph. fut. ܢܣܗܕ–fut. tense, masc. gender. In the fut. Aph. 3d. masc. usually we find ـَ in the last syllable ; but sometimes as here we have ـ̈ (§23.2, where are examples, with ـ̈ in the last syllable. Compare §19, Tables I and II). The future tense is here used in the sense of the subjunctive mood imperfect tense (§61. 3. A. b) and agrees with its nominative ܕ. ܕ is a relative pronoun–3d

pers. singular, masculine–a prefix–nominative case to ܕܢܣܗܕ (¶ 18. *t*).

19) V. 7. w. 5., ܥܠ *to, against, on account of, of*–preposition governing ܢܘܗܪܐ.

20) V. 7. w. 6., ܢܘܗܪܐ *light*–verbal noun from ܢܗܪ *to shine*–declension fourth, 3d pers. singular, masculine, emphatic state, ablative case and governed by ܥܠ (¶18. y).

21) V. 7. w. 7., ܕܟܠܢܫ–compounded of ܕ *that*, ܟܠ *all, every*, and ܢܫ *man*–ܕ is a conjunction (§85. 3 & 4, *d*)–prefix connecting ܕܢܣܗܕ and ܢܗܝܡܢ. ܟܠ *every, all*, is a pronoun, but here used as an adjective (§58. B. 2. *b. a*) and belongs to ܢܫ. For declension, etc. vid. ¶18. *l.* ܢܫ *man*, is a noun from ܐܢܫ—declension first, but is somewhat irregular–3d pers. singular, masc. absolute state, nom. case to ܢܗܝܡܢ. For further explanations, vid. ¶ 18. 1.

22) V. 7. w. 8., ܢܗܝܡܢ *might believe*–a verb doubly irregular, ܦܐ and ܢ, and is placed among the defective verbs (§35. 2. *c*). In the Aph. conjugation. Pe. ܐܡܢ, Aph. ܗܝܡܢ, future Aph. ܢܗܝܡܢ–active voice–intransitive–3d pers. singular masc.–future tense and used in the sense of the subjunctive mood, imperfect tense, and agrees with its nominative ܢܫ (comp. ¶18. 18).

23) V. 7. w. 9., ܒܐܝܕܗ *through* or *by the hand of him*. For parsing, vid. ¶ 18. *m.*, where the same expression occurs.

24) V. 8. w. 1., ܠܐ *not*, is an adverb and qualifies ܗܘܐ.

25) V. 8. w. 2., ܗܘ *he*, is a personal pronoun separate–3d pers. singular masc. and nominative case to ܗܘܐ (comp. ¶18. *e*).

26) V. 8. w. 3., ܗܘܐ *was*–an irregular verb agreeing with ܗܘ for its nominative (vid. ¶18. *n*).

27) V. 8. w. 4., ܢܘܗܪܐ *light*–a noun and nominative case after ܗܘܐ (vid. ¶18. *y*).

28) V. 8. w. 5., ܐܠܐ *but*–a conjunction, a contraction of ܠܐ *not*, and ܐܢ *if*; it continues the sense. Following this and preceding the next word, there is something implied; after ܐܠܐ supply ܐܬܐ ܠܣܗܕܘܬܐ *came for a witness*, the same which is expressed in verse 7. For the remaining three words of this verse, vid.¶18. 18, 19, 20.

29) V. 9. w. 1 and 2., ܐܝܬܘܗܝ ܗܘܐ *was*–a verb and agrees with ܢܘܗܪܐ understood, ܗܘ ܢܘܗܪܐ *that light*, being implied. For parsing this verb fully, vid. ¶18. *b.* & *c.*

30) V. 9. w. 3., ܓܝܪ *for*, is a conjunction continuing the sense.

31) V. 9. w. 4., ܢܘܗܪܐ *light*–a noun–nominative case after ܐܝܬܘܗܝ ܗܘܐ (vid. ¶18. *y*).

32) V. 9. w. 5., ܕܫܪܪܐ *of truth*–compounded of ܕ *of*, and ܫܪܪܐ *truth.* ܫܪܪܐ is a noun derived from the verb ܫܪܪ *to be convinced*–declension first (vid. §48. A. decl. 1. Rem.)–singular. Construct and absolute, ܫܪ or ܫܪܪ, emphatic ܫܪܪܐ forming the emphatic state, from ܫܪ. ◌ܰ falls away on account of the addition at the end (§15. 3), then ܕܫ presenting two vowelless consonants, ܕ takes the new vowel ◌ܰ (§15. 4. *b*)–3d pers. singular, masc.–genitive case after ܕ (§74. 2. *a*). The expression ܢܘܗܪܐ ܕܫܪܪܐ is an instance in which the abstract noun ܫܪܪܐ has the sense of an adjective, and the phrase is properly rendered *the true light.*

33) V. 9. w. 6., ܕܡܢܗܪ *which shineth*, or *having shone*–compounded of ܡܢܗܪ *shineth*, or *having shone*, and ܕ *which.* ܡܢܗܪ is an Aph. participle from ܢܗܪ, absolute

with ܕ (¶18. 5). ܕ *which*, is a relative pronoun, nominative absolute with ܡܢܗܪ (§76. 1; ¶18. 3).

34) V. 9. w. 7., ܠܟܠܐܢܫ *upon every man*, compounded of ܠ *upon*, ܟܠ *every* and ܐܢܫ *man*. ܠ is a preposition governing the accusative or dative. ܟܠ is a pronoun used adjectively and belongs to ܐܢܫ (vid. 18. *l*). ܐܢܫ is a noun in the accusative and governed by ܠ (¶18. 1, 9, 21).

35) V. 9. w. 8., ܕܐܬܐ *who comes*, composed of ܕ *who*, and ܐܬܐ *comes*. ܐܬܐ is a verb–Peal conjugation, present tense, and agrees with its nominative ܕ (¶18. 16).

36) V. 9. w. 9., ܠܥܠܡܐ *into the world*–compounded of ܠ *into*, and ܥܠܡܐ *the world*. ܠ is a preposition governing the accusative. ܥܠܡܐ is a noun from ܥܠܡ second declension. Absolute and construct ܥܠܡ, emphatic ܥܠܡܐ. In ܥܠܡ the final vowel ܰ falls away in the emphatic state as a syllable is added (§15. 3)–3d pers. singular, masc. accusative case and governed by ܠ.

37) V. 10. w. 8., (the seven preceding words are explained above). ܝܕܥܗ *knew him*–compounded of ܗ *him*, and ܝܕܥ *knew*. ܝܕܥ is a verb with a suffix pronoun attached to it–derived from the Hebrew יָדַע *to know*, doubly anomalous. ܦܐ and ܠܐ–Peal preterit –3d pers. singular, masc. indicative mood and agrees with ܥܠܡܐ. By taking a suffix the usual form is changed. The common form of the Peal preterit is ܝܕܰܥ. ܰ falls away and ܰ falls back upon the first radical when the verb takes a suffix (vid. §36). ܗ is a suffix pronoun with its union vowel (§16. Tab. *a*) 3d pers. singular, masc.–accusative, and governed by ܝܕܥ (§54. B. 1).

CHRESTOMATHY.

CHRESTOMATHY.

FIRST LESSONS IN TRANSLATING.

John i. 1—10.

1 ܒܪܫܝܬ ܐܝܬܘܗܝ ܗܘܐ ܡܠܬܐ . ܘܗܘ ܡܠܬܐ ܐܝܬܘܗܝ
ܗܘܐ ܠܘܬ ܐܠܗܐ . ܘܐܠܗܐ ܐܝܬܘܗܝ ܗܘܐ ܗܘ ܡܠܬܐ .
2 ܗܢܐ ܐܝܬܘܗܝ ܗܘܐ ܒܪܫܝܬ ܠܘܬ ܐܠܗܐ .
3 ܟܠ ܒܐܝܕܗ ܗܘܐ . ܘܒܠܥܕܘܗܝ ܐܦܠܐ ܚܕܐ ܗܘܬ ܡܕܡ
ܕܗܘܐ .
4 ܒܗ ܚܝܐ ܗܘܐ . ܘܚܝܐ ܐܝܬܘܗܝ ܢܘܗܪܐ ܕܒܢܝܢܫܐ
5 ܘܗܘ ܢܘܗܪܐ ܒܚܫܘܟܐ ܡܢܗܪ ܆ ܘܚܫܘܟܐ ܠܐ ܐܕܪܟܗ ܀
6 ܗܘܐ ܓܒܪܐ ܕܐܫܬܕܪ ܡܢ ܐܠܗܐ ܆ ܫܡܗ ܝܘܚܢܢ .
7 ܗܢܐ ܐܬܐ ܠܣܗܕܘܬܐ ܕܢܣܗܕ ܥܠ ܢܘܗܪܐ . ܕܟܠܢܫ ܢܗܝܡܢ
ܒܐܝܕܗ .
8 ܠܐ ܗܘܐ ܗܘ ܗܘܐ ܢܘܗܪܐ . ܐܠܐ ܕܢܣܗܕ ܥܠ ܢܘܗܪܐ .
9 ܐܝܬܘܗܝ ܗܘܐ ܢܘܗܪܐ ܕܫܪܪܐ ܆ ܕܡܢܗܪ ܠܟܠܢܫ ܕܐܬܐ
ܠܥܠܡܐ .
10 ܒܥܠܡܐ ܗܘܐ . ܘܥܠܡܐ ܒܐܝܕܗ ܗܘܐ . ܘܥܠܡܐ ܠܐ
ܝܕܥܗ .

MATTHEW ii. 1—10.

1 *ܟܕ ܕܝܢ ܐܬܝܠܕ ܝܫܘܥ ܒܒܝܬ ܠܚܡ ܕܝܗܘܕܐ: ܒܝܘܡܝ
ܗܪܘܕܣ ܡܠܟܐ. ܐܬܘ ܡܓܘܫܐ ܡܢ ܡܕܢܚܐ ܠܐܘܪܫܠܡ
2 ܘܐܡܪܝܢ. *ܐܝܟܘ ܡܠܟܐ ܕܝܗܘܕܝܐ ܕܐܬܝܠܕ: ܚܙܝܢ ܓܝܪ
3 ܟܘܟܒܗ ܒܡܕܢܚܐ ܘܐܬܝܢ ܠܡܣܓܕ ܠܗ. *ܫܡܥ ܕܝܢ
ܗܪܘܕܣ ܡܠܟܐ ܘܐܬܕܠܚ. ܘܟܠܗ ܐܘܪܫܠܡ ܥܡܗ.
4 *ܘܟܢܫ ܟܠܗܘܢ ܪܒܝ ܟܗܢܐ ܘܣܦܪܐ ܕܥܡܐ ܘܡܫܬܐܠ
5 ܗܘܐ ܠܗܘܢ ܕܐܝܟܐ ܡܬܝܠܕ ܡܫܝܚܐ. *ܗܢܘܢ ܕܝܢ ܐܡܪܘ
ܒܒܝܬ ܠܚܡ ܕܝܗܘܕܐ. ܗܟܢܐ ܓܝܪ ܟܬܝܒ ܒܢܒܝܐ:
6 *ܐܦ ܐܢܬܝ ܒܝܬ ܠܚܡ ܕܝܗܘܕܐ: ܠܐ ܗܘܝܬܝ ܒܨܝܪܐ
ܒܡܠܟܐ ܕܝܗܘܕܐ. ܡܢܟܝ ܓܝܪ ܢܦܘܩ ܡܠܟܐ: ܕܗܘ
7 ܢܪܥܝܘܗܝ ܠܥܡܝ ܐܝܣܪܝܠ: *ܗܝܕܝܢ ܗܪܘܕܣ
ܒܛܘܫܝܐ ܩܪܐ ܠܡܓܘܫܐ ܘܝܠܦ ܡܢܗܘܢ. ܒܐܝܢܐ ܙܒܢܐ
8 ܐܬܚܙܝ ܠܗܘܢ ܟܘܟܒܐ. *ܘܫܕܪ ܐܢܘܢ ܠܒܝܬ ܠܚܡ ܘܐܡܪ
ܠܗܘܢ. ܙܠܘ ܒܥܘ ܥܠ ܛܠܝܐ ܒܚܦܝܛܘܬܐ ܘܡܐ
ܕܐܫܟܚܬܘܢܝܗܝ ܬܘ ܚܘܐܘܢܝ. ܕܐܦ ܐܢܐ ܐܬܐ ܐܣܓܘܕ
9 ܠܗ. *ܗܢܘܢ ܕܝܢ ܟܕ ܫܡܥܘ ܡܢ ܡܠܟܐ ܐܙܠܘ. ܘܗܐ
ܟܘܟܒܐ ܗܘ ܕܚܙܘ ܒܡܕܢܚܐ ܐܙܠ ܗܘܐ ܩܕܡܝܗܘܢ ܥܕܡܐ
10 ܕܐܬܐ ܩܡ ܠܥܠ ܡܢ ܐܝܟܐ ܕܐܝܬܘܗܝ ܗܘܐ ܛܠܝܐ. *ܟܕ ܕܝܢ
ܚܙܐܘܗܝ ܠܟܘܟܒܐ: ܚܕܝܘ ܚܕܘܬܐ ܪܒܬܐ ܛܒ.

Mark xiv. 32—42.

32 *ܘܐܬܘ ܠܕܘܟܬܐ ܐܝܕܐ ܕܡܬܩܪܝܐ ܓܕܣܡܢ. ܘܐܡܪ ܠܬܠܡܝܕܘܗܝ.
33 ܬܒܘ ܗܪܟܐ ܥܕ ܡܨܠܐ ܐܢܐ. *ܘܕܒܪ ܥܡܗ ܠܟܐܦܐ ܘܠܝܥܩܘܒ
34 ܘܠܝܘܚܢܢ. ܘܫܪܝ ܠܡܬܡܗܘ ܘܠܡܬܟܪܝܘ. *ܘܐܡܪ ܠܗܘܢ.
ܟܪܝܐ ܗܝ ܠܗ ܠܢܦܫܝ ܥܕܡܐ ܠܡܘܬܐ. ܩܘܘ ܗܪܟܐ ܘܐܬܬܥܝܪܘ.
35 *ܘܩܪܒ ܩܠܝܠ ܘܢܦܠ ܥܠ ܐܪܥܐ. ܘܡܨܠܐ ܗܘܐ ܕܐܢ ܡܫܟܚܐ
36 ܬܥܒܪ ܡܢܗ ܫܥܬܐ. *ܘܐܡܪ ܐܒܐ ܐܒܝ. ܟܠ ܡܕܡ ܡܫܟܚ ܐܢܬ.
37 ܐܥܒܪ ܡܢܝ ܟܣܐ ܗܢܐ. ܐܠܐ ܠܐ ܕܨܒܐ ܐܢܐ ܐܠܐ ܕܨܒܝܬ. *ܘܐܬܐ
ܐܫܟܚ ܐܢܘܢ ܟܕ ܕܡܟܝܢ. ܘܐܡܪ ܠܟܐܦܐ. ܫܡܥܘܢ ܕܡܟܬ ܠܟ.
38 ܠܐ ܐܫܟܚܬ ܚܕܐ ܫܥܐ ܠܡܬܬܥܝܪܘ. *ܐܬܬܥܝܪܘ ܘܨܠܘ ܕܠܐ ܬܥܠܘܢ
39 ܠܢܣܝܘܢܐ. ܪܘܚܐ ܨܒܝܐ ܘܡܛܝܒܐ. ܐܠܐ ܦܓܪܐ ܟܪܝܗ. *ܘܐܙܠ
40 ܬܘܒ ܨܠܝ ܘܗܕܐ ܡܠܬܐ ܐܡܪ. *ܘܗܦܟ ܐܬܐ ܬܘܒ ܐܫܟܚ
ܐܢܘܢ ܟܕ ܕܡܟܝܢ. ܡܛܠ ܕܥܝܢܝܗܘܢ ܝܩܝܪܢ ܗܘܝ. ܘܠܐ ܝܕܥܝܢ
41 ܗܘܘ ܡܢܐ ܢܐܡܪܘܢ ܠܗ. *ܘܐܬܐ ܕܬܠܬ ܙܒܢܝܢ ܘܐܡܪ ܠܗܘܢ.
ܕܡܟܘ ܡܟܝܠ ܘܐܬܢܝܚܘ. ܡܛܬ ܚܪܬܐ ܘܐܬܬ ܫܥܬܐ. ܘܗܐ
42 ܡܫܬܠܡ ܒܪܗ ܕܐܢܫܐ ܒܐܝܕܝܗܘܢ ܕܚܛܝܐ. *ܩܘܡܘ ܢܐܙܠ. ܗܐ
ܡܛܐ ܗܘ ܕܡܫܠܡ ܠܝ.

Luke xxiii. 18—27.

18 *ܘܩܥܘ ܟܠܗ ܟܢܫܐ ܘܐܡܪܝܢ. ܫܩܘܠܝܗܝ ܠܗܢܐ ܘܫܪܐ
19 ܠܢ ܠܒܪܐܒܐ. *ܗܘ ܐܝܢܐ ܕܡܛܠ ܐܣܛܣܝܣ ܕܗܘܬ ܒܡܕܝܢܬܐ

ܘܩܛܠܐ ܕܚܒܝܫ ܗܘܐ ܒܝܬ ܐܣܝܪܐ. *ܬܘܒ ܕܝܢ ܡܠܠ ܠܗܘܢ 20
ܦܝܠܛܘܣ ܟܕ ܨܒܐ ܕܢܫܪܐ ܠܝܫܘܥ. *ܗܢܘܢ ܕܝܢ ܩܥܝܢ ܗܘܘ 21
ܘܐܡܪܝܢ. ܨܠܘܒܝܗܝ ܨܠܘܒܝܗܝ. *ܗܘ ܕܝܢ ܕܬܠܬ ܙܒܢܝܢ 22
ܐܡܪ ܠܗܘܢ. ܡܢܐ ܓܝܪ ܕܒܝܫ ܥܒܕ ܗܢܐ. ܡܕܡ ܕܚܝܒ ܡܘܬܐ
ܥܠܬܐ ܠܐ ܐܫܟܚܬ ܒܗ. ܐܪܕܝܘܗܝ ܗܟܝܠ ܘܐܫܪܝܘܗܝ.
*ܗܢܘܢ ܕܝܢ ܐܬܚܦܝܘ ܗܘܘ ܒܩܠܐ ܪܡܐ: ܘܫܐܠܝܢ ܗܘܘ ܠܗ 23
ܕܢܙܕܩܦ. ܘܥܫܢ ܗܘܐ ܩܠܗܘܢ ܕܗܢܘܢ ܘܕܪܒܝ ܟܗܢܐ.
*ܦܝܠܛܘܣ ܕܝܢ ܦܣܩ ܕܬܗܘܐ ܫܐܠܬܗܘܢ. *ܘܫܪܐ ܠܗܘܢ ܠܗܘ 24 25
ܕܡܛܠ ܐܣܛܣܝܣ ܘܩܛܠܐ ܕܚܒܝܫ ܗܘܐ ܒܝܬ ܐܣܝܪܐ ܗܘ ܕܫܐܠܘ.
ܠܝܫܘܥ ܕܝܢ ܐܫܠܡ ܠܨܒܝܢܗܘܢ. *ܘܟܕ ܡܘܒܠܝܢ ܠܗ: 26
ܐܚܕܘ ܠܫܡܥܘܢ ܩܘܪܝܢܝܐ ܕܐܬܐ ܡܢ ܩܪܝܬܐ: ܘܣܡܘ ܥܠܘܗܝ
ܙܩܝܦܐ ܕܢܫܩܘܠ ܒܬܪܗ ܕܝܫܘܥ. *ܘܐܬܐ ܗܘܐ ܒܬܪܗ ܟܢܫܐ 27
ܕܥܡܐ. ܘܢܫܐ ܐܝܠܝܢ ܕܡܪܩܕܢ ܗܘܝ ܘܒܟܝܢ ܥܠܘܗܝ.

Luke xxiii. 33---42.

*ܘܟܕ ܐܬܘ ܠܕܘܟܬܐ ܚܕܐ ܕܡܬܩܪܝܐ ܩܪܩܦܬܐ: ܙܩܦܘܗܝ ܬܡܢ. 33
ܘܠܗܢܘܢ ܥܒܕܝ ܒܝܫܬܐ: ܚܕ ܡܢ ܝܡܝܢܗ ܘܚܕ ܡܢ ܣܡܠܗ◆
*ܗܘ ܕܝܢ ܝܫܘܥ ܐܡܪ ܗܘܐ. ܐܒܐ ܫܒܘܩ ܠܗܘܢ. ܠܐ ܓܝܪ 34
ܝܕܥܝܢ ܡܢܐ ܥܒܕܝܢ. ܘܦܠܓܘ ܢܚܬܘܗܝ ܘܐܪܡܝܘ ܥܠܝܗܘܢ
ܦܣܐ. *ܘܩܐܡ ܗܘܐ ܕܝܢ ܥܡܐ ܚܙܐ. ܘܡܡܝܩܝܢ ܗܘܘ ܒܗ 35

ܐܦ ܐܪ̈ܟܘܢܐ ܘܐܡܪܝܢ. ܠܐܚܪ̈ܢܐ ܐܚܝ. ܢܦܫܗ ܢܚܐ. ܐܢ ܗܘܝܘ
36 ܡܫܝܚܐ ܓܒܝܐ ܕܐܠܗܐ. *ܘܡܒܙܚܝܢ ܗܘܘ ܒܗ ܐܦ
ܐܣܛܪ̈ܛܝܘܛܐ ܟܕ ܩܪܒܝܢ ܠܗ ܘܡܩܪܒܝܢ ܠܗ ܚܠܐ.
37 38 *ܘܐܡܪܝܢ ܠܗ. ܐܢ ܐܢܬ ܗܘ ܡܠܟܐ ܕܝܗܘ̈ܕܝܐ ܐܚܐ ܢܦܫܟ. *ܐܝܬ
ܗܘܐ ܕܝܢ ܐܦ ܟܬܒܐ ܕܟܬܝܒ ܥܠܘܗܝ ܒܟܬܒܐ: ܝܘܢܐܝܬ ܘܪܗܘܡܐܝܬ.
39 ܘܥܒܪܐܝܬ. ܗܢܘ ܡܠܟܐ ܕܝܗܘ̈ܕܝܐ. *ܚܕ ܕܝܢ ܡܢ ܗܢܘܢ ܓܒܪ̈ܐ
ܥܒ̈ܕܝ ܒܝܫܬܐ ܕܙܩܝܦܝܢ ܗܘܘ ܥܡܗ: ܡܓܕܦ ܗܘܐ ܥܠܘܗܝ ܘܐܡܪ.
40 ܐܢ ܐܢܬ ܗܘ ܡܫܝܚܐ: ܦܨܐ ܢܦܫܟ ܘܦܨܢ ܐܦ ܠܢ. *ܘܟܐܐ ܒܗ
ܚܒܪܗ ܘܐܡܪ ܠܗ. ܐܦ ܠܐ ܡܢ ܐܠܗܐ ܕܚܠ ܐܢܬ: ܕܐܦ ܐܢܬ
41 ܒܗ ܐܢܬ ܒܕܝܢܐ: *ܘܚܢܢ ܟܐܢܐܝܬ. ܐܝܟ ܕܫܘܝܢ ܗܘܝܢ ܓܝܪ
ܐܝܟ ܕܥܒܕܢ ܐܬܦܪܥܢ. ܗܢܐ ܕܝܢ ܡܕܡ ܕܣܢܐ ܠܐ ܥܒܕ ܠܗ.
42 *ܘܐܡܪ ܠܝܫܘܥ. ܐܬܕܟܪܢܝ ܡܪܝ ܡܐ ܕܐܬܝܬ ܒܡܠܟܘܬܟ.

Luke xxiii. 43—53.

43 *ܐܡܪ ܠܗ ܝܫܘܥ. ܐܡܝܢ ܐܡܪ ܐܢܐ ܠܟ: ܕܝܘܡܢܐ ܥܡܝ ܬܗܘܐ
44 ܒܦܪܕܝܣܐ. *ܐܝܬ ܗܘܬ ܕܝܢ ܐܝܟ ܫܥ̈ܐ ܫܬ. ܘܗܘܐ ܚܫܘܟܐ ܥܠ
45 ܟܠܗ ܐܪܥܐ: ܥܕܡܐ ܠܫ̈ܥܐ ܬܫܥ. *ܘܚܫܟ ܫܡܫܐ. ܘܐܨܛܪܝ ܐܦܝ
46 ܬܪܥܐ ܕܗܝܟܠܐ ܡܢ ܡܨܥܬܗ. *ܘܩܥܐ ܝܫܘܥ ܒܩܠܐ ܪܡܐ ܘܐܡܪ.
47 ܐܒܝ ܒܐܝ̈ܕܝܟ ܣܐܡ ܐܢܐ ܪܘܚܝ. ܗܕܐ ܐܡܪ ܘܫܠܡ. *ܟܕ ܚܙܐ ܕܝܢ
ܩܢܛܪܘܢܐ ܡܕܡ ܕܗܘܐ ܫܒܚ ܠܐܠܗܐ ܘܐܡܪ. ܫܪܝܪܐܝܬ ܗܢܐ

ܓܒܪܐ ܙܕܝܩܐ ܗܘܐ. *ܘܟܠܗܘܢ ܟܢܫܐ ܐܝܠܝܢ ܕܐܬܟܢܫܘ ܗܘܘ 48
ܠܚܙܝܬܐ ܗܕܐ. ܟܕ ܚܙܘ ܡܕܡ ܕܗܘܐ܆ ܗܦܟܘ ܟܕ ܡܢܩܫܝܢ ܥܠ
ܚܕܝܗܘܢ. *ܘܩܝܡܝܢ ܗܘܘ ܡܢ ܪܘܚܩܐ ܟܠܗܘܢ ܝܕ̈ܘܥܘܗܝ 49
ܕܝܫܘܥ. ܘܢܫ̈ܐ ܐܝܠܝܢ ܕܐܬܝ̈ ܗܘ̈ܝ ܥܡܗ ܡܢ ܓܠܝܠܐ܆ ܘܚܙܝܢ
ܗܘ̈ܝ ܗܠܝܢ܀ *ܓܒܪܐ ܕܝܢ ܚܕ ܕܫܡܗ ܝܘܣܦ ܒܘܠܘܛܐ܆ ܡܢ 50
ܪܡܬܐ ܡܕܝܢܬܐ ܕܝܗܘܕ܆ ܓܒܪܐ ܗܘܐ ܛܒܐ ܘܙܕܝܩܐ. *ܗܢܐ ܠܐ 51
ܫܠܡ ܗܘܐ ܠܪܥܝܢܗܘܢ ܘܠܣܘܥܪܢܗܘܢ. ܘܡܣܟܐ ܗܘܐ
ܠܡܠܟܘܬܐ ܕܐܠܗܐ. *ܗܢܐ ܩܪܒ ܠܘܬ ܦܝܠܛܘܣ܆ ܘܫܐܠ 52
ܦܓܪܗ ܕܝܫܘܥ. *ܘܐܚܬܗ ܘܟܪܟܗ ܒܣܕܘܢܐ ܕܟܬܢܐ. ܘܣܡܗ 53
ܒܩܒܪܐ ܦܣܝܠܐ ܒܟܐܦܐ. ܗܘ ܕܠܐ ܐܢܫ ܥܕܟܝܠ ܐܬܬܣܝܡ ܗܘܐ
ܒܗ.

Acts xvii. 22—32.

*ܟܕ ܩܡ ܦܘܠܘܣ ܒܐܪܝܘܣ ܦܓܘܣ ܐܡܪ. ܓܒܪܐ ܐܬܢܝ̈ܐ܆ 22
ܚܙܐ ܐܢܐ ܠܟܘܢ܆ ܕܒܟܠܡܕܡ ܡܝܬܪܝܢ ܐܢܬܘܢ ܒܕܚܠܬ ܫܐܕܐ. *ܟܕ 23
ܓܝܪ ܡܬܚܕܪ ܗܘܝܬ ܘܚܙܐ ܗܘܝܬ ܒܝܬ ܕܚܠܬܟܘܢ. ܐܫܟܚܬ
ܡܕܒܚܐ ܚܕ܆ ܕܟܬܝܒ ܗܘܐ ܥܠܘܗܝ. ܕܐܠܗܐ ܟܣܝܐ. ܗܘ
ܗܟܝܠ ܕܠܐ ܝܕܥܝܢ ܐܢܬܘܢ ܘܕܚܠܝܢ ܐܢܬܘܢ ܠܗ܆ ܠܗ ܠܗܢܐ
ܐܢܐ ܡܟܪܙ ܐܢܐ ܠܟܘܢ. *ܐܠܗܐ ܓܝܪ ܕܥܒܕ ܥܠܡܐ ܘܟܠܡܕܡ ܕܐܝܬ 24
ܒܗ. ܘܗܘܝܘ ܡܪܐ ܕܫܡܝܐ ܘܕܐܪܥܐ܆ ܒܗܝܟܠܐ ܕܥܒܕ ܐܝܕܝܐ ܠܐ
ܥܡܪ. *ܘܠܐ ܡܫܬܡܫ ܡܢ ܐܝܕܝ̈ ܒܢܝ̈ܢܫܐ. ܘܠܐ ܡܕܡ ܠܐ 25

26 ܣܢܝܩ. ܡܛܠ ܕܗܘ ܝܗܒ ܠܟܠܢܫ ܚܝܐ ܘܢܦܫܐ. *ܘܥܒܕ
ܡܢ ܕܡܐ ܚܕ ܟܠܗ ܥܠܡܐ ܕܒܢܝ̈ܢܫܐ. ܕܢܗܘܘܢ ܥܡܪܝܢ ܥܠ ܐܦܝ
ܐܪܥܐ ܟܠܗ. ܘܦܪܫ ܙܒܢܐ ܒܦܘܩܕܢܗ: ܘܣܡ ܬܚܘܡܐ
27 ܠܥܡܘܪܬܐ ܕܒܢܝ̈ܢܫܐ. *ܕܢܗܘܘܢ ܒܥܝܢ ܠܐܠܗܐ ܘܡܬܒܨܝܢ: ܘܡܢ
ܒܪܝܬܗ ܡܫܟܚܝܢ ܠܗ. ܡܛܠ ܕܐܦ ܠܐ ܗܘܐ ܪܚܝܩ ܡܢ ܟܠ
28 ܚܕ ܡܢܢ. *ܒܗ ܗܘ ܓܝܪ ܚܝܝܢܢ ܘܡܬܬܙܝܥܝܢܢ ܘܐܝܬܝܢ. ܐܝܟ
ܕܐܦ ܐܢܫܐ ܡܢ ܚܟܝܡܐ ܕܠܘܬܟܘܢ ܐܡܪܘ ܕܡܢܗ ܗܘ ܓܢܣܢ.
29 *ܐܢܫܐ ܗܟܝܠ ܕܓܢܣܐ ܗܘܝܢ ܡܢ ܐܠܗܐ ܗܘ: ܠܐ ܫܘܝܢܢ ܠܡܣܒܪ
ܕܠܕܗܒܐ ܐܘ ܠܣܐܡܐ. ܐܘ ܠܟܐܦܐ ܕܓܠܝܦܐ ܒܐܘܡܢܘܬܐ
30 ܘܒܡܚܫܒܬܐ ܕܒܪܢܫܐ ܕܡܝܐ ܐܠܗܘܬܐ. *ܙܒܢܐ ܓܝܪ ܕܛܘܥܝܝܐ ܐܥܒܪ
ܐܠܗܐ. ܘܒܙܒܢܐ ܗܢܐ ܦܩܕ ܠܟܠܗܘܢ ܒܢܝ̈ܢܫܐ: ܕܟܠ ܐܢܫ
31 ܒܟܠ ܐܬܪ ܢܬܘܒ. *ܡܛܠ ܕܐܩܝܡ ܝܘܡܐ ܕܒܗ ܥܬܝܕ ܕܢܕܘܢ
ܐܪܥܐ ܟܠܗ ܒܟܐܢܘܬܐ. ܒܝܕ ܓܒܪܐ ܐܝܢܐ ܕܦܪܫܗ. ܘܐܦܢܝ ܠܟܠ
32 ܐܢܫ ܠܗܝܡܢܘܬܗ ܟܕ ܐܩܝܡܗ ܡܢ ܒܝܬ ܡܝ̈ܬܐ. *ܘܟܕ ܫܡܥܘ
ܩܝܡܬܐ ܕܡܢ ܒܝܬ ܡܝ̈ܬܐ: ܡܢܗܘܢ ܡܡܝܩܝܢ ܗܘܘ.
ܘܡܢܗܘܢ ܐܡܪܝܢ ܗܘܘ. ܙܒܢܐ ܐܚܪܢܐ ܢܫܡܥܟ ܥܠ ܗܕܐ.

Romans vi. 1—10.

1 *ܡܢܐ ܗܟܝܠ ܢܐܡܪ. ܢܩܘܐ ܒܗ ܒܚܛܝܬܐ ܕܢܣܓܐ ܛܝܒܘܬܐ.
2 *ܚܣ. ܐܝܠܝܢ ܓܝܪ ܕܡܝܬܢ ܠܚܛܝܬܐ. ܐܝܟܢܐ ܬܘܒ ܒܗ ܢܚܐ.

*ܐܘ ܠܐ ܝܕܥܝܢ ܐܢܬܘܢ ܕܐܝܠܝܢ ܕܥܡܕܢ ܒܝܫܘܥ ܡܫܝܚܐ. ܒܡܘܬܗ 3
ܗܘ ܥܡܕܢ. *ܐܬܩܒܪܢ ܓܝܪ ܥܡܗ ܒܡܥܡܘܕܝܬܐ ܠܡܘܬܐ. ܕܐܝܟܢܐ 4
ܕܩܡ ܝܫܘܥ ܡܫܝܚܐ ܡܢ ܒܝܬ ܡܝܬܐ ܒܫܘܒܚܐ ܕܐܒܘܗܝ:
ܗܟܢܐ ܐܦ ܚܢܢ ܒܚܝܐ ܚܕܬܐ ܢܗܠܟ. *ܐܢ ܓܝܪ ܐܟܚܕܐ ܐܬܢܨܒܢ 5
ܥܡܗ ܒܕܡܘܬ ܡܘܬܗ: ܗܟܢܐ ܐܦ ܒܩܝܡܬܗ ܢܗܘܐ.
*ܝܕܥܝܢ ܓܝܪ ܕܒܪܢܫܢ ܥܬܝܩܐ ܐܙܕܩܦ ܥܡܗ. ܕܢܒܛܠ ܦܓܪܐ 6
ܕܚܛܝܬܐ. ܕܠܘ ܬܘܒ ܢܫܬܥܒܕ ܠܚܛܝܬܐ. *ܐܝܢܐ ܓܝܪ ܕܡܝܬ ܐܬܚܪܪ 7
ܠܗ ܡܢ ܚܛܝܬܐ. *ܐܢ ܗܟܝܠ ܡܝܬܢ ܥܡ ܡܫܝܚܐ: ܢܗܝܡܢ 8
ܕܢܚܐ ܥܡ ܡܫܝܚܐ ܬܘܒ. *ܝܕܥܝܢ ܓܝܪ ܕܡܫܝܚܐ ܩܡ ܡܢ 9
ܒܝܬ ܡܝܬܐ. ܘܬܘܒ ܠܐ ܡܐܬ. ܘܡܘܬܐ ܠܐ ܡܫܬܠܛ ܒܗ.
*ܕܡܝܬ ܓܝܪ ܠܚܛܝܬܐ ܗܘ ܡܝܬ ܚܕܐ ܙܒܢ. ܘܕܚܝ ܚܝ ܗܘ 10
ܠܐܠܗܐ.

Colossians iii. 1—15.

*ܐܢ ܗܟܝܠ ܩܡܬܘܢ ܥܡ ܡܫܝܚܐ: ܕܠܥܠ ܒܥܘ. ܐܬܪ ܕܡܫܝܚܐ 1
ܝܬܒ ܥܠ ܝܡܝܢܐ ܕܐܠܗܐ. *ܕܠܥܠ ܐܬܪܥܘ ܘܠܐ ܕܒܐܪܥܐ. 2
*ܡܝܬܬܘܢ ܠܟܘܢ ܓܝܪ. ܘܚܝܝܟܘܢ ܟܣܝܢ ܥܡ ܡܫܝܚܐ ܒܐܠܗܐ. 3
*ܘܐܡܬܝ ܕܡܫܝܚܐ ܢܬܓܠܐ ܕܐܝܬܘܗܝ ܚܝܝܢ. ܗܝܕܝܢ ܐܦ ܐܢܬܘܢ 4
ܬܬܓܠܘܢ ܥܡܗ ܒܫܘܒܚܐ. *ܡܝܬܘ ܗܟܝܠ ܗܕܡܝܟܘܢ 5
ܕܒܐܪܥܐ. ܙܢܝܘܬܐ ܘܛܢܦܘܬܐ ܘܚܫܐ ܘܪܓܬܐ ܒܝܫܬܐ. ܘܥܠܘܒܘܬܐ
ܕܐܝܬܝܗ ܦܘܠܚܢ ܦܬܟܪܐ. *ܡܛܠ ܗܠܝܢ ܓܝܪ ܐܬܐ ܪܘܓܙܗ 6

7 ܕܐܠܗܐ ܥܠ ܒܢܝܐ ܕܠܐ ܡܬܛܦܝܣܢܘܬܐ. *ܒܗܠܝܢ ܐܦ ܐܢܬܘܢ
8 ܗܠܟܬܘܢ ܡܢ ܩܕܝܡ. ܟܕ ܡܬܗܦܟܝܢ ܗܘܝܬܘܢ ܒܗܝܢ. *ܗܫܐ
ܕܝܢ ܐܪܦܘ ܡܢܟܘܢ ܟܠܗܝܢ ܪܘܓܙܐ. ܚܡܬܐ. ܒܝܫܘܬܐ.
9 ܓܘܕܦܐ. ܡܡܠܠܐ ܛܢܦܐ. *ܘܠܐ ܬܗܘܘܢ ܡܟܕܒܝܢ ܚܕ ܥܠ ܚܕ. ܐܠܐ
ܫܠܚܘܗܝ ܠܒܪܢܫܐ ܥܬܝܩܐ ܥܡ ܟܠܗܘܢ ܣܘܥܪܢܘܗܝ.
10 11 *ܘܠܒܫܘ ܚܕܬܐ ܕܡܬܚܕܬ ܒܝܕܥܬܐ ܒܕܡܘܬܐ ܕܒܪܘܝܗ. *ܐܝܟܐ ܕܠܝܬ
ܝܗܘܕܝܐ ܘܐܪܡܝܐ. ܘܠܐ ܓܙܘܪܬܐ ܘܥܘܪܠܘܬܐ. ܘܠܐ ܒܪܒܪܝܐ ܘܣܩܘܬܝܐ.
12 ܘܠܐ ܥܒܕܐ ܘܒܪ ܚܐܪܐ: ܐܠܐ ܟܠ ܘܒܟܠܢܫ ܡܫܝܚܐ ܗܘ. *ܠܒܫܘ
ܗܟܝܠ ܐܝܟ ܓܒܝܐ ܕܐܠܗܐ ܩܕܝܫܐ ܘܡܚܒܒܐ: ܪ̈ܚܡܐ ܘܒܣܝܡܘܬܐ
ܘܡܟܝܟܘܬܐ. ܘܡܟܝܟܘܬ ܪܥܝܢܐ. ܘܢܓܝܪܘܬ ܪܘܚܐ.
13 *ܘܗܘܝܬܘܢ ܡܣܝܒܪܝܢ ܚܕ ܠܚܕ ܘܡܫܒܩܝܢ ܚܕ ܠܚܕ: ܘܐܢ ܐܝܬ
ܠܐܢܫ ܥܠ ܚܒܪܗ ܪܥܡܬܐ: ܐܝܟܢܐ ܕܡܫܝܚܐ ܫܒܩ ܠܟܘܢ:
14 ܗܟܢܐ ܐܦ ܐܢܬܘܢ ܫܒܘܩܘ. *ܘܥܡ ܗܠܝܢ ܟܠܗܝܢ ܚܘܒܐ
15 ܕܗܘܝܘ ܐܣܪܐ ܕܓܡܝܪܘܬܐ. *ܘܫܠܡܗ ܕܡܫܝܚܐ ܢܕܒܪ
ܠܒܘܬܟܘܢ. ܕܠܗ ܐܬܩܪܝܬܘܢ ܒܚܕ ܦܓܪ. ܘܗܘܝܬܘܢ ܡܘܕܝܢ
ܠܡܫܝܚܐ:

Revelations v. 1—10.

1 *ܘܚܙܝܬ ܥܠ ܝܡܝܢܗ ܕܗܘ ܕܝܬܒ ܥܠ ܟܘܪܣܝܐ: ܟܬܒܐ
ܕܟܬܝܒ ܡܢ ܠܓܘ ܘܡܢ ܒܣܬܪ. ܕܚܬܝܡ ܒܫ̈ܒܥܐ ܚܬܡܐ.
2 *ܘܚܙܝܬ ܡܠܐܟܐ ܚܝܠܬܢܐ ܕܡܟܪܙ ܒܩܠܐ ܪܒܐ: ܡܢܘ ܐܝܬܘܗܝ

ܕܗܘܐ ܠܡܦܠܚ ܠܐܕܡܬܐ. ܘܠܡܛܪ ܠܦܪܕܝܣܐ ܕܝܠܗ. *ܘܠܐ 3
ܐܝܬ ܡܬܡܨܝܐ ܗܘܐ ܡܥܕܪܢܐ ܠܟܠܠ: ܘܠܐ ܥܠ ܐܪܥܐ. ܘܠܐ ܠܡܣܥܪ
ܡܢ ܐܪܥܐ. ܠܡܦܠܚ ܠܐܕܡܬܐ ܘܠܐ ܠܡܫܩܝܘܬܗ. *ܘܡܥܝܢܐ ܗܘܐ 4
ܢܦܩ. ܡܛܠ ܕܠܐ ܐܝܬ ܐܢܫ ܕܗܘܐ ܠܡܦܠܚ ܠܐܕܡܬܐ ܘܠܐ
ܠܡܫܩܝܘܬܗ. *ܘܣܒ ܡܢ ܗܢܘܢ ܡܝܐ ܐܡܪ ܠܗ ܠܐ ܛܒܐ. 5
ܗܘ ܐܝܬ ܐܢܫܐ ܗܘ ܕܡܢ ܦܪܕܝܣܐ ܕܝܗܘܒܐ: ܗܘ ܥܦܪܐ ܕܕܡ. ܗܘ
ܢܦܫ ܠܐܕܡܬܐ. ܘܠܡܛܪܐ ܚܠܡܬܐ ܕܝܠܗ. *ܘܚܙܐ ܘܡܫܡܠܝܐ 6
ܕܗܢܘܢ ܡܝܐ: ܐܡܪܐ ܕܦܐܡ ܐܝܟ ܢܦܫܐ. ܕܐܝܬ ܠܗ ܦܪܝܬܐ
ܡܢܗ. ܘܩܝܡܐ ܡܢܗ. ܗܠܝܢ ܕܐܬܗܘܝ ܡܢܗ ܕܘܟܝܐ ܕܟܠܗܘܢ:
ܗܠܝܢ ܕܐܬܦܪܫܝ ܠܚܠܬܗ ܐܪܥܐ. *ܘܐܬܐ ܘܢܦܩ ܚܝܘܬܐ ܡܢ 7
ܡܥܢܝܢܗ ܕܗܘ ܕܢܦܩ ܥܠ ܬܪܝܢܘܗܝ. *ܘܡܢ ܢܦܫܗ ܠܚܝܘܬܐ. 8
ܗܢܝܢ ܐܪܒܥ ܚܝܘܬܐ. ܘܗܢܘܢ ܚܫܝܢ ܘܐܪܒܥܐ ܡܝܢܐ: ܢܦܠܘ
ܡܦܩܘܗܝ ܕܐܡܪܐ. ܟܕ ܐܝܬ ܠܚܠܝܢ ܚܕ ܡܢܗܘܢ ܡܠܐܟܐ ܘܫܠܛܐ
ܕܕܘܟܐ ܕܡܬܬܠܝܢ ܡܢ ܫܡܝܐ: ܗܠܝܢ ܕܐܬܗܘܝ ܠܟܠܬܐ
ܕܡܝܢܐ. *ܘܡܬܩܪܝܢ ܬܫܒܘܚܬܐ ܚܕܬܐ ܟܕ ܐܡܪܝܢ: ܕܗܘܐ 9
ܐܢܫ ܠܡܦܠܚ ܠܐܕܡܬܐ: ܘܠܡܛܪܘ ܠܚܝܘܬܐ ܕܝܠܗ. ܡܛܠ
ܕܬܢܝܢܗ ܘܚܫܒܗ ܠܝ ܠܐܠܗܐ ܡܪܝܐ ܕܝܠܗ. ܡܢ ܟܠ ܦܪܕܝܣܐ
ܘܟܠܢܐ ܘܟܠܢܐ ܘܐܘܡܬܐ: *ܘܡܛܝܒ ܐܢܘܢ ܠܐܠܗܐ ܕܝܠܝ ܡܠܟܬܐ 10
ܘܟܘܢܐ. ܘܡܬܟܢܫܝܢ ܥܠ ܐܪܥܐ.

Revelations xxii. 1—10.

1 *ܘܚܘܝܢܝ ܠܝ ܢܗܪܐ ܕܡܝܐ ܚܝܐ ܢܨܝܚܐ (ܐܝܟ) ܩܪܘܣܛܠܘܣ
2 ܕܢܦܩ ܡܢ ܬܪܘܢܘܣ ܕܐܠܗܐ. ܘܕܐܡܪܐ. *ܒܡܨܥܬܗ ܕܫܘܩܐ
ܫܘܩܐ ܕܝܠܗ. ܘܡܟܐ ܢܗܪܐ ܡܢ ܗܪܟܐ ܘܡܢ ܠܗܠ: ܩܝܣܐ
ܕܚܝܐ. ܕܥܒܕ ܦܐܖ̈ܐ ܬܪܬܥܣܪ. ܕܒܟܠ ܝܪܚܐ ܝܗܒ ܟܠ ܚܕ ܦܐܖ̈ܐ
3 ܕܝܠܗ. ܘܛܪܦܝܗܘܢ ܕܩܝܣܐ. ܠܐܣܝܘܬܐ ܕܥܡܡܐ. *ܘܟܠ ܚܪܡܐ
ܠܐ ܢܗܘܐ ܬܡܢ. ܘܬܪܘܢܘܣ ܕܐܠܗܐ ܘܕܐܡܪܐ ܒܗ ܢܗܘܐ.
4 ܘܥܒܕܘܗܝ ܢܫܡܫܘܢܝܗܝ. *ܘܢܚܙܘܢ ܦܪܨܘܦܗ ܕܝܠܗ.
5 ܘܫܡܗ ܕܝܠܗ ܥܠ ܒܝܬ ܥܝܢܝܗܘܢ. *ܘܠܠܝܐ ܠܐ ܢܗܘܐ
ܬܡܢ. ܘܠܐ ܢܗܘܐ ܠܗܘܢ ܣܘܢܩܢܐ ܕܢܘܗܪܐ ܕܫܪܓܐ. ܘܕܢܘܗܪܐ
ܕܫܡܫܐ. ܡܛܠ ܕܡܪܝܐ ܐܠܗܐ ܡܢܗܪ ܠܗܘܢ. ܘܢܡܠܟܘܢ
6 ܠܥܠܡ ܥܠܡܝܢ. *ܘܐܡܪ ܠܝ. ܗܠܝܢ ܡܠܐ ܡܗܝܡܢܢ ܘܫܪܝܪܢ.
ܘܡܪܝܐ ܐܠܗܐ ܕܪܘܚܐ ܕܢܒܝܐ ܫܕܪ ܠܝ ܠܡܠܐܟܐ ܕܝܠܗ.
ܠܡܚܘܝܘ ܠܥܒܕܘܗܝ ܕܝܠܗ. ܗܠܝܢ ܕܘܠܐ ܠܡܗܘܐ ܥܓܠ.
7 *ܘܗܐ ܐܬܐ ܐܢܐ ܥܓܠ. ܛܘܒܘܗܝ ܠܗܘ ܕܢܛܪ ܠܡܠܐ ܕܢܒܝܘܬܐ ܕܟܬܒܐ
8 ܗܢܐ. *ܘܐܦ ܐܢܐ ܝܘܚܢܢ ܗܘ ܕܫܡܥ ܘܚܙܐ ܗܠܝܢ: ܘܟܕ ܫܡܥܬ
ܐܦ ܚܙܝܬ: ܢܦܠܬ ܠܡܣܓܕ ܩܕܡ ܪܓܠܘܗܝ ܕܡܠܐܟܐ ܗܘ
9 ܕܡܚܘܐ ܗܘܐ ܠܝ ܗܠܝܢ. *ܘܐܡܪ ܠܝ ܚܙܝ. ܠܐ. ܟܢܬܟ ܕܝܠܟ
ܐܢܐ. ܘܕܐܚܝܟ ܢܒܝܐ. ܘܕܗܠܝܢ ܕܢܛܪܝܢ ܠܡܠܐ ܕܟܬܒܐ
10 ܗܢܐ. ܠܐܠܗܐ ܣܓܘܕ. *ܘܐܡܪ ܠܝ ܠܐ ܬܚܬܘܡ ܠܡܠܐ ܕܢܒܝܘܬܐ
ܕܟܬܒܐ ܗܢܐ. ܗܘ ܙܒܢܐ ܓܝܪ ܕܩܪܝܒ ܐܝܬܘܗܝ.

Revelations xxii. 11—21.

11 *ܘܗܘ ܕܡܥܘܠ. ܢܥܘܠ ܬܘܒ. ܘܗܘ ܕܛܢܦ. ܢܛܢܦ ܬܘܒ.
12 ܘܙܕܝܩܐ ܙܕܝܩܘܬܐ ܢܥܒܕ ܬܘܒ. ܘܩܕܝܫܐ ܢܬܩܕܫ ܬܘܒ. *ܗܐ
ܐܬܐ ܐ̱ܢܐ ܥܓܠ. ܘܐܓܪܐ ܕܝܠܝ ܥܡܝ. ܠܡܦܪܥ ܠܟܠܢܫ ܐܝܟ
13 ܕܐܝܬܘܗܝ ܥܒܕܐ ܕܝܠܗ. *ܐܢܐ ܐ̱ܢܐ ܐܠܦ ܘܬܘ. ܗܘ ܩܕܡܝܐ
14 ܘܗܘ ܐ̱ܚܪܝܐ. ܗܘ ܪܫܐ ܘܗܘ ܫܘܠܡܐ. *ܛܘܒܝܗܘܢ ܐܝܠܝܢ ܗܢܘܢ
ܕܥܒܕܝܢ ܠܦܘܩܕܢܘܗܝ ܕܝܠܗ. ܐܝܟܢܐ ܕܢܗܘܐ ܫܘܠܛܢܐ ܕܝܠܗܘܢ.
15 ܥܠ ܩܝܣܐ ܕܚܝܐ ܘܒܬܪܥܐ ܢܥܠܘܢ ܠܡܕܝܢܬܐ. *ܠܒܪ ܟܠܒܐ
ܘܚܪܫܐ ܘܙܢܝܐ. ܘܩܛܘܠܐ ܘܦܠܚܝ ܦܬܟܪܐ. ܘܟܠ ܕܪܚܡ ܘܥܒܕ
16 ܕܓܠܘܬܐ. *ܐܢܐ ܝܫܘܥ ܫܕܪܬ ܠܡܠܐܟܐ ܕܝܠܝ: ܠܡܣܗܕܘ ܠܟܘܢ
ܗܠܝܢ ܩܕܡ ܥܕܬܐ. ܐܢܐ ܐܝܬܝ ܗܘ ܥܩܪܐ ܘܫܪܒܬܐ ܕܕܘܝܕ. ܐܝܟ
17 ܗܘ ܟܘܟܒܐ ܢܗܝܪܐ: ܗܘ ܕܨܦܪܐ. *ܘܪܘܚܐ ܘܟܠܬܐ ܐܡܪܝܢ.
ܬܐ. ܘܗܘ ܕܫܡܥ ܢܐܡܪ. ܬܐ. ܘܗܘ ܕܨܗܐ ܢܐܬܐ. ܘܗܘ ܕܨܒܐ.
18 ܢܣܒ ܡܝܐ ܚܝܐ ܡܓܢ. *ܡܣܗܕ ܐ̱ܢܐ ܠܟܠ ܕܫܡܥ ܠܡܠܐ
ܕܢܒܝܘܬܐ ܕܟܬܒܐ ܗܢܐ. ܕܐܢ ܐ̱ܢܫ ܢܘܣܦ ܥܠܝܗܝܢ: ܢܘܣܦ
19 ܐܠܗܐ ܥܠܘܗܝ ܠܡܚܘܬܐ ܕܟܬܝܒܢ ܒܟܬܒܐ ܗܢܐ. *ܘܐܢ ܐ̱ܢܫ
ܢܒܨܪ ܡܢ ܡܠܐ ܕܟܬܒܐ ܕܢܒܝܘܬܐ ܗܕܐ. ܢܒܨܪ ܐܠܗܐ ܡܢܬܗ
ܡܢ ܩܝܣܐ ܕܚܝܐ. ܘܡܢ ܡܕܝܢܬܐ ܗܝ ܩܕܝܫܬܐ: ܕܟܬܝܒܢ
20 ܒܟܬܒܐ ܗܢܐ. *ܐܡܪ ܗܘ ܕܡܣܗܕ ܗܠܝܢ. ܐܝܢ. ܐܬܐ ܐ̱ܢܐ ܥܓܠ
21 ܐܡܝܢ. ܬܐ ܡܪܝܐ ܝܫܘܥ. *ܛܝܒܘܬܗ ܕܡܪܢ ܝܫܘܥ ܡܫܝܚܐ ܥܡ
ܟܠܗܘܢ ܩܕܝܫܐ. ܐܡܝܢ܀

Psalm xlv. 1---10.

1 *ܐܪܛܢ ܠܒܝ ܡܠܬܐ ܛܒܬܐ. ܘܐܡܪ ܥܒܕܝ̈ ܠܡܠܟܐ: ܠܫܢܝ
2 ܩܢܝܗ ܕܣܦܪܐ ܡܗܝܪܐ. *ܫܦܝܪ ܒܫܘܦܪܗ ܡܢ ܒܢܝ̈ܢܫܐ: ܐܬܢܫܝܒܬ
3 ܛܝܒܘܬܐ ܥܠ ܣܦܘܬܟ. ܡܛܠܗܢܐ ܒܪܟܟ ܐܠܗܐ ܠܥܠܡ. *ܐܣܘܪ
4 ܣܝܦܐ ܒܚܨܝ̈ܟ ܓܢܒܪܐ. *ܗܕܪܟ ܘܫܘܒܚܟ ܐܬܐ: ܪܟܒ ܥܠ
ܡܠܬܐ ܕܩܘܫܬܐ ܘܡܟܝܟܘܬܐ ܕܙܕܝܩܘܬܐ. ܢܠܦܘܢܟ ܒܕܚܠܬܐ
5 ܝܡܝܢܟ: *ܓܐܪ̈ܝܟ ܚܪ̈ܝܦܝܢ ܘܥܡ̈ܡܐ ܢܦܠܘܢ ܬܚܬܝܟ. ܒܠܒܐ
6 ܕܒܥܠܕܒܒ̈ܘܗܝ ܕܡܠܟܐ: *ܟܘܪܣܝܟ ܐܠܗܐ ܠܥܠܡ ܥܠܡܝܢ.
7 ܫܒܛܐ ܦܫܝܛܐ ܫܒܛܐ ܕܡܠܟܘܬܟ: *ܪܚܡܬ ܙܕܝܩܘܬܐ ܘܣܢܝܬ
ܥܘܠܐ. ܡܛܠܗܢܐ ܡܫܚܟ ܐܠܗܐ ܐܠܗܟ: ܡܫܚܐ ܕܚܕܘܬܐ ܝܬܝܪ
8 ܡܢ ܚܒܪ̈ܝܟ. *ܡܘܪܐ ܘܩܛܝܐ ܘܐܩܨܝܥܬܐ: ܡܢ ܠܒܘܫܝ̈ܟ ܡܢ ܗܝܟܠ̈ܐ
9 ܠܫܢܝܟ. ܡܢ ܗܕܐ ܕܫܢܐ ܘܡܢ ܠܟܘܢ ܚܕܝܘܟ: *ܒܢ̈ܬ
ܡܠܟܐ ܒܐܝܩܪܟ ܩܡܬ. ܘܡܠܟܬܐ ܡܢ ܝܡܝܢܟ: ܒܠܒܘܫܐ
10 ܕܕܗܒܐ ܕܐܘܦܝܪ. *ܫܡܥܝ ܒܪܬܝ ܘܚܙܝ: ܘܪܟܢܝ ܐܕܢܟܝ:
ܘܐܬܢܫܝ ܥܡܟܝ ܘܒܝܬ ܐܒܘܟܝ.

Psalm li. 1---10.

1 *ܪܚܡ ܥܠܝ ܐܠܗܐ ܐܝܟ ܛܝܒܘܬܟ: ܘܐܝܟ ܣܘܓܐܐ ܕܪ̈ܚܡܝܟ
2 ܥܛܝ ܚܛܗ̈ܝ. *ܐܣܓܝ ܐܚܠܠܝܢܝ ܡܢ ܥܘܠܝ: ܘܡܢ ܚܛܗ̈ܝ
3 ܕܟܝܢܝ. *ܡܛܠ ܕܥܘ̈ܠܝ ܝܕܥ ܐܢܐ: ܘܚܛܗ̈ܝ ܠܘܩܒܠܝ
4 ܐܝܟ ܒܟܠܙܒܢ. *ܠܟ ܒܠܚܘܕܝܟ ܚܛܝܬ: ܘܒܝܫܬܐ ܩܕܡܝܟ

ܥܒܕܬ. ܡܛܠ ܕܬܙܕܕܩ ܒܡܠܝܟ ܘܬܙܟܐ ܒܕܝܢܝܟ: *ܡܛܠ 5
ܕܒܥܘܠܐ ܐܬܒܛܢܬ ܘܒܚܛܗܐ ܒܛܢܬܢܝ ܐܡܝ: *ܐܢܬ ܕܝܢ 6
ܒܩܘܫܬܐ ܨܒܝܬ. ܘܟܣܝ̈ܬܐ ܕܚܟܡܬܟ ܐܘܕܥܬܢܝ: *ܪܘܣ 7
ܥܠܝ ܒܙܘܦܐ ܘܐܬܕܟܐ. ܢܚܠܠܢܝ ܒܗ ܘܡܢ ܬܠܓܐ ܐܚܘܪ:
*ܐܫܡܥܝܢܝ ܒܣܘܣܝ ܘܚܕܘܬܝ. ܘܢܪܘܙܘܢ ܓܪ̈ܡܝ ܡܟܝ̈ܟܐ: 8
*ܐܗܦܟ ܐܦܝܟ ܡܢ ܚܛܗ̈ܝ. ܘܟܠܗܘܢ ܣܟܠܘ̈ܬܝ ܥܛܝ: 9
*ܠܒܐ ܕܟܝܐ ܒܪܝ ܒܝ ܐܠܗܐ. ܘܪܘܚܐ ܬܪܝܨܬܐ ܚܕܬ ܒܓܘܝ: 10

Psalm civ. 1—10.

*ܒܪܟܝ ܢܦܫܝ ܠܡܪܝܐ. ܡܪܝܐ ܐܠܗܝ ܪܒܬ ܛܒ: ܐܝܩܪܐ ܘܗܕܪܐ 1
ܠܒܫܬ. *ܘܐܬܥܛܦܬ ܢܘܗܪܐ ܐܝܟ ܡܪܛܘܛܐ: ܡܬܚ ܫܡܝܐ ܐܝܟ 2
ܝܪ̈ܝܥܬܐ. *ܕܡܛܠܠ ܒܡ̈ܝܐ ܥܠܝܘܗܝ: ܘܣܐܡ ܥܠ ܥܢ̈ܢܐ ܡܪܟܒܬܗ. 3
ܘܡܗܠܟ ܥܠ ܟܢ̈ܦܝ ܪܘܚܐ: *ܕܥܒܕ ܡܠܐܟܘܗܝ ܪܘܚܐ. 4
ܘܡܫܡܫܢܘܗܝ ܢܘܪܐ ܝܩܕܐ: *ܐܫܬܐܣ ܐܪܥܐ ܥܠ ܡܬܩܢܘܬܗ. ܕܠܐ 5
ܬܙܘܥ ܠܥܠܡ ܠܥܠܡܝܢ: *ܬܗܘܡܐ ܐܝܟ ܡܪܛܘܛܐ ܟܣܝܬܗ. 6
ܥܠ ܛܘܪ̈ܐ ܢܩܘܡܘܢ ܡ̈ܝܐ: *ܡܢ ܟܐܬܟ ܢܥܪܩܘܢ. ܘܡܢ ܩܠܐ ܕܪܥܡܟ 7
ܢܬܕܚܠܘܢ: *ܣܠܩܝܢ ܛܘܪ̈ܐ ܘܢܚܬܝܢ ܒܩܥܬܐ. ܠܐܬܪܐ ܕܫܬܐܣܬ 8
ܠܗܘܢ: *ܬܚܘܡܐ ܣܡܬ ܠܗܘܢ. ܕܠܐ ܢܥܒܪܘܢ ܘܢܗܦܟܘܢ ܠܐܪܥܐ: 9
*ܡܫܕܪ ܡܒ̈ܘܥܐ ܒܢ̈ܚܠܐ. ܘܒܝܢܝ ܛܘܪ̈ܐ ܡܗܠܟܝܢ: 10

CHRESTOMATHY.

NOTES ON THE READING LESSONS.

After having analyzed the first page of the Chrestomathy, and thus given a specimen of the manner in which the learner should proceed in reading his first lessons in Syriac, it will only be necessary, in respect to the remaining pages of the Chrestomathy, to explain the derivation and formation of the most difficult words which there occur. Thus the student will be thrown upon his own resources, and be induced, it is hoped, to assiduously study his grammar.

EXPLANATIONS.

Matthew ii. 1—10.

1) Verse 1. word 3., ܐܬܝܠܕ is a verb in the Ethpeel conjugation, from ܝܠܕ.

2) V. 1. w.7., ܒܝܘܡܝ is compounded of ܒ a preposition and ܝܘܡܝ a noun of the fourth decl. construct plural, from ܝܘܡ.

3) V. 1. w. 10., ܐܬܘ is a verb from ܐܬܐ Pe. pret. 3d. masc. plural (vid. ¶18. 16).

4) V. 2. w. 5., ܝܠܝܕ is a verb from ܝܠܕ.

5) V. 2. w. 10., ܠܡܣܓܕ is a verb in the infin. pret., from ܣܓܕ.

6) V. 3. w. 5., ܐܬܬܙܝܥ is a verb in Ethpeel conjugation, from ܙܘܥ or ܙܥ.

7) V. 4. w. 1., ܟܢܫ is a verb in Pa. conjugation, from ܟܢܫ.

8) V. 4. w. 2., ܒܢܰܝܗܽܘܢ-from ܒܪ and takes the noun suffix-3d masc. plural.

9) V. 4. w. 3., ܕܶܒܪ̈ܰܝ-constr. plural from ܕܒܪ.

10) V. 4. w. 7., ܡܫܰܠܶܠ-is a part. from ܫܠܠ.

11) V. 4. w. 8 and 11., ܗܘܳܐ——ܡܫܰܠܰܡ. These two words indicate the imperfect tense, the latter word being a passive participle (vid. § 64. 2. B. *a;* § 65. B. *a*).

12) V. 6. w. 6., ܗܘܰܝܬܽܘܢ is a verb in the second person from ܗܘܳܐ.

13) V. 6. w. 12., ܢܶܥܡܽܘܕ-third, masc. fut. Pe., from ܥܡܕ.

14) V. 6. w. 15., ܢܶܕܟܪܽܘܢܳܗ is a verb in the fut. with suffix, from ܕܟܪ.

15) V. 7. w. 8., ܡܳܐܢܳܐ is compounded of ܐܢܐ and ܡ (vid. Lexicon).

16) V. 7. w. 10., ܐܶܬܚܰܣܝ is a verb in Ethpe. pret. from ܚܣܐ.

17) V. 8. w. 6., ܐܙܶܠܘ is a verb in the imperative from ܐܙܠ (vid. §28. 1 and 2).

18) V. 8. w. 7., ܥܡܽܕܘ, imperative from ܥܡܕ.

19) V. 8. w. 12., ܕܐܰܠܡܶܕܬܽܘܢܳܝܗܝ is composed of ܝܗܝ-meaning *him*-3d. masc. suffix, ܕ *that* a conjunction*-and ܐܰܠܡܶܕܬܽܘܢ a verb in Aph. conjugation, 2d. plural, from ܠܡܕ.

20) V. 8. w. 13., ܬܘ is a verb 2d. pl. masc. (vid. § 28. 2. Rem.)-imperative from ܐܬܐ *to come.*

21) V. 8. w. 14., ܢܛܰܪܽܘܢܳܝܗܝ is a verb from ܢܛܰܪ——2d. masc. plural, imperative, with a suffix pronoun (vid. § 37. table of verbs ܠܐ with suffixes ; § 37. 3).

22) V. 10. w. 5., ܚܰܘܘ is a verb from ܚܘܐ.

23) V. 10. w. 7., ܪܰܒܰܬ is an adjective noun, fem. sing. construct, from ܪܒ.

*In connection with the preceding word ܡܳܐ, it forms a compound conjunction meaning *when.* (vid. § 85. 4. *d. a*).

Mark xiv. 32—42.

24) V. 32. w. 4., ܕܡܬܩܪܝܐ is composed of ܡܬܩܪܝܐ and ܕ. The relative ܕ with the preceding pronoun should be rendered *that which* (vid. § 56. 3. *a*)–ܡܬܩܪܝܐ is an Ethpe. pass. participle, from ܩܪܐ.

25) V. 32. w. 8., ܬܒܘ–imperative from ܝܬܒ (§ 29. 2. Rem).

26) V. 32. w. 11., ܡܨܠܐ–Pa. act. participle from ܨܠܐ.

27) V. 33. w. 7., ܠܡܬܡܗܘ is composed of the prefix preposition and the verb—infinitive Ethpe.

28) V. 33. w. 8., ܘܠܡܬܟܪܝܘ is composed of the conjunction ܘ, the prep. ܠ and the verb in the infinitive from ܟܪܐ or ܟܪܝ.

29) V. 34. w. 9., ܩܘܘ– imperative from ܩܘܐ.

30) V. 34. w. 11., ܘܐܬܬܥܝܪܘ–imperative, Ethpe. from ܥܘܪ or ܥܪ.

31) V. 35. w. 9., ܡܫܟܚܐ–Aph. fem. participle, from ܫܟܚ.

32) V. 35. w. 10., ܬܥܒܪ–Pe. future, from ܥܒܪ.

33) V. 37. w. 5., ܕܡܟܝܢ is a participle, plural from ܕܡܟ and that from the verb ܕܡܟ.

34) V. 37. w. 15., ܠܡܬܬܥܝܪܘ–infinitive, Ethpe. from ܥܘܪ or ܥܪ.

35) V. 38. w. 2., ܨܠܘ *pray*–imperative, Pa. from ܨܠܐ.

36) V. 38. w. 4., ܬܥܠܘܢ (ye) *shall enter*–Pe. fut. 2nd. plural, from ܥܠܠ or ܥܠ.

37) V. 38. w. 8., ܡܛܝܒܐ *willing*–act. part. f. Pa. from ܛܘܒ.

38) V. 40. w. 9., ܥܝܢܝܗܘܢ *their eyes*–from ܥܝܢܐ with a plural suffix pronoun.

39) V. 40. w. 10., ܝܩܝܪܢ *heavy*–an adjective in the plural, from ܝܩܝܪ.

40) V. 40. w. 13., ܝܕܥܝܢ *knew*–from ܝܕܥ.

41) V. 41. w. 8., ܐܬܬܢܝܚܘ *rest ye*–Ethpe. imperative from ܢܘܚ or ܢܚ.

42) V. 41. w. 14., ܡܫܬܠܡ *being betrayed*–Ethpe. participle from ܫܠܡ.

43) V. 42. w. 2., ܢܐܙܠ future of ܐܙܠ *to go.*

44) V. 42. w. 6., ܡܫܠܡ *betraying*–Aph. participle from ܫܠܡ.

Luke xxiii. 18—27.

45) V. 18. w. 1., ܩܥܘ *cried out*–3d. masc. plural, from ܩܥܐ.

46) V. 18. w. 6., ܫܩܘܠܝܗܝ *take him away*–2nd. masc. plural, imperative, with suffix pronoun (vid. § 36. E table of suffixes).

47) V. 20. w. 8., ܢܫܪܐ–future from ܫܪܐ *to release.*

48) V. 21. w. 6., ܐܙܩܦܝܗܝ *crucify him*–imperative, with a suffix from ܐܙܩܦ.

49) V. 22. w. 19., ܐܪܕܝܘܗܝ–*I will chastise him*–fut. 1st. sing. Pe. from ܪܕܐ with a suffix pronoun.

50) V. 22. w. 21., ܐܫܒܩܝܘܗܝ–*I will let him go*–future, Pe. 1st. singular, with a suffix pronoun, from ܫܒܩ.

51) V. 23. w. 3., ܡܬܟܒܝܢ with ܗܘܘ *urged*–a part. from ܐܬܟܒ.

52) V. 23. w. 10., ܢܙܩܦܘܢܝܗܝ (that) *they shall crucify him*–pret. Pe. fut. 3d. masc. plural, with suffix pronoun, from ܙܩܦ (vid. § 36. Table).

53) V. 24. w. 4., ܬܗܘܐ *should be*–future of ܗܘܐ.

54) V. 24. w. 5., ܫܐܠܬܗܘܢ (according to) *their desire*–a feminine, sing. noun, with a plural suffix (§ 16. Table).

55) V. 25. w. 16., ܨܒܝܢܗܘܢ *their will*–a noun with a suffix plural from ܨܒܝܢ.

56) V. 26. w. 2., ܡܘܒܠܝܢ *leading* or *causing to lead away*–Aph. part. plural from ܝܒܠ.

57) V. 26. w. 4., ܐܚܕܘܗ *laid hold of*–from ܐܚܕ.

58) V. 26. w. 13., ܢܛܥܢ *might carry*–future from ܛܥܢ.

59) V. 27. w. 8., ܡܪܩܕܝܢ *bewailing*–Aph. part. from ܪܩܕ.

Luke xxiii. 33—42.

60) V. 33. w. 5., ܡܬܩܪܐ *called*–Ethpe. pass. participle, from ܩܪܐ.

61) V. 34. w. 7., ܫܒܘܩ *forgive*–imperative, from ܫܒܩ.

62) V. 34. w. 16., ܐܪܡܝܘ *cast*–Aph. 3d. plural from ܪܡܐ.

63) V. 35. w. 1., ܩܐܡ *standing*–participle from ܩܘܡ.

64) V. 35. w. 12., ܠܐܚܪ̈ܢܐ *to others*–plural from ܐܚܪܝܢ–with the prefix prep. Lomad.

65) V. 35. w. 13., ܐܚܝ *saved*–Aph. pret. from ܚܝܐ.

66) V. 35. w. 14., ܢܚܐ *shall save*–Aph. future, from ܚܝܐ.

67) V. 36. w. 1., ܡܒܙܚܝܢ *mocking*–part. from ܒܙܚ.

68) V. 37. w. 8., ܐܚܐ *save*–imperat. Aph. from ܚܝܐ.

69) V. 42. w. 3., ܐܬܕܟܪܝܢܝ *remember me*–imperat. Ethpe. with suf. from ܕܟܪ.

Luke xxiii. 43—53.

70) V. 45. w. 3., ܐܨܛܪܝ *was rent*–Ethpe. part. from ܨܪܐ. ܬ is transposed and changed into ܛ (§ 12. 2. Rem.).

71) V. 46. w. 3., ܩܠܐ *voice*–with a prefix preposition.

72) V. 46. w. 7., ܒܐܝܕܝܟ *into thy hands*–from ܐܝܕ with a prefix preposition, and a suffix pronoun.

73) V. 46. w. 8., ܣܐܡ *confiding*–Pe. act. participle from ܣܘܡ.

74) V. 48. w. 4., ܐܬܟܢܫܘ *came together*–Aph. pret. plural from ܟܢܫ.

75) V. 48. w. 16., ܬܕ̈ܝܗܘܢ *their breasts*–from ܬܕܝܐ with suf. plural.

76) V. 49. w. 1., ܩܝ̈ܡܝܢ *standing*–part. Pe. plural from ܩܘܡ.

77) V. 49. w. 6., ܝܕ̈ܘܥܘܗܝ *his acquaintance*–from ܝܕܘܥܐ with suffix.

78) V. 51. w. 7., ܡܣܟܝܢ̈ܐ *waiting*–participle from ܣܟܐ.

79) V. 53. w. 1., ܐܚܬܗ *took down*–Aph. pret. from ܢܚܬ.

80) V. 53. w. 8., ܢܩܝܪܐ *dug out*–part. passive, Peal from ܢܩܪ.

81) V. 53. w. 13., ܐܬܬܣܝܡ *was laid*–Ethpe. pret. from ܣܘܡ. ܬ is doubled (vid. § 12. 2. Rem ; § 31. 2).

Acts xvii. 22—32.

82) V. 23. w. 3., ܡܬܥܒܪ *passing by*–Ethpe. part. from ܥܒܪ.

83) V. 23. w. 9., ܐܫܟܚܬ *I found*–Aph. pret. 1st. singular from ܫܟܚ.

84) V. 23. w. 14., ܥܠܘܗܝ *on it* ܥܠ with a suffix.

85) V. 23. w. 29., ܡܣܒܪ *declare*–Pa. part. from ܣܒܪ.

86) V. 25. w. 2., ܡܫܬܡܫܝܢ *worshipping*–Ethpa. part. from ܫܡܫ.

87) V. 26. w. 8., ܢܗܘܘܢ *shall be*, with ܥܡܪܝܢ *should dwell*–Pe. fut. 3d. plural of the defective verb ܗܘܐ.

88) V. 27 w. 2., ܒܥܝܢ *seeking*–participle from ܒܥܐ.

89) V. 27. w. 4., ܡܓܫܫܝܢ *seeking, feeling*–Pael pass. participle from ܓܫܫ.

90) V. 28. w. 4., ܚܝܝܢ *our life*–pl. absolute form with suf. ܝܢ from ܚܝ̈ܐ.

91) V. 28. w. 5., ܡܬܬܙܝܥܝܢ *our moving*–Ethpe. part. and suffix from ܙܘܥ or ܙܥ.

92) V. 28. w. 6., ܐܝܬܝܢ *are*–1st. person plural from ܐܝܬ.

93) V. 28. w. 12., ܕܥܡܟܘܢ *who with you*–composed of ܟܘܢ *you;* ܥܡ *with* and ܕ *who.*

94) V. 28. w. 16., ܬܘܠܕܬܢ *our offspring*–from ܬܘܠܕܬܐ with suffix pronoun.

95) V. 29. w. 8., ܚܘܒܬܢ *our debt,* from ܚܘܒܐ with a suffix.

96) V. 29. w. 9., ܡܣܒܪ *to think*–infinitive, Pe. from ܣܒܪ.

97) V. 29. w. 15., ܓܠܝܦܐ *written* or *graven*–participle, Pe. from ܓܠܦ.

98) V. 29. w. 16., ܒܐܘܡܢܘܬܐ *by art,* from ܐܘܡܢܘܬܐ.

99) V. 30. w. 15., ܢܬܘܒ *shall repent*–future Pe. from ܬܘܒ or ܬܒ.

100) V. 31. w. 6., ܕܢܕܘܢ *that shall judge*–future Pe. from ܕܢ with the prefix ܕ.

101) V. 31. w. 14., ܘܐܘܕܥ *and showed, made known*–Aph. from ܝܕܥ.

102) V. 32. w 8., ܡܡܝܩܝܢ *mocking*–participle, Pa. from ܡܝܩ.

Romans vi. 1—10.

103) V. 1. w. 4., ܢܩܘܐ *shall remain*–Pa. future from ܩܘܐ.

104) V. 1. w. 8., ܬܬܝܬܪ *shall be abundant*–Ethpa. future from ܝܬܪ.

105) V. 2. w. 7., ܢܚܐ *shall live*–future Pe. from ܚܝܐ.

106) V. 3. w. 6., ܕܥܡܕܢ *who were baptized*–pret. Pe. 1st. pl. com. from ܥܡܕ with the prefix ܕ.

107) V. 4. w. 1., ܐܬܩܒܪܢ *are buried*–Ethpe. pret. 1st. pl. com. from ܩܒܪ.

108) V. 4. w. 14., ܕܐܒܘܗܝ *of his father*–a noun in the suffix state,

3d. masc. singular, from ܐܒ with the prefix ܕ.

109) V. 4. w. 20., ܢܗܠܟܘܢ *should walk*–future Pa. from ܗܠܟ.

110) V. 5. w. 4., ܐܬܢܨܒ *have been planted*–Ethpe. pret. from ܢܨܒ.

111) V. 5. w. 11., ܢܗܘܐ *shall be*–future Pe. from ܗܘܐ.

112) V. 6. w. 1., ܝܕܥܝܢܢ *knowing*–participle, with a suffix from ܝܕܥ.

113) V. 6. w. 5., ܐܙܕܩܦ *is crucified*–Ethpe. pret. from ܙܩܦ.

114) V. 6. w. 7., ܕܢܬܒܛܠ *that should be destroyed*–Ethpa. from ܒܛܠ with the prefix ܕ.

115) V. 8. w. 6., ܢܗܝܡܢ *believe*–Aph. future from ܐܡܢ.

116) V. 8 w. 10., ܢܚܐ *shall live*–future Pe. from ܚܝܐ.

117) V. 9. w. 13., ܡܬܚܝܠ *being powerful*–Ethpa. participle from ܚܝܠ.

118) V. 10. w. 9., ܡܚܐ *living*–part. Aph. from ܚܝܐ.

COLOSSIANS iii. 1—15.

119) V. 1. w. 7., ܒܥܘ *seek*–imperative of ܒܥܐ.

120) V. 2. w. 2., ܐܬܪܥܘ *let your affections be placed*–Ethpe. imperative, from ܪܥܐ.

121) V. 3. w. 4., ܘܚܝܝܟܘܢ *your life*–from ܚܝܐ with a suffix pron. and the prefix ܘ.

122) V. 4. w. 9., ܬܬܚܙܘܢ (ye) *shall appear*–future Ethpe. from ܚܙܐ.

123) V. 5. w. 1., ܐܡܝܬܘ *mortify*–Aph. imperative from ܡܝܬ.

124) V. 5. w. 3., ܗܕܡܝܟܘܢ *your members*–Suffix state, 2nd. masc. plural from ܗܕܡܐ.

125) V. 5. w. 11 and 12., ܕܗܘܝܘ ܗܘܝܘ. These pronouns seem to include the substantive verb (comp. § 54. 3. *a*).

126) V. 7. w. 8., ܡܬܗܦܟܝܢ *turning* or *having turned*-Ethpa. from ܗܦܟ.

127) V. 8. w. 3., ܐܢܝܚܘ *put away*-Aph. from ܢܘܚ or ܢܚ.

128) V. 9. w. 2., ܬܗܘܘܢ *ye shall be*-future from ܗܘܐ.

129) V. 9. w. 3., ܡܕܓܠܝܢ *lying, deceitful*-participle Pa., from ܕܓܠ.

130) V. 9. w. 7., ܫܠܘܚܘܗܝ *put off, cast away*-imperative Pe., from ܫܠܚ. It takes a suffix.

131) V. 9. w. 12., ܗܘܦܟ̈ܘܗܝ *his deeds*-suff. state, plural from ܗܘܦܟܐ.

132) V. 10. w. 3., ܕܡܬܚܕܬܐ *who being renewed*-Ethpa. part. passive from ܚܕܬ with the prefix ܕ.

133) V. 10. w. 6., ܕܒܪܝܗ *who created him*-from ܒܪܐ with a suf. pronoun, with the prefix ܕ.

134) V. 12. w. 7., ܘܚܒܝ̈ܒܐ *and beloved*-plural from ܚܒܝܒܐ with the prefix ܘ.

135) V. 13. w. 1., ܘܗܘܝܬܘܢ *and ye*-from ܗܘܐ with the verbal termination-2nd. pl. with the prefix ܘ.

136) V. 13. w. 2., ܡܣܝܒܪܝܢ *forbearing*-Pa. part. from ܣܒܪ.

137) V. 15. w. 1., ܘܫܠܡܗ *and his peace*, from ܫܠܡܐ with suf. pronoun, and prefix ܘ.

138) V. 15. w. 4., ܠܒܘܬܟܘܢ *your hearts*, from ܠܒܐ with suf. pron.

139) V. 15. w. 6., ܐܬܩܪܝܬܘܢ *ye are called*-Eth. 2nd. plural from ܩܪܐ.

140) V. 15. w. 10., ܡܘܕܝܢ *thankful*-part. active Aph. from ܝܕܐ.

Revelations v. 1—10.

141) V. 1. w. 1., ܘܚܙܝܬ *and I saw*–Aph. pret. 1st. sing. from ܚܙܐ with prefix ܘ.

142) V. 2. w. 10., ܠܡܦܬܚ *to open*–Pe. infinitive from ܦܬܚ with prefix ܠ.

143) V. 3. w. 17., ܠܡܚܙܝܗ *to look on it*–infin. with suffix from ܚܙܐ with the prefix ܠ.

144) V. 4. w. 2., ܗܘܝܬ *it is*–formed from ܐܝܬ and ܗܘ, ܐ being dropped. The phrase, including the word preceding and the one following, means literally, *it is weeping much.*

145) V. 4. w. 7., ܐܫܬܟܚ *was found*–Ethpe. from ܫܟܚ.

146) V. 5. w. 8., ܬܒܟܐ literally *thou shalt weep*–2nd. per. fut. masc–put for the imperative (vid. § 61. B. *a*).

147) V. 6. w. 6., ܕܩܐܡ *to stand.* ܩܐܡ is a participle from ܩܘܡ (vid. § 64. 3. B. Rem.).

148) V. 6. w. 8., ܢܟܝܣܬܐ *slain*–pass. part. Peal. fem. from ܢܟܣ.

149) V. 6. w. 21., ܕܐܫܬܕܪ̈ܝ *who were sent*–3d. per. f. plural, Ethpa. from ܫܕܪ.

Revelations xxii. 1—10.

150) V. 2. w. 23., ܘܛܪ̈ܦܘܗܝ *and leaves of it*–from ܛܪܦܐ with a suffix, and prefix ܘ.

151) V. 3. w. 4., ܢܗܘܐ *shall be*–future of ܗܘܐ.

152) V. 3. w. 14., ܢܫܡܫܘܢܝܗܝ *shall serve him*–fut. 3d. masc. plural, Pa. from ܫܡܫ with a suffix.

153) V. 5. w. 16., ܡܢܗܪ *causing to shine*–Aph. part. masc. from ܢܗܪ.

154) V. 6. w. 15., ܠܡܚܘܝܘ *to show*–infinitive, Pa. from ܚܘܐ.

155) V. 8. w. 13., ܠܡܣܓܕ *to worship, to praise*–infinitive, Peal from ܣܓܕ.

156) V. 11. w. 7., ܢܬܛܡܐ *shall be filthy*–fut. Ethpa. from ܛܡܐ.

157) V. 14. w. 15., ܢܥܠܘܢ *they shall enter in*–fut. 3d. masc. Peal from ܥܠ.

158) V. 17. w. 4., ܬܐ *come*–imperative of ܐܬܐ.

159) V. 19. w. 3., ܢܒܨܪ *shall take away*–Peal future from ܒܨܪ.

POETRY.

We present a few specimens of Syriac poetry, taken from the Peshito Bible, published by the British and Foreign Bible Society, in 1826. It will be observed that the text does not appear in a rhythmical form, nor are there any divisions into verses. The Peshito or *literal* version was made near the close of the first, or beginning of the second century, while the divisions into chapters and verses were introduced in the thirteenth century. Points, in addition to *Ribui*, will be noticed over and under particular letters. These are intended to mark the occurrence of *Kushoi* and *Rukok*.

Psalm xlv. 1—10.

1) Verse 2. word 9., ܡܛܠܗܢܐ *therefore.* This is composed of the conjunction ܡܛܠ and the suffix pronoun ܗܢܐ. Conjunctions as well as other particles often take suffixes.

2) V. 3. w. 1., ܐܪܡܐ *cast* (gird)–Aph. imperative, from ܪܡܐ. See a similar instance in Matt. xvii. 27.

Psalm li. 1—10.

3) V. 2. w. 1., ܐܣܓܝ *multiply*–imperative, Aph. from ܣܓܝ used here adverbially in the sense of *very much.*

4) V. 2. w. 2., ܐܚܠܠܝܢܝ *wash me*–imperative, Aph. from ܚܠܠ with a suffix pronoun.

5) V. 2. w. 7., ܕܟܝܢܝ *cleanse me*–imperative, *Pa.* from ܕܟܳܐ with a suffix pronoun.

6) V. 3. w. 8., ܒܟܠܙܒܢ *in all time, always*–from ܟܠ *all*, ܙܒܢ *time* and the prefix preposition, ܒ *in*.

7) V. 4. w.8., ܕܬܙܕܕܩ *that thou mightest be just–Ethpa.* 2nd. sing. masc. future from ܐܙܕܩ. The preformative falls away as the conjunction ܕ precedes.

8) V. 6. w. 7., ܐܘܕܥܬܢܝ *thou makest me to know*–2nd. sing. pret. Aph. from ܝܕܥ with a suffix pronoun.

9) V. 9. w. 7., ܠܚܝ *blot out*–imperative Pe. from ܠܚܐ.

Psalm civ. 1—10.

10) V. 5. w. 1., ܐܬܩܢ *prepared, laid–Ethpe.* from ܬܩܢ.

11) V. 5. w. 4., ܡܬܩܢܢܗ–participle with a suffix pronoun from ܬܩܢ.

12) V. 7. w. 7., ܡܬܪܗܒܝܢ *hastening*–an *Ethpe.* participle, from ܪܗܒ.

13) V. 9. w. 6., ܘܢܟܣܘܢܗ *and* (that) *they should not cover*–3d. plural, Pa. from ܟܣܐ with a suffix pronoun, and the conjunction ܘ preceding.

SYRIAC LEXICON.

ܐܰܒ, ܐܰܒܳܐ, suf. ܐܰܒܽܘܗܝ a father, pl. ܐܰܒܳܗܳܬܳܐ ܐܰܒܳܗ̈ܶܐ parents.

ܐܒܰܕ to perish, Aph. to cause to perish, to destroy.

ܐܶܒܰܠ to be sad, to be disturbed.

ܐܰܒܢܺܝܠ *Abnil* (name of an idol).

ܐܰܒܪܳܗܳܡ Abraham.

ܐܰܓܪܳܐ m. a reward.

ܐܶܓܰܪܬܳܐ a letter, a writing.

ܐܶܕܢܳܐ an ear.

ܐܰܘ or.

ܐܳܘ O! (mark of the vocative).

ܐܰܘܟܺܝܠ namely, that is (from ܐܰܘ and ܟܺܝܠ).

ܐܽܘܡܳܢܽܘܬܳܐ skill, ability.

ܐܽܘܡܬܳܐ f. a nation.

ܐܽܘܦܺܝܪ Ophir (a proper name).

ܐܽܘܪܗܳܝ Edessa in Mesopotamia (a proper name).

ܐܽܘܪܚܳܐ a way.

ܐܽܘܪܳܝܬܳܐ the law book of Moses, the Pentateuch.

ܐܽܘܪܺܫܠܶܡ Jerusalem.

ܐܶܙܰܠ to go, to go away.

ܐܰܚܳܐ brother.

ܐܶܚܰܕ to hold, to seize, to lay hold of.

ܐܰܚܪܳܝܳܐ the last, the end.

ܐ̱ܚܪܺܢ, ܐ̱ܚܪܺܢܳܐ another; fem. ܐ̱ܚܪܺܬܳܐ, pl. m. ܐ̱ܚܪ̈ܢܶܐ, ܐ̱ܚܪ̈ܢܳܐ.

ܐܰܝܓܽܘܦܛܳܝܳܐ an Egyptian.

ܐܰܝܓܽܘܦܛܳܐܺܝܬ *Adverb*, like the Egyptians.

ܐܺܝܕܳܐ hand—in Hebrew יָד.

ܐܰܝܕܳܐ who, which, fem. of ܐܰܝܢܳܐ.

ܐܰܝܟ so as, according to, as to, (*secundum*) nearly, ܐܰܝܟ ܕ just as, therewith.

ܐܰܝܟܳܐ where? ܐܰܝܟܳܐ ܕ there, where; ܠܰܐܝܟܳܐ whither? ܡܶܢ ܐܰܝܟܳܐ whence?

ܐܰܝܟܰܘ where.

ܐܝܟ.

ܐܝܟ, ܐܝܟܢܐ how? ܐܝܟܢܐ ܕ so that.

ܐܝܠܝܢ pl. they.

ܐܝܢ truly, certainly, yes.

ܐܝܢܐ who, what–ܒܐܝܢܐ at what.

ܐܝܣܚܩ Isaac (a proper name).

ܐܝܣܪܐܝܠ Israel (a proper name).

ܐܝܩܪܐ honor, a mark of esteem, a solemn procession.

ܐܝܬ it is, ܐܝܬܝ I am, etc.

ܐܟܕܢܐ serpent (ἔχιδνα).

ܐܟܚܕ at the same time–together.

ܐܟܠ to eat, to consume.

ܐܟܘܬܐ just as, ܐܟܘܬܐ ܕ of such a quality (*qualis*).

ܐܟܣܢܝܐ a stranger, a guest (ξένος).

ܐܠܐ but, yet (ἀλλά), if not (= ܠܐ ܐܢ).

ܐܠܐ to lament.

ܐܠܗܐ God.

ܐܠܗܝܐ godly.

ܐܠܗܘܬܐ f. divinity, the godhead.

ܐܠܟܣܢܕܪܝܐ an Alexandrian.

ܐܠܦ Olaph, the first letter of the alphabet.

ܐܢܫ̈ܐ.

ܐܠܦ to learn, Aph. to cause to learn, to teach.

ܐܠܦܐ a ship.

ܐܠܨ to constrain, to compel, to urge any one, ܐܠܝܨ oppressed.

ܐܠܝܨܐ oppressed.

ܐܡܐ mother.

ܐܡܝܕ *Amida* in Mesopotamia (a proper name).

ܐܡܝܢ, ܐܡܝܢܐ, surely, firmly.

ܐܡܢ *Aph.* ܗܝܡܢ, fut. ܢܗܝܡܢ to believe.

ܐܡܝܢܐܝܬ Adv. constantly.

ܐܡܪ to say, to speak.

ܐܡܪܐ a lamb.

ܐܡܬܝ (with ܕ following) if.

ܐܢ if.

ܐܢܐ I, pl. ܚܢܢ we.

ܐܢܘܢ m. ܐܢܝܢ f., that (*as Acc.*)

ܐܢܛܝܢܘܣ *Antinum* (a proper name).

ܐܢܚ *Ethpa.* to sigh.

ܐܢܫ man, a certain man, pl. ܐܢܫ̈ܐ and ܐܢܫܐ.

ܐܢܫܘܬܐ humanity, *as concrete*, mankind.

ܐܢܬ m. ܐܢܬܝ f. thou; pl. ܐܢܬܘܢ m.

ܐܢܬܝܢ f. you.

ܐܢܬܬܐ a woman, a wife.

ܐܣܝܘܬܐ a healing.

ܐܣܘܪܐ a bound, pl ܐܣܘܪܐ ܒܝܬ a prison.

ܐܣܛܘܢܪܐ stylite (according to Assem.)

ܐܣܛܣܝܣ sedition.

ܐܣܛܘܟܐ oil of cinnamon.

ܐܣܛܪܛܝܘܛܐ a soldier.

ܐܣܟܝܡܐ external appearance, dress, (σχῆμα).

ܐܣܟܝܡܬܢܐ hypocrite

ܐܦ also, ܐܦܠܐ neither.

ܐܦܐ, ܐܦܝ face, ܐܦܝ ܟܠ over, ܠܐܦܝ according to, towards.

ܐܦܣܩܘܦܐ a bishop.

ܐܩܦ to be anxious, uneasy.

ܐܪܒܥܐ ܐܪܒܥ four.

ܐܪܛܝܩܐ heterodox.

ܐܪܝܐ a lion.

ܐܪܝܘܣ Arius.

ܐܪܝܘܣ ܦܓܘܣ Areopagite.

ܐܪܟܘܢܐ a ruler, a chief man.

ܐܪܡܝܐ a Syrian, a Gentile.

ܐܪܣܝܘܛܐ an errorist, a heretic.

ܐܪܣܝܣ heresy (αἵρεσις).

ܐܪܥܐ earth, land, country.

ܐܫܟܚ to find, *Ethpe.* to be found.

ܐܫܬܐ ܝܘܡܝܢ the six days work, the creation.

ܐܬܐ to come, *Aph.* to lead, to bring, to conduct.

ܐܬܪ, ܐܬܪܐ a place, a region.

ܒ.

ܒ in, from, through, to.

ܒܠܢܝܐ a possessor of a bath.

ܒܐܡ, ܒܐܡܐ a pulpit (βῆμα).

ܒܗܪܟܐ hence.

ܒܗܬ to be ashamed, *Aph.* to make ashamed.

ܒܗܬܬܐ shame, disgrace.

ܒܘܠܘܛܐ, ܒܘܠܘܛܝܣ a counselor.

ܒܘܣܡܐ agreeableness, amiableness.

ܒܘܪܐ awkward, uneducated.

ܒܙܚ. | ܒܪܟ.

ܒܙܚ *Pa.* ܒܙܚ to deride, to mock.

ܒܚܪܬܐ (from ܐܚܪܬܐ end) finally.

ܒܛܠ to cease, to destroy.

ܒܛܢ to conceive.

ܒܛܢܬܐ pregnant.

ܒܝܢܝ among, between.

ܒܝܫ m. ܒܝܫܬܐ evil.

ܒܝܫ m. an evil person—pl. ܒܝ̈ܫܝ, ܒܝܫܬܐ.

ܒܝܫܘܬܐ malice.

ܒܝܫܘܝ Besoe (a monk—proper name).

ܒܝܬ = ܒܝܢܬ between, by; ܒܝܢܬ ܡܢ ܒܝܢܬ out; ܢܗܪ̈ܝܢ ܒܝܬ Mesopotamia.

ܒܝܬ, ܒܝܬܐ a house, ܪ̈ܗܘܡܝܐ ܒܝܬ the Roman dominion.

ܒܝܬܠܚܡ Bethlehem (a proper name).

ܒܟܐ to weep.

ܒܠܥܕ without.

ܒܢܝܐ pl. m. sons. ܒܢ̈ܝ ܐܢܫܐ *Const.* ܒܢܝ̈ܢܫܐ men, lit. sons of men. ܒܪ is always used in the sing. for son.

ܒܣܐ to despise. *Part.* P. ܒܣܐ despised.

ܒܣܝܠܝܘܣ Basilius (a proper name.

ܒܣܝܡܘܬܐ f. joy, benignity.

ܒܣܬܪܐ m. back.

ܒܣܡ to perfume.

ܒܣܡܐ odors.

ܒܥܐ to seek, with ܡܢ to entreat, to demand.

ܒܥܠܕܒܒܐ enemy, an adversary.

ܒܥܬܐ the seeking, the finding out.

ܒܨܪ to take away.

ܒܨܝܪ m. small—ܒܨܝܪܬܐ feminine.

ܒܨܝܪܘܬܐ a small matter (for the *Adj.* small).

ܒܨܐ to explore, to discover, *Ethpa.* with ܒ to contemplate.

ܒܩܐ a gnat, a midge.

ܒܪ, ܒܪܐ son. ܒܪ ܡܕܝܢܬܐ ܒܢ̈ܝ an inhabitant of the city.

ܒܪܐ to create.

ܒܪܐܒܐ Barabbas (a proper name).

ܒܪܒܪܝܐ a Barbarian.

ܒܪܕܝܨܢ Bardesanes (a proper name).

ܒ̈ܬܐ houses, pl. feminine.

ܒܪܟ to fall down, to bend the knees, *Ethpa.* to receive a benediction, to bless one's-self.

ܒܪܡ.

ܒܪܡ but, yet.
ܐܬܒܪܢܫ *Ethpa.* to become man.
ܒܪܢܫܐ man.
ܒܪܩܐ the lightning, brightness.
ܒܪܬܐ, ܒܪܬ a daughter. pl. ܒܢܬܐ.
ܒܬܘܠܐ, ܒܬܘܠܬܐ a young woman, a maiden.
ܒܬܪ after, ܒܬܪܟܢ afterwards.
ܒܬܪ ܩܠܝܠ soon, (literally), shortly thereupon.

ܓ

ܓܐܪܐ, ܓܪܐ an arrow, dart.
ܓܒܐ to choose, to select.
ܓܒܐ a side, a part, ܓܒܬܐ
ܓܒܐ ܕܣܛܪܐ the wrong side, i. e. an enemy.
ܓܒܝܐ the choice.
ܓܒܝܠܬܐ a formation, a creature.
ܓܒܪ, ܓܒܪܐ a man, a person.
ܓܕܣܡܢܝ Gethsemane (a proper name).
ܓܕܦ *Pa.* ܓܕܦ to blaspheme.
ܓܕܫ to meet with any one, to happen to any one.
ܓܘ in the midst, ܠܓܘ within.
ܓܘܕܐ a troop, a multitude.

ܓܪܡܐ.

ܓܘܕܦܐ m. blasphemy.
ܓܘܢܝܐ shame, disgrace.
ܓܘܪܝܐ Guria (proper name of a woman).
ܓܙܘܪܬܐ circumcision.
ܓܚܟ to laugh, to mock.
ܓܝܪ for.
ܓܠܐ to uncover, to discover, *Ethpe.* to be discovered, to be made known.
ܓܠܙ to rob, *Ethpe.* to be robbed.
ܓܠܝܐܝܬ public, free.
ܓܠܝܠܐ Galilee (a proper name).
ܓܠܝܢܐ a revelation.
ܓܠܦ to engrave.
ܓܡܝܪܘܬܐ an accomplishment, perfection.
ܓܡܪ to fulfill, to finish.
ܓܢܒܪܐ mighty.
ܓܢܙ *Pass. Part.* ܓܢܝܙܐ hidden, unknown.
ܓܙܦ to lend.
ܓܢܣ, ܓܢܣܐ race, family (γένος), offspring.
ܓܢܐ *Aph.* ܐܓܢܐ to lie down.
ܓܥܪ to scold, with ܒ.
ܓܪܒܝܐ the north.
ܓܪܡܐ a bone, a limb.

ܕ.

ܕ mark of the *Genitive; Relative Pronoun*; while, that, therewith, in order that.

ܕܒܚ to offer, *Pa.* the same.

ܕܒܚܬܐ an offering.

ܕܒܪ to carry, to take, *Ethpe.* to be conducted, to conduct oneself.

ܕܓܠ to lie, *Pa.* ܕܓܠ.

ܕܓܠܘܬܐ a falsehood.

ܕܗܒܐ gold.

ܕܘܒܪܐ behavior.

ܕܘܝܕ David, sometimes written ܕܘܝܕ (a proper name).

ܕܘܟ, ܕܘܟܐ, ܕܘܟܬܐ, place.

ܕܘܫ, ܕܫ to crush.

ܕܚܠ to fear, to worship.

ܕܚܠܬܐ fear, terror, ܕܚܠܬ ܦܬܟܪ̈ܐ superstition.

ܕܝܘܐ an evil spirit, the Devil.

ܕܝܘܢܐ to be possessed of an evil spirit.

ܕܝܠ* a word accompanying the *Possessive Pron.* § 16, ܕܝܠܝ who is my, or my.

ܕܝܠܟ thy, or who is thy.

ܕܝܢ but (δὲ).

ܕܝܢܐ a Judge.

ܕܝܢܐ judgment.

* This is formed from ܕ and ܠ. Vid. reference above. Tr.

ܕܝܨ.

ܕܝܨܢ Daison (the proper name of a river).

ܕܝܪܐ a cloister.

ܕܝܪܝܐ a monk.

ܕܝܪܝܘܬܐ monastic life.

ܕܝܬܝܩܝ testament (διαθήκη).

ܕܟܐ, ܕܟܝܐ pure, clean.

ܕܟܐ Pa. ܕܟܝ to purify.

ܕܟܪ to remember.

ܕܡ, and ܕܡܐ the blood.

ܕܡܘܬܐ a resemblance, an image, a likeness.

ܕܡܝܐ similar.

ܕܡܝܐ *Constr. St.* ܕܡܝ value.

ܕܡܟ to sleep.

ܕܡܝܟ sleeping; Matt. viii. 24, pl. ܕܡܝܟܝܢ.

ܕܡܥ to weep.

ܕܡܪ *Ethpa.* to wonder at, to be astonished.

ܕܢ to judge, *Pass. Part.* ܕܝܢ judged.

ܕܢܚܐ the feast of the appearance of Christ; Epiphany.

ܕܩܢܐ the beard.

ܕܪܟ *Aph.* ܐܕܪܟ to comprehend.

ܕܪܥܐ an arm.

ܕܪܫ to encounter, to speak with any one.

ܗܐ.

ܗ.

ܗܐ lo!

ܗܕܐ *Pa.* ܗܰܕܺܝ to lead, to guide.

ܗܳܕܶܐ this, she, *Pron.* (*Chal.*, הָדָא).

ܗܰܕܳܡܶܐ members.

ܗܕܪܐ honor, glory.

ܗܘ m. ܗܝ f. and ܗܰܘ m. ܗܳܝ f. that, the former; ܗܰܘ ܕ who; ܡܶܢ ܗܳܝ ܕ since.

ܗܘܳܐ to be (*Verb Subst.*) *Fut.* ܢܶܗܘܶܐ.

ܗܘܝ he, she.

ܗܢܘܢ them.

ܗܘܦܟܶܐ customs, deeds.

ܗܰܝܕܶܝܢ there, then.

ܗܰܝܟܠܐ a temple, a palace.

ܗܰܝܡܳܢܽܘܬܐ faith, belief, doctrine, ܗܝܡܢܘܬܐ ܡܚܝܢܝܬܐ the saving faith.

ܗܟܘܬ in like manner.

ܗܟܝܠ therefore.

ܗܳܟܰܢ, ܗܳܟܰܢܐ so, in this manner.

ܗܠ, ܠܗܠ hence, for, there.

ܗܰܠܶܟ *Pa.* to wander, to go forth, to walk.

ܗܠܶܝܢ they, these.

ܗܳܢ, ܗܳܢܳܐ m. ܗܳܕܶܐ f. plur. ܗܳܠܶܝܢ m. ܗܳܠܶܝܢ f. this.

ܙܢܘܒܝܣ.

ܗܢܝܐܢܐ advantage, pleasure.

ܗܦܰܟ to return, *Aph.* to lead back.

ܗܶܪܳܘܕܶܣ Herod (a proper name.)

ܗܳܪܟܳܐ here, hither.

ܗܫ, ܗܳܫܳܐ now, at present.

ܘ.

ܘ, ܘܐܘ the letter *Vau*, and.

ܙ.

ܙܒܰܢ to redeem, *Fut.* ܢܶܙܒܽܘܢ, *Pa.* ܙܰܒܶܢ.

ܙܒܰܢ, ܙܒܢܳܐ time, pl. ܙܒܢܐ Acts xvii. 26.

ܙܒܢܬܐ, ܕܬܪܬܝܢ ܙܒܢܝܢ or ܬܪܬܝܢ ܙܒܢܝܢ twice; ܬܠܬ ܙܒܢܝܢ thrice; ܙܒܢ ܩܕܡ ܡܢܩܕܡ before.

ܙܡ to grow dumb, to put to silence.

ܙܰܕܺܝܩܳܐ just, upright.

ܙܕܩ to be just, ܙܳܕܶܩ it befits, it is suitable, it is becoming.

ܙܕܩܘܬܐ agreement, correspondence.

ܙܕܩܬܐ alms.

ܙܗܝܪܐܝܬ *Adv.* carefully.

ܙܗܪ *Ethpa.* to beware.

ܙܘܚܐ praise, show, splendor.

ܙܢܘܒܝܣ Zenobius (a proper name).

ܙܘܥ.

ܙܘܥ, ܙܳܥ to move, to be restless.

ܙܰܘܥܳܐ a moving, a dance.

ܙܽܘܦܳܐ hyssop.

ܙܺܝܘܳܐ honor, splendor.

ܙܺܝܙܳܢܳܐ a weed.

ܙܰܝܶܢ to arm.

ܙܟܳܐ to conquer, to vanquish.

ܙܳܟܽܘܝܳܐ a conqueror.

ܙܡܺܝܪܬܳܐ a song.

ܙܢܳܐ species, kind.

ܙܢܳܐ, ܙܳܢܝܳܐ m. fornication.

ܙܳܢܝܽܘܬܳܐ fornication.

ܙܥܽܘܪ, ܙܥܽܘܪܳܐ little, ܠܳܐ ܒܙܥܽܘܪ not small.

ܙܥܶܩ to cry, to call.

ܙܩܺܝܦܳܐ cross.

ܙܩܰܦ to crucify, to torture.

ܚ.

ܚܺܐܪܳܐ free, ܒܰܪ ܚܺܐܪܶܐ free.

ܚܰܒ ought.

ܚܒܽܘܫܝܳܐ quiet, concealed residence.

ܚܰܒܺܝܒܳܐ beloved, pl. ܚܰܒܺܝܒܶܐ.

ܚܰܒܺܝܒ Habib (a proper name).

ܚܰܒܪܳܐ an associate, the other, any one.

ܚܒܰܫ to enclose.

ܚܰܓܳܐ a feast, a feast day.

ܚܓܪ.

ܚܰܓܺܝܪܳܐ lame.

ܚܰܕ m. ܚܕܳܐ f. one, a certain one, any one ܚܰܕ ܒܫܰܒܳܐ sunday.

ܚܕܳܐ, ܚܕܺܝ to rejoice; ܚܕܳܐ ܚܕܽܘܬܳܐ to rejoice very much.

ܚܰܕܽܘܬܳܐ rejoicing.

ܚܕܳܕܶܐ mutual, reciprocal.

ܚܰܕܘܳܐ, ܚܰܕܽܘܬܳܐ gladness.

ܚܶܕܘܳܐ joy.

ܚܰܕܝܳܐ the breast, pl. suff. Luke, xxiii. 48.

ܚܕܰܪ to surround, to flow around.

ܗܶܕܪܳܐ honor, majesty.

ܚܕܳܪ around.

ܚܰܕܶܬ to renew.

ܚܰܕܬܳܐ new, pl. ܚܰܕܬܳܬܳܐ.

ܚܘܳܐ, *Pa.* ܚܰܘܺܝ to show, to indicate.

ܚܽܘܒܳܐ love.

ܚܽܘܡܣܳܢܳܐ perseverance, patience.

ܚܽܘܣܳܪܳܐ injury.

ܚܙܳܐ to see *Ethpe.* to be seen, to appear.

ܚܶܙܘܳܐ a vision, pl. ܚܶܙܘܳܢܶܐ an apparition.

ܚܙܺܝܪܳܢ June.

ܚܙܰܩ to bind.

ܚܙܘܩܐ bond, union.
ܚܙܬܐ a view.
ܚܛܐ to err, to sin.
ܚܛܗܐ m. sin, crime, pl. ܚܛ̈ܐ, ܚܛܗ̈ܐ and ܚܛܗܝܢ.
ܚܛܝܬܐ f. sin.
ܚܛܬܐ wheat, pl. ܚܛ̈ܐ.
ܚܝܐ to live, *Aph.* ܐܚܝ.
ܚܝ̈ܐ and ܚܝ̈ܐ life. (It always has the plural form but generally a singular signification.
ܚܝܒ m. a debtor, pl. ܚܝܒ̈ܝܢ.
ܚܝܘܬܐ living creature, an animal, a monster.
ܚܝܠ, ܚܝܠܐ a force, an army.
ܚܝܠ to strengthen.
ܚܝܠܬܢ and ܚܝܠܬܢܐ strong.
ܚܝܘܪܐ linen, fine linen.
ܚܟܝܡ, ܚܟܝܡܐ wise, plural ܚܟܝܡ̈ܝܢ and ܚܟܝܡ̈ܐ.
ܚܟܡܬܐ wisdom.
ܚܠܐ vinegar.
ܚܠܘܬܐ a gnat. a fly.
ܚܠܛ to mingle, *Ethpa.* to take part, to associate with any one.
ܚܠܝܡ, ܚܠܝܡܐ sound, healthy.
ܚܠܠ to wash.
ܚܠܡ to dream, *Ethpe.* to recover.
ܚܠܦ for, instead of.
ܚܡܬ *Ethpe.* to be angry.
ܚܡܬܐ anger, wrath.
ܚܢܚܬܐ a sigh.
ܚܢܢ we, us, pl. c. from ܐܢܐ.
ܚܢܦܐ a heathen, an idolater.
ܚܣ, ܚܘܣ far be it.
ܚܣܝܢ vehement, strong.
ܚܣܡ to envy, with ܒ.
ܚܦܐ to cover *Ethpa.* to conceal one's-self.
ܚܦܝܛܐܝܬ diligently.
ܚܦܪ *Aph.* to blush, to be ashamed.
ܚܨܐ the back, the loins.
ܚܘܪ to be white.
ܚܪ to see, to look out.
ܚܪܡ, ܐܚܪܡ to curse, to detest.
ܚܪܪ *Pa.* to liberate.
ܚܪܫܐ a magician, a sorcerer.
ܚܪܬܐ f. from ܐܚܪܝܬܐ finally, the end, enough.
ܚܫܐ endurance, suffering.
ܚܫܘܟ, ܚܫܘܟܐ darkness, pl ܚܫܘܟ̈ܝܢ Eph. iv. 18.
ܚܬܡ to mark, to seal.
ܚܬܡܐ a seal.

ܛ.

ܛܒܐ a rumor, a report.

ܛܒ *Adj.* good. *Adv.* very.

ܛܒܝܥ *Part.* P. m. sealed.

ܛܒܥܐ seal.

ܛܘܒ *Pa.* ܛܝܒ to be ready, to be willing.

ܛܘܒܢܐ the pious, the good.

ܛܘܒܬܢܐ happy, blessed.

ܛܘܗܡ, and ܛܘܗܡܐ kind, family, offspring.

ܛܘܛܠܝܬܐ vine, branch.

ܛܘܝܒܐ readiness.

ܛܘܡܣܐ a part (*tomus.*)

ܛܘܦ, ܛܦ to swim over anything, to overflow.

ܛܘܪܐ a mountain.

ܛܘܪܕܐ distress, misfortune.

ܛܘܫܝܐ that which is concealed, ܒܛܘܫܝܐ secret.

ܛܝܒܘ, ܛܝܒܘܬܐ goodness, excellence, benevolence, grace.

ܛܟܣ to order, (τάσσειν).

ܛܟܣܐ an arrangement, order, state (τάξις).

ܛܠܐ, ܛܠܝܐ a young man, a youth.

ܛܠܝܬܐ a girl, a maiden.

ܛܥܢ to carry.

ܛܥܡ *Ethpa.* to be dispersed.

ܛܢܦܐ foul, detestable.

ܛܢܦܐ unclean.

ܛܢܦܘܬܐ uncleanness.

ܛܥܐ to wander, to wander around, to forget, with ܠ to fall from something, to apostatize, *Aph.* to mislead, to deceive, to cheat.

ܛܘܥܝܘܬܐ error, heresy.

ܛܥܡ to taste, to taste well.

ܛܥܢ to be laden, to bear, *Aph.* to cause to carry, to bring.

(ܛܘܦ = ܛܦ) ܛܦ to overrun. *Aph.* ܐܛܝܦ to overflow, to fill.

ܛܦܣ, *Ethpe.* ܐܬܛܦܣ to acquiesce, to obey.

ܛܪܕ to chase away, to drive away.

ܛܪܦ to strike, *Ethpe.* ܐܬܛܪܦ.

ܛܪܦܐ a leaf.

ܝ.

ܝܐܐ, ܝܐܝܐ fine, suitable, proper.

ܝܐܒ to wish very much, *Ethpa.* the same.

ܝܒܠ to lead, to lead away.

ܝܒܫ to dry up.

ܝܕ.

ܝܕ, ܐܝܕܐ hand, ܒܝܕ by, with help, on account of.

ܝܕܐ Aph. ܐܘܕܝ to thank, with ܒ to believe in something, to confess.

ܝܕܝܥܐ m. acknowledged, known.

ܝܕܥܬܐ f. knowledge.

ܝܕܥ to know, to be acquainted with; *Ethpe.* to be known; *Aph.* to make known, to indicate.

ܝܕܘܥܐ, ܝܕܥܐ an acquaintance, one known.

ܝܕܥܬܐ knowledge, insight, device.

ܝܗܒ to give, *Imperative* ܗܒ; with ܢܦܫܐ to give up one's life.

ܝܗܘܕܐ, ܝܗܘܕ Judæa, ܝܗܘܕܝܐ pl. Jews.

ܝܘܒܝܢܝܢܘܣ Jovinian (a proper name).

ܝܘܚܢܢ John (a proper name.)

ܝܘܣܦ Joseph (a proper name).

ܝܘܠܝܘܣ Julius (a proper name).

ܝܘܠܝܢܘܣ Julian (a proper name).

ܝܘܠܦܢܐ a doctrine, teaching.

ܝܘܡ, ܝܘܡܐ day, ܒܐܝܡܡܐ by day, ܝܘܡܢ, ܝܘܡܢܐ to day, now; ܟܠܝܘܡ daily.

ܝܬܪ.

ܝܘܢܝܐ a Greek, ܝܘܢܐܝܬ *Adverb.* in the Greek manner, according to the Greeks.

ܝܘܬܪܢ, ܝܘܬܪܢܐ use, advantage.

ܝܚܝܕܝܐ a hermit.

ܝܠܕ to bring forth, *Ethpe.* to be born.

ܝܠܕܐ birth.

ܝܠܘܕܐ a small boy, a child.

ܝܠܘܦܐ a teacher, a learned man.

ܝܠܦ to learn, *Aph.* to inform.

ܝܡܐ the sea.

ܝܡܐ to swear, *Aph.* to cause to swear, to swear to.

ܝܡܝܢܐ the right hand, the right.

ܝܢܘܩܐ a suckling, a baby.

ܝܣܦ *Aph.* to add.

ܝܣܓܐ to increase rapidly.

ܝܥܩܘܒ Jacob (a proper name).

ܝܨܘܦܐ one who takes care.

ܝܩܕ to burn.

ܝܩܕܐ flame, holocaust.

ܝܩܝܪ, ܝܩܝܪܐ illustrious, honored, great.

ܝܬܪ to be great, to increase (in respectability).

ܝܪܚܐ.

ܝܪܚܐ a month.

ܝܪܝܥܬܐ, ܝܪܝܥܬܐ a tent.

ܝܫܘܥ Jesus.

ܐܝܬ being, essence.

ܝܬܒ to remain, to dwell, to settle, to sit.

ܝܬܝܪ ܡܢ more than.

ܝܬܝܪܘܬܐ superfluity.

ܝܬܪ to win, to abound.

ܟ.

ܟܐܐ to prevent, to rebuke.

ܟܐܒ, ܟܐܒܐ passion.

ܟܐܢܐܝܬ justly.

ܟܐܢܘܬܐ justice, righteousness.

ܟܐܦܐ a stone, a rock, Cephas, or Peter.

ܟܐܬܐ f. a rebuke.

ܟܒܪ perhaps.

ܟܕ as, during (pleonastic before the *Part.*).

ܟܗܢܐ a priest.

ܟܗܢܘܬܐ the priesthood.

ܟܘܚܕܐ shame.

ܟܘܟܒܐ m. a star, *pl.* ܟܘܟܒ̈ܐ Matt. xxiv. 29.

ܟܘܡܪܐ a priest.

ܟܘܣ, ܟܘܣܐ m. a cup.

ܟܘܪܚܐ a cell.

ܟܪܐ.

ܟܘܪܣܝܐ a throne.

ܟܚܕ *Ethpa.* ܐܬܟܚܕ to blush.

ܟܝܪܘܛܘܢܝܐ the laying on or extending of the hand (χειροτονία).

ܟܠ all, every, ܟܠ ܚܕ each.

ܟܠܒܐ a dog.

ܟܠܝܠܐ, ܟܠܝܠܐ a crown.

ܟܠܡܕܡ every thing, any thing.

ܟܠܬܐ a bride.

ܟܡܐ how much, how much more.

ܟܡܪ to be amazed, to be sad.

ܟܢܐ to give a surname.

ܟܢܬܐ a fellow servant.

ܟܢܦܐ bosom, lap.

ܟܢܫ to assemble, to collect together, *Ethpa.* to be assembled.

ܟܢܫܐ an assembly.

ܟܣܐ a cup.

ܟܣܐ to conceal, *Pa.* to cover, *Ethpa.* to hide one's-self.

ܟܣܐ, ܟܣܝܐ, ܟܣܝܐ concealed, *pl.* ܟܣܝ̈ܢ.

ܟܦܢܐ famine.

ܟܦܪ to deny, to refuse, to desert (with ܒ).

ܟܪ where, ܠܟܪ there where.

ܟܪܐ to feel pain, ܟܪܝܐ ܠܝ it pains one.

ܟܪܝܐ.

ܟܪܝܐ sad, sorrowful, *Ethpe.* to pass by, to go.

ܟܪܝܗ, ܟܪܝܗܐ infirm, weak.

ܟܪܙ *Aph.* to announce (χηρυσσειν).

ܟܪܣܛܝܢܐ a christian.

ܟܪܟ to involve, to roll up, to pass by.

ܟܪܟܐ a roll, a scroll.

ܟܫܠܐ a collision, a shock.

ܟܫܦ *Ethpa.*, ܐܬܟܫܦ to humbly entreat.

ܟܬܒ to write, *Aph.* the same.

ܟܬܒܐ a writing, a book.

ܟܬܢܐ flax, linen.

ܟܬܦܐ a shoulder.

ܟܬܪ to remain, to remain behind.

ܠ.

ܠܐ not, no; ܕܠܐ lest, without.

ܠܒܐ heart.

ܠܒܒ to arouse, to cheer.

ܠܒܘܫܐ dress, a garment.

ܠܒܘܒܝܬܐ a decision, reliance.

ܠܒܟ to hold, to take hold.

ܠܒܪ outside, without.

ܠܒܫ to clothe, to cover.

ܠܘܐ *Pa.* to accompany, *Ethpa.* to be accompanied, to be confirmed.

ܡܓܘܫܐ.

ܠܘܛܬܐ abuse, insult.

ܠܘܩܒܠ against, towards.

ܠܘܬ to, by, besides, with.

ܠܚܐ to blot out.

ܒܠܚܘܕ, ܠܚܘܕ only, alone.

ܠܚܡܐ bread.

ܠܠܐ, ܠܠܝܐ, ܠܝܠܝܐ night, *pl.* ܠܠܝܘܬܐ, &c.

ܠܝܬ it is not.

ܠܠܐ an insane person.

ܠܥܠ over, up; ܡܢ ܠܥܠ before, besides.

ܠܥܣ to eat.

ܠܩܘܒܠܐ opponent.

ܠܫܢ, ܠܫܢܐ tongue, language.

ܡ.

ܡܐ that, what; ܡܐ ܕ when.

ܡܐܡܪܐ word, discourse, a part of speech.

ܡܐܢܐ a handle, a covering.

ܡܒܘܥܐ spring, fountain.

ܡܒܪܟܘܬܐ a blessing, a benediction.

ܡܓܠܐ, ܡܓܠܬܐ scroll, volume, roll.

ܡܓܢ freely.

ܡܓܘܫ, ܡܓܘܫܐ a wise man, *pl.* ܡܓܘܫܐ.

ܡܕܒܚܐ an altar.

ܡܕܒܪܐ a desert.

ܡܕܒܪܢܘܬܐ redemption.

ܡܕܝܪܐ a cloister, a chamber.

ܡܕܝܢ thus, thence, therefore.

ܡܕܝܢܐ, ܡܕܝܢܬܐ a town, a city.

ܡܕܡ something, ܠܐ ܡܕܡ nothing.

ܡܕܢܚܝܐ eastern, ܡܕܢܚܐ the East.

ܡܕܪܫܐ a song, a hymn.

ܡܗܝܡܢܐ believing, with ܬܪܝܨܐ orthodox.

ܡܗܝܪܐ prompt, ready.

ܡܘܗܒܬܐ a gift.

ܡܘܩ, *Pa.* ܡܝܩ to deride.

ܡܘܪܐ myrrh.

ܡܘܬܐ death.

ܡܚܐ to strike, to prick, to bite.

ܡܚܘܬܐ a blow, plague, *pl.* ܡܚ̈ܘܬܐ.

ܡܚܝܠܐ weak, humble.

ܡܚܪ on the morrow.

ܡܚܫܘܠܐ a tempest, *pl.* waves.

ܡܛܐ to go, to come, to arrive, 3 *f. Pret.* ܡܛܬ.

ܡܛܠ from, of, over, on account of; ܡܛܠ ܕ while.

ܡܛܥܝܢܐ a heretic, a seducer.

ܡܛܫܝܐܝܬ secretly.

ܡ̈ܝܐ water.

ܡܝܬ to die, *Aph.* to cause to die, to mortify.

ܡܝܬܪ distinguished, excellent.

ܡܟܝܟܘܬܐ humility, modesty.

ܡܟܝܟܐ affable, modest.

ܡܟܝܠ now, immediately.

ܡܟܝܟܘܬܐ lowliness, intelligence.

ܡܟ, ܡܟܟ to be depressed.

ܡܠܐ to be full, *Pa.* to fill, *Ethpe.* to be filled.

ܡܠܐ word, saying, *plur.* ܡ̈ܠܐ.

ܡܠܐܟܐ an angel, a messenger.

ܡܠܚܐ a captain.

ܡܠܟ to advise, to consult, to reign.

ܡܠܟ, ܡܠܟܐ a king.

ܡܠܟܘܬܐ a kingdom.

ܡܠܠ to speak, to converse.

ܡܠܬܐ *Abs.* word.

ܡܠܬܐ *Emph.*, word *pl.* ܡ̈ܠܐ.

ܡܠܦܢܐ a teacher, a learned man.

ܡܠܦܢܘܬܐ learning.

ܡܡܠܠܐ speech.

ܡܰܢ. — ܡܰܫܟܰܒܬܳܐ.

ܡܰܢ who? ܕ ܡܰܢ that, which, ܡܰܢܽܘ who is this?

ܡܶܢ certainly (μέν); it often is superfluous.

ܡܶܢ of, from, on account of, since; ܡܶܢ ܠܗܳܠ from, of; ܡܶܢ ܐܳܚܪܳܢܳܐ afterwards, hereafter, with suff. ܡܶܢܰܢ of us.

ܡܳܢܳܐ what?

ܡܗܰܝܡܢܳܐ a faithful servant.

ܡܢܰܪܬܳܐ a candlestick.

ܡܢܳܬܳܐ a part.

ܡܣܰܝܒܪܳܢܽܘܬܳܐ patience.

ܡܣܟܺܢܳܐ poor.

ܡܰܥܡܽܘܕܺܝܬܳܐ f. baptism.

ܡܥܰܪܳܐ, ܡܥܰܪܬܳܐ a hollow, a cavern.

ܡܦܰܫܩܳܢܳܐ an interpreter, an explainer.

ܡܨܝܳܐ, ܡܨܝܳܢܳܐ possible.

ܡܨܳܐ to be able, *Ethpe.* the same, to have power to do (with ܒ by, through).

ܡܨܰܡܨܡܽܘܬܳܐ splendor, light.

ܡܨܰܥܬܳܐ in the midst.

ܡܨܰܥܬܳܐ midst.

ܡܳܪܳܐ, ܡܳܪܝܳܐ, ܡܳܪܢܳܐ Lord, Sir, ܡܳܪܝ *literally* my Lord (title for bishop or any other ecclesiastical person), ܡܳܪܰܢ our Lord, (i. e. Christ); ܡܳܪܬ title for ecclesiastical ladies.

ܡܰܪܓܳܢܺܝܬܳܐ a pearl, a precious stone.

ܡܪܰܛ to fall off, to cast away, to make free.

ܡܶܪܛܽܘܬܳܐ a falling off, an injury.

ܡܰܪܚܳܐ bold, impudent, *Adv.* ܡܰܪܚܳܐܝܬ.

ܡܰܪܛܽܘܛܳܐ a garment.

ܡܰܪܺܝܪܳܐ bitter, sorrowful.

ܡܰܪܟܰܒܬܳܐ a chariot, a throne.

ܡܳܪܳܝܳܐ that which relates to Christ.

ܡܰܪܥܺܝܬܳܐ a flock, an assembly, a community.

ܡܫܰܕܪܳܐ a messenger.

ܡܫܰܚ to anoint.

ܡܫܰܚܠܦܳܐ changable, variegated.

ܡܫܺܝܚܳܐ the Anointed, the Messiah.

ܡܫܰܘܕܥܳܐ known, distinguished.

ܡܫܰܡܠܝ complete, perfect.

ܡܫܰܡܫܳܢܳܐ a deacon, a minister.

ܡܫܰܡܫܳܢܽܘܬܳܐ the office of a deacon.

ܡܫܰܪܝܳܐ a person sick of the palsy.

ܡܫܟܰܒܬܳܐ a position, a bed.

ܡܫܬܡܥܢܘܬܐ f. obedience.

ܡܬܚ to extend.

ܡܬܚܐ time, a period.

ܡܬܪܓܡܢܐ an interpreter.

ܡܬܐܠܨܢܘܬܐ necessity.

ܡܬܠܡܕܢܐ a catechumen.

ܢ.

ܢܒܝܐ m. a prophet, Matt. i. 22. *pl.* ܢܒܝ̈ܐ.

ܢܒܝܘܬܐ f. prophecy.

ܢܓܝܪܘܬ drawing out, patience, suffering.

ܢܗܝܪ shining, bright.

ܢܗܪ to shine, *Aph.* to light, *Ethpa.* to be bright.

ܢܗܪܐ a river.

ܢܘܗܪܐ m. light, from ܢܗܪ to shine.

ܢܘܚ, ܢܚ to repose, to be appeased, *Aph.* to lay aside, to put away.

ܢܘܚ, ܢܘܚܐ rest.

ܢܘܟܪܝ, ܢܘܟܪܝܐ a stranger, ܢܘܟܪܝܬܐ f. also *Neuter*.

ܢܘܡ, ܢܡ to sleep.

ܢܘܦܩܐ distribution, expending.

ܢܘܪܐ fire.

ܢܙܝܪܘܬܐ abstemiousness.

ܢܚܠܐ a valley.

ܢܚܬ to go down, to descend, *Aph.* to lay down, to take down, to bring, to deliver.

ܢܚܬܐ m. a garment, *pl.* ܢܚܬܝܢ, ܢܚ̈ܬܐ.

ܢܛܦ to drop.

ܢܛܪ to take care of, to watch.

ܢܝܚܘܬܐ f. lenity, meekness.

ܢܝܩܝܐ Nicæa (a proper name).

ܢܝܪ, ܢܝܪܐ a yoke, a bow.

ܢܟܝܢ guilt, injury, crime.

ܢܟܣ to augment, to honor, to sacrifice, to slay.

ܢܡܘܣ law.

ܢܣܒ to take, to receive.

ܢܣܝܘܢܐ temptation.

ܢܣܟ to pour, *Ethpe.* ܐܬܢܣܟ.

ܢܣܩ to ascend.

ܢܦܐܫܐ refreshment.

ܢܦܠ to fall.

ܢܦܩ to go out, *Aph.* to take out, ܢܦܝܨ spread.

ܢܦܫܐ the soul, reflexive, self.

ܢܨܐ to fight, to attack.

ܢܨܒ to plant.

ܢܨܚܢܐ.

ܢܨܚܢܐ a victory, an exploit.

ܢܨܝܒܝܢ Nesibis in Mesopotamia (a proper name).

ܢܨܝܚܐ victorious, superior, clear.

ܢܩܡ *Ethpa.* to be avenged .

ܢܩܦ to adhere, to follow.

ܢܩܪ to dig, to dig out.

ܢܫܐ (*pl.* ܐܢ̈ܬܬܐ) a woman.

ܢܬܪܐ a downfall, a curse.

ܣ.

ܣܐܡܐ silver, money.

ܣܐܬܐ a bushel.

ܣܒܐ an old man, *Adj.* old.

ܣܒܝܟܐ dense, extensive.

ܣܒܠܬܐ an ode, a song.

ܣܒܥ to be satisfied.

ܣܒܪ to believe, *Pa.* to declare, to forbear, *Aph.* to suppose.

ܣܒܪܐ hope.

ܣܓܐ to multiply, to increase.

ܣܓܕ to worship, to honor.

ܣܓܕܬܐ worship, honor.

ܣܓܘܠܐ a cluster.

ܣܓܝ, ܣܓܝܐܐ much, *Adv.* very.

ܣܓܝܐܘܬܐ a multitude.

ܣܘܪܝܐܝܬ.

ܣܕܪ to order, to arrange.

ܣܗܕ to testify, to witness, *Aph.* to die as a martyr.

ܣܗܕܐ *Emph.* of ܣܗܕ a witness, a martyr ($=$μάρτυρ).

ܣܗܕܘܬܐ testimony, witness, martyred one.

ܣܘܓܐܐ a multitude.

ܣܘܓܦܢܐ offense.

ܣܘܚ to long for something, to take pleasure in.

ܣܘܟܠܐ thought.

ܣܘܠܩܐ reception, ascension to heaven.

ܣܘܡ, ܣܝܡ to place, to inter, to add, ܒܪܝܫ to shut, ܡܐܡܪܐ to write or compose books, ܒܪܝܫܐ to punish with death, *Ethpe.* to be interred, to be buried.

ܣܘܢܗܕܘܣ synod (σὺνοδος).

ܣܘܢܩܢܐ indigence, poverty, need.

ܣܘܥܪܢܐ a deed, an occurrence.

ܣܘܪܝܐ Syria.

ܣܘܪܝܐܝܬ *Adv.* Syriac, in the Syriac.

ܣܘܪܝܝܐ a Syrian, *Adj.* Syrian.

ܣܚܦ to pull down, *Pa.* to destroy, *Ethpa.* to be dispersed.

ܣܛܢܐ Satan (a proper name).

ܣܛܪܐ a side, a page.

ܣܝܒܪ to bear, to endure, to tolerate.

ܣܝܡ the laying on (of hands).

ܣܝܥܬܐ an assembly.

ܣܝܦܐ a sword (ξίφος).

ܣܟܐ to expect, *Pa.* ܣܟܝ to wait.

ܣܟܠܘܬܐ transgression.

ܣܠܩ to ascend.

ܣܡ, ܣܘܡ to place, to lay upon, to commit.

ܣܡܟ to support, ܣܡܟܐ to take refreshment, to tarry.

ܣܡܠܐ left, wrong.

ܣܢܐ to hate.

ܣܢܝܐ hated, mean.

ܣܢܩ to need, ܣܢܝܩ *Part. Pass. Pe.*

ܣܥܪ to make, to do, to visit (the sick).

ܣܦܪܐ a scribe, *pl.* ܣܦܪܐ, ܣܦܪܝܢ.

ܣܦܝܢܐ, ܣܦܝܢܬܐ a ship.

ܣܦܪ, ܣܦܪܐ a book.

ܣܦܬܐ, *pl.* ܣܦܘܬܐ the mouth, the lips.

ܣܪܚ *Pa.* to dishonor, to violate.

ܥ.

ܥܐܕܐ a feast, a feast-day.

ܥܒܕ to do, to perform, to yield, to make something (with a double Accusative).

ܥܒܕܐ m. servant, *pl.* ܥܒܕܝܢ, ܥܒܕܐ Mat. xiii. 27.

ܥܒܘܕܐ creator.

ܥܒܪ to pass by, to pass over; with ܒ, to pass around.

ܥܒܪܐܝܬ Hebrew, Ad. Hebraically.

ܥܓܠ, ܒܥܓܠ shortly.

ܥܓܠܐ, ܥܓܠܬܐ a young cow.

ܥܕ until, ܥܕܟܝܠ ܠܐ not yet; ܥܕܡܐ until, ܥܕܡܐ ܕ until that; ܥܕܢܐ, ܥܕܢ time.

ܥܕܪ *Pa.* to support, to aid.

ܥܕܬܐ church.

ܥܘܠ to act unjustly.

ܥܘܠ, ܥܘܠܐ unjust, sinful.

ܥܘܠܐ wicked, ungodly.

ܥܘܡܪܐ a habitation, an abode.

ܥܘܢܕܢܐ death.

ܥܘܢܝܬܐ an answer, an alternative song.

ܥܘܩ, ܥܩ *Ethpe.* to be troubled.

ܥܘܪܠܘܬܐ uncircumcision.

ܥܘܪ or ܥܪ to watch.

ܥܛܐ to blot.

ܥܝܕܐ custom.

ܥܝܢ, ܥܝܢܐ eye.

ܥܝܪ to arouse, *Aph.* to stir up.

ܥܝܪܐ a guardian angel.

ܥܠ over, to, against, on account of; ܥܠ ܕ because.

ܥܠܘܒܘܬܐ avarice.

ܥܠܐ, ܥܠܬܐ cause.

ܥܠܬܐ an altar, Acts xvii. 23.

ܥܠܠ, ܥܠ to go, with ܒ to go into, with ܥܠ to carry on prohibited intercourse with any one, *Ethpe.* to go into, *Aph.* to lead, to lead into.

ܥܠܡ, *Emph.* ܥܠܡܐ world, race, generation.

ܥܡ with, above.

ܥܡ, ܥܡܐ a nation, *pl.* ܥܡܡܝܢ, ܥܡܡܐ.

ܥܡܕ to suffer one's self to be dipped, to suffer one's-self to be baptized.

ܥܡܕܐ dipping, baptism.

ܥܡܘܕܐ a pillar.

ܥܡܘܪܐ an inhabitant.

ܥܡܠܐ trouble, labor.

ܥܡܪ to dwell.

ܥܢܐ to hear, to answer, *Ethpe.* to converse.

ܥܢܘܝܘܬܐ piety.

ܥܢܝܕܐ one who is dead.

ܥܢܢܐ a cloud.

ܥܣܪܝܢ twenty.

ܥܦܐ *Pa.* to inter.

ܥܨܝܢܐ aversion, opposition.

ܥܩܒ *Pael*, to inquire.

ܥܩܪܐ a root.

ܥܪܩ to flee.

ܥܫܢ to avail, to prevail.

ܥܬܝܕ prepared, *Part.* (put for the future).

ܥܬܝܩܐ ancient, old, f. ܥܬܝܩܬܐ.

ܥܬܝܪ, ܥܬܝܪܐ rich.

ܦ.

ܦܐܪܐ fruit, *pl.* ܦܐܪ̈ܐ.

ܦܓܥ to meet, to happen to (with ܒ).

ܦܓܪ, ܦܓܪܐ body.

ܦܘܚ.

ܦܘܚ, ܦܳܚ to blow, to sound.
ܦܰܘܠܳܘܣ Paul (a proper name).
ܦܽܘܠܚܳܢܳܐ work.
ܦܘܡ, ܦܽܘܡܳܐ mouth.
ܦܽܘܩܕܳܢܳܐ a command.
ܦܘܪ *Ethpe.* to be unwilling.
ܦܽܘܪܓܳܐ a tower (πύργος).
ܦܽܘܪܥܳܢܳܐ a reward, a recompense.
ܦܽܘܪܩܳܢܳܐ redemption, salvation.
ܦܽܘܪܫܳܢܳܐ separation.
ܦܘܫ, ܦܳܫ to remain, to come to any one.
ܦܽܘܫܳܟܳܐ doubt.
ܦܽܘܫܳܩܳܐ an explanation.
ܦܝܳܠܺܐ a phial.
ܦܺܝܠܳܣܘܦܳܐ a philosopher.
ܦܺܝܠܰܛܳܘܣ Pilate (a proper name).
ܦܝܳܣܳܐ mediation, entreaty.
ܦܰܪܰܡܘܢܳܪܳܐ a servant of the church.
ܦܰܟܳܐ cheek, jole.
ܦܠܰܓ to divide, *Ethpa.* to doubt.
ܦܠܰܚ, *Part.* ܦܳܠܰܚ to work, to serve.
ܦܢܳܐ to return, *Pa.* to answer, *Aph.* to lead back, to make known; *Ethpe.* to turn one's-self.

ܦܫܩ.

ܦܶܢܛܰܣܝܳܐ an apparition, an enchantment.
ܦܢܺܝܬܳܐ a limit, an end.
ܦܣܣ, ܦܰܣ to free, *Aph.* to permit.
ܦܶܣܳܐ a lot, a portion, *pl.* ܦܶܣܶ̈ܐ.
ܦܥܠܽܘܬܳܐ a work, labor.
ܦܨܳܐ, *Pa.* ܦܰܨܺܝ to free, to deliver.
ܦܩܶܕ to command.
ܦܽܘܩܕܳܢ, ܦܽܘܩܕܳܢܳܐ precept, command.
ܦܩܰܥܬܳܐ a camp, a valley.
ܦܰܪܕܰܝܣܳܐ paradise.
ܦܳܪܽܘܩܳܐ a redeemer, a deliverer.
ܦܳܪܽܘܩܳܝܳܐ salutiferous, saving.
ܦܳܪܣ Persia.
ܦܳܪܣܳܝܳܐ a Persian.
ܦܪܰܥ to recompense, *Ethpa.* to be rewarded.
ܦܰܪܨܽܘܦܳܐ face, presence.
ܦܪܰܩ to preserve, to deliver.
ܦܪܰܫ to separate, to divide, *Ethpe.* to be divided, to appoint.
ܦܪܰܬ to break.
ܦܫܰܛ to extend, to spread.
ܦܫܺܝܛܳܐ just, right.
ܦܫܰܩ to interpret.

ܦܬܓܡܐ.

ܦܬܓܡܐ a word, a matter.

ܦܬܐ, ܦܬܝܐ wide.

ܦܬܚ to open.

ܦܬܟܪܐ *pl.* m. idols, images.

ܦܬܟܪܐ an idol, an image of a false god.

ܨ.

ܨܐܐ to be filthy.

ܨܐܐ vile, filthy.

ܨܒܐ to be willing, to wish.

ܨܒܝܢܘܬܐ will, ܨܒܝܢܬ, ܢܦܫܗ, ܡܢ of one's-self, freely.

ܨܒܝܐ willing, ready.

ܨܒܝܢ will.

ܨܒܝܢܐ will, purpose.

ܨܗܐ to thirst.

ܨܘܡ, ܨܡ to fast.

ܨܘܡܐ days of fasting, fast days.

ܨܘܪܬܐ a figure, a pretence.

ܨܠܐ to incline, *Pa.* to pray, with ܥܠ to pray for any one, to bless.

ܨܠܐ, ܨܠܝܐ inclined.

ܨܠܒ *Ethpe.* to be crucified.

ܨܠܘܬܐ a prayer, an entreaty.

ܩܘܡܛܪܝܘܢ.

ܨܠܝܒܐ a cross.

ܨܠܡܐ a figure, an image.

ܨܦܪܐ early time, dawn.

ܨܪܐ *Ethpe.* to be separated, to burst.

ܩ.

ܩܒܠ *Pa.* to receive; ܐܬܩܒܠ to happen, to come to pass.

ܩܒܪ to bury.

ܩܒܪܐ, ܩܒܘܪܐ a sepulchre.

ܡܢ ܩܕܝܡ from the beginning.

ܩܕܡ for, to, ܡܢ ܩܕܡ ܕ ere, before.

ܩܕܡܝ, ܩܕܡܝܐ the first.

ܩܕܝܫܐ holy.

ܩܘܐ to remain, to stop.

ܩܘܒܠܐ a reception, an entertainment.

ܩܘܕܫܐ holiness.

ܩܘܡ, ܩܡ to stand up, to stand, *Aph.* to erect, to set up, to conclude, to appoint, to determine; with ܩܪܒܐ ܥܠ preceding, to make war with any one.

ܩܘܡܛܪܝܘܢ a church-yard, burying-ground.

ܩܘܢܕܠܐ.

ܩܘܢܕܠܐ a servant of the church, sexton.

ܩܘܣܛܢܛܝܢܘܣ Constantine (a proper name).

ܩܘܪܝܐ a town, a city.

ܩܘܪܝܢܝܐ a Cyrenean (a proper name).

ܩܘܫܬܐ truth.

ܩܛܘܠܐ m. a murderer, a robber.

ܩܛܝܢ cunning, ingenious.

ܩܛܠܐ slaughter, murder.

ܩܝܡܐ a league, ܒܢܬ ܩܝܡܐ consecrated virgins.

ܩܝܡܬܐ resurrection.

ܩܝܢܬܐ a song.

ܩܝܣܐ a tree, bark, a book.

ܩܝܬܪܐ Cithara, harp.

ܩܝܬܪܘܕܐ a player on the cithara.

ܩܠ, ܩܠܐ a voice.

ܩܠܝܠ little.

ܩܠܝܪܘܣ the clergy.

ܟܠܬܐ a bride.

ܩܢܐ to acquire; *Aph.* to grant, to bring.

ܩܢܝܐ a pen, a reed.

ܩܢܛܪܘܢܐ a centurion.

ܩܣܪܝܐ Cæsarea (a proper name).

ܩܥܐ to call, to cry.

ܪܓܠ.

ܩܦܐܕܘܩܝܐ Cappadocia (a proper name).

ܩܣܝܐ cassia.

ܩܪܐ to name, to call, to choose.

ܩܪܒ to approach, to draw near, *Pa.* to conduct, to bring; ܩܘܪܒܢܐ to sacrifice.

ܩܪܒܐ war

ܩܪܘܣܛܠܠܘܣ a crystal.

ܩܪܝܒ near.

ܩܪܝܢܐ reading.

ܩܪܝܬܐ a field, a country.

ܩܪܢܐ a horn.

ܩܪܩܦܬܐ calvary.

ܩܫܝܫܐ a priest, an elder.

ܪ.

ܪܒ much, great, loud, chief; 2) a teacher, *Emphat.* ܪܒܐ *Abs. pl.* ܪܒܐ *Const. pl.* ܪܒܝ.

ܪܒܐ to grow, *Pa.* to bring up, to educate.

ܪܒܘ a myriad, *pl.* ܪܒܘܢ.

ܪܒܘܬܐ greatness, a multitude.

ܪܓܓ, ܪܓ to wish very much, to desire, *Ethpa.* the same.

ܪܓܙ to be angry.

ܪܓܠ, ܪܓܠܐ foot.

ܪܓܡ.

ܪܓܡ to stone.

ܪܓܫ to mark, to feel, *Aph.* the same, with ܒ to perceive, to remark.

ܪܓܬܐ a wish, a desire.

ܪܕܐ to go, to chastise; with and without ܒܐܠܦܐ to ship.

ܪܕܘܦܐ a persecutor.

ܪܕܘܦܝܐ persecution.

ܪܗܒ to hasten, to tremble, *Ethpe.* to be afraid, to be terrified.

ܪܗܘܡܝܐܝܬ Roman, *Adv.* romaically, Latin.

ܪܗܛ to run, to hasten.

ܪܘܓܙܐ anger, misfortune.

ܪܘܚ m. spirit.

ܪܘܚܐ f. wind, breath, spirit.

ܪܘܚܢܝܐ spiritual.

ܪܘܚܡܐ bowel love, bowels of mercies.

ܪܘܚܩܐ distance ܡܢ ܪܘܚܩܐ from a distance.

ܪܘܡ *Aph.* ܐܪܝܡ to raise up, to elevate.

ܪܘܡܡܢܐ a gift.

ܪܘܡܒܐ a quarrel.

ܪܘܩܥܐ a cloth, a rag.

ܪܡܐ.

ܪܘܪܒܢܐ a prince, a person of rank.

ܪܘܫܡܐ a sign.

ܪܚܝܡ beloved.

ܪܚܡ to love, *Ethpa.* with ܥܠ to feel compassion.

ܪܚܡܐ *pl.* compassion, benevolence, love.

ܪܚܡܬܐ love.

ܪܚܦ to lie, to float.

ܪܚܩ to be far distant.

ܪܝܚܐ smell.

ܪܝܩܐ spittle.

ܪܝܫܐ the first named.

ܪܝܫܝܬܐ, ܪܝܫܝܬ firstling, beginning, *pl.* ܪܫܝܬܐ.

ܪܝܫܟܘܡܪܐ the high priest.

ܪܝܫܢܐ a person of rank.

ܪܟܒ to ride.

ܪܟܢ *Ethpa.* to feel inclined, to be moved.

ܪܡ, ܪܡܐ f. ܪܡܬܐ high, loud, *pl.* ܪܡܐ James iv. 6.

ܪܡܐ to lie, to be placed, *Aph.* to cast, to send; with ܚܠܡ to administer; with ܢܦܫܐ to lose life.

ܪܡܝܐ.

ܪܡܝܐ *Part. P.* thrown down, given up.

ܪ̈ܡܬܐ hills, Luke xxiii. 30.

ܪܡܚܣܘܬܐ patience, long suffering.

ܪܡܫܐ evening.

ܪܣܣ to sprinkle.

ܪܥܐ *Pa.* ܪܥܝ to obtain again, *Ethpa.* to be reconciled.

ܪܬܡܬܢܐܝܬ mournful, deeply moved.

ܪܥܝܐ a herdsman.

ܪܥܝܢ, ܪܥܝܢܐ sense, mind.

ܪܥܡ *Ethpe.* to be angry.

ܪܥܡܐ thunder.

ܪܩܕ to dance, to mourn, to lament.

ܪܫܝܥܐ sinful, a transgressor.

ܪܫܡ to make a sign.

ܪܬܚ to be inflamed, to rejoice.

ܫ.

ܫܐܒܘܪ Sapores (a proper name).

ܫܐܕܐ an evil spirit.

ܫܐܠ to entreat, *Pa.* to ask; with ܒܐܠ to ask after some one.

ܫܐܠܬܐ, ܫܐܠܬܐ entreaty.

ܫܝܢ, ܫܐܢ to reconcile, to calm.

ܫܒܒܘܬܐ nearness.

ܫܘܙܒ.

ܫܒܚ to praise.

ܫܒܝܐ captivity, destruction.

ܫܒܝܚܐ praise-worthy.

ܫܒܫܬܐ a vine.

ܫܒܛܐ a sceptre.

ܫܒܠ to guide, to lead.

ܫܒܥ, ܫܒܥܐ seven, ܫܒܥܝܢ seventy.

ܫܒܩ to leave, to give up, to permit, to let go.

ܫܒܬܐ a week.

ܫܓܘܫܝܐ an uproar.

ܫܓܝܫܐ restless, uneasy.

ܫܓܪ to kindle.

ܫܓܫ *Ethpe.* to be moved, to be indignant.

ܫܕܐ to throw, to precipitate.

ܫܕܪ *Pa.* to send, *Ethpa.* ܐܫܬܕܪ is sent.

ܫܗܪ to awake.

ܫܘܐ to be worthy, *Ethpe.* to be considered as worthy.

ܫܘܐ, ܫܘܝܐ equal. *pl.* ܫܘ̈ܝܐ.

ܫܘܒܗܪܐ renown.

ܫܘܒܚܐ praise, renown, glory.

ܫܘܓ, ܫܓ to wash.

ܫܘܙܒ to free, to tear away.

ܫܘܝܛܐ.

ܫܘܝܛܐ dishonor, shame.

ܫܘܚܠܦܐ change, exchange.

ܫܘܠܡܐ consummation, end.

ܫܘܛ, ܫܛ to despise.

ܫܘܠܛܢܐ power, authority, right.

ܫܘܩܐ way, street.

ܫܘܪܐ a wall.

ܫܘܪܝܐ beginning.

ܫܘܪܪܐ confirmation.

ܫܘܬܪܢܐ gain, advantage.

ܫܛܘܪܐ awkward, stupid.

ܫܝܛܐ despised, small, inferior.

ܫܟܚ *pl.* f. ܫܟܝܚܢ present, *Aph.* ܐܫܟܚ to be able, to find.

ܫܠܚ to send, to put away.

ܫܠܐ, ܫܠܝ to cease, to rest.

ܫܠܝܐ, ܫܠܝܐ rest, ܫܠܝ ܫܠܝܐ, ܫܠܝܘܬܐ sudden.

ܫܠܝܚܐ an apostle.

ܫܠܛ *Pa.* ܫܠܛ to be able, to be powerful.

ܫܠܡ to approach fulfillment, *Pa.* to fulfill, to complete; with ܫܠܡܐ to salute, *Aph.* to deliver up; ܪܘܚܐ to give up the ghost, to die.

ܫܦܝܪ.

ܫܠܡܐ *pl.* m. ܫܠܡܐ peace.

ܫܡ, ܫܡܐ a name.

ܫܡܘܢܐ Samona (a proper name).

ܫܡܥܘܢ Simon (a proper name).

ܫܡܝܐ heaven.

ܫܡܝܫܛ Samosata (a proper name).

ܫܡܠܝ to finish, to complete.

ܫܡܥ to hear.

ܫܡܥܘܢ Simeon, Simon (a proper name).

ܫܡܫ to serve.

ܫܡܫܐ the sun.

ܫܢܐ *Pa.* to go away, ܠܥܠܡܗ or ܠܘܬ ܡܪܗ to die.

ܫܢܐ, ܫܢܝܐ insane, foolish.

ܫܢܐ, ܫܢܬܐ year.

ܫܢܕܐ torment, pain, torture.

ܫܢ, ܫܢܐ tooth.

ܫܢܝܢܐ sharp.

ܫܥܐ *Ethpa.* ܐܫܬܥܝ to relate.

ܫܥܐ, ܫܥܬܐ an hour; ܒܫܥܬܐ ܒܗ forthwith.

ܫܥܝܐ jest, play.

ܫܦܝܪ beautiful, good, *fem. pl.* ܫܦܝܪܬܐ also the *neuter*, goodness.

ܫܡܥ.

ܫܡܰܥ to hear, to take; *Aph.* with ܡܶܢ to go away.

ܫܳܪܝܳܐ an inhabitant.

ܫܪܳܐ to dwell; with ܥܰܠ to besiege, *Pa.* to begin.

ܫܪܒ, ܫܰܪܒܳܐ generation, biography.

ܫܪܳܓܳܐ a light, wax light, a candle.

ܫܪܓܪܓܺܝܬܳܐ a spectre, an apparition.

ܫܰܪܟܳܐ the remainder, the rest.

ܫܪܰܪ, ܫܰܪ *Ethpa.* to be convinced.

ܫܰܪܺܝܪܳܐ true, *Adv.* ܫܰܪܺܝܪܳܐܺܝܬ truly, really.

ܫܪܳܪܳܐ truth.

ܫܬ six.

ܫܬܺܝܩܳܐܺܝܬ *Adv.* silently.

ܫܬܶܩ to be silent, to be dumb.

ܬ.

ܬܰܓܳܪܳܐ a merchant.

ܬܳܐܘܡܳܐ, ܬܳܐܘܡܰܐܣ Thomas, (a proper name).

ܬܶܐܘܦܺܝܠܳܘܣ Theophilus (a proper name).

ܬܠܐ.

ܬܰܐܠܳܢܳܐ not clear, dirty. 2) dregs, that which is most objectionable.

ܬܒܰܥ to demand.

ܬܓܰܪ to carry on trade, *Ethpa.* to win (by trade), to be added.

ܬܶܕܡܽܘܪܬܳܐ wonder.

ܬܗܳܘܡܳܐ an abyss.

ܬܰܗܺܝܪܳܐ wonderful.

ܬܗܰܪ to be surprised.

ܬܰܘ *Tav*–last letter of the Alphabet.

ܬܘܒ or ܬܳܒ to repent, to turn, to return.

ܬܽܘܒ again.

ܬܘܰܗ to be astonished.

ܬܽܘܪܓܳܡܳܐ interpretation.

ܬܳܘܬܳܐ repentance.

ܬܚܽܘܡܳܐ a limit, bound.

ܬܚܶܝܬ, ܬܚܽܘܬ, ܬܚܶܝܬ under, ܬܚܶܝܬ ܡܶܢ from below, ܠܬܚܶܝܬ ܡܶܢ under.

ܬܰܚܡܶܝܬܳܐ shame.

ܬܰܚܢܽܘܬܳܐ repentance.

ܬܟܰܦ to urge, *Part.* ܬܳܟܶܦ, Luke xxv. 23.

ܬܠܳܐ to hang up, to raise up.

ܬܠܓ.

ܬܠܓܐ snow.

ܬܠܝܬܝܘܬܐ the Trinity.

ܬܠܡܕ to make a scholar, *Ethpa.* to be learned, to be a scholar.

ܬܠܡܝܕܐ a scholar.

ܬܠܬ, *f.* ܬܠܬܐ *m.* three.

ܬܡܗ to wonder, to be astonished.

ܬܡܝܗܐ wonderful, remarkable.

ܬܡܝܡ, ܬܡܝܡܐ honest, genuine.

ܬܡܢܐ *f.* eight.

ܬܡܢ there, in that place.

ܬܢܐ to repeat, *Pa.* to narrate.

ܬܫܥܝܬܐ.

ܬܩܝܦܐ great, strong.

ܬܪܓܡ to explain, to interpret.

ܬܪܬܝܢ, ܬܪܝܢ two; ܬܪܝܢܐ the second.

ܬܪܝܨܐ right, true, faithful.

ܬܪܥܐ a door, a gate.

ܬܪܥܝܬܐ mind, opinion.

ܬܫܒܘܚܬܐ a hymn, a song of praise

ܬܫܡܫܬܐ service, attendance.

ܬܫܥ *f.* ܬܫܥܐ *m.* nine.

ܬܫܥܝ to narrate, from ܫܥܐ.

ܬܫܥܝܬܐ a narration.

www.ingramcontent.com/pod-product-compliance
Lightning Source LLC
Chambersburg PA
CBHW071226230426
43668CB00011B/1325

* 9 7 8 1 6 2 5 6 4 0 3 1 4 *